MW01518031

VISUAL QUICKPRO GUIDE

ADOBE AIR
(ADOBE INTEGRATED RUNTIME)
WITH AJAX

Larry Ullman

 Peachpit Press

Visual QuickPro Guide
Adobe AIR (Adobe Integrated Runtime) with Ajax
Larry Ullman

Peachpit Press

1249 Eighth Street
Berkeley, CA 94710
510/524-2178
510/524-2221 (fax)

Find us on the Web at: www.peachpit.com
To report errors, please send a note to: errata@peachpit.com
Peachpit Press is a division of Pearson Education.

Copyright © 2008 by Larry Ullman

Editor: Rebecca Gulick
Copy Editor: Anne Marie Walker
Production Coordinator: Myrna Vladic
Compositor: Debbie Roberti
Indexer: Rebecca Plunkett
Cover Production: Louisa Adair
Technical Reviewer: Prayank Swaroop

Notice of rights
All rights reserved. No part of this book may be reproduced or transmitted in any form by any means, electronic, mechanical, photocopying, recording, or otherwise, without the prior written permission of the publisher. For information on getting permission for reprints and excerpts, contact permissions@peachpit.com.

Notice of liability
The information in this book is distributed on an "As Is" basis, without warranty. While every precaution has been taken in the preparation of the book, neither the author nor Peachpit Press shall have any liability to any person or entity with respect to any loss or damage caused or alleged to be caused directly or indirectly by the instructions contained in this book or by the computer software and hardware products described in it.

Trademarks
Visual QuickPro Guide is a registered trademark of Peachpit Press, a division of Pearson Education. Adobe AIR and Adobe Integrated Runtime are registered trademarks of Adobe Systems, Inc., in the United States and in other countries. Macintosh and Mac OS X are registered trademarks of Apple Computer, Inc. Microsoft and Windows are registered trademarks of Microsoft Corp. Other product names used in this book may be trademarks of their own respective owners. Images of Web sites in this book are copyrighted by the original holders and are used with their kind permission.

Many of the designations used by manufacturers and sellers to distinguish their products are claimed as trademarks. Where those designations appear in this book, and Peachpit was aware of a trademark claim, the designations appear as requested by the owner of the trademark. All other product names and services identified throughout this book are used in editorial fashion only and for the benefit of such companies with no intention of infringement of the trademark. No such use, or the use of any trade name, is intended to convey endorsement or other affiliation with this book.

ISBN-13: 978-0-321-52461-4
ISBN-10: 0-321-52461-6

9 8 7 6 5 4 3 2 1

Printed and bound in the United States of America

Dedication:

To the Kavounis family

Special thanks to:

Top-notch editor and champion of books and writers, Rebecca Gulick.

Anne Marie Walker, for her excellent attention to detail and for improving writing that is often too vague.

Debbie Roberti and Myrna Vladic, for putting together the puzzle that is this book out of the pieces I created.

Rebecca Plunkett, for creating the index.

Everyone else at Peachpit Press, naturally, for all of the work they do!

Prayank Swaroop, for jumping in and providing a most helpful technical review.

Nicole, for helping with the kids so that I can write these books.

Jessica, Zoe, and Sam, for making it so much fun not to be sitting at my computer writing and programming.

TABLE OF CONTENTS

TABLE OF CONTENTS

TABLE OF CONTENTS

INTRODUCTION

Adobe AIR (Adobe Integrated Runtime) is a fantastic new technology that greatly expands the ways in which you can create desktop applications. Traditionally, programs like Microsoft Word, the Firefox Web browser, and Adobe Reader have been written in a programming language like C or C++. Learning such technologies, while not hard, takes some effort, and making graphical applications, let alone cross-platform apps, using them is an even larger hurdle. Now, with Adobe AIR you can use whatever Web development know-how you have— be it Adobe Flash, Adobe Flex, or standard Ajax (HTML and JavaScript)—to create fully functional desktop applications that will run equally well on Windows, Mac OS X, and Linux.

This book, which focuses solely on the Ajax (HTML and JavaScript) approach, covers everything you need to know to begin creating useful Adobe AIR applications today. With a minimum of technical jargon and lots of practical examples, this easy-to-follow text is the perfect introduction for how you can apply your Web development skills in new ways. Whether you're creating programs for your own use, developing company software, or repurposing a Web site to broaden its reach, Adobe AIR is the right tool for the job.

With so many ways to create desktop applications, the natural question is: Why should I use Adobe AIR? The first and most compelling reason is that *using Adobe AIR is easy*. In all likelihood you'll just apply the knowledge you already have. In the worst-case scenario, if you have limited to no experience with HTML and JavaScript, rest assured that few technologies are as approachable as these. The learning curve for using Adobe AIR is therefore short but the upside is huge.

A second but very strong reason to use Adobe AIR is that it automatically generates *cross-platform applications*. The programs you create will run equally well on Windows, Mac OS X, and Linux regardless of the operating system on which they were written. Adobe AIR was designed specifically with this in mind, and there are but few areas in which operating system-specific steps need to be taken.

A third consideration to note is that with Adobe AIR you're creating *graphical applications*: programs that are visible, that run outside of any console window or terminal application, and that can take full advantage of the user's mouse and keyboard. This may not sound revelatory to you, but when using other technologies (like C or C++) to make an application, creating a graphical application as opposed to a command-line utility isn't that simple.

The Adobe AIR applications you develop can

- Access files and directories on the user's computer

- Integrate a client-side database

- Securely store data in an encrypted format

- Contain custom windows and menus

- Interact with network resources, like Web sites and servers

- Tap into the computer's clipboard, supporting cut, copy, paste, plus drag in and out functionality

- Play sounds and videos

- Display PDFs

In short, an application written in AIR can do pretty much anything you can think of!

If you still need convincing, consider that the tools required for creating and running AIR applications are free and supported by an excellent company, Adobe. If the way in which Adobe handled the invention, promotion, and distribution of the Portable Document Format (PDF) is any gauge, the future looks bright for Adobe AIR.

About This Book

This book covers everything you need to know to develop desktop applications using Adobe AIR. Although there are three primary technologies that you can use with AIR—Ajax, Flash, and Flex—this book focuses solely on just the Ajax (which is to say HTML and JavaScript) method. I've chosen to only use Ajax code because:

- HTML and JavaScript are easier to learn than Flash and Flex (in my opinion).

- HTML and JavaScript are understood by a larger audience.

- Far more applications can be used to generate HTML and JavaScript code.

There are 16 chapters in all, and they can pretty much be read in any order you like. I would, however, highly recommend that you initially read the first four chapters in order. They cover the most basic information, knowledge that the other chapters will assume you already have.

In keeping with the approach I take to any subject, I hope you'll find that the content in this book, while accurate and appropriate, is never too complicated or overloaded with technical jargon. Also, a real emphasis has been placed on using practical, real-world examples. With few exceptions, most of the demonstrations portray actions that desktop applications would actually perform.

Because there are limits to what a book can discuss, not everything that's possible in AIR is covered here. As stated earlier, the book does not discuss how to write AIR applications using Flash or Flex (I don't think a good book could actually cover multiple AIR development methods). Beyond that, a small subset of topics has been omitted, for example, taking command-line arguments or using digital rights management (DRM) for media files. Rest assured that I only made such omissions for subjects that the vast majority of readers will not need to know and that are also adequately covered in the online documentation (a fact that can't be said for every topic).

What You'll Need

Fortunately, the requirements for developing Adobe AIR applications with Ajax are quite manageable. In fact, you don't even need to spend any money! To run an AIR application, you'll need to download and install the Adobe AIR runtime, which Chapter 1, "Running AIR Applications," covers. The runtime works on Microsoft Windows 2000, XP, or Vista and on Mac OS X version 10.4.9 or later. At the time of this writing (April 2008), an alpha version of the runtime for Linux was just released.

To create an AIR application, you'll need to download and install the Software Development Kit (SDK). Chapter 2, "Creating an Application," walks you through those steps. The SDK does require that you have either the Java Runtime Environment (JRE) or the Java Development Kit (JDK) installed on your computer. Both are freely available from `http://java.sun.com` (as part of what is called the Java Standard Edition, Java SE).

To develop an Adobe AIR application—to create the HTML and JavaScript code involved, you'll need a text editor or an Integrated Development Environment (IDE). If you already have a text editor that you like, that's perfect. Chapter 2 leads you through the steps you would take when using a text editor. If you prefer an IDE, like Aptana Studio or Adobe Dreamweaver, that's fine, too. Chapter 3, "AIR Development Tools," shows you how to use both of these programs to create AIR applications.

Other than the software requirements, this book does assume that you are comfortable with HTML. If not, there are many fine books available on the subject, including Elizabeth Castro's most excellent *HTML, XHTML, and CSS, Sixth Edition: Visual QuickStart Guide* (Peachpit Press, 2006). Some familiarity with JavaScript (or any programming language, really) will help make the code easier to follow.

Getting Help

Should you have problems with Adobe AIR in general or the contents of this book in particular, there are many resources to which you can turn. The first, naturally, is Adobe's supporting Web site for AIR: `www.adobe.com/go/air/`. At that site you can download the AIR runtime and the SDK, as well as many sample programs and code. From there you can also find Adobe's Developer Center pages for AIR (`www.adobe.com/devnet/air/ajax/`), which contain articles and tutorials.

I would also highly recommend that you bookmark two areas of Adobe's site. The first is the online documentation provided by Adobe for developing AIR applications using Ajax at `www.adobe.com/go/learn_air_html`. These pages discuss and demonstrate how to tackle different tasks.

The second link you'll frequently use is the JavaScript Language Reference at `www.adobe.com/go/learn_air_html_jslr`. This is a more technical set of pages but provides a detailed reference for all the JavaScript functionality you'll use in your AIR applications. In short, if you forget what features a certain widget has, these pages will quickly provide that information.

A simple search will also turn up plenty of third-party Web sites that discuss Adobe AIR. When using these sites, just pay attention as to whether the site's content specifically addresses AIR applications written using Ajax, Flash, or Flex. Many of these sites have support forums that are quite useful for getting quick answers to questions (there's one on Adobe's site, too).

Of course, you can (and probably should) also use the supporting Web site I created especially for this book. You'll find it at `www.DMCInsights.com/air/`. There you'll be able to download all of this book's code, access a supporting forum where you can ask questions, find corrections for any errors that may be present in the book, and contact me directly.

Running AIR Applications

Rather than starting to develop your own Adobe AIR (Adobe Integrated Runtime) application right out of the box, this first chapter instead covers how to run any AIR application. This knowledge, and some of the initial setup, are required when it's time to test your own work. More important, these are the steps that any potential user of your program needs to take to see the magic you've created.

To begin, I cover how to install the Adobe Integrated Runtime on both Windows and Mac OS X (Linux support for AIR will be added in later versions of the technology). After the runtime has been successfully installed, you'll see how easy it is to install any AIR application. Finally, you'll run that application on your computer. Some of the choices you make when developing your own AIR applications will affect the installation and running of it, so pay attention to the details discussed herein.

Installing the Runtime

You can install AIR on the following platforms:

◆ Windows XP with Service Pack 2

◆ Windows Vista Ultimate

◆ Mac OS X 10.4.8 or later (PowerPC)

◆ Mac OS X 10.4.8 or later (Intel)

This is true as of the beta version of AIR, with Linux support expected sometime after the first official release.

I'll run through the installation process using Windows XP Pro with all the latest patches and services packs, as well as Mac OS X 10.4.9 (Intel). The figures you'll see are a mix of the two operating systems, but the steps are the same regardless.

To install the runtime:

1. Download the AIR installer from Adobe.

   Head to www.adobe.com/go/air/ (**Figure 1.1**). Click Download Adobe AIR Now, which takes you to the proper download area (**Figure 1.2**).

2. Run the downloaded installer (**Figure 1.3**).

   On Windows, the name of the file is AdobeAIRInstaller.exe. Double-click that to run the installer.

   On Mac OS X, the name of the down-loaded file is AdobeAIR.dmg. Double-click that to mount the disk image (if it doesn't mount automatically), and then double-click the installer found within the disk image (**Figure 1.3**).

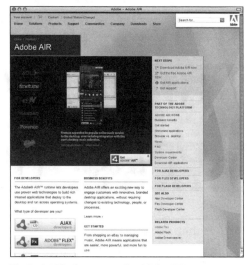

Figure 1.1 The home page for Adobe AIR.

Figure 1.2 The Adobe AIR download page, which also provides links to sample AIR applications.

Figure 1.3 The Adobe AIR runtime installer.

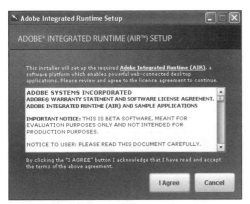

Figure 1.4 To install the runtime, you first have to agree to the license.

Figure 1.5 Hooray! You can now install AIR applications.

3. Read and agree to the license (**Figure 1.4**). The license is a legally binding document, so you should read it, have your lawyer look it over, see if it conflicts with any other agreement you've entered into, and so on. Or, you can just click I Agree. It's really up to you.

4. When the installation is complete (**Figure 1.5**), click Finish.

✔ Tips

■ As updated versions of the AIR runtime are released, you can install them (to update the version of the runtime on your computer) using these same steps.

■ Since one of the biggest benefits of AIR applications is their ability to run on multiple operating systems without change, expect Adobe's support for various operating systems to grow over time.

■ The AIR runtime gets installed and exists behind the scenes. It's not a program that is run on its own. You can confirm the successful installation of the AIR runtime by installing an AIR application.

Uninstalling the Runtime

Most people shouldn't need to uninstall the runtime, but doing so is simple enough. To uninstall the runtime on Windows, use the Add or Remove Programs control panel. To uninstall the runtime on Mac OS X, double-click the Adobe AIR Uninstaller program, which should be in your `Applications` directory.

INSTALLING THE RUNTIME

Installing an Application

The AIR runtime needs to be installed only once on your computer for you to be able to install any number of AIR applications. Throughout the course of this book you'll create several AIR apps (which is the point of the book, after all), but many apps are available and can be downloaded from the Internet as well. Along with any number of third-party AIR applications, Adobe provides some of its own, one of which I'll use in these steps.

To install an AIR application:

1. Download an application from the Internet.

   You can find a handful of applications on Adobe's Web site (see www.adobe.com/devnet/air/flex/samples.html) and find more by searching the Web. For this example, I'll install a playful application from Adobe called ScreenBoard. Note that the app file you'll download is generally not operating-system-specific.

2. Double-click the downloaded file (**Figure 1.6**) to begin the installation process.

   AIR applications use a .air extension and display a simple icon (it looks like a cardboard box).

   When you install the very first AIR application, you'll get a security warning about opening the Adobe AIR Application Installer for the first time (**Figure 1.7**). Click Open to proceed with the installation, and you won't see this message again.

Figure 1.6 The ScreenBoard application, with its .air extension that indicates it uses the Adobe Integrated Runtime.

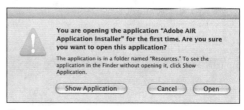

Figure 1.7 AIR applications are installed using the Adobe AIR Application Installer. On most systems, you'll need to approve this application running the first time it is requested.

Figure 1.8 The installation process begins with detailed information about the application, its creator, and the security implications.

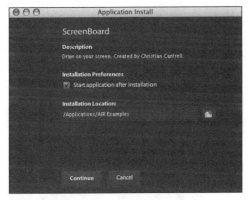

Figure 1.9 The installer allows the user to specify where the program should be located.

Figure 1.10 The Windows installer provides the option of adding a desktop shortcut for the new application.

3. Read and pay attention to everything on the initial screen (**Figure 1.8**). Then click Install if you still want to install the application.

This installation screen is very important and worth looking at (more so than for most applications you might install). For starters, you'll see the application's publisher (the company or person who created it) and the name of the application. In the next chapter you'll learn how to set these values when making your own program.

The installer also indicates what system access the program will have. It's very important that AIR application creators, and the people who use the programs, are aware of the associated security issues. Adobe AIR allows Web developers to create desktop applications, which means that an AIR application can do damage to the user's computer, something that could never happen with a standard Web site (with a few exceptions). The security issues are topics that are repeatedly addressed throughout this book and in Chapter 15, "Security Techniques," in particular.

4. On the next screen (**Figure 1.9**) decide where the application should be installed and whether it should automatically be started after installation. Click Continue.

On Windows, the default is to install the application within the Program Files directory, just like any other application. Windows users are also given the option of creating a desktop shortcut to the application (**Figure 1.10**).

continues on next page

INSTALLING AN APPLICATION

On Mac OS X, the default is to install AIR programs within the Applications folder, just like any other application.

Some programs will also indicate where they think they should be installed. With the ScreenBoard example, its default option is to store it within a special AIR Examples folder (within the Applications or Program Files directories).

Ta-da! That's it. No big deal. If you checked the corresponding box in the previous step (Figures 1.9 and 1.10), the application will start when the installation finishes.

Figure 1.11 Running the installer for the same version of an application already installed gives this result.

✔ Tip

■ If you attempt to install an AIR application that has already been installed, you will be alerted to the existing installation (**Figure 1.11**). If you install a newer version, you will be given the option of replacing the original installation with the update.

Uninstalling an Application

On Windows you can uninstall an AIR application as you would any other application by using the Add or Remove Programs control panel. On Mac OS X, you can quickly uninstall an application by trashing its file (found in Applications, by default). Alternatively, on both platforms, if you attempt to reinstall that same application, you are provided with an uninstall option (see Figure 1.11).

Figure 1.12 The shortcut to the ScreenBoard application, as found on the Windows desktop.

Figure 1.13 AIR applications are listed among All Programs on the Windows Start menu.

Figure 1.14 The ScreenBoard application on Mac OS X.

Figure 1.15
The ScreenBoard application is placed on the Dock.

Running an Application

After you've successfully installed an AIR application, you'll have myriad ways to run it. You could probably figure out all these on your own, but the point is that once you've installed the runtime and the application, you'll see that AIR applications behave just like any other program on your computer.

To run an application:

◆ Check the Start application after installation box during the installation process (Figures 1.9 and 1.10).

◆ On Windows, use the desktop shortcut if one was created (**Figure 1.12**).

◆ On Windows, use the Start menu (**Figure 1.13**).

◆ On Mac OS X, double-click the application's icon (most applications will be installed in the Applications folder by default) (**Figure 1.14**).

◆ On Mac OS X, add the application to your Dock so it can be launched from there (**Figure 1.15**).

RUNNING AN APPLICATION

✔ Tips

- In each of the images, the ScreenBoard icon happens to be the default AIR application icon. You can create custom icons for your AIR applications to be used instead.

- The ScreenBoard application lets you draw on your screen, on top of every other program (**Figure 1.16**). This isn't the most important use of the AIR technology, but it does allow for some legal, nondestructive graffiti.

- If you have created or modified a file called `mms.cfg`, which is used by the Flash Player, it can cause problems when running AIR applications. Temporarily remove it from its primary location (e.g., `C:\winnt\system32\macromedia\flash\mms.cfg` on Windows XP or `/Library/Application Support/Macromedia/mms.cfg` on Mac OS X) to fix the conflict. This shouldn't be a problem for most users, however.

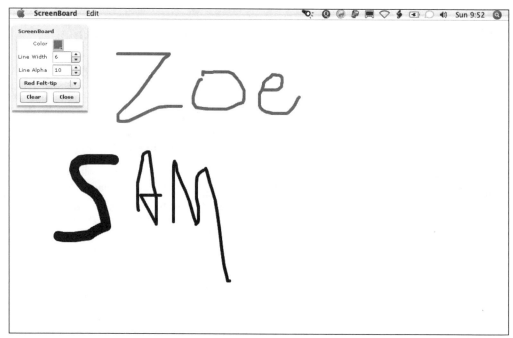

Figure 1.16 The actual ScreenBoard program in action (on Mac OS X).

CREATING AN APPLICATION

When creating an Adobe AIR application, you have your choice of technologies and development tools. The three technology options are Ajax (HTML and JavaScript), Adobe Flex, and Adobe Flash. In this book I focus solely on programs based on Ajax. The list of development tools you could use is practically limitless. In this chapter I go through the steps for creating an AIR application using any text editor and Adobe's AIR SDK (Software Development Kit). In the next chapter I show you how to use the Dreamweaver CS3 and Aptana Studio Integrated Development Environments (IDEs) instead.

Creating an AIR application starts with laying out a project folder. Next, you'll create two text files: an HTML file and an XML file. The final step is to use the Adobe AIR SDK tools to test and build the application from the two files. Because you'll need these AIR utilities, the first couple of sections of this chapter cover the installation of the SDK and any configuration of your operating system that is required. These initial steps are only necessary once.

Installing the SDK

The Adobe AIR SDK is a separate entity from the AIR runtime you need to install to run your applications. The SDK contains lots of goodies:

◆ Two command-line tools for testing and packaging applications

◆ Frameworks (libraries of useful code)

◆ Samples (like application icons)

◆ An XML file template

The SDK requires you to install either the Java Runtime Environment (JRE) or the Java Development Kit (JDK) on your computer. Both are freely available from http://java. sun.com (as part of what is called the Java Standard Edition, Java SE). After you've installed either program (the JRE is likely already installed if you have a Mac; you may need to install it if you're running Windows), you can follow these next steps.

To install the SDK:

1. Download the SDK for your operating system from Adobe (**Figure 2.1**).

The SDK is available at http://www. adobe.com/products/air/tools/sdk/. As of this writing, the SDK is available for both Windows and Mac OS X.

2. Open and expand the downloaded file (**Figure 2.2**).

Windows users need to expand the ZIP archive. Mac users need to mount the .dmg (disc image) file.

3. Copy the entire contents of the downloaded file to another location on your computer.

Where you place the SDK folder is up to you. You might want it on your desktop or within a folder in your home directory. Whichever location you choose, you'll need to remember it for subsequent steps.

4. Update your system path so that it includes the SDK bin directory.

What this means and how you accomplish it are both discussed in the next two sections of the chapter.

✔ Tips

■ JRE and JDK are requirements of only the AIR SDK. End users only need to install the Adobe AIR runtime (see Chapter 1, "Running AIR Applications").

■ Along with the SDK, you can also download lots of AIR development documentation, sample applications, and source code from Adobe's site.

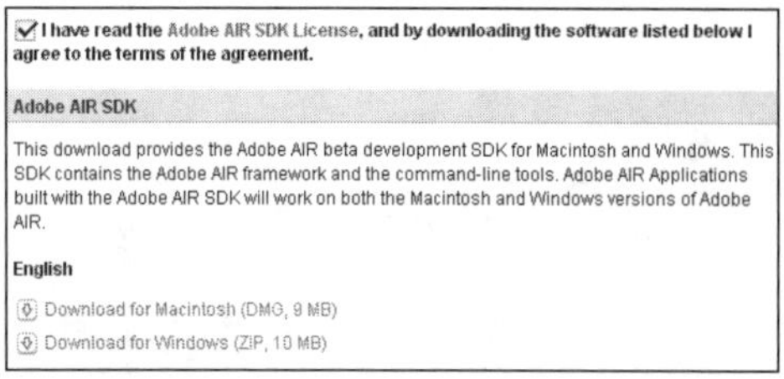

☑ I have read the Adobe AIR SDK License, and by downloading the software listed below I agree to the terms of the agreement.

Adobe AIR SDK

This download provides the Adobe AIR beta development SDK for Macintosh and Windows. This SDK contains the Adobe AIR framework and the command-line tools. Adobe AIR Applications built with the Adobe AIR SDK will work on both the Macintosh and Windows versions of Adobe AIR.

English

◉ Download for Macintosh (DMG, 9 MB)
◉ Download for Windows (ZIP, 10 MB)

Figure 2.1 Download the SDK for your operating system (you'll need to agree to the license as well).

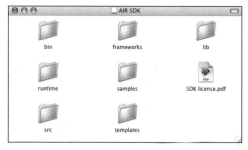

Figure 2.2 The contents of the Adobe AIR SDK.

Figure 2.3 Accessing the System Properties.

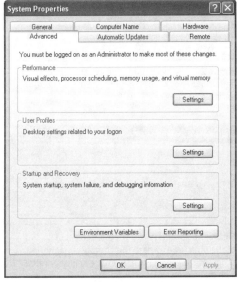

Figure 2.4 The system path is editable via the Environment Variables button on the Advanced tab.

Updating Your Path on Windows

The two tools installed by the SDK—the AIR Development Tool (adt) and the AIR Debug Launcher (adl)—are used from the command line. This means you'll run them, on Windows, through a console prompt, not in a graphical interface. The command line syntax is really easy to use, but there is one catch: Both programs must be "known" by your computer. To accomplish this, you need to add the SDK folder's `bin` directory (see Figure 2.2) to your system's *path*.

The path is simply a listing of where the computer can find programs that might be invoked. You probably don't normally deal with a path because you don't normally run applications from the command line. But follow these simple steps and you'll be fine.

To modify your system's path:

1. Close any open console windows.

   The path change you're about to make takes effect for any console windows (aka DOS prompts) opened after making the change. To avoid confusing problems later, close any open console windows prior to changing the path.

2. Bring up the System Properties dialog by right-clicking on My Computer and selecting Properties (**Figure 2.3**).

3. Within the System Properties dialog, click the Advanced tab (**Figure 2.4**).

4. Click Environment Variables.

   You can see this button at the bottom of Figure 2.4.

continues on next page

5. In the Environment Variables dialog, click Path in the System variables listing to select it (**Figure 2.5**).

6. Click Edit to bring up the Edit System Variable dialog.

7. At the end of Variable value, add a semi-colon plus the full path to the SDK `bin` directory (**Figure 2.6**).

   It's very important that you *add* the SDK path to the existing value; you *should not replace* the existing value with just the SDK path.

   To confirm the correct full path, you can open the SDK folder in an Explorer window (**Figure 2.7**) and copy the address. Make sure that what you're adding to the Variable value includes the final *\bin*, because that's the most important part here.

8. Click OK in all three dialogs to close them.

✔ Tip

■ You don't technically need to modify the path to use the command-line tools. But if you don't, when it comes time to invoke them, you'll need to type something like `C:\"Documents and Settings"\"Larry Ullman"\Desktop\SDK\bin\adt` instead of just `adt`. Changing the path is a worthwhile shortcut.

Figure 2.5 The list of editable system variables is found in the bottom half of the Environment Variables window.

Figure 2.6 For the Path variable, the value lists all of the directories where the computer might find programs to execute. Each directory is separated by a semicolon.

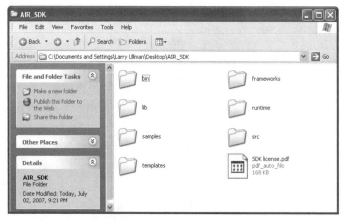

Figure 2.7 The SDK folder, located on my desktop, with its path (or address) viewable in an Explorer window.

UPDATING YOUR PATH ON WINDOWS

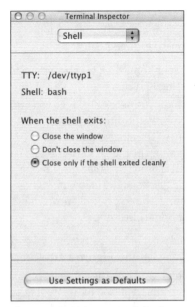

Figure 2.8 On Unix systems, including Mac OS X, you need to know which shell you're using to successfully change the path. The current shell can be found in the Terminal Inspector.

Updating Your Path on Mac OS X

The two tools installed by the SDK—the AIR Development Tool (adt) and the AIR Debug Launcher (adl)—are used from the command line. This means you'll run them, on Mac OS X, through the Terminal application, not in a graphical interface. The command-line syntax is really easy to use, but there is one catch: Both programs must be "known" by your computer. To accomplish this, you need to add the SDK folder's `bin` directory to your system's *path*.

The path is simply a listing of where the computer can find programs that might be invoked. You probably don't normally deal with a path because you don't normally run applications from the command line. But follow these simple steps and you'll be fine.

To modify your system's path:

1. Close any open Terminal windows.

   The path change you're about to make takes effect for any Terminal windows opened after making the change. To avoid confusing problems later, close any open Terminal windows before changing the path.

2. Confirm which shell you are using by selecting Terminal > Window Settings to bring up the Terminal Inspector (**Figure 2.8**).

continues on next page

How you change the path depends on which shell you're using (if you're really curious about what shells are, search the Web for "unix shell"). The Shell page of the Terminal Inspector names the shell in use. The most common shells are called (the program's actual name is in parentheses):

▲ Bourne (*sh*)

▲ Bourne Again Shell (*bash*, and I'm not making that up).

▲ C shell (*csh*)

▲ T shell or T C shell (*tsch*)

▲ Korn shell (*ksh*)

The most recent versions of Mac OS X are preset to use the bash shell (as in Figure 2.8). For these instructions, I'll assume you are using the bash shell. If your Terminal Inspector says otherwise, you'll need to do an online search for how to change that particular shell's path.

3. Open a Terminal window (File > New Shell or Command + N), if one is not already open (**Figure 2.9**).

4. Move to your home directory by typing cd and pressing Return.

This shouldn't be necessary since you're likely in your home directory when you create a new Terminal window, but follow this step just to be safe. The cd command is used to change the directory. Invoking it without any following values (like naming a directory) will move you into your home directory.

5. List all the current files by typing ls -a and pressing Return (**Figure 2.10**).

The ls command lists the contents of a directory; the -a option indicates that all the files should be listed, including hidden ones.

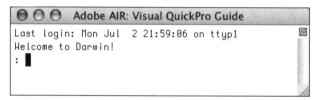

Figure 2.9 A new Terminal window.

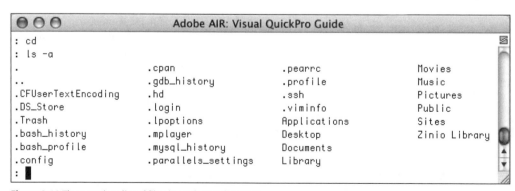

Figure 2.10 The complete list of files in my home directory.

6. If there is not a file called `.bash_profile` in the directory listing (Figure 2.10), create one by typing `touch .bash_profile`.

Files that begin with a period are normally special, hidden files. This particular file, `.bash_profile`, is used to affect how the bash shell behaves. If the file does not already exist, the `touch` command will create it.

7. Open the `.bash_profile` file in any text editor (**Figure 2.11**).

I use the popular (and most excellent) BBEdit text editor, so I can open the file by typing `bbedit .bash_profile` from the command line. You can also use Bare Bones' free TextWrangler (`www.barebones.com`) for this purpose or one of the many command-line editors: vi, vim, emacs, pico, and so on.

8. In the `.bash_profile` file, add this line:

```
export PATH="$PATH:/path/to/AIR/
→ SDK/bin/"
```

The `export PATH` command changes the path for the bash shell. The value of the path should be the current path (represented by `$PATH`) plus the full path to the SDK `bin` directory (you'll need to use the actual path in place of `/path/to/`, see

the first Tip that follows). Each directory in the path is separated by a colon.

If your `.bash_profile` document already has an `export PATH...` line, just add the colon plus the full path to the current value.

9. Save and close the file.

10. Close the Terminal window.

The change to the path will take effect the next time a Terminal window is opened.

✔ Tips

■ In most Mac OS X programs you can insert into a file the full path to a folder by dragging that folder onto the file. For example, if you grab the SDK `bin` folder in the Finder and drag it into the `.bash_profile` file in BBEdit, the full path to `bin` will be inserted into `.bash_profile` wherever you release the mouse button.

■ You don't technically need to modify the path to use the command-line tools. But if you don't, when it comes time to invoke them, you'll need to type something like `/Users/larryullman/Desktop/AIR/SDK/bin/adt` instead of just `adt`. Changing the path is a worthwhile shortcut.

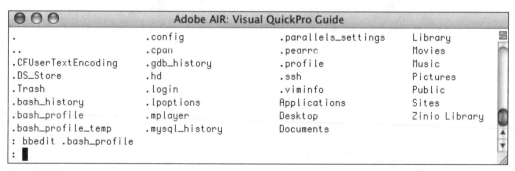

Figure 2.11 The `bbedit .bash_profile` command opens `.bash_profile` in BBEdit.

Creating the Project's Structure

Although it's not mandatory to create some sort of exact directory structure to make AIR applications, I think doing so is for the best. Just like any seasoned Web developers will logically organize their sites' files and assets, so will smart programmers. Not every project mandates the same structure and you might prefer to use different naming schemes, but the principles put forth in these steps are well worth heeding.

Note that in the following steps I go through some best practices for any project you create. The specific example you'll make in this chapter won't need, for example, folders for CSS and JavaScript files, but I mention them here just to be thorough.

To create an application's structure:

1. Create a new folder somewhere on your computer for your AIR application development.

You absolutely know how to do this, I'm certain (right-click and then choose New > Folder on Windows; Command + Shift + N or choose File > New Folder on Mac OS X). For example, you might, within your documents directory or on your desktop, create a folder called AIR Development. It's important that all of your AIR work be stored in the same area, so it'll be easier and faster to begin developing and building apps.

2. Within the folder you created in step 1, create a new folder for each new project.

Create a new folder for each new application but put all of these folders within the same parent folder (the AIR Development folder)

3. Give the new folder the same name as the application (**Figure 2.12**).

For this first sample application, I'll create a good old-fashioned *Hello, World!* program (it's a mainstay of any programming text). So I'll create a folder called *HelloWorld* into which all my files will go.

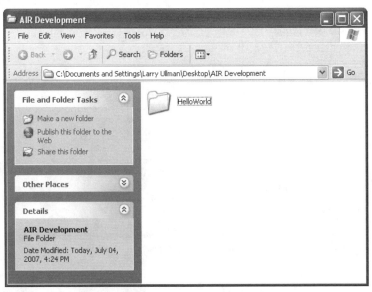

Figure 2.12 The HelloWorld folder will contain the first sample application's files.

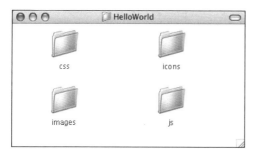

Figure 2.13 A basic application folder layout.

4. Within the application folder named in step 3, create a folder for Cascading Style Sheets.

I'll call this new folder *css*, for obvious reasons. It'll store any CSS files used by the application. Keep in mind that because HTML is the basis for the AIR application, you could logically organize your AIR program folder as you would a Web site.

5. Within the application folder, create a folder for JavaScript.

Not surprisingly, I'll call this folder *js*. Any JavaScript files will be stored here.

6. Within the application folder, create a folder for images.

This one will be called (…drumroll…) *images*. You might also call it *assets* or *imgs*. It doesn't really matter, but the graphics used by the program will go here.

7. Within the application folder, create a folder for icons (**Figure 2.13**).

On a whim, I've decided to call this folder *icons*. As you'll see in Chapter 16, "Deploying Applications," you can create icons unique to your program. These are different than the images and graphics used within the program.

✔ Tip

■ Other folders you might have in your application directory include *audio* (for storing sounds used by the program); *docs* (for any documentation); or *resources* (for other assets). Again, these names and folders aren't obligatory, just prudent suggestions.

Creating the HTML File

The first file in the application that I'll create will be the base HTML file (aka the "top-level" page). When creating Adobe AIR applications using HTML and JavaScript, this HTML file will essentially be the application.

One of the great advantages of AIR is that you can leverage your existing Web development knowledge to create desktop applications. This means that you can use the same skills and technologies you have for creating a Web page's look to create an application's look. Also, you can run the application's HTML file in a Web browser, and it will look exactly like the application when it's run on its own.

For this demonstration example, I'll go with the classic (i.e., done to death) *Hello, World!* page. The resulting application won't do anything useful, but these steps of developing, packaging, and running your own AIR applications will apply to the rest of the book.

To create an HTML file:

1. Begin a new HTML document in your text editor or IDE (**Script 2.1**).

```
<html>
<head>
   <title>Hello, World!</title>
</head>
```

Because you're not actually making a Web site, you can eliminate some of the extra HTML stuff, like the DOCTYPE, the META tags, and so on.

2. Add the HTML body.

```
<body>
   <h1>Hello, World!</h1>
</body>
```

As mentioned earlier, this won't be the most impressive app you've ever done, but you can take solace in seeing how simple it'll be to create your own cross-platform desktop applications.

3. Complete the HTML.

```
</html>
```

4. Save the file as `HelloWorld.html` in your application folder.

The file should be saved in the root of the application folder, not within any subdirectories.

✔ Tips

■ The HTML rendering engine—the thing that interprets HTML code to create a graphical appearance—used by AIR is called WebKit (`www.webkit.org`). This same engine is at the heart of Apple's Safari Web browser, so Safari will display the best imitation of how the actual program will look and function. Safari is available for both Macs and Windows as of version 3.

■ AIR applications can be based on Ajax, Flash, or Flex. Ajax AIR programs have a base `.html` file. Flash and Flex AIR applications have a base SWF (Shockwave format) file instead.

Script 2.1 This HTML file is the basis of the sample AIR application.

```
1    <html>
2    <head>
3       <title>Hello, World!</title>
4    </head>
5    <body>
6       <h1>Hello, World!</h1>
7    </body>
8    </html>
```

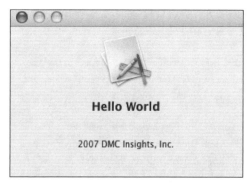

Figure 2.14 The application's About window, which shows the program's name, copyright, and creator.

Figure 2.15 Some of the information in the application descriptor file is used on the installation screen.

Creating the XML File

Along with an HTML file, your AIR applications must also have an XML file, which is referred to as the application descriptor file. This file provides all of the *metadata* (information about the program) for the application. This includes:

◆ Name

◆ Version

◆ Creator

◆ Description

◆ Copyright

◆ Icons

◆ Default installation folder

◆ Window appearance and behavior

◆ And more

Much of this information is reflected in an application's About menu (**Figure 2.14**) and also appears during the installation process (**Figure 2.15**).

If you've never worked with XML before, don't worry: It's not that much different than an HTML file. I'll go through everything you need to know in these steps. I do focus here on the *required* XML data. In other chapters, you'll see what other settings you might set here, and in Chapter 16 a few more of the optional elements are covered.

To create the XML file:

1. Begin a new XML document in your text editor or IDE (**Script 2.2**).

   ```
   <?xml version="1.0" encoding=
   → "utf-8" ?>
   ```

   XML files are just plain-text documents that can be created in most applications. XML files start with the XML declaration (this line), which indicates the XML version being used (1.0 is fine) and the encoding (see the first Tip that follows).

2. Add the root application tag.

   ```
   <application>
   </application>
   ```

   All XML files have one base tag (just like HTML files have the base html tag). For the AIR application descriptor file, this should always be application. The rest of the XML data goes between the opening and closing application tags.

3. Add the xmlns attribute to the opening application tag.

   ```
   <application xmlns="http://ns.adobe.
   → com/air/application/1.0">
   ```

   This attribute stands for *XML namespace*. Namespaces are an advanced programming concept that you don't need to know. What you do need to know is that the value of the attribute indicates the earliest version of the AIR runtime that the application supports. The value here refers to the first official release of AIR. Programs written using that namespace should be able to run on any version of the AIR runtime that comes later.

Script 2.2 The XML file is the application descriptor file, and is required by every AIR program.

```
1   <?xml version="1.0" encoding="utf-8" ?>
2   <application xmlns="http://ns.adobe.com/
    air/application/1.0">
3
4       <id>com.dmci.air.HelloWorld</id>
5
6       <filename>Hello World</filename>
7
8       <version>1.0</version>
9
10      <initialWindow>
11
12          <content>HelloWorld.html</content>
13
14          <visible>true</visible>
15
16      </initialWindow>
17
18  </application>
```

4. Between the opening and closing `application` tags, add an `id` element.

`<id>com.dmci.air.HelloWorld</id>`

The `id` value is the unique AIR reference for a program. The recommendation is to use a syntax like *com.company.application*. This can (and will) be a made-up value, but you should use something unique and meaningful. For example, an Adobe AIR application would have an `id` of *com.adobe.air.something*. For this application created by my company (DMC Insights, Inc.), I'll use *com.dmci.air. HelloWorld*. You should change this to something applicable to you.

You are limited to using the letters A–Z, the numbers 0–9, the period, and the dash. You cannot use spaces. The maximum length of the `id` is 255 characters.

5. Between the opening and closing `application` tags, add a `filename` element.

`<filename>Hello World</filename>`

This is the name of the application as the users will know and see it. The application name appears in its About menu (Figure 2.14), in shortcuts (**Figure 2.16**), in the Start menu (on Windows), and so forth. Conversely, the `appID` value is a behind-the-scenes reference to the program, which the end user will likely never see.

6. Between the opening and closing `application` tags, add a `version` element.

`<version>1.0</version>`

This refers to the version of this application. It's a made-up value but should be meaningful. Beta versions of applications are normally given a number less than 1. As a convention, from version 1 on, major updates get the next logical value (from 1 to 2, 2 to 3, etc.) and minor updates are normally assigned as a decimal (a minor update to version 1.1 would be 1.2). The most important thing is that updated versions of an application are given higher version numbers so that it's clear to the end user when a version constitutes an upgrade.

As you can see in Script 2.2, every other element (or tag pair) is placed between the opening and closing application tags. It does not matter the order in which they're written.

7. Between the opening and closing `application` tags, add an `initialWindow` element.

`<initialWindow>`

`</initialWindow>`

The `initialWindow` element will contain values dictating the content and appearance of the application's primary window.

continues on next page

Figure 2.16 The shortcut to the installed application, which uses the application's `filename` from the XML file.

8. Between the opening and closing `initialWindow` tags, add a `content` element.

   `<content>HelloWorld.html</content>`

   The value of the `content` element is the exact name of the base HTML file (Script 2.1). It's really best to store both the HTML and XML files in the same folder, so just the HTML file's name would be the value. If you choose not to put both files in the same place, you'll need to make this a relative path to the HTML file from this XML file (for example, `../HelloWorld.html` or `content/HelloWorld.html`).

9. Between the opening and closing `initialWindow` tags, add a `visible` element.

   `<visible>true</visible>`

   In these steps I want to focus on the required elements of the application descriptor file. The `visible` element, part of `initialWindow`, is not required but, for some very strange reason, its default value is `false`. What this means is that, by default, the application you write, test, and build, will run but won't be visible! Assuming that you actually want the user to be able to see your program when it's running, add this line.

10. Save the file as `application.xml` in the same directory as `HelloWorld.html`.

    You can give this file any name (with a `.xml` extension), but `application.xml` is conventional. You could also call it `HelloWorld.xml` or `HelloWorld-app.xml` (indicating it's a descriptor file for the Hello World application).

✔ Tips

■ Encoding refers to the types of characters that the file will support. UTF-8 is perhaps the most popular encoding choice and should be safe for your XML files.

■ One nice feature of some AIR IDEs (like Dreamweaver with the AIR Extension or Aptana) is that they'll help create the XML file for you. See Chapter 3, "AIR Development Tools," for more.

■ If you created two AIR applications with the same `id`, they would be considered the same program by the runtime and both could not be installed. Two applications can have the same `filename`, although that would be confusing to the end user.

CREATING THE XML FILE

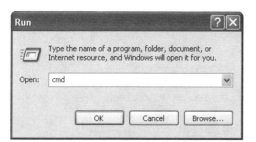

Figure 2.17 Use the Run command to get to the console window on Windows.

Figure 2.18 A DOS prompt or console window on Windows (although yours will likely have white text on a black background).

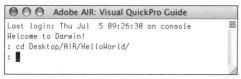

Figure 2.19 Moving into the HelloWorld application folder within a Terminal window on Mac OS X.

Testing the Application

Once the entire application has been created (in this case, that's just one HTML file and one XML file), it can be tested and then built (building is the final step, where you make the installable file). To test an application, you can use the command-line AIR Debug Launcher (adl), which is installed as part of the SDK. The syntax is simply:

```
adl ApplicationXMLFile.xml
```

Being able to test applications as you're developing them is an important feature. The alternative is to build the entire application, install it, and then see how it runs. But by following the steps in this section, you can cut to the chase, and then only build the application once you've finalized it.

To test an AIR application:

1. Access your computer via a command-line interface.

On Windows, select the Run option in the Start menu, and then enter cmd in the prompt (**Figure 2.17**). **Figure 2.18** shows the result.

Mac OS X users just need to open the Terminal application (Applications > Utilities). If a window doesn't open automatically, select File > New Shell or press Command + N.

2. Move to the project directory by typing cd path/to/HelloWorld and pressing Enter/Return (**Figure 2.19**).

You'll need to change the exact command (the part after the cd) so that it matches your computer and location of the application folder. As a trick, you can type cd, followed by a space, and then drag the HelloWorld folder into this window to automatically enter its full path.

continues on next page

3. Type the following and press Enter/Return (**Figure 2.20**).

```
adl application.xml
```

This should launch the application in a separate window (**Figure 2.21**). Because the XML file contains the name of the root document (the HTML file), this simple command is all you need to type to test the application.

If you see a message about Java not being a recognized command (**Figure 2.22**), that means you haven't yet installed the JRE, so you'll need to do that and then return to this step. If you see a message about adl not being a recognized command, that means the adl utility is not in your system path (see the steps for updating your path earlier in the chapter).

4. Quit the adl utility to close the application and return to the command line.

Testing in a Web Browser

Because the AIR applications being built in this book are based on Ajax (aka HTML and JavaScript), they can often be tested in a Web browser as well. AIR uses the same rendering engine as Apple's Safari, so that browser will provide the most accurate results (and it's available on both Mac OS X and Windows, as of version 3). Firefox, which also runs on both platforms, should also work well. Firefox has an additional benefit—its excellent JavaScript debugging tools.

Although you could, theoretically, test your applications in Internet Explorer, I would advise against doing so for two reasons. First, the JavaScript may not behave the same in IE as it will in your AIR apps (this is a common Ajax problem). Second, IE is a notoriously tricky browser that makes even Web development and testing much harder than it should be (in my opinion, at least).

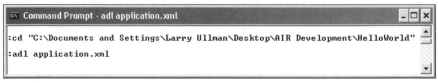

Figure 2.20 Invoking the AIR Debug Launcher on Windows.

Figure 2.21 Running the sample application.

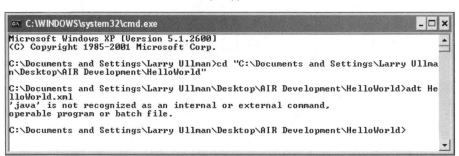

Figure 2.22 If the adl program cannot find the Java Runtime Environment (JRE), you'll see an error like this.

Creating a Certificate

Once you've successfully tested (and debugged) your AIR application, you can build it, which turns it into a distributable format for end users to install. However, as a security measure, every AIR application requires a *digital signature certificate*. This is intended to prove the authenticity of a program, thereby reassuring the end user that it's safe to install the application.

There are two kinds of certificates you can use. The first is purchased from an accredited company like Thawte or VeriSign. These certificates imply the highest level of security because those companies will verify your credentials. The second option is a *self-signed* certificate, something you create that allows you to build installable AIR applications but offers no real assurance to the application's end users. This option is free but essentially means that you're the one telling end users that you are legitimate. If they don't know you, that's not worth much. But for testing purposes, creating a self-signed signature makes sense. In these next steps, I'll show you how to do so using the command-line ADT (AIR Development Tool) utility.

To create a certificate:

1. Access your computer via a command-line interface.

   I go through the specific operating-system steps for both Windows and Mac OS X in the preceding section of the chapter.

2. Move to your AIR development directory by typing cd *path/to/AIR Development* and pressing Enter/Return.

   It'd be best to create the certificate in your AIR development directory (assuming you created one per the recommendations earlier in the chapter). You'll need to change the exact command (the part after the cd) so that it matches your computer and location of that folder.

   If you'd rather create the certificate somewhere else (like on your desktop), that's fine, but still use the cd command to make sure that you're in that directory before proceeding.

3. Type the following and press Enter/Return (**Figure 2.23**).

   ```
   adt -certificate -cn
     ↪ CertificateCommonName 1024-RSA
     ↪ certName.pfx somePassword
   ```

   continues on next page

continues on next page

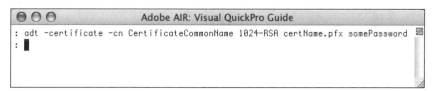

Figure 2.23 Creating a new self-signed certificate called *certName.pfx*.

This line creates a self-signed certificate using only the required options (and I've italicized values you'll likely want to change). The *CertificateCommonName* string should be replaced with a "common name" you provide for the certificate. This might be your company's name or something else useful and indicative of you, the creator of the application that will use this certificate.

The *certName.pfx* is the name of the generated certificate file. Again, give this a meaningful name (like *MySelfSignedCert*) but you must use a .pfx extension. Finally, the *somePassword* text will be the password associated with this certificate. You'll need to provide this when building the application (in the next series of steps).

The 1024-RSA text indicates the type of key used for this certificate (which impacts how tough, security-wise, it is). A tougher alternative is to use 2048-RSA.

4. Check the folder's contents for the newly created certificate.

✔ Tips

■ For a full list of certificate-generation options, type adt --help or see the Adobe AIR official documentation for all the details.

■ Each certificate created by ADT will be unique, even if you duplicate the steps taken to make them. When creating updated versions of an application, be certain to use the same certificate as was originally associated with that program.

■ The self-signed certificate will be valid for five years from the time it was created. This also means, per the first tip, that any application created using a self-signed certificate can be updated for five years. After that you'll need to release the program as a new entity, using a new certificate.

Building the Application

When your application is completed, debugged, and working as it should, you can build, or *package*, the application. This step is where you'll create the `.air` file that can be distributed and installed.

The syntax for using `adt` to build an application is:

```
adt -package -storetype pkcs12
→ -keystore certName.pfx AIRFileName.air
→ ApplicationXMLFile.xml
→ MainHTMLFile.html …
```

The `-package` argument specifies that you want to build a packaged application. The `-storetype pkcs12 -keystore certName.pfx` identifies the certificate to use for this application (as created using the previous steps). The next argument is the name of the `.air` file that should be generated. You then list the XML file, the base HTML file, and every other asset that needs to be packaged together. To be clear, every file, folder, or resource that an application uses needs to be mentioned on the `adt` line.

To include directories in the build, which you'll need to do if those directories contain CSS files, JavaScript, images, and so forth, you would use

```
adt -package -storetype pkcs12 -
→ keystore certName.pfx AIRFileName.air
→ ApplicationXMLFile.xml
→ MainHTMLFile.html css icons images js …
```

Let's use this information to package the Hello, World! test program.

To build an application:

1. Access your computer via a command-line interface.

   I go through the specific operating-system steps for both Windows and Mac OS X earlier in the chapter.

2. Move to the project directory by typing `cd path/to/HelloWorld` and pressing Enter/Return.

   Again, you'll need to change the exact command (the part after the `cd`) so that it matches your computer and location of the application folder.

3. Type the following and press Enter/Return (**Figure 2.24**).

   ```
   adt -package -storetype pkcs12
   → -keystore /path/to/certName.pfx
   → HelloWorld.air application.xml
   → HelloWorld.html
   ```

continues on next page

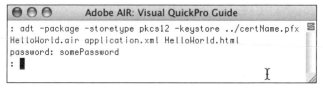

Figure 2.24 The `adt` program creates the `.air` file by packaging together all of the named elements.

BUILDING THE APPLICATION

You'll need to change the */path/to/certName*.pfx part of this command to correspond to the actual location of your self-signed certificate, relative to this folder. For example, when I executed this command (Figure 2.24), I was within the `HelloWorld` folder, which itself is within the `AIR Development` directory. Also within AIR Development is `certName.pfx`, the certificate created in the previous series of steps. So the actual command I used was `../certName.pfx`, which means go up one directory and you'll find `certName.pfx` there. The only other caveat is that this entire command needs to be entered on one line (i.e., you can't hit Enter or Return midway through).

After typing in all this and pressing Enter or Return, you'll be prompted for the certificate's password.

4. Confirm the success of the operation by looking for the new `HelloWorld.air` file in the application's folder (**Figure 2.25**).

5. Install and run `HelloWorld.air` using the steps outlined in Chapter 1.

✔ Tip

■ At a minimum, you could get away with calling the `adt` using just

```
adt -package -package -storetype
→ pkcs12 -keystore certName.pfx
→ AIRFileName.air
→ ApplicationXMLFile.xml .
```

The period represents everything in the current directory, so that line will package the HTML file and all directories together. This is functional, but heavy handed. It's best to be specific as illustrated in the previous steps.

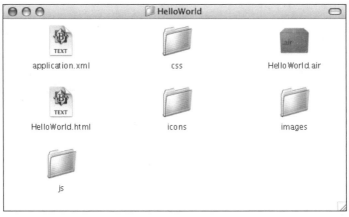

Figure 2.25 The newly generated `HelloWorld.air` file is the distributable and installable version of the application.

AIR DEVELOPMENT TOOLS

Chapter 2, "Creating an Application," walks you through developing AIR applications using HTML and JavaScript. Doing so requires the installation of the SDK (Software Development Kit), which includes the AIR Debug Launcher (ADL) and the Air Development Tool (ADT). Along with these tools, that chapter shows how to use any text editor to write the application's HTML and JavaScript. If you're the kind of person who prefers a simple text editor, continuing to follow those steps for developing and building AIR applications is fine. Some people, however, prefer to use more sophisticated development tools—two of which are covered here.

This chapter demonstrates how to write, test, and build AIR applications using two different IDEs (Integrated Development Environments). The first is Aptana Studio, a free product written in Java that runs on most operating systems. The second IDE is Adobe's own Dreamweaver, a commercial application. Along with instructions for creating AIR applications in Aptana Studio and Dreamweaver, the chapter also teaches you how to create a digital signature using these programs (a digital signature is necessary to build installable AIR applications).

Using Aptana Studio

Aptana Studio, available at www.aptana.com, is an open-source IDE written in Java. Because it's a Java application, it runs on pretty much every operating system, as long as the Java runtime has already been installed (keep in mind that you also need the Java runtime to use the ADL and ADT development tools). Aptana Studio is available in two versions, a free Community Edition and a Professional Edition (listed at $199 US at the time of this writing). The commercial version supports a few more features than the free version and comes with better support. Naturally, you can install the Community Edition and upgrade later, should you have the need.

Aptana Studio is a wonderful IDE with many potential uses. It's perfect for basic Web development, because it has HTML, JavaScript, and CSS support. But it can also be used for programming in PHP, using Ruby on Rails, or even developing software for the iPhone. Most important, in terms of this book, Aptana Studio makes developing Adobe AIR applications a snap. Although I normally use a text editor and command-line tools for pretty much everything I do, I've found Aptana Studio to be a much easier, faster, and more foolproof way to create AIR applications. Being able to write, debug, and build an application without changing applications is such a convenience.

In the following steps, I'll show you how to create, test, and build an AIR application using Aptana Studio. But first, make sure you've installed the Java runtime and Aptana Studio, and have configured Aptana Studio for AIR development. I'll start by running through those steps, which you should only need to ever follow once. (Note that throughout the book the images will come from both Windows and Mac OS X, although the steps are the same.)

To install Aptana Studio:

1. Install the Java runtime, if you have not previously.

   Mac OS X comes with Java installed, as do some versions of Windows. If you don't know if the Java runtime has been installed, type java -version at a command prompt (a DOS/console window on Windows, the Terminal application on Mac OS X). That command will result in either an error or a reporting of the version of Java installed (**Figure 3.1**).

   The Java runtime is available free of charge at http://java.sun.com. You'll want to install the Java Runtime Environment (JRE) for the Java SE (Standard Edition).

2. Download Aptana Studio.

   Again, it's up to you whether you download the Community Edition or the Professional Edition (which requires the purchase of a license).

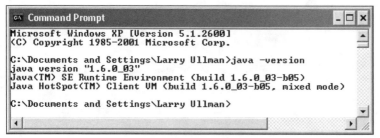

Figure 3.1 This command confirms that Java is installed (specifically version 1.6).

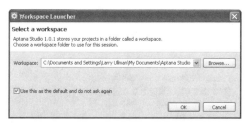

Figure 3.2 Tell Aptana Studio where all of your project files should be stored.

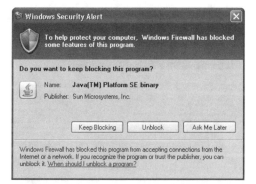

Figure 3.3 Windows' built-in firewall will block some activity made by the Java Runtime Engine. Click Unblock to avoid future problems.

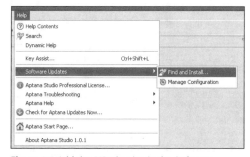

Figure 3.4 Add the AIR plug-in via the Software Updates option on the Help menu.

3. Install Aptana Studio.

The installer works much like every other installer you've used, so there shouldn't be any surprises and there's nothing for me to add here.

4. Start Aptana Studio.

How you do this depends on your operating system and the choices you made in step 3, but I'll assume you can figure out this part. The first time you load the program, you'll be prompted to select the location of your workspace—the default location for the projects you create (**Figure 3.2**). You may also be notified of updates to be installed. If (on Windows) you are notified that the Java SE is being blocked by the firewall (**Figure 3.3**), click Unblock.

5. Choose Help > Software Updates > Find and Install (**Figure 3.4**).

After installing and starting Aptana Studio, the next step is to install the necessary plug-in for developing AIR applications using the program. To start, use the Software Updates option on the Help menu.

continues on next page

6. Choose "Search for new features to install" and click Next (**Figure 3.5**).

Use the other option when you want to check for updates for everything already installed.

7. Select Aptana: Support for Adobe AIR and click Finish (**Figure 3.6**).

8. In the Search Results window, select Aptana: Support for Adobe AIR and click Next (**Figure 3.7**).

The preceding steps essentially search for the plug-in. Now that it's been found, click Next to actually install it.

Figure 3.5 Select which of the two updates you want to perform: update installed software or install new. To add the AIR plug-in for the first time, go with the second choice.

Figure 3.6 Support for AIR is one of many plug-ins that you can install in Aptana Studio.

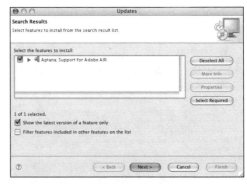

Figure 3.7 Click Next to begin the installation process.

Figure 3.8 The final step for installing the AIR plug-in is to click Finish here.

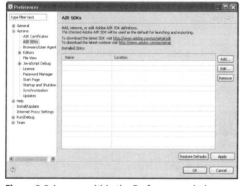

Figure 3.9 An area within the Preferences window is where you identify the AIR SDK to use for your development.

9. Complete the installation by accepting (and maybe even reading) the license agreement and confirming the installation location (**Figure 3.8**).

10. Restart Aptana Studio.

11. Select Window > Preferences > AIR SDKs (**Figure 3.9**).

You'll need to tell Aptana where the AIR SDK is located. This is done in the Preferences window, which is accessed from the Window menu.

12. Click Add.

Aptana Studio allows you to build Adobe AIR applications using different versions of the SDK. To start, you'll need to add at least one.

13. In the resulting window (**Figure 3.10**), find the location of the SDK on your computer and give the SDK a meaningful name.

Instructions for installing the SDK are in Chapter 2.

14. Click OK in the Add Adobe AIR SDK (Figure 3.10) and Preferences (Figure 3.9) windows.

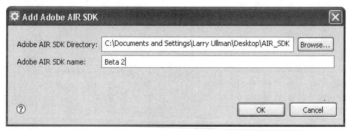

Figure 3.10 Use this window to identify the AIR SDK to use for developing applications.

To create an AIR application:

1. Launch Aptana Studio, if it is not already open.

2. Choose File > New > Project (**Figure 3.11**). Each AIR application should be its own project.

3. In the New Project window, select AIR Project and click Next (**Figure 3.12**).

4. In the Create an Adobe AIR project window, give the project a name (**Figure 3.13**).

   Other options here include changing the location of the project, if you don't want to use the default, and changing the name of the application's main HTML file (which is *ProjectName*.html by default).

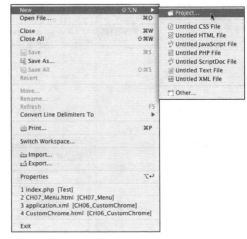

Figure 3.11 Start developing an AIR application by creating a new project.

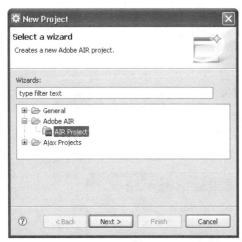

Figure 3.12 After installing support for Adobe AIR, AIR Project will be one of the possible project types.

Figure 3.13 Personalize the project by choosing its name, location on your computer, and root HTML file using this window.

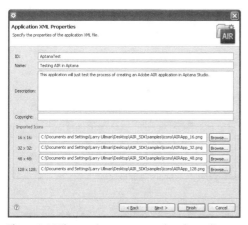

Figure 3.14 These values correspond to those discussed in Chapter 2, which are written into the XML descriptor file.

5. If desired, enter the application's ID, Name, Description, and Copyright, and then click Finish (**Figure 3.14**).

The ID is the `appID` value that goes in the application descriptor XML file (see Chapter 2). This should be a unique reference, like *com.dmci.air.HelloWorld*. The Name is the name of the application as it'll appear in the user's operating system (in shortcuts, in the Start menu on Windows, and so forth). The Description appears in the application's installer and About or application menu, as does the Copyright value. Discussion of the icons appears in Chapter 16, "Deploying Applications."

After you click Finish, Aptana Studio should create the main HTML file (**Figure 3.15**). This file should have some HTML and JavaScript already in it (based on an AIR application template).

continues on next page

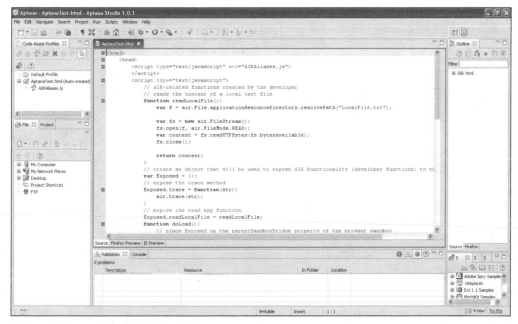

Figure 3.15 The resulting file after creating a new AIR project.

6. To run an application, click the Run button (green circle with the right-pointing white triangle) (**Figure 3.16**).

This will run the AIR application using the ADL. Of course, there are other ways to run the program—using keyboard commands, the Run menu, or right-clicking in the proper places—but this is the easiest way. To close the running application and return to Aptana Studio, quit the ADL.

7. To build the application, click the Export Adobe AIR Package icon (**Figure 3.17**).

In the resulting window, you can tweak some of the parameters and indicate which files need to be included in the package (**Figure 3.18**). This window serves the same purpose as the command-line ADT tool (see Chapter 2).

As for the digital signature option, you can use the default certificate that comes with Aptana Studio or create your own, as covered later in this chapter.

✔ Tips

■ Applications written in Java are notorious for being memory hogs and often running slowly. Although I have no problems using Aptana Studio on my computer (Mac PowerBook Pro with Intel Core Duo 2.16 GHz chip and 2 GB RAM), you may find that Aptana Studio performs poorly on your system.

■ By choosing the Run option on the Run menu, you'll be prompted to adjust how the application is executed. This is useful if you want to try running a program using a different application descriptor XML file or a different SDK, or while providing command-line arguments.

Figure 3.16 Click once on the Run button to test an application you're developing.

Figure 3.17 When you've completed developing a program, click this icon to create its .air file, which can then be installed on users' computers.

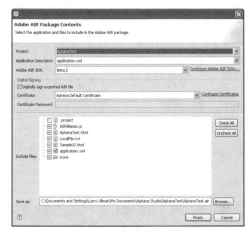

Figure 3.18 This window mimics the step taken using the ADT on the command-line to create the package.

USING APTANA STUDIO

Figure 3.19 To start developing an AIR application using Dreamweaver, create a new site for the project.

Figure 3.20 A bare-bones HTML page, which will also serve as the test AIR application.

Using Dreamweaver

Dreamweaver is perhaps the most popular IDE available for Web developers. Because AIR and Dreamweaver are Adobe products (Dreamweaver became so after Adobe purchased Macromedia), it's no surprise that you can use Dreamweaver to create AIR applications. Unlike Aptana Studio, Dreamweaver is a commercial application only, but you can download a 30-day trial version at www.adobe.com.

To develop AIR applications in Dreamweaver, you must install the AIR Extension, which is simple enough, so there's no need to walk you through it. Just download the extension at http://labs.adobe.com/wiki/index.php/AIR:Dreamweaver_CS3_Extension. It works with Dreamweaver CS3 on Windows (XP or Vista) and Mac OS X (10.4 or later), and can be installed using Dreamweaver's Extension Manager. Once you have the extension installed (remember to restart Dreamweaver afterwards), follow these steps to write, debug, and build an AIR application.

To create an AIR application:

1. Open Dreamweaver.

2. Create a new site for your AIR application (**Figure 3.19**).

    You'll likely want to create a new site for each AIR application you develop. If you don't already know how to do so, it's simply a matter of choosing Site > New Site to bring up the window (Figure 3.19), filling out the prompts, and then clicking OK.

3. Create a new HTML page (**Figure 3.20**).

    continues on next page

Again, if you don't know how to do this, start by selecting File > New. In the resulting window (**Figure 3.21**), choose HTML for the Page Type, <none> for the Layout, and None for the DocType (if you want to create something prettier, use a different layout). Then create the look you want in the resulting HTML page (Figure 3.20). Later in the book you'll learn how to add functionality to your pages so they actually do something.

4. Save the HTML page as `HelloWorld.html`. Make sure you save this file in the site's main directory.

5. To preview the application, click the Preview/Debug in Browser button and choose Preview in Adobe AIR (**Figure 3.22**).

This opens the application using the ADL, providing you with the exact same look and experience as the end user will have.

6. To build the application, select Site > AIR Application Settings to bring up the AIR Application and Installer Settings window (**Figure 3.23**).

Much of the information entered into this window goes into the application descriptor XML file, which Dreamweaver makes for you. This includes the program's name and ID, its window style, and icons. You'll see that some of the information will be generated automatically; other details, including those required, need to be filled in.

Figure 3.21 Dreamweaver's New Document window.

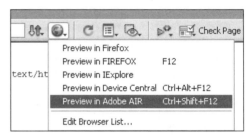

Figure 3.22 After installing the AIR Extension, Dreamweaver creates a Preview in Adobe AIR option.

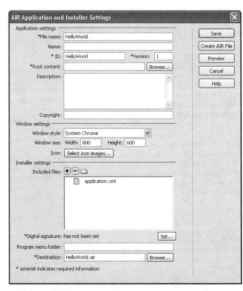

Figure 3.23 The initial settings when opening the AIR Application and Installer Settings window for a project.

USING DREAMWEAVER

Figure 3.24 To build the program, a digital signature must be chosen. Select an existing one using this prompt.

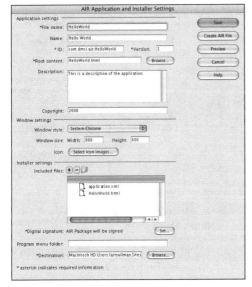

Figure 3.25 The final settings to create the .air program file.

7. Choose the application's root content.

   One of the required pieces of information is the root content, which is the primary HTML file for the application. In this example it would be HelloWorld.html. Click Browse and navigate to that file.

8. Click Set to bring up the window for identifying the digital signature (**Figure 3.24**).

   Digital signatures are discussed in Chapter 2, where you also learned how to create your own self-signed certificate. If you followed those steps, you can use the certificate you created then. Otherwise, see the next section in this chapter to create your own certificate using Dreamweaver.

9. When you've finished configuring everything in the AIR Application and Installer Settings window (**Figure 3.25**), click Create AIR File.

   Unless you changed the destination, the AIR package will be created in the site's directory.

✔ Tip

- The Installer settings section in the AIR Application and Installer Settings window (Figures 3.23 and 3.25) replicate the choices you would make when using the command-line ADT to create an .air file.

Creating Digital Signatures

Added to the second beta version of AIR is the ability to associate a digital signature—a certificate of authenticity—to an application. This is part of AIR's security model and is meant to be a reassurance to end users. In fact, you can't even create a .air file without associating it with a certificate.

There are two kinds of certificates you can use. The first is purchased from an accredited company like Thawte or VeriSign. These certificates imply the highest level of security because those companies will verify your credentials. The second option is a self-signed certificate: something you create that allows you to build installable AIR applications but offers no real assurance to the application's end users. This option is free but essentially means that you're the one telling end users that you are legitimate. If they don't know you, that's not worth much.

But for testing purposes, creating a self-signed signature makes sense. Both Aptana Studio and Dreamweaver include tools for doing so, which is discussed in the following steps (Chapter 2 shows how to create a certificate using the command-line ADT).

Creating a certificate using Aptana Studio

Another reason I like using Aptana Studio for AIR development is that it comes with its own self-signed certificate. Thus, you can build AIR applications without going through the extra effort of creating a new certificate. But if you want a more personalized program, follow these steps.

To create a certificate in Aptana Studio:

1. Open Aptana Studio, if it is not already open.

2. Click the Export Adobe AIR Package icon. You do not need to have an AIR file open to follow these steps.

3. In the resulting window, click Configure Certificates (**Figure 3.26**).

Figure 3.26
The Adobe AIR Package Contents window.

4. In the resulting window (**Figure 3.27**) click Add.

5. Give the certificate a name (**Figure 3.28**).

The name here is a reference to this certificate for Aptana Studio's purposes. It won't appear in the final, installed application.

6. Select the Create new certificate option.

7. For the Certificate Location, enter *somename*.pfx.

The certificate should use a .pfx extension and be given a meaningful name (replace *somename* with an actual value you choose). It's a little confusing, but you don't want to use the Browse button to enter the location unless you're overwriting an existing certificate.

8. For the Publisher Name, enter your name or your company's name.

This value is important and will be displayed to the end user. It should be obviously related to the name used as the creator of the application (i.e., if the application is created by Widgets, Inc., but the certificate is signed by Jane Doe, the installing user may be suspicious). You can also fill out the Organization Unit and Organization Name, if necessary (e.g., to represent a subset of a larger company).

9. Enter your country.

This is optional but is a good idea.

continues on next page

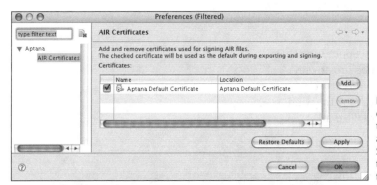

Figure 3.27 This window lists all the certificates you've made available to Aptana Studio (allowing you to choose from among them for each project).

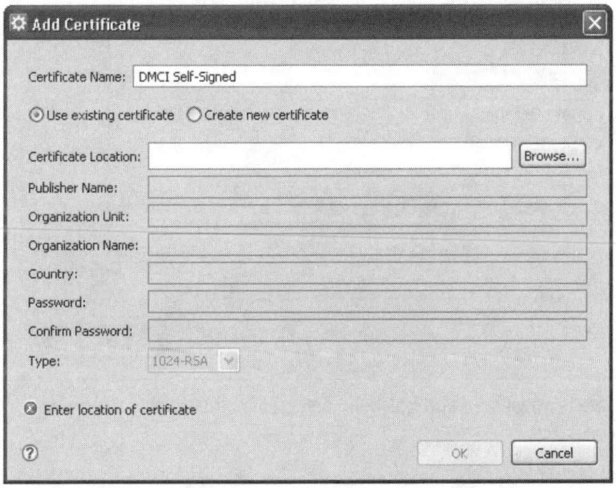

Figure 3.28 The Add Certificate window.

CREATING DIGITAL SIGNATURES

10. Enter a secure password, twice.

As with any password, it should not be chosen cavalierly. Come up with something secure containing several characters using both uppercase and lowercase letters as well as numbers and punctuation.

11. Choose a Type (**Figure 3.29**).

The options are 1024-RSA and 2048-RSA, which represent two different encryption algorithms. The latter is more secure.

12. Click OK to generate the certificate.

13. Back in the Preferences window, select the check box next to the new certificate to use it (**Figure 3.30**).

14. Click OK to exit the Preferences window.

✔ Tip

■ When creating an AIR application that uses your certificate, be sure to enter the certificate's password in the export window (Figure 3.26 shows the window without the password filled in).

Figure 3.29 As of AIR version 1, you have a choice of two encryptions for the certificate.

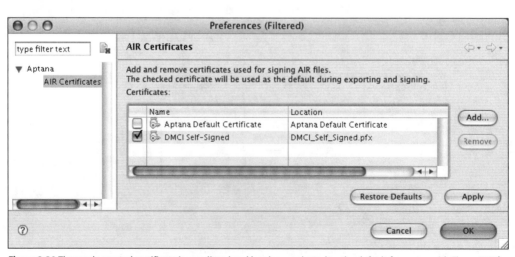

Figure 3.30 The newly created certificate is now listed and has been selected as the default (compare with Figure 3.27).

CREATING DIGITAL SIGNATURES

Figure 3.31 New certificates are generated by first accessing the AIR Application and Installer Settings window.

Figure 3.32 The Digital Signature window is where you select, or create, a certificate to associate with a program.

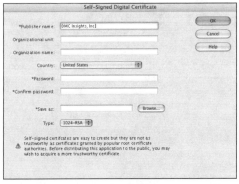

Figure 3.33 The window for creating your own self-signed certificate.

Creating a certificate using Dreamweaver

Unlike Aptana Studio, Dreamweaver does not provide a certificate you can use, so you have to create (or buy) your own. You can use the steps in Chapter 2 to do so or create one using Dreamweaver.

To create a certificate in Dreamweaver:

1. Open Dreamweaver, if it is not already open.

2. Select Site > AIR Application Settings. You do not need to have an AIR file open to follow these steps.

3. In the resulting window, click the Set button after Digital signature (**Figure 3.31**).

4. In the Digital Signature window, click Create (**Figure 3.32**).

5. Enter your name or your company's name as the Publisher name (**Figure 3.33**).

   This value is important and will be displayed to the end user. It should be obviously related to the name used as the creator of the application (i.e., if the application is created by Widgets, Inc., but the certificate is signed by Jane Doe, the installing user may be suspicious). You can also fill out the Organization Unit and Organization Name, if necessary (e.g., to represent a subset of a larger company).

6. Use the pull-down menu to select your country.

   United States is the default.

continues on next page

CREATING DIGITAL SIGNATURES

7. Enter a secure password, twice.

As with any password, it should not be chosen cavalierly. Come up with something secure containing several characters using both uppercase and lowercase as well as numbers and punctuation.

8. For the Save as value, enter *somename*.pfx.

The certificate should use a .pfx extension and be given a meaningful name (replace *somename* with an actual value you choose). You can also use the Browse button to choose the destination folder, and then in that prompt type *somename*.pfx as the name (**Figure 3.34**).

9. Choose a Type (**Figure 3.35**).

The options are 1024-RSA and 2048-RSA, which represent two different encryption algorithms. The latter is more secure.

10. Click OK to generate the certificate.

11. Back in the Digital Signature window, use the pull-down menu to choose the certificate to use (**Figure 3.36**).

When creating an AIR application that uses your certificate, be sure to enter the certificate's password in the export prompt (Figure 3.36 shows the prompt without the password filled in).

12. Click OK to exit the Digital Signature window.

Figure 3.34 Click the Browse button on the Self-Signed Digital Certificate window (see Figure 3.33) to decide where you'd like the certificate saved. You'll also need to name the file.

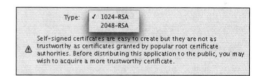

Figure 3.35 As of AIR version 1, you have a choice of two encryptions for the certificate.

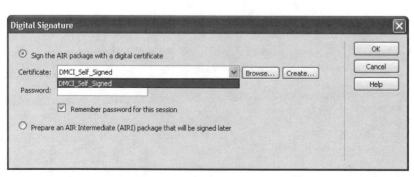

Figure 3.36 The newly created certificate is now listed and has been selected as the default (compare with Figure 3.32).

BASIC CONCEPTS AND CODE

As the simple test case in Chapter 2, "Creating an Application," shows, with Adobe AIR you can make an executable desktop application using just HTML. The problem is that with HTML alone your program won't do anything useful. To make a functional application, you'll need to use additional technologies, starting with JavaScript.

Although JavaScript can produce some nice results, there's no reason to stop there. It's easy enough to use ActionScript and Flash, even if you're not terribly familiar with either. An introduction to these programs plus how to tie them into an HTML application is what you'll find in this chapter. You'll also learn the fundamentals of the `XMLHttpRequest` object, a standard JavaScript tool for communicating between any two pages. Before getting to all of that, this chapter provides some general technical knowledge and background. Taken all together, the material in this chapter goes through every basic concept and code snippet that you'll want to use in your Adobe AIR applications.

Technological Background

Adobe AIR provides the power to create desktop applications using just HTML, CSS, and JavaScript, but there are several other technologies and concepts involved. Because this book assumes very little about what you might already know, I'll briefly introduce each.

WebKit

The first technology involved is WebKit (www.webkit.org). AIR uses WebKit as its HTML *rendering engine*, which is to say that WebKit translates HTML code into the result you see in a Web browser (for example, turning `<b>word</b>` into **word**). WebKit also handles the JavaScript, Document Object Model (DOM), and Cascading Style Sheets (CSS).

The use of a single rendering engine is one of Adobe AIR's best features. Every Web browser uses one rendering engine or another, but not often the same one. This is why different browsers give slightly or even drastically different results with the same HTML, CSS, or JavaScript. If you're a seasoned Web developer, you've probably become used to adding extra bits of code, formatting, or hacks to make your site behave properly in all browsers. Thankfully, the AIR applications you write should look and function essentially the same on different computers (thanks to WebKit).

WebKit is also the engine of choice for Apple's Safari Web browser (in fact, for Apple's operating system as a whole). An HTML page that looks and functions like you want it to in Safari will reliably look and function the same as an AIR application. (Even though Safari is made by Apple, it also now runs on Windows.)

JavaScript

The second technology involved in making AIR applications is JavaScript. Certainly you've heard of and have, I hope, dabbled with JavaScript already. HTML, by definition, dictates the appearance of a Web page or AIR application. JavaScript adds the functionality (so-called *client-side* functionality, which takes place within the browser or application; server-side functionality uses PHP, ASP.NET, and other technologies).

This book does assume that you have some comfort with JavaScript. You don't need to be able to program JavaScript like a pro, but understanding how to write and call functions, declare and use variables, and so forth will make this book's instructions more accessible. I'm conversant with several languages and can honestly say that JavaScript is really easy to work with, particularly once you've done away with the browser-specific issues.

Object-oriented programming

Object-oriented programming (OOP) is a serious subject that requires years of experience and learning to master. This book doesn't teach OOP, but that's not a problem, because you can easily use OOP without any mastery at all. The premise of OOP is as follows.

You first define a *class*, which is a blueprint that maps out the variables and functions required to work with a certain thing. For example, a blueprint of a rectangle would have variables that store its length and width. It would also have functions that calculate its perimeter and its area. Confusing matters just a little bit, the variables in a class are normally called *attributes* or *properties*, and the functions are normally called *methods*.

To use a class, you can create a variable of that class type using the new keyword:

```
var r = new Rectangle();
```

Now the r variable is an object of type `Rectangle` (r is called an *instance* of `Rectangle`). To access the object's attributes and methods, use the dot syntax:

```
r.length = 20;
var a = r.getArea(); // Call the method.
```

That's the basics of creating and using objects! Defining the classes is really the hard part, and in this book that'll always already be done for you (creating your own JavaScript classes is something you *can* do, it just won't be necessary for any of the examples in this book). But there will be some exceptions to how you use objects.

First, you won't always create an object initially. Some class functions can be used without creating an object, and some objects are created automatically for you. For example, a Web browser, or AIR HTML page, starts with a `document` object.

Second, the dot syntax can often be chained together, saving you steps by making the code a bit more complicated. For example, take this line of JavaScript that changes an item's CSS class:

```
document.getElementById('thing').
→ className = 'newClassName';
```

This code starts by calling the `getElement-ById()` method of the `document` object. That method returns an element in the page that matches the given ID (*thing* in this example). Then the `className` attribute of the `thing` element is assigned a new value (of *newClass-Name*). This is just a shortcut way of writing:

```
var thing = document.
→ getElementById('thing');
thing.className = 'newClassName';
```

I introduce all of this because JavaScript, among others, is an object-oriented language. Familiarity with these terms and the syntax will help minimize confusion

as you start to work with JavaScript code (the Document Object Model also uses objects, as its name implies).

APIs

An API is an *application programming interface*, which is to say it's an easy way for one technology to interact with another technology. For example, Google provides several different APIs for interacting with its many services. With respect to AIR applications, two important tools are the AIR API and the Flash API. Both provide access to features not normally associated with browser-based JavaScript. The most important of these are

◆ File system access

◆ Working with sounds and images

◆ Support for native windows (which are different than standard JavaScript-created windows)

◆ Working with the computer's clipboard

◆ Interacting with databases

The AIR and Flash APIs are accessible in JavaScript through `window.runtime` (by comparison, lots of standard JavaScript starts with `document`, as in the previous code). For example, to access the computer's file system, you would start by creating a new object of the `File` type:

```
var fp = new window.runtime.flash.
→ filesystem.File();
```

That line represents a JavaScript call to Flash functionality.

In your Adobe AIR applications you'll frequently go back and forth between conventional JavaScript and using the AIR and Flash APIs. Often, you won't need to think about the distinction at all, but there will be times that understanding that you're using the AIR or Flash API will be relevant.

Security model

Of the many new concepts you'll need to learn to fully adapt your existing Web development knowledge to creating desktop applications, none is more important than security. The Web browser has its own security model: Web pages are quite limited in what they can do with respect to the user's computer. Since AIR applications behave like standard programs, the rules are significantly different.

The AIR security model uses the concept of *sandboxes*: the realm in which an application can "play," which is to say where it can read data from or write data to. AIR builds on the Flash security model, which defines two sandboxes: one for the *local filesystem* (i.e., the user's computer) and another for *remote computers* (i.e., the Internet, other networked computers, etc.). AIR adds to these a third sandbox—*application*—which refers to the files and content that reside in the application's folder.

For example, the user installs an AIR application. When that program runs, it loads the main HTML page. This is the *application* sandbox. If that program retrieves content from the user's computer (i.e., from another directory), that's the *local* sandbox. If the program loads content from a Web site, that's the *remote* sandbox. The distinctions are important because they affect what a program can do with the content, as well as what security measures need to be taken. This topic is thoroughly covered in Chapter 15, "Security Techniques."

Universal Resource Identifiers

One of the most basic terms any Web developer knows is *URL*, which stands for Uniform Resource Locator (it used to mean Universal Resource Locator). If you want someone to access your site, you provide them with a URL, such as `http://www.example.com`. The *http://* part of the URL is the protocol; common alternatives are *https://* and *ftp://*. The *www.example.com* is the address; although, an IP address can also be used.

Naturally, your Adobe AIR applications will use URLs, but not every resource in an AIR application will be found online. Along with *http://*, *https://*, and *ftp://*, AIR supports:

◆ *file://*

◆ *app:/*

◆ *app-storage:/*

(There's also a plan to support *feed://* and *mailto://* in future versions of AIR.) Taken together, these are all Universal Resource Identifiers (URIs).

As you may already know, *file://* is supported by the Web browser, too, as a way to open local or networked documents. But the other two listed URIs are new to Adobe AIR. The first, *app:/* (notice there's only one slash), always refers to the directory where the AIR application is installed: the application's root. If you create an application whose main file is called *index.html*, no matter what operating system that application is installed on or where the user chose to install it, `app:/index.html` points to that main page. The second new URI, *app-storage:/* (again, one slash), refers to the application's storage directory, which will be a folder on the user's computer, different than the application's root directory.

From a security perspective, content within *app:/* has full privileges. In other words, this content can do the most harm to the user's computer! Any content an application loads from *app-storage:/*, *http://*, and the others, is more limited as to what it can do.

Using AIRAliases.js

As mentioned earlier, your AIR applications will make frequent and extensive use of the AIR and Flash APIs, resulting in lines like

```
var fp = new window.runtime.flash.
→ filesystem.File();
```

To make code easier to type, read, and debug, Adobe has created the `AIRAliases.js` file. This is a JavaScript document that creates shortcuts to the most commonly used AIR and Flash APIs. You'll find this file in the SDK's `frameworks` folder.

By using the aliases file, instead of the line as written above, you can just type

```
var fp = new air.File();
```

To use `AIRAliases.js` in any application, you must do two things:

- Include it in your HTML page, as you would any other JavaScript file.

- Include it when you build the application for distribution.

I'll walk you through this in more detail in the next sequence of steps.

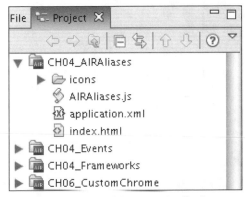

Figure 4.1 The project tab in Aptana Studio shows what files and folders are part of the project.

To use AIRAliases.js:

1. Begin a new AIR project in your text editor or IDE.

   The exact steps for doing so are outlined in Chapter 2 and Chapter 3, "AIR Development Tools." In those two chapters I explain how you'd use a text editor, Aptana Studio, or Dreamweaver for this purpose.

2. Copy the `AIRAliases.js` file to the project folder created in step 1.

   You'll find `AIRAliases.js` in the `frameworks` folder within the SDK folder (created when you installed the SDK following the instructions in Chapter 2).

   If you're using Aptana Studio, the `AIRAliases.js` file is automatically part of the project. You can see it in the project tab on the left side of the application (**Figure 4.1**).

   Ordinarily I would recommend creating a separate folder in which your JavaScript files, like `AIRAliases.js`, would be stored. But for this simple example, I won't spend the time doing so.

3. Add the following to the head of the main HTML document:

   ```
   <script src="AIRAliases.js"
   → type="text/javascript"></script>
   ```

   If you do place the file in a special JavaScript folder, you'll need to change this code accordingly.

   Aptana Studio automatically creates a reference to `AIRAliases.js` in the main HTML file, so you can skip this step, or just update the code to reflect the location of the file in a subdirectory if you chose to go that route.

continues on next page

4. When you build the final application, be sure to include `AIRAliases.js`.

If you're building the application using the command-line tools (as demonstrated in Chapter 2), the requisite instruction would be something like (**Figure 4.2**)

```
adt -package -storetype pkcs12
→ -keystore ~/Desktop/AIR/
→ MyCert.pfx AIRAliases.air
→ application.xml index.html
→ AIRAliases.js
```

Aptana Studio automatically includes the file as long as it's listed in the project tab (see Figure 4.1). If you're using

Dreamweaver, make sure the file is included in the AIR Application and Installer Settings window (**Figure 4.3**).

✔ Tips

- You can see the full list of AIR aliases by opening the JavaScript file in any text editor or IDE.

- If you appreciate the convenience of aliases, you can add your own to the `AIRAliases.js` file. Or better yet create a new `MyAIRAliases.js` file that won't have the potential of being overwritten by new releases of the AIR SDK.

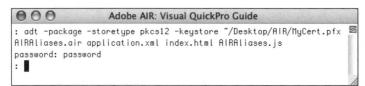

Figure 4.2 When building an AIR application using the command-line tool, be sure to include all of the program's required files, like `AIRAliases.js`.

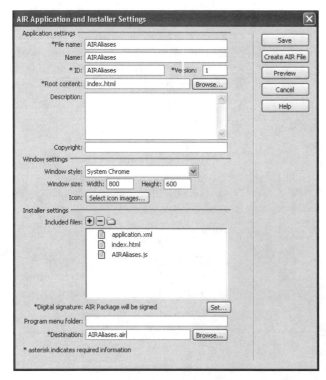

Figure 4.3 In Dreamweaver's AIR Application and Installer Settings window, you can choose which files and folders should be included in the build.

JavaScript Frameworks

A *framework* is an established library of code designed to perform common tasks. Instead of having to write, test, and debug the code necessary to do a particular thing, you can save yourself a lot of time and hassle by using a framework.

A ton of JavaScript frameworks are available, each with their own strengths and weaknesses. Frameworks you might want to consider include (in no particular order):

◆ Yahoo! User Interface (YUI) Library (`http://developer.yahoo.com/yui/`)

◆ Dojo (`www.dojotoolkit.org`)

◆ Rico (`www.openrico.org`)

◆ qooxdoo (`www.qooxdoo.org`)

◆ Ext JS (`www.extjs.com`)

◆ mootools (`www.mootools.net`)

◆ script.aculo.us (`http://script.aculo.us`)

Most are free of charge (others require licenses for some uses). Which you use on any project is up to you. How you use each specific framework is far too complicated to discuss here, but I will demonstrate the basics of incorporating one into your AIR applications.

Figure 4.4
The YUI calendar widget creates a calendar you can use in your AIR applications (or Web pages, naturally). It's scrollable by month and allows the user to select any date.

To use a framework:

1. Determine which framework you'd like to use and download it.

To make that decision, start by looking at the framework's features: Does it do what you need it to do in your program? As part of this question, make sure the framework functions perfectly in Apple's Safari Web browser. Because Safari uses the same HTML and JavaScript rendering engine as Adobe AIR, if the framework is good for Safari, it's good for your AIR application.

A second but still important consideration is the quantity and quality of documentation available for the framework (including tutorials or articles put together by third parties). The point of a framework is to save you time; spending hours figuring out how to use a framework defeats that purpose.

For these next steps, let's use the Yahoo! User Interface (YUI) Library, which was at version 2.4.1 at the time of this writing.

2. Begin a new AIR project in your text editor or IDE.

3. Copy any required files to your project's directory.

This may be the hardest step because it requires a thorough understanding of how the framework will be used. For example, to use the YUI calendar widget (**Figure 4.4**), you need to copy three files from the downloaded code into the project folder (all are within the `build` directory found in the YUI download):

▲ `yahoo-dom-event/yahoo-dom-event.js`

▲ `calendar/calendar-min.js`

▲ `calendar/assets/skins/sam/calendar.css`

continues on next page

I put the two JavaScript files into a folder called js, the CSS file into a folder called css, and some images into an assets folder (**Figure 4.5**).

4. Include the framework files in your HTML page (**Script 4.1**):

```
<html><!-- Script 4.1 -->
  <head>
    <script type="text/javascript"
→ src="js/AIRAliases.js">
→ </script>
    <link rel="stylesheet"
→ type="text/css" href="css/
→ calendar.css">
    <script type="text/javascript"
→ src="js/yahoo-dom-event.js">
→ </script>
    <script type="text/javascript"
→ src="js/calendar-min.js">
→ </script>
  </head>
```

Figure 4.5 All of the files and folders in this project, as shown in Aptana Studio's project window.

Script 4.1 By including and using the Yahoo! User Interface framework, a few lines of code can create a complete calendar (see Figure 4.4).

```
1    <html><!-- Script 4.1 -->
2        <head>
3            <script type="text/javascript" src="js/AIRAliases.js"></script>
4            <link rel="stylesheet" type="text/css" href="css/calendar.css">
5            <script type="text/javascript" src="js/yahoo-dom-event.js"></script>
6            <script type="text/javascript" src="js/calendar-min.js"></script>
7        </head>
8        <body class="yui-skin-sam">
9            <div id="calendarDIV"></div>
10           <script type="text/javascript">
11           var c = new YAHOO.widget.Calendar("calendarDIV");
12           c.render();
13           </script>
14       </body>
15   </html>
```

As with any JavaScript file you use, you must include it in your HTML page to be able to use its functionality. Here the three files from YUI (mentioned in step 3) are included, along with the `AIRAliases.js` file.

5. Use the framework in your HTML page as needed:

```
<body class="yui-skin-sam">
    <div id="calendarDIV"></div>
    <script type="text/javascript">
    var c = new YAHOO.widget.
    → Calendar("calendarDIV");
    c.render();
    </script>
</body>
</html>
```

These lines are all that's necessary to make the AIR application shown in Figure 4.4. Whenever you use a framework, most of the code in the HTML page will be derived from the framework's documentation, modified to suit your application. For this YUI calendar widget, a `DIV` is created, and then a new `YAHOO.widget.Calendar` object is created. Finally, the object's `render()` method is called to actually generate the calendar.

6. Be sure to include the framework files when building the application!

How you do this depends on what you're using to build the application. With Aptana Studio, all files listed in the project window (see Figure 4.5) will automatically be included. With Dreamweaver, you just need to make sure you add all the files in the AIR Application and Installer Settings window (see Figure 4.3 for the previous example). If you're using the command-line `adt`, all of the files and directories must be listed in the command (see Figure 4.2 for the previous example).

✔ Tips

- When creating Web pages, factor in the file size of the framework when selecting one to use. Forcing a user to download 300 KB of JavaScript to use a 4 KB HTML file is absurd. However, with an AIR application, that same 300 KB is perfectly reasonable to include.

- If you'd rather make sure the application works before you finesse it, copy the entire framework into the project folder and remove files you think are unnecessary after you're certain it works.

ActionScript Libraries

Along with the AIR and Flash APIs, and existing JavaScript frameworks, another way to add functionality to your applications is to tie into an ActionScript library. ActionScript, in case you're not familiar with it, is a scripting language commonly used in Flash. But as of version ActionScript 3, it can now be used with Adobe AIR.

ActionScript libraries are compiled as .swf files (Shockwave Format). These can be used in an AIR application after including them as you would any JavaScript file:

```
<script src="somefile.swf" type=
→ "application/x-shockwave-flash">
→ </script>
```

Note that you should explicitly use the type attribute with a value of *application/ x-shockwave-flash*.

If you're comfortable with JavaScript, learning ActionScript isn't too much of a leap. But even if you never write your own code, you'll likely still use some ActionScript in your AIR applications thanks to servicemonitor.swf. The AIR SDK comes with this one precompiled library and is found in the same SDK frameworks directory as AIRAliases. js. It defines the functionality for detecting network connectivity (which can be used, for example, to see if the user is currently connected to the Internet or not—a valuable piece of information).

To use ActionScript libraries:

1. Begin a new AIR project in your text editor or IDE.

   The exact steps for doing so are outlined in Chapter 2 and Chapter 3.

2. Add a new folder named as to your project's directory (**Figure 4.6**).

   As in the steps for using frameworks, I recommend creating a separate folder in which your ActionScript files will be stored.

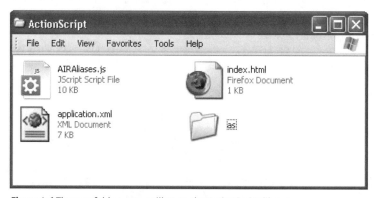

Figure 4.6 The new folder—as—will store the ActionScript library.

ACTIONSCRIPT LIBRARIES

3. Copy the `servicemonitor.swf` file to the folder created in step 2.

You'll find `servicemonitor.swf` in the `frameworks` folder within the SDK folder (created when you installed the SDK following the instructions in Chapter 2).

4. Add the following to the head of the main HTML document:

```
<script src="as/servicemonitor.swf"
→ type="application/x-shockwave-
→ flash"></script>
```

If you used a different name for the ActionScript folder (created in step 2), you'll need to change this code accordingly.

5. Use the ActionScript code as needed in your program.

You'll see examples of this in Chapter 13, "Networking."

6. When you build the final application, be sure to include the as folder and the `.swf` file.

If you're building the application using the command-line tools (as demonstrated in Chapter 2), the requisite instruction would be something like (**Figure 4.7**)

```
adt -package -storetype pkcs12
→ -keystore C:\Documents and
→ Settings\Larry Ullman\My Documents/
→ MyCert.pfx ActionScript.air
→ application.xml index.html
→ AIRAliases.js as
```

Aptana Studio automatically includes the file as long as it's listed in the project (see Figure 4.5 for an earlier example). With Dreamweaver, make sure you add all the files and folders in the AIR Application and Installer Settings window (see Figure 4.3 for an earlier example).

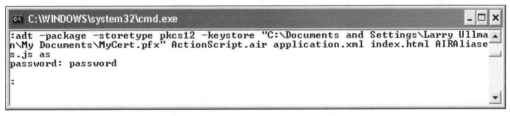

Figure 4.7 Building the application on Windows using the command-line adt.

Handling Events

Another basic idea you'll need to grasp to create many AIR applications is how to handle an event. If you've worked with JavaScript even a little, you probably already have a sense of this. In the Web browser, an event might be when the cursor moves over an item (like an image or a link) or when a form is submitted. In AIR, you can still use JavaScript events, like calling a function when a button is clicked:

```
<input type="button" value="Click This!"
→ onclick="callThisFunction();">
```

Continuing to use this kind of event handling is fine for basic JavaScript stuff. Unfortunately, this method won't work for Flash and AIR API events (things that happen within `window. runtime` as opposed to `document`).

Handling so-called *runtime* events is a two-step process:

◆ Create a function that will handle the event

◆ Indicate for what event the function should be called

For the first step, define a function that does whatever should be done. The particulars will vary according to the event being handled: If the event is a window closing, the function would do X; if it's the user going offline, the function would do Y. In every case, you'll want to write this function so that it takes one argument, which will be an event object:

```
function someFunction(event) {
    // Code.
}
```

For the second step, you'll use the `addEventListener()` method applied to a corresponding object. Its first argument is the type of event that should be monitored. The event type will be a *constant*: a static value associated with a name (normally written in all capital letters) that has special meaning. The `addEventListener()` method takes a second argument, the name of the function to be called when that event occurs

As a concrete example of this, say you write a program that should do something special when it's activated. "Activated" means that the application is already open, the user switches to another application, and then returns to—*activates*—this one. That particular event is represented by the constant `air.Event.ACTIVATE` (or written without the AIRAliases.js alias, `window.runtime.flash. events.Event.ACTIVATE`).

Along with knowing the event to watch for, the function to be called must be defined:

```
function nowActive(event) {
    alert('This is now the active
    → program.');
}
```

Finally, you need to call the `addEvent- Listener()` for the proper object. In this example, the object is the application itself, accessed via `air.NativeApplication. nativeApplication`. The final code is therefore:

```
air.NativeApplication.nativeApplication.
→ addEventListener(air.Event.ACTIVATE,
→ nowActive);
```

In this code, note that the second argument is the name of the function to be called without parentheses or quotation marks.

HANDLING EVENTS

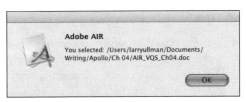

Figure 4.8 This AIR application simply reports back to the user which file the user selected.

Script 4.2 In this Adobe AIR program, the `File` class (part of the Flash API) is used to create a prompt for the user (see Figure 4.9) in which the user can select a file on the computer. The selected file's name and location is then repeated in a JavaScript dialog.

```
1   <html><!-- Script 4.2 -->
2     <head>
3        <script type="text/javascript"
          src="AIRAliases.js"></script>
4        <script type="text/javascript">
5
6          // Create an object of File type:
7          var file = new air.File();
8
9          // Add the event listener:
10         file.addEventListener(air.Event.
           SELECT, fileWasSelected);
11
12         // Create the Open prompt:
13         file.browseForOpen('Choose a file:');
14
15         // Define a function that will be
             called when
16         // the event occurs:
17         function fileWasSelected(event) {
18
19             // Use an alert to print the
                 selected file's name.
20             alert ('You selected: ' +
                 file.nativePath);
21
22         } // End of fileWasSelected()
             function.
23
24       </script>
25     </head>
26     <body>
27        <h1>Handling Events</h1>
28     </body>
29   </html>
```

To hammer this point home, let's run through another example. In it, an event listener will be created that reports what file a user selected (**Figure 4.8**). This uses some code you haven't seen before (which will be covered in more detail in Chapter 9, "Files and Directories") but will still be easy enough to follow.

To create an event handler:

1. Begin a new AIR project in your text editor or IDE.

   Make sure that you include the `AIRAliases.js` file (described earlier in this chapter), because shortcuts defined in it will be used by this program.

2. Within a JavaScript block, define an object of `File` type (**Script 4.2**):

   `var file = new air.File();`

   The `File` class defines all the functionality necessary for dealing with files on the user's computer. To start, create an object of this type using the new keyword and the AIR alias.

3. Add an event listener to the file selection event:

   ```
   file.addEventListener(air.Event.
   → SELECT, fileWasSelected);
   ```

   This line adds an event listener to the file object. The specific event being watched for is `air.Event.SELECT`, which occurs when a user selects a file in a Open dialog window. When such an event occurs, the `fileWasSelected()` function will be called. It'll be written in step 5.

   continues on next page

4. Create the browse prompt:

```
file.browseForOpen('Choose a file:');
```

Again, you haven't seen any of this file-related code before, but it shouldn't be too confusing. This line generates the dialog in which the user can select a file (**Figure 4.9**).

5. Define the `fileWasSelected()` function:

```
function fileWasSelected(event) {
  alert ('You selected: ' +
  → file.nativePath);
}
```

This function states the full path to the file that was selected by the user (see Figure 4.8). It does so by referring to the `nativePath()` method of the file object.

6. Save, test, debug, and run the application.

Notice that the application does away with normal niceties and immediately prompts the user to select a file. Later in the book you'll see examples for doing this same thing more professionally.

✔ Tips

■ Some application events are common and will therefore be automatically handled by Adobe AIR (for example, closing the application's main window). You never need to write event handlers for such events, but you can if you'd like to overrule the default behavior. Not all default event behavior can be altered, though.

■ The `removeEventListener()` method gets rid of event handlers created by `addEventListener()`.

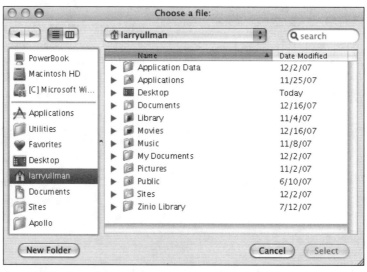

Figure 4.9 The Open dialog window allows the user to select a file on the computer.

The XMLHttpRequest Object

The XMLHttpRequest object, which is part of JavaScript, has been around for years but has really gained popularity recently thanks to the rise of Ajax. XMLHttpRequest is a class that defines the functionality for HTTP (HyperText Transfer Protocol) interactions. Even if that sounds like gibberish to you, you're actually quite familiar with the concept: When you load a Web page in your browser, you're making an HTTP request (normally). Using XMLHttpRequest, JavaScript in one page can make that same kind of transaction behind the scenes (i.e., without the browser leaving the current page). The JavaScript can use the response from the second page as needed, most likely to update the first page's content in some way.

As an example of how you might use this, say you wanted to create an iTunes-like application with a search feature. The user enters some text—a song or album title, or an artist's name—in a box, and then clicks an icon or presses Enter. This would queue the JavaScript, which would use Ajax to send the search term to another page. That page would, unbeknownst to the user, actually perform the search and return the results to the original page. The JavaScript in that page would then update the application window, showing the results of the search.

There are many ways this kind of functionality can be added to an application by using the AIR API. But it's worth knowing how to make an XMLHttpRequest using plain old JavaScript, so let's work through an example.

To use XMLHttpRequest, start by creating an object of type XMLHttpRequest:

```
var xhr = new XMLHttpRequest();
```

Next, provide to the open() method the type of request to make—normally GET or POST—and the file to be communicated with:

```
xhr.open('get', 'filename.ext');
```

This line opens a connection to filename.ext, to which it will make a GET request. If you're not familiar with what GET and POST mean, search the Web for (probably too detailed) answers. Or, for the time being, simply understand that you'll generally use GET, because it's the standard method for requesting information from a page, whereas POST is used to send information to a page.

The next step is to name the function to be called when `filename.ext` returns its results. The `onreadystatechange` property takes this value. This property is one of five important `XMLHttpRequest` object properties listed in **Table 4.1** (remember that in object-oriented programming a *property* or *attribute* is a variable defined in a class). Assign to this property the name of the function without any parentheses or quotation marks:

```
xhr.onreadystatechange =
→ callThisFunction;
```

So the JavaScript will send the request to `filename.ext`, that page will send back a reply, and at that time the `callThisFunction()` function will be called. This function, defined shortly, will take the returned data and update the page content accordingly.

The last step in this sequence is to send the request. For `GET` requests, you should provide the value `null` as the `send()` method's only argument:

```
xhr.send(null);
```

That wraps up the "making the request" JavaScript; next is the handling of the returned results (what `filename.ext` sends back). Remember that this will be done within the `callThisFunction()` function. But you'll first want to confirm that the request was successful. To do so, check that the `readyState` is equal to 4 (see **Table 4.2** for the list of `readyState` values):

```
function callThisFunction () {
    if (xhr.readyState == 4) {
        // Handle the returned data.
```

The `readyState` attribute indicates the status of the request process. At first the `readyState` value is uninitialized (which equals 0, see Table 4.2). When the request is made, the server page starts to load, making the `readyState` value 1. Then the server page finishes

Table 4.1 Performing XMLHttpRequests relies upon the XMLHttpRequest properties listed here.

XMLHttpRequest Properties

PROPERTY	CONTAINS THE...
onreadystatechange	Name of the function to be called when the readyState property changes
readyState	Current state of the request (see Table 4.2)
responseText	Returned data as a string
responseXML	Returned data as XML
status	HTTP status code returned

Table 4.2 Of the five readyState values listed here, the last one is the most important for knowing when to handle the returned data.

XMLHttpRequest readyState Values

VALUE	MEANING
0	uninitialized
1	loading
2	loaded
3	interactive
4	complete

Script 4.3 This bit of a text (a quote from Homer Simpson, naturally) will be retrieved using an XMLHttpRequest.

```
1    They have the Internet on computers now.
```

loading, making readyState 2. Some interaction will occur between the two pages, making readyState 3, and eventually the request is completed, giving readyState a value of 4. Often, these states will change very quickly, but in terms of handling the response, getting a readyState of 4 is most important.

Having created the XMLHttpRequest object, performed the transaction, and confirmed the results, the final step is to use the returned data to alter the page content. The easiest way to access that data is to refer to the responseText property. This attribute stores the result of the request, which is what the requested page would display if loaded directly in a Web browser. If the result of the request is XML data, you would use responseXML instead.

Once you have the page's response, you can use it however the application dictates. You might write the response content to the page, use it to change some existing values, and so on. To help demonstrate this concept and to provide you with some usable code, let's run through a basic example of an XMLHttpRequest.

To use XMLHttpRequest:

1. Begin a new AIR project in your text editor or IDE.

   For this particular program, it's not necessary to include the AIRAliases.js file, although it's not a big deal if you do.

2. Create a plain text file named message.txt that contains some text (**Script 4.3**).

   The contents of this file will be read in by the XMLHttpRequest object and printed in the main application page.

continues on next page

3. Within the body of the main HTML file, add the following (**Script 4.4**):

```
<h1 id="response" style="color:
→ red;"></h1>
```

```
<button id="do" onclick=
→ "getMessage()">Get the message!
→ </button>
```

Script 4.4 This is the primary HTML file for the XMLHttpRequest AIR application. It performs the actual request, updating the body of the page using the results.

```
1    <html><!-- Script 4.4 -->
2        <head>
3            <script type="text/javascript">
4
5                // Create an XMLHttpRequest object:
6                var xhr = new XMLHttpRequest();
7
8                // This function is called when the user clicks the button:
9                function getMessage() {
10
11                    // Open the connection:
12                    xhr.open('get', 'message.txt');
13
14                    // Identify the function to handle the ready state change:
15                    xhr.onreadystatechange = printMessage;
16
17                    // Send the request:
18                    xhr.send(null);
19
20                } // End of getMessage() function.
21
22                // This function updats the page after the request is made:
23                function printMessage() {
24
25                    // Only do something when the readyState is complete:
26                    if (xhr.readyState == 4) {
27                        document.getElementById( 'response' ).innerText = xhr.responseText;
28                    }
29
30                } // End of printMessage() function.
31
32            </script>
33        </head>
34        <body>
35            <h1 id="response" style="color: red;"></h1>
36            <button id="do" onclick="getMessage()">Get the message!</button>
37        </body>
38    </html>
```

Figure 4.10 The application as it appears when it first opens.

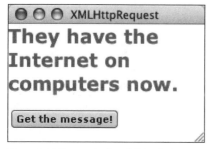

Figure 4.11 The result after clicking the button.

The body of this application is just a button (**Figure 4.10**) that, when clicked, invokes the XMLHttpRequest functionality. That JavaScript will update this empty H1 with the response from the text file (**Figure 4.11**).

4. Within the head of the main HTML file, begin a section of JavaScript and create an XMLHttpRequest object:

```
<script type="text/javascript">
var xhr = new XMLHttpRequest();
```

5. Define the getMessage() function:

```
function getMessage() {
    xhr.open('get', 'message.txt');
    xhr.onreadystatechange =
    → printMessage;
    xhr.send(null);
}
```

This function will be called when the user clicks the button (see the code in step 3). The first step within the function is to invoke the open() method of xhr (that variable is accessible within the function because it was defined outside of the function, per JavaScript scope behavior). The first argument is the HTTP method to use and the second is the name of the file to request, which in this case is message.txt, created earlier.

Next, assign to the onreadystatechange attribute the name of the function to be called when the readyState value changes. Finally, make the request by calling send().

continues on next page

The XMLHttpRequest Object

6. Define the printMessage() function:

```
function printMessage() {
  if (xhr.readyState == 4) {
    document.getElementById(
    → 'response' ).innerText =
    → xhr.responseText;
  }
}
```

This function will be called whenever the readyState value changes (it will actually change several times). The code in this function will not do anything until readyState has a value of 4. At that time, the innerText—the value between the tags—of the H1 with an ID of *response* will be assigned the value of the textual response of message.txt. This will literally be the contents of that file (see step 2).

7. Complete the JavaScript section:

```
</script>
```

8. Save, test, debug, run, and build the application.

Make sure that the message.txt file is in the same directory as index.html and that it's included when you build the application.

✔ Tip

■ XMLHttpRequests in Adobe AIR also differ from those in a Web browser in that they can be performed across domains. For security purposes, in a Web browser you cannot use XMLHttpRequest to access www.example2.com/page.html from www.example1.com/page.html. In Adobe AIR, allowing this behavior means that a program on your computer can use XMLHttpRequest to access www.example1.com/page.html.

DEBUGGING

One of the most important aspects of learning any new programming language or technology is knowing how to debug a problem when it occurs. No matter how skilled or smart you are, problems will occur, bugs will creep into your code, and something just won't work the way it should. In this chapter, you'll learn about some specific techniques and actual code you can use to help solve the problems you encounter as you develop your own AIR applications.

Because this book addresses AIR development using HTML and JavaScript, the bulk of the debugging information herein pertains just to JavaScript. This includes using simple alert dialogs or the JavaScript tools included in the excellent Firefox Web browser. The AIR API (see the previous chapter) has its own utility that aids in the debugging process, so you'll see how to use it, too. There are even steps you can take when using *adl* (AIR Debugging Launcher) that can make testing your code or project a little easier. The chapter concludes with some other recommendations and considerations to keep in mind as you continue working your way through this book.

Using JavaScript Dialogs

Simply put, debugging is always a two-step process:

1. Figure out where the problem is.

2. Figure out what the solution is to that problem.

Put like that, debugging seems easy, but it rarely is. Sometimes it takes forever to determine what's causing the problem, and other times you might discover what's causing the problem but still not know what the fix is. But you have to get through step 1 to even attempt step 2, and that's where JavaScript dialogs come in handy.

The best way to identify the problem is to confirm what an application (or, more specifically, the JavaScript code) is or is not doing and what values your variables have. To achieve both, use an alert dialog:

```
alert ('This is the text.');
alert ('name: ' + name);
```

There are many ways you might use an alert dialog as a debugging tool.

To use JavaScript dialogs:

◆ To print the value of a variable, use (**Figure 5.1**):

```
alert('myVar = ' + myVar);
```

This simple line of code is one of the most useful debugging techniques available.

◆ To print the value of an object, use (**Figure 5.2**):

```
var stuff = '';
for (var i in myVar) {
   stuff += myVar[i] + "\n";
}
alert('myVar = ' + stuff);
```

Figure 5.1 The name and value of a variable can be easily confirmed using an alert dialog.

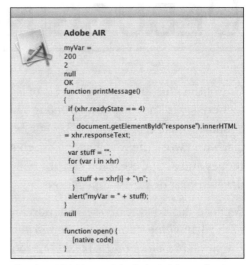

Figure 5.2 This is a partial printing of the attributes and methods found within the xhr object, created in Chapter 4, "Basic Concepts and Code."

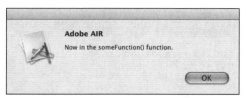

Figure 5.3 By using an alert such as this, you can be certain that a function is being executed.

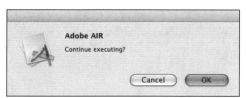

Figure 5.4 A confirmation dialog adds a Cancel option, which an alert dialog does not have.

Because the structure of object variables is more complex than other variables, they cannot be printed using just `alert(myVar)`. Instead, you can use a loop to access every element in an object. As you can see in the figure, this includes the values of all attributes and the names of all methods.

◆ To indicate that a function is being called, use (**Figure 5.3**):

```
function someFunction() {
    alert('Now in the someFunction()
    → function.');
}
```

Sometimes the most useful piece of debugging information is confirmation as to what sections of code are or are not being executed.

✔ Tips

■ The preceding listings represent just three ways you might use an alert dialog. There are other options, but the important point is that you use the JavaScript to help you in the debugging process.

■ An alternative to `alert()` is `confirm()`. It also creates a window, but one that gives the user an option of clicking Cancel or OK (**Figure 5.4**). For debugging purposes, a confirmation dialog could give you the choice of continuing to execute the JavaScript or stopping. For example, to terminate the execution of a function, use:

```
if (!confirm('Continue executing?'))
→ return false;
```

USING JAVASCRIPT DIALOGS

Using Trace

JavaScript dialogs are an easy and effective way to identify the values of variables, what code is being executed, and so forth. But if you use them a lot, particularly in the same bit of code, dealing with all those dialogs can be tiresome. An alternative is to use the `trace()` method that's part of the AIR API. This method takes a string that will be written to the console:

```
window.runtime.trace('Print this
→ message.');
```

If you include the `AIRAliases.js` file (see Chapter 4, "Basic Concepts and Code"), you can abbreviate this to just

```
air.trace('Print this message.');
```

You might not be familiar with what the console is, and the fact is that the answer depends on how you're testing and running the application. If you use the command-line `adl` utility, the console is the program in which you invoked `adl`. This would be a DOS prompt or console window on Windows (**Figure 5.5**) or the Terminal window on Mac OS X (**Figure 5.6**). If you are using Aptana Studio, the console is part of that application (**Figure 5.7**).

The `trace()` method is best used exactly as I suggest for `alert()` in the previous section of this chapter.

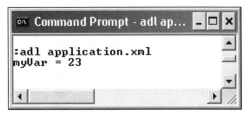

Figure 5.5 When using `adl` on Windows, `trace()` writes messages to the DOS prompt.

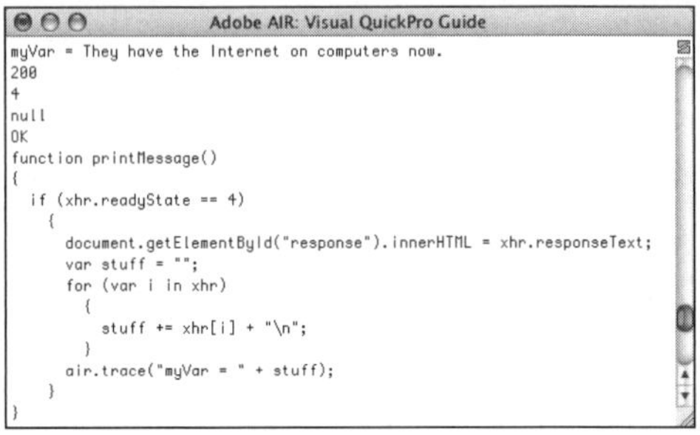

Figure 5.6 When using `adl` on Mac OS X, `trace()` writes messages to the Terminal window.

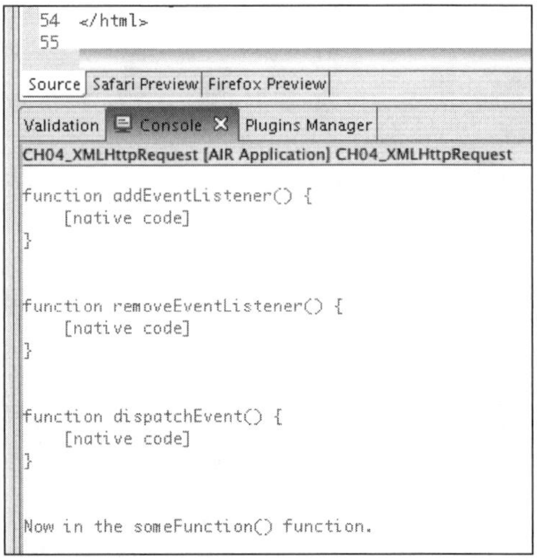

Figure 5.7 Aptana Studio has a console window built into the application. That's where you'll see any `trace()` messages.

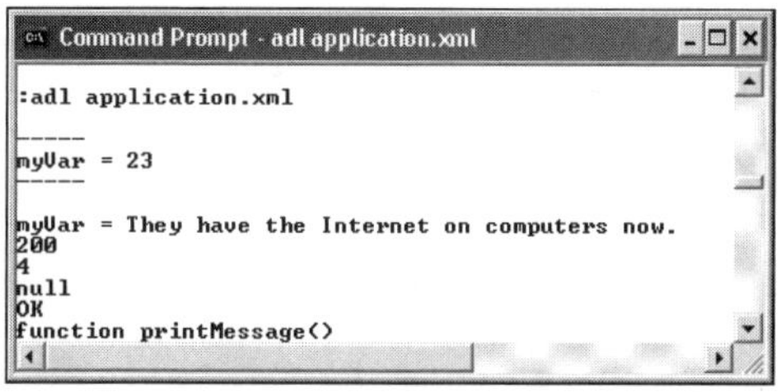

Figure 5.8 Improve the legibility of your trace messages by adding newlines and other characters.

To use trace:

♦ To print the value of a variable, use (see Figure 5.5):

```
air.trace('myVar = ' + myVar);
```

♦ To print the value of an object, use (see Figure 5.6):

```
var stuff = '';
for (var i in myVar) {
    stuff += myVar[i] + "\n";
}
air.trace('myVar = ' + stuff);
```

♦ To indicate that a function is being called, use (see Figure 5.7):

```
function someFunction() {
    air.trace('Now in the
→ someFunction() function.');
}
```

♦ Add spacing to your trace messages by printing a newline character (\n):

```
air.trace('Print this message.\n');
```

Or to make your debugging messages easier to read, you can add even more spacing and extra characters (**Figure 5.8**):

```
air.trace('\n-----\nPrint this
→ message. \n-----\n ');
```

✔ Tip

■ Although I focus on using trace() as a debugging tool, it can also be used in live, running applications. However, most users don't access console windows with any frequency, so it would be a somewhat special application that would make use of this feature.

Using the AIR Introspector

Included with the AIR SDK (Software Development Kit) is a JavaScript file called AIRIntrospector.js (found within the frameworks folder). If you include this file in an AIR application, you can launch an extremely useful debugging tool while the program is running. It will pop up in a separate window and allow you to:

◆ See the code associated with program elements (**Figure 5.9**)

◆ Use a console to interact with the JavaScript

◆ See the underlying HTML (**Figure 5.10**)

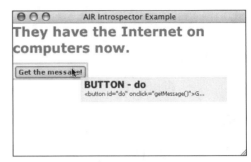

Figure 5.9 When the AIR Introspector is enabled, moving the cursor over the program's interface will show the HTML associated with its various parts.

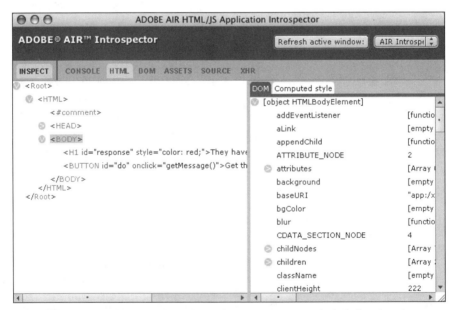

Figure 5.10 The utility's HTML tab shows the window's HTML source code, including alterations made by DOM scripting.

◆ Navigate and manipulate the page's Document Object Model

◆ List a program's assets (included files, images, etc.)

◆ View the entire source code for the program (including JavaScript)

◆ Inspect the values of XMLHttpRequest objects (**Figure 5.11**)

The following steps walk you through what you need to do to use this utility.

To use AIRIntrospector.js:

1. Copy the AIRIntrospector.js file from the SDK frameworks directory to your project's folder.

2. Add the file to an application using this line:

```
<script type="text/javascript"
→ src="AIRIntrospector.js"></script>
```

If you place the file within a subdirectory, you'll need to change the src value.

3. Run the application using the AIR Debug Launcher (adl).

Logically, you'll want to use the AIR Introspector while developing and debugging a project, so you'll probably only ever use it when testing a program.

4. To launch the AIR Introspector, press F12 while the program is running.

5. For specific information on using the AIR Introspector, see the Adobe AIR online documentation.

✔ Tips

■ The AIR Introspector should only be included in a project while you're developing it. It should never be included and enabled in a program distributed to end users.

■ Also found in the SDK's frameworks directory is a file called AIRSourceViewer.js. If you include this file in a project, you can allow a user to view the application's source code. See the AIR online documentation for details.

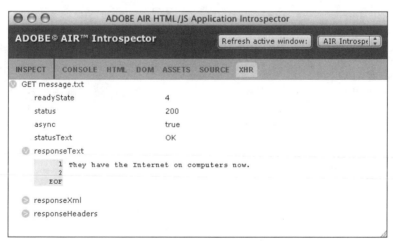

Figure 5.11 The values of an XMLHttpRequest object's properties are also revealed by the AIR Introspector (this is, again, the example from Chapter 4).

Other Debugging Techniques

In this chapter, I suggest a number of techniques—both specific and more general—you can use to help debug your AIR applications. The bulk of these centers around the JavaScript code: the heart of the AIR applications discussed in this book.

Over the course of the rest of the book, different topics will imply their own particular debugging steps. At those times, you'll see tips and recommendations toward that end. For example, when the book covers network-related tasks, there'll be hints as to the common problems that might occur and how you would go about solving them. Still, I want to place a few thoughts together here to get you in a good "debugging mindset" as you continue on through the book.

The most important debugging technique I've come up with in my years of programming and Web development is this: *Step away from the computer and take a break!* I've solved many computer problems by taking showers, going for a walk, or watching really bad television.

If that's what you should do, in general, here's what you shouldn't do: Take wild guesses to solve a problem. As a writer I've see far too many readers compound relatively simple issues by taking stabs at possible fixes. Taking steps you don't fully understand almost never fixes a problem, and more often than not creates new errors that muddle things even more.

Debugging with Firefox

Naturally this chapter focuses on debugging techniques you would take within an AIR application. But to expand your debugging toolbox, turn to the Firefox Web browser (`www.mozilla.com`). When it comes to debugging JavaScript, Firefox offers tools and add-ons that can't be beat. There is one rather significant caveat: Not everything you can do in an AIR application will work in Firefox. Any basic JavaScript that you write should run just fine, but any use of the Flash and AIR APIs will fail because they are part of AIR, not part of JavaScript. In simpler terms, any code that starts with `air` or `window.runtime` won't work in a browser.

To use Firefox for debugging purposes, here are the highlights of what you'd want to do:

- Use the Error Console (found under the Tools menu).

- Open the DOM Inspector (also under Tools).

- Install the Web Developer widget (`www.chrispederick.com/work/web-developer/`).

- Install Firebug (`www.getfirebug.com`).

- Install JavaScript Debugger (`https://addons.mozilla.org/en-US/firefox/addon/216`).

- Enable strict JavaScript in Firefox's configuration.

More adl Options

Chapter 2, "Creating an Application," went through the steps involved in making an AIR program using a text editor and the command-line tools that come with the AIR SDK (Software Development Kit). Of these two tools, the AIR Debug Launcher (adl) is the one used for testing an application without having to build and formally install it. Although this program probably won't be the first line of defense in debugging your applications, it can be useful in the right circumstances.

The program is used quite simply by providing it with the name of the application descriptor XML file associated with the project:

```
adl ApplicationXMLFile.xml
```

The application descriptor file has the most important settings for how an application runs, for example, the visibility, size, and other properties of the primary window, the version of Adobe AIR it requires, and the types of files that the program might control. One way you might use adl is to create different descriptor files for your program, and then test it using each.

To debug AIR applications:

◆ Use multiline comments to deactivate problematic sections of code.

If you wrap the multiline comment markers—/* and */—around a block of code, that code will no longer be operational. This can be a good way to deactivate blocks of code that may be causing a problem. Just be sure not to create syntax errors when using this technique (e.g., by starting a multiline comment inside of a function but closing it outside of the function).

If you're using a JavaScript debugging tool, you can also use breakpoints to execute only part of the JavaScript code.

◆ When working with XML or JSON data, independently confirm that the data is *well-formed*.

XML (Extensible Markup Language) and JSON (JavaScript Object Notation) are two common formats that data can be stored in. If your AIR application is reading data in these formats, problems will occur if the data is not well-formed (which is to say written in exactly the proper syntax). In such cases, examine the data independent of the AIR application to confirm that it's correct. You can also validate the format of XML and JSON data using online tools.

◆ Test database queries independently.

When working with databases, problems can occur in several places. The most common problems are incorrect queries; correct queries but unexpected results; and correct queries with expected results but incorrect handling of the results. To narrow the field just among these three, you should confirm what your query is, and then run it using a separate interface to confirm the results.

◆ Test external pages independently.

This is much the same as the previous two suggestions, and it comes down to this: Don't assume that your program is receiving what you think it should. Instead, confirm this for yourself. For example, if the program interacts with Google Maps, try that interaction outside of the AIR application so you know that it works.

◆ Be sure to use unique variable and function names in your JavaScript.

Avoid using reserved words for either variables or classes, because doing so will lead to annoying bugs. Also, watch what variables and functions you use in included files, so as to avoid conflicts.

◆ Watch out for variable scope.

A common cause of bugs in any language but in JavaScript in particular is *variable scope*. Scope is the realm in which a variable exists. Variables declared outside of a function have *global* scope, meaning they are available everywhere. Variables declared within a function without using the var keyword are also global, once that function is called. Variables declared within a function using the var keyword are *local* to that function. Scope pertains to debugging because you could inadvertently be using or changing a global variable when you thought you were working with a local one.

◆ Pay attention to the versions of the Adobe AIR runtime and SDK being used.

The different versions of AIR will support different features, so don't ignore this vital bit of information. If an application used to work but no longer does, see if it's not due to an update in AIR.

MAKING
WINDOWS

The window is the heart of any graphical application and is where all of the action takes place, or at the very least, starts. And most applications use more than one window: Along with the primary application window, secondary windows might be used for adjusting the program's preferences, taking some sort of user input (like a search box), or whatever. In this chapter you'll learn everything you need to know about making and customizing windows.

Adobe AIR applications written using HTML and JavaScript can create and manipulate two types of windows: standard HTML windows, the same as those in a Web browser, and *native windows*. Native windows require more code but are more customizable and may fit in better with the operating system as a whole. The chapter begins with a quick discussion of standard HTML windows, but most of the content focuses on the relevant information regarding native windows.

Creating a New Window

The first way that you can create a new AIR application window is exactly the same as it is in a Web browser:

```
window.open("pagename.html", "title",
→ properties);
```

The *properties* argument is where you would specify the window's dimensions and other attributes, which are listed in **Table 6.1**.

The benefit of creating a window in this way is that it's simple to do and requires little code. The downside is that the amount of control that the primary window has over the new window is limited, and the new window will not look and behave like standard application windows. The alternative, creating a new native window (discussed throughout the rest of this chapter), has the opposite strengths and weaknesses.

To make a new window:

1. In your project's primary HTML file, begin a new JavaScript function (**Script 6.1**):

```
<script type="text/javascript">
function createWindow() {
}
</script>
```

The function is called *createWindow*. It takes no arguments.

2. Within the createWindow() function, add the code that opens a new window:

```
window.open("new.html", "NewWindow",
→ "height=300,width=300");
```

This line opens a new window with a title of *NewWindow* and a size of 300 pixels by 300 pixels. The contents of the window will be the HTML file new.html.

Script 6.1 This application creates a new HTML window when the user clicks a button.

```
1   <html><!-- Script 6.1 -->
2       <head>
3           <script src="AIRAliases.js"
            type="text/javascript"></script>
4           <script type="text/javascript">
5           function createWindow() {
6               window.open("new.html",
                "NewWindow",
                "height=300,width=300");
7           }
8
9           </script>
10          <title>HTML Window</title>
11      </head>
12      <body>
13          <button onclick="createWindow();">
            Open a New HTML Window</button>
14      </body>
15  </html>
```

Table 6.1 These window properties can all be used with HTML windows to adjust their look and behavior. The default value is *no* for any *yes/no* option.

Window Properties		
NAME	**MEANING**	**VALUES**
width	width in pixels	any integer
height	height in pixels	any integer
resizable	is resizable	yes/no
status	has a status bar	yes/no
toolbar	has a toolbar	yes/no
scrollbars	has vertical scrollbars	yes/no
menubar	has a menu bar	yes/no
location	has an address bar	yes/no

Script 6.2 This script will be the content of the new HTML window.

```
              Script
1  <html><!-- Script 6.2 -->
2      <head>
3          <title>New Window</title>
4      </head>
5      <body>
6          <h1>Wow! It's a new window.</h1>
7      </body>
8  </html>
```

Creating Your Own Projects

For all of the steps in this chapter, you'll just see the relevant code and instructions demonstrating the new technique. For the most part, you won't be told to create a new project folder, make the application descriptor XML file, and start a basic HTML file. Those steps are covered in the chapters leading up to this point, and the assumption here is that you already know how to do all that. In addition, if you're using Dreamweaver with the AIR Extension or Aptana Studio, most of this is already done for you. This does mean that most of the scripts will include code that wasn't explicitly mentioned in the steps, but none of it should come as a surprise. Also note that these examples will assume inclusion of the `AIRAliases.js` file, which is discussed in Chapter 4, "Basic Concepts and Code."

3. Within the HTML page, create an element that will call the `createWindow()` function:

```
<button onclick="createWindow();">
→ Open a New HTML Window</button>
```

The application needs some impetus for creating the new window. In general, the new window should open as a response to a user action (it's pretty annoying to just have windows pop up randomly). Clicking this button invokes the JavaScript `createWindow()` function, thereby creating the new window. You could also use a link, an image, or what have you.

4. Create a second HTML page called `new.html` (**Script 6.2**):

```
<html><!-- Script 6.2 -->
    <head>
        <title>New Window</title>
    </head>
    <body>
        <h1>Wow! It's a new window.</h1>
    </body>
</html>
```

In other examples in this book, you'll see how to do something useful with the new window, but for demonstration purposes, this content will suffice.

continues on next page

5. Save, test, debug, and run the completed application (**Figures 6.1** and **6.2**).

Click the link to create the new window.

✔ Tips

- If you need to be able to refer to a new window from the first window, you'll want to assign the result of calling `window.open()` to a variable:

  `var window2 = window.open("pagename.`
  `→ html", "title", properties);`

- The newly created window can use all of the JavaScript `window` object's methods, such as `close()`, `moveTo()`, `moveBy()`, and so forth.

- A window's content can be established when the window is created (the first argument in `window.open()`), set using `window.location`, or tweaked using the Document Object Model (DOM).

- New windows created using `window.open()` cannot initially use the Flash and AIR APIs. To add that functionality, execute this line of JavaScript within the new window:

  `window.runtime = window.opener.`
  `→ runtime;`

  The new window will also need to include the `AIRAliases.js` file if it's to use any of those aliases.

Figure 6.1 The main page of the application.

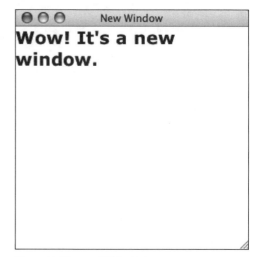

Figure 6.2 The new HTML window.

Using Dialog Boxes

Short of a whole new window but also useful is the ability to make dialog boxes. JavaScript has several kinds: alert, confirm, prompt, and file browser. Unfortunately, the last two are not supported in the early versions of AIR.

Creating an alert is simple:

```
alert('whatever message here');
```

Whereas an alert just needs to be acknowledged by the end user (by clicking OK), a confirm dialog box gives the user the options Cancel and OK. So the confirm dialog box is normally invoked as part of a conditional that reacts to the response:

```
if (confirm('message')) {
    // User clicked OK.
} else {
    // User clicked Cancel.
}
```

There are a couple of details to note with these types of dialog boxes. First, they use plain text for the message, not HTML. Therefore, you cannot create spacing using paragraph or break tags. Instead, use the newline character (\n) to start the next part of a message on the following line.

Second, dialog boxes by themselves cannot really do much (in comparison, a new window could load the application's Preferences page or create a box for editing text). Dialog boxes can only be used for communicating messages, and with a confirmation dialog box, fetch a simple response from the user.

In Web pages, these dialog boxes can be irksome, interrupting the user experience. In desktop applications, the user expectations are different, but you should still only use these judiciously. That being said, I use alerts frequently in this book, as they provide a quick and easy way to indicate that an action has occurred.

CREATING A NEW WINDOW

Creating a New Native Window

The second way to create a new application window (besides using `window.open()`) is to create a *native window*. A native window looks and behaves like the primary application window so it'll better fit into the operating system. Native windows can also be more controlled and customized (see "Creating a New Look" later in the chapter).

To make a new native window, start by creating an object of type `NativeWindowInitOptions`:

```
var options = new air.
→ NativeWindowInitOptions();
```

This object will be used to establish the window's attributes. Once you have this object, the easiest way to create the window is to use the `createRootWindow()` method of the `HTMLLoader` object:

```
var popup = air.HTMLLoader.
→ createRootWindow(true, options,
→ false, rect);
```

The first argument is a Boolean indicating whether the window should be visible or not. The second is the `NativeWindowInitOptions` object. The third is a Boolean indicating whether the window should have scrollbars or not. And the fourth argument should be an object of type `Rectangle`. You can create one of those using

```
var rect = new air.Rectangle(x, y, w, h);
```

The first two arguments are the location on the screen where the rectangle should start (where its upper-left corner is located). The third argument is the window's width in pixels; the last is its height in pixels (**Figure 6.3**).

```
var rect = new air.Rectangle(60, 45,
→ 150, 90);
```

The final step is to load the page's content. To do so, invoke the `HTMLLoader` object's `load()` method:

```
popup.load(content);
```

Of course, there's some effort in indicating the content to be used (did I mention that native windows require a bit more code?). The argument to the `load()` method needs to be in the form of a `URLRequest` object. To get to that point, start by identifying the file that will be used for the content:

```
var page = air.File.
→ applicationDirectory.
→ resolvePath('page.html');
```

You'll learn more about referring to files on the computer in Chapter 9, "Files and Directories." For now, understand that this line returns a `File` object associated with `page.html`. The `applicationDirectory. resolvePath` part indicates that the `page.html` should be in the application directory: The place where the application's main files are installed. This means that `page.html` should be in the same folder as the application's main HTML page, and that it also needs to be included when building the application.

But you can't just use the `page` variable in `popup.load()`, because it's a `File` object. Instead, create a new `URLRequest()` object.

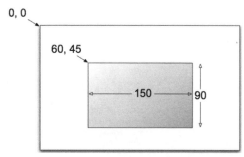

Figure 6.3 The larger rectangle represents the screen, where the origin is the upper-left corner. The smaller rectangle represents a new window with an x value of 60, a y of 45, a width of 150, and a height of 90.

Script 6.3 In this application, a new native window is created.

```
000                 📄 Script
1    <html><!-- Script 6.3 -->
2        <head>
3            <script src="AIRAliases.js"
             type="text/javascript"></script>
4            <script type="text/javascript">
5
6            // Function for making new native
             windows.
7            // Takes no arguments.
8            function makeNativeWindow() {
9
10               // For window options:
11               var options = new air.
                 NativeWindowInitOptions();
12
13               // Window size and location:
14               var rect = new air.Rectangle(50,
                 50, 200, 200);
15
16               // Create the window:
17               var popup = air.HTMLLoader.
                 createRootWindow(true, options,
                 false, rect);
18
19               // Load the content:
20               var page = air.File.
                 applicationDirectory.
                 resolvePath('new.html');
21               popup.load(new air.
                 URLRequest(page.url));
22
23           } // End of makeNativeWindow()
             function.
24           </script>
25           <title>New Native Window</title>
26       </head>
27       <body>
28           <button onclick=
             "makeNativeWindow();">Make a new
             native window.</button>
29       </body>
30   </html>
```

The `URLRequest()` *constructor* (the method automatically called when you create an object of that type) takes one argument, which is a URL to be loaded. You can get this from `page` by referring to `page.url`.

So, finally, this line provides the `URLRequest` to the `load()` method:

```
popup.load(new air.URLRequest(page.url));
```

In the end, creating a new native window requires at least five objects and a few lines of code, but as you'll see in this chapter, it's almost always worth that extra effort. And before long, these steps, to be reinforced in this next example, will be all too familiar.

To make a new native window:

1. In your project's primary HTML file, begin a new JavaScript function (**Script 6.3**):

   ```
   <script type="text/javascript">
   function makeNativeWindow() {
   }
   </script>
   ```

   This function is called *makeNativeWindow*. It takes no arguments.

2. Within the `makeNativeWindow()` function, create an object of `NativeWindowInitOptions` type:

   ```
   var options = new
   → air.NativeWindowInitOptions();
   ```

   Although this script won't tweak the window options at all, a `NativeWindowInitOptions` object will still be necessary.

3. On the next line, create a new `Rectangle` object:

   ```
   var rect = new air.Rectangle(50,
   → 50, 200, 200);
   ```

   The rectangle starts at 50, 50 (50 pixels in from the left side of the screen, 50 pixels down from the top) and is 200 pixels wide and 200 pixels high.

continues on next page

CREATING A NEW NATIVE WINDOW

4. On the next line, create the window:

```
var popup = air.HTMLLoader.
→ createRootWindow(true, options,
→ false, rect);
```

This window, assigned to the variable popup, will be visible, uses the options object for its settings, will not have scroll-bars, and uses the rect object for its size and location on the screen.

5. Next, load the actual content:

```
var page = air.File.
→ applicationDirectory.
→ resolvePath('new.html');

popup.load(new air.URLRequest
→ (page.url));
```

The page variable will represent the content to be used in the window. It will be a File object referencing the document new.html found in the application directory. This object's url attribute (*page.url*) is then used as an argument in the creation of a new URLRequest object, which is what popup.load() needs.

6. In the body of the page, create a button that calls the JavaScript function:

```
<button onclick=
→ "makeNativeWindow();">
→ Make a new native window.</button>
```

In other examples in this book, you'll see how to do something useful with the new window, but for demonstration purposes, this content will suffice.

7. Copy new.html (Script 6.2) to this project's directory.

8. Save, test, debug, and run the completed application (**Figures 6.4** and **6.5**).

Remember to include new.html when you actually build the application. To test the running program, click the button in the main window to create the second window.

✔ Tips

■ Although the native window created here (Figure 6.5) looks the same as the HTML window created earlier (see Figure 6.2), what can be done with native windows is the distinguishing trait. Keep reading to learn more!

■ The value of page.url will be *app:/new.html*. The *app:/* part of that is the *scheme* (see Chapter 4) and refers to the application's directory where the application was installed, like C:\Programs and Files\ThisAIRApp (Windows) or /Applications/ThisAIRApp (Mac OS X).

■ As mentioned in Chapter 4, where content comes from dictates the security rules and concerns involved. If a new native window loads content from the application directory, it runs with the same powers as the primary application window. If the content comes from elsewhere, its powers will be more limited. Chapter 15, "Security Techniques," explains this concept in detail.

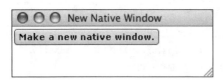

Figure 6.4 The main page of the application.

Figure 6.5
The new native window, whose content is the same as the HTML window created earlier in the chapter (see Figure 6.2).

Figure 6.6
From bottom to top, a normal, lightweight, and utility window on Windows. The lightweight window has no visible frame (i.e., no chrome).

Figure 6.7
From bottom to top, a normal, lightweight, and utility window on Mac OS X. The lightweight window has no visible frame (i.e., no chrome).

Table 6.2 These six attributes are used to adjust the appearance and behavior of a native window. All are found within the `NativeWindowInitOptions` object.

NativeWindowInitOptions Attributes

ATTRIBUTE	VALUES
maximizable	true/false
minimizable	true/false
resizable	true/false
systemChrome	"none"/"standard"
transparent	true/false
type	"normal"/"lightweight"/"utility"

Customizing Windows

The previous section showed how to create a new native window without any modifications. Once you have that working, you can start using the `NativeWindowInitOptions` object to tweak some of the window's behavior.

Table 6.2 lists all of the possible settings. The defaults—which the previous example implicitly demonstrated—are used to create a normal window using the standard system chrome (see the "What Is the Chrome?" sidebar) with no transparency and to create a window that is resizable, maximizable, and minimizable.

The most interesting of these settings is the window type, of which there are three possibilities: *normal*, *lightweight*, and *utility*. **Figure 6.6** shows all three on Windows; **Figure 6.7** shows them on Mac OS X.

What Is the Chrome?

Several places in this chapter use the terms *chrome* and *system chrome*. The chrome refers to the frame that windows have, including the coloring of the frame, the icons used for minimizing, maximizing, and closing the window, and so forth. Put another way, the content goes within a window; the chrome goes around that content.

AIR application windows that use the *system chrome* will look like other standard windows on the host computer (i.e., they will look like standard Windows windows on Windows and like standard Mac OS X windows on Mac OS X). For a more dramatic effect, you can forgo the system chrome and create your own. By doing so, you can use unique buttons, make a window transparent, and even create nonrectangular shapes. This will be discussed toward the end of the chapter.

A normal window is the default; it looks and behaves like any standard window for the operating system. The lightweight window has a minimal amount of chrome or none at all (see Figures 6.6 and 6.7). Note that the lightweight window type must have a systemChrome of *none*.

The utility type of window has a minimal amount of chrome and a shorter title bar than the standard window. With both the lightweight and utility window types, the windows will not appear in the Microsoft Windows taskbar or the OS X Window menu (some applications in OS X have a menu called *Windows*, which lists the program's windows by name).

Other settings, like the window's title, will come from the HTML file (when using HTMLLoader().createRootWindow()). The window's location on the screen, its size, its visibility, and the presence of scrollbars are set when the window is created (again, in the invocation of createRootWindow()). Still, more tweaks can be made by using a NativeWindow object. This will be demonstrated later in the chapter. But to start learning how to customize a window, let's take the previous example and change the window's type.

To customize a native window:

1. Open Script 6.3 in your text editor or IDE, if it is not already.

2. After creating the options variable, add this line (**Script 6.4**):

   options.type = air.NativeWindowType.
   → UTILITY;

Script 6.4 By adding one line of code, the script has been updated to create a new window of type utility.

```
1   <html><!-- Script 6.4 -->
2     <head>
3       <script src="AIRAliases.js"
        type="text/javascript"></script>
4       <script type="text/javascript">
5
6       // Function for making new native
        windows.
7       // Takes no arguments.
8       function makeNativeWindow() {
9
10        // For window options:
11        var options = new
          air.NativeWindowInitOptions();
12
13        // Change the type:
14        options.type =
          air.NativeWindowType.UTILITY;
15
16        // Window size and location:
17        var rect = new air.Rectangle(50,
          50, 200, 200);
18
19        // Create the window:
20        var popup = air.HTMLLoader.
          createRootWindow(true, options,
          false, rect);
21
22        // Load the content:
23        var page = air.File.
          applicationDirectory.
          resolvePath('new.html');
24        popup.load(new air.
          URLRequest(page.url));
25
26        } // End of makeNativeWindow()
          function.
27      </script>
28      <title>New Native Window</title>
29    </head>
30    <body>
31      <button onclick=
        "makeNativeWindow();">Make a new
        native window.</button>
32    </body>
33  </html>
```

CUSTOMIZING WINDOWS

Figure 6.8 After clicking the button in the main content window, the new utility window appears in the upper-left corner of the screen. Compare it with the same content in a normal window in Figure 6.5.

To set a window's type, you can assign it a literal string such as *utility*, but it's best if you use an AIR constant. The other two constants are `air.NativeWindowType.LIGHTWEIGHT` and `air.NativeWindowType.NORMAL`.

3. Save, test, debug, and run the completed application (**Figure 6.8**).

✔ Tips

- If *minimizable* and *maximizable* are set to *false*, those buttons will not be active (depending on the operating system and the window type).

- For Mac OS X, both *resizable* and *maximizable* must be set to *false* to make a window a fixed size (i.e., to disallow resizing).

- While you can dictate the window type for a newly created window, the application's primary window will always be of type *normal* (you cannot change this in the application descriptor XML file). However, you can create a unique look for the primary window by customizing the chrome.

- Adjusting the chrome and using some of the other techniques covered later in the chapter will also be necessary to make a lightweight window more useful.

- Being able to change a window's type is a big advantage that the native window has over the standard HTML window. The latter, created using `window.open()`, will always be a normal window with the system chrome.

CUSTOMIZING WINDOWS

Accessing a New Native Window

As mentioned in the previous section, some window settings can be adjusted by referring to a `NativeWindow` object (**Table 6.3**). For example, you can alternatively create a new native window by using this code:

```
var popup = new
→ air.NativeWindow(options);
```

Then you can set the window's title, for example, using:

```
popup.title = 'New Title';
```

This is not possible using the window creation technique outlined in this chapter—

```
var popup = air.HTMLLoader.
→ createRootWindow(true, options,
→ false, rect);
```

—because the popup variable is an object of type `HTMLLoader`, not `NativeWindow`. But there are several ways to access the `NativeWindow` object, one of which is to refer to `window.nativeWindow`. This line of code will work if executed within a new native window:

```
window.nativeWindow.title = 'New Title';
```

But obviously that line can't be used to change the title of a different window, because `window.nativeWindow` always points to the current window (i.e., the window executing that code). But you can access all the windows open in an application this way:

```
var allWindows = air.NativeApplication.
→ nativeApplication.openedWindows;
```

The `openedWindows` property is an array of `NativeWindow` objects, one for each window currently open in the application. Because arrays begin indexing at 0, the second native window open would be at 1. So to change a

second window's title from within the first window, you would use

```
allWindows[1].title = 'New Title';
```

To further demonstrate this, let's create an application that allows the user to adjust the new native window's size from within the application's primary window.

To access a native window:

1. In your project's primary HTML file, create an anonymous function (**Script 6.5**):

   ```
   <script type="text/javascript">
   window.onload = function() {

   }
   </script>
   ```

   Instead of defining a function that creates the window, the window will be created within an anonymous function that is automatically run when the page is loaded. By using this technique, the JavaScript for creating the native window is only executed after the page has completely loaded, as opposed to being executed while the page is loading, which would be the case if no function was used.

continues on page 88

Table 6.3 These ten properties also affect the look and behavior of a native window, but these are accessed directly through a `NativeWindow` object.

NativeWindow Attributes	
alwaysInFront	true/false
bounds	Rectangle object
height	integer (in pixels)
maxSize	Point object
menu	NativeMenu object
minSize	Point object
title	string
visible	true/false
width	integer (in pixels)
x	integer (in pixels)
y	integer (in pixels

Script 6.5 In this AIR application, a new native window is automatically created. The user can then change its dimensions using text inputs in the application's primary window.

```
1    <html><!-- Script 6.5 -->
2        <head>
3            <script src="AIRAliases.js" type="text/javascript"></script>
4            <script type="text/javascript">
5
6            // Create the new native window:
7            window.onload = function() {
8
9                var options = new air.NativeWindowInitOptions();
10               var rect = new air.Rectangle(50, 50, 200, 200);
11               var popup = air.HTMLLoader.createRootWindow(true, options, false, rect);
12               var page = air.File.applicationDirectory.resolvePath('new.html');
13               popup.load(new air.URLRequest(page.url));
14
15           } // End of anonymous function.
16
17           // Function for changing the window's size:
18           // Function takes two arguments:
19           // - which dimension to change
20           // - its new size in pixels
21           function changeSize(which, size) {
22
23               // Get a reference to the new window:
24               var thatWindow = air.NativeApplication.nativeApplication.openedWindows[1];
25
26               // Adjust the size based upon the value
27               // of the first argument:
28               if (which == 'width') {
29                   thatWindow.width = size;
30               } else if (which == 'height') {
31                   thatWindow.height = size;
32               }
33
34           } // End of changeSize() function.
35
36           </script>
37           <title>Accessing Native Windows</title>
38       </head>
39       <body>
40           <p>Window width: <input type="text" name="width" size="4" value="200"
              onchange="changeSize('width', this.value);"></p>
41           <p>Window height: <input type="text" name="height" size="4" value="200"
              onchange="changeSize('height', this.value);"></p>
42       </body>
43   </html>
```

ACCESSING A NEW NATIVE WINDOW

2. Within the anonymous function, create the new native window:

```
var options = new
→ air.NativeWindowInitOptions();
var rect = new air.Rectangle(50,
→ 50, 200, 200);
var popup = air.HTMLLoader.
→ createRootWindow(true, options,
→ false, rect);
var page = air.File.
→ applicationDirectory.
→ resolvePath('new.html');
popup.load(new air.URLRequest
→ (page.url));
```

All of this code, down to which page is used for the window's content, has already been explained in this chapter. Feel free to change any of the particulars—like the window's size or type, if you like.

3. Create a function that resizes the window:

```
function changeSize(which, size) {
}
```

This function takes two arguments: which dimension—width or height—is being resized and the new size.

4. Within the changeSize() function, create an object reference to the new native window:

```
var thatWindow =
→ air.NativeApplication.
→ nativeApplication.openedWindows[1];
```

As already explained, air. NativeApplication.nativeApplication. openedWindows is an array of objects representing every open window in the application. The second window in the application will be indexed at 1. So this line assigns to the thatWindow variable a NativeWindow object that refers to the new native window.

5. Within the changeSize() function, complete the code that resizes the window:

```
if (which == 'width') {
    thatWindow.width = size;
} else if (which == 'height') {
    thatWindow.height = size;
}
```

Based on the value of which, this conditional will change the corresponding dimension of the window. As an extra precaution, you could include code here that makes sure the size value is a positive integer and that the value is not larger than the screen's width or height (see the Tips).

6. Within the HTML, create inputs for adjusting the window's size:

```
<p>Window width: <input type="text"
→ name="width" size="4" value="200"
→ onchange="changeSize('width',
→ this.value);"></p>

<p>Window height: <input type="text"
→ name="height" size="4" value="200"
→ onchange="changeSize('height',
→ this.value);"></p>
```

Both inputs, when changed, invoke the changeSize() function. The function will be passed the dimension being changed—*width* or *height*—and the value entered into the text box (represented by this.value).

7. Save, test, debug, and run the completed application (**Figures 6.9** and **6.10**).

✔ Tips

- The screen size is available in `air.Capabilities.screenResolutionX` and `air.Capabilties.screenResolutionY`.

- The maximum window size that the operating system supports is available through `air.NativeWindow.systemMaxSize`. The smallest possible window size can be found in `air.NativeWindow.systemMinSize`.

Figure 6.9 The primary window and the custom new native window when the application is first started.

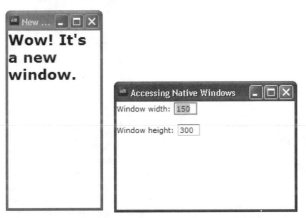

Figure 6.10 After changing the numbers in the primary window, the native window is resized.

Creating Full-screen Windows

If you've gone through this chapter exercise by exercise, you might be thinking that everything about native windows is complicated. Rest assured that there's one easy task when it comes to native windows: creating a full-screen window.

You've probably seen full-screen windows at some point. They, as the name implies, take up the entire screen and also eliminate most, if not all, menus and utility windows in the process. The purpose of full-screen windows is to provide the maximum amount of workspace possible. Microsoft Word has a full-screen mode, as does Internet Explorer 7, among other applications.

To put a window in full-screen mode, change its `stage.displayState` value:

```
window.nativeWindow.stage.displayState =
→ runtime.flash.display.
→ StageDisplayState.FULL_SCREEN;
```

As an operating system convention, the user can press the Escape key to exit full-screen mode. The next example will also demonstrate how JavaScript can be used to change the full-screen mode.

To create a full-screen window:

1. In your project's HTML file, begin a new JavaScript function (**Script 6.6**):

   ```
   <script type="text/javascript">
   function makeFullScreen() {
   } // End of makeFullScreen ()
   → function.
   </script>
   ```

   This function takes no arguments.

2. Within the `makeFullScreen()` function, change the `stage.displayState` property:

   ```
   window.nativeWindow.stage.
   → displayState = runtime.flash.
   → display.StageDisplayState.
   → FULL_SCREEN;
   ```

   This rather verbose line is all you need to enable full-screen mode.

3. Within the `makeFullScreen()` function, change the HTML button:

   ```
   document.getElementById('btn').
   → onclick = makeNormalScreen;
   document.getElementById('btn').
   → innerHTML = 'Normal (or press
   → Escape)';
   ```

   The HTML page will have a button that the user clicks to enter full-screen mode (**Figure 6.11**). After clicking this button, there's no need to have it around with the same text and purpose, so both will be changed, giving the user a visual instruction and mouse option for returning to normal screen size (**Figure 6.12**).

   continues on page 92

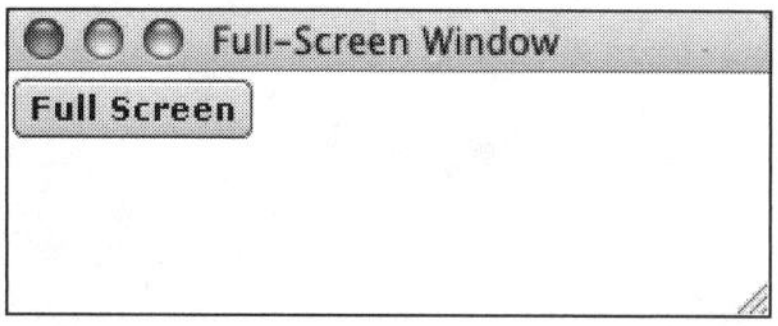

Figure 6.11 The window when first running the program.

Figure 6.12 After the user clicks the button in the application window (Figure 6.11), the window changes to full-screen mode (not shown in this figure), and the button's label and functionality are changed.

Script 6.6 An HTML button in the application's main window will trigger JavaScript functions that both enable and disable full-screen mode.

```
1    <html><!-- Script 6.6 -->
2        <head>
3            <script src="AIRAliases.js" type="text/javascript"></script>
4            <script type="text/javascript">
5
6            // Function for enabling full-screen mode:
7            function makeFullScreen() {
8
9                // Change the window:
10               window.nativeWindow.stage.displayState = runtime.flash.display.StageDisplayState.
                 FULL_SCREEN;
11
12               // Change the button:
13               document.getElementById('btn').onclick = makeNormalScreen;
14               document.getElementById('btn').innerHTML = 'Normal (or press Escape)';
15
16           } // End of makeFullScreen () function.
17
18           // Function for disabling full-screen mode:
19           function makeNormalScreen() {
20
21               // Change the window:
22               window.nativeWindow.stage.displayState = runtime.flash.display.StageDisplayState.NORMAL;
23
24               // Change the button:
25               document.getElementById('btn').onclick = makeFullScreen;
26               document.getElementById('btn').innerHTML = 'Full Screen';
27
28           } // End of makeNormalScreen() function.
29
30           </script>
31           <title>Full-Screen Window</title>
32       </head>
33       <body>
34           <button onclick="makeFullScreen();" id="btn">Full Screen</button>
35       </body>
36   </html>
```

CREATING FULL-SCREEN WINDOWS

4. Make a second function that does the opposite of the makeFullScreen() function:

```
function makeNormalScreen() {
   window.nativeWindow.stage.
   →displayState = runtime.flash.
   →display.StageDisplayState.
   →NORMAL;
   document.getElementById('btn').
   →onclick = makeFullScreen;
   document.getElementById('btn').
   →innerHTML = 'Full Screen';
}
```

This function undoes the actions of the makeFullScreen() function. So when the user clicks the original button and enters full-screen mode, the button's label and onclick behavior is modified. Clicking the modified button returns the screen to normal mode and reestablishes the button's behavior.

5. Within the HTML page, create a button with an id of *btn*:

```
<button onclick="makeFullScreen();"
→id="btn">Full Screen</button>
```

6. Save, test, debug, and run the completed application (see Figures 6.11 and 6.12).

✔ Tip

■ You may notice that if the user (i.e., you) presses the Esc key instead of clicking the HTML button, the window exits full-screen mode but the button's label and onclick functionality is not changed. This is because pressing the Esc key doesn't trigger the JavaScript function. To fix this, an event listener can be added that calls the makeNormalScreen() function when Esc is pressed. A tip at the end of the next section shows that code.

Handling Window Events

With native windows, many things that the user might do with the window—maximize, minimize, resize, move, and close—count as *events*. Handling events in general is discussed in Chapter 4, but you'll need to know how to handle specific types of window events to do some of the exercises that follow in this chapter.

As a quick recap, the process for handling any event is

- Create a function to be called when an event occurs.

- Tell the window to associate that event with that function.

You accomplish this second task by adding an *event listener*. With window events, you add the event listener to the `NativeWindow` object:

```
windowName.addEventListener(type,
→ someFunction);
```

The function will be called when the event happens and can do whatever is necessary. It

can even, if desired, cancel the event. **Table 6.4** lists the window-related event types.

As an example, the last series of steps demonstrates how to change a window to full-screen mode. That change involves two events: `DISPLAY_STATE_CHANGING` and `DISPLAY_STATE_CHANGE`. To do something when the state has changed, you would use:

```
window.nativeWindow.addEventListener
→ (air.NativeWindowDisplayStateEvents.
→ DISPLAY_STATE_CHANGE, functionName);
```

(In that line I used `window.nativeWindow` instead of *windowName* because there was no variable associated with the primary application window.)

In this next example, the AIR application will confirm that the user wants to close the window (which may also mean quitting the application). To do so, the application needs to watch for a `CLOSING` event. The application can stop an event from happening by calling the `preventDefault()` method of the `Event` object. This method cancels an event's default behavior (if it can; not all events can be canceled).

Table 6.4 These 12 items are the common window-related events. You'll need to know the class in which an event is defined to properly add a listener for it.

Window-related Events	
EVENT	CLASS
ACTIVATE	Event
CLOSE	Event
CLOSING	Event
DEACTIVATE	Event
FOCUS_IN	Event
FOCUS_OUT	Event
MOVE	NativeWindowBoundsEvents
MOVING	NativeWindowBoundsEvents
RESIZE	NativeWindowBoundsEvents
RESIZING	NativeWindowBoundsEvents
DISPLAY_STATE_CHANGE	NativeWindowDisplayStateEvents
DISPLAY_STATE_CHANGING	NativeWindowDisplayStateEvents

To handle window events:

1. In your project's HTML file, begin a new JavaScript function (**Script 6.7**):

```
<script type="text/javascript">
function confirmClose(e) {
}
```

The function named confirmClose()
will be called when a window closing
event occurs. When this function is
invoked, it will automatically be passed
the event as an argument to be assigned
to the variable e. This value will be used
later in the function.

Script 6.7 This application uses an event listener to call a function when the user closes the window. The function will confirm the closing.

```
1    <html><!-- Script 6.7 -->
2        <head>
3            <script src="AIRAliases.js" type="text/javascript"></script>
4            <script type="text/javascript">
5
6            // Function confirms the window closing.
7            // Takes one argument: the Event object.
8            function confirmClose(e) {
9
10               // Prompt the user:
11               if (!confirm('Are you sure you want to close this window?')) {
12                   e.preventDefault(); // Stop the event.
13               }
14
15           } // End of confirmClose() function.
16
17           // Add the event listener:
18           window.nativeWindow.addEventListener(air.Event.CLOSING, confirmClose);
19
20           </script>
21           <title>Handling Events</title>
22        </head>
23        <body>
24            <p>Try to close this window, I dare you!</p>
25        </body>
26    </html>
```

2. Within the confirmClose() function, cancel the closing event if the user clicks Cancel:

```
if (!confirm('Are you sure you want
→ to close this window?')) {
    e.preventDefault();
}
```

The confirmation prompt (**Figure 6.13**) makes the user take one more step before the window is closed. If the user clicks OK, the closing event will go on without interruption. If the user clicks Cancel, this conditional will be true, and the event will be canceled by calling e.preventDefault().

3. Outside of the function, add the event listener to this window:

```
window.nativeWindow.addEventListener
→ (air.Event.CLOSING, confirmClose);
```

This process is very simple once you understand the right syntax. To add the event listener to the window, you call the addEventListener() method that's part of (technically, inherited by) the window. nativeWindow object. The first argument should be the event to be watched, which is represented by a constant. As shown in Table 6.4, the CLOSING event is part of the Event class, so the constant is air.Event. CLOSING. The second argument is the

name of the function to call when that event happens.

4. If you want, add some text to the HTML page:

```
<p>Try to close this window, I dare
→ you!</p>
```

5. Save, test, debug, and run the completed application (**Figure 6.14**).

✔ Tips

■ Many actions a user might take will send two events. For example, the act of closing a window first triggers an Event. CLOSING event, which indicates that a request has been made to close the window. If that request is not interrupted, the window will be closed, which triggers an Event.CLOSE event.

■ To fix the button issue mentioned in the Tip in the "Creating Full-screen Windows" section, add this code:

```
window.nativeWindow.addEventListener
→ (air.NativeWindowBoundsEvent.
→ RESIZE, fixButton);
function fixButton() {
    document.getElementById('btn').
    → onclick = makeFullScreen;
    document.getElementById('btn').
    → innerHTML = 'Full Screen';
}
```

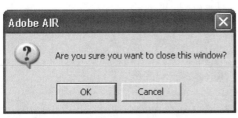

Figure 6.13 The confirmation dialog box forces the user to click OK before the window is actually closed (a little annoying, yes, but it demonstrates the concept well).

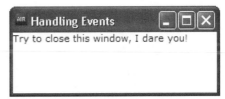

Figure 6.14 The application's main window, whose closing event is being listened for.

Creating a New Look

When you create any window, including the primary application window, you have an option as to what chrome to use. If you use the system chrome, the window will look and behave like any application window on that operating system (you've seen many examples of this in the book already). With AIR you can create a new chrome to give your application a unique appearance.

Custom chrome windows are much more customizable than the standard chrome windows. They can be transparent (see the "Transparent Windows" sidebar) and of any shape. Conversely, system chrome windows cannot be transparent and are always rectangular. Of course, there's one little snag.

The system chrome handles not just the look of a window but also the functionality, offering close, minimize, and maximize buttons. Your custom chrome must create these buttons plus include the JavaScript that handles the corresponding events (when the user clicks one of the buttons). Fortunately, for each of these buttons there is a corresponding method in the `NativeWindow` object:

windowName.close();

windowName.minimize();

windowName.maximize();

In this next example, let's get rid of the system chrome and see how that works!

Transparent Windows

If you are not using the system chrome, you have the option of creating a transparent window. One reason you might want to use a transparent window is to create a nonrectangular window.

To create a transparent window, set the `NativeWindowInitOptions` object's `systemChrome` attribute to *none* and its `transparent` attribute to *true*:

```
var options = new
→ air.NativeWindowInitOptions();
options.systemChrome = "none";
options.transparent = true;
```

This has to be done before the window is created; an existing window's transparency cannot be altered.

A couple of words of caution: First, transparent windows do not have a default background, so you must create one. Second, rendering and dealing with transparent windows demands more of a computer's resources, so your application's performance will likely degrade if you use this option.

Script 6.8 To use your own chrome in an application's primary window, the application descriptor file must set the systemChrome value to *none*.

```
1   <?xml version="1.0" encoding="utf-8" ?>
2   <application xmlns="http://ns.adobe.com/
    air/application/1.0">
3
4       <!-- Script 6.8 -->
5
6       <id>NewChrome</id>
7       <filename>NewChrome</filename>
8       <version>1.0</version>
9       <initialWindow>
10          <content>script_06_09.html</content>
11          <systemChrome>none</systemChrome>
12          <visible>true</visible>
13      </initialWindow>
14
15  </application>
```

Script 6.9 This application will use not use the system chrome but will instead rely on CSS for the look. HTML buttons and JavaScript will replicate the closing, minimizing, and maximizing functionality that's expected of most application windows.

```
1   <html><!-- Script 6.9 -->
2       <head>
3           <script src="AIRAliases.js"
            type="text/javascript"></script>
4           <script type="text/javascript">
5
6           // This window:
7           var win = window.nativeWindow;
8
9           </script>
10
11          <style type="text/css">
12
13          body {
14              background: #FC0;
15              color: #666
16          }
17
```

(script continues on next page)

To create your own chrome:

1. In the application descriptor XML file, set the systemChrome attribute to *none* (**Script 6.8**):

    ```
    <?xml version="1.0" encoding=
    → "utf-8" ?>
    <application xmlns="http://ns.adobe.
    → com/air/application/1.0">
        <!-- Script 6.8 -->
        <id>NewChrome</id>
        <filename>NewChrome</filename>
        <version>1.0</version>
        <initialWindow>
        <content>script_06_09.html
        → </content>
        <systemChrome>none</systemChrome>
        <visible>true</visible>
        </initialWindow>
    </application>
    ```

    For this descriptor file, I've just defined the minimum of required settings.

2. In the project's main HTML file, assign the current window to a variable (**Script 6.9**):

    ```
    <script type="text/javascript">
    var win = window.nativeWindow;
    </script>
    ```

    To be able to easily call this window's methods, a variable is assigned the value of this NativeWindow object.

    continues on next page

3. Add the CSS for the page:

```
<style type="text/css">
body {
    background: #FC0;
    color: #666
}
</style>
```

To give the application a modicum of styling, CSS will be used. (Keep in mind that without the system chrome you lose almost all of the default styling.)

4. Add CSS to format the buttons:

```
.button {
    position: absolute;
    top: 5px;
    font-family: monospace;
    color: #900;
    font-size: 12px;
}
#close {
    width: 50px;
    right: 5px;
}
#min {
    width: 40px;
    right: 55px;
}
#max {
    width: 40px;
    right: 95px;
}
```

Script 6.9 *continued*

```
18      .button {
19          position: absolute;
20          top: 5px;
21          font-family: monospace;
22          color: #900;
23          font-size: 12px;
24      }
25
26      #close {
27          width: 50px;
28          right: 5px;
29      }
30
31      #min {
32          width: 40px;
33          right: 55px;
34      }
35
36      #max {
37          width: 40px;
38          right: 95px;
39      }
40
41      </style>
42
43      <title>Custom Chrome</title>
44
45  </head>
46  <body>
47      <p>Spam Spam Spam Spam Spam</p>
48      <p>Spam Spam Spam Spam Spam</p>
49      <p>Spam Spam Spam Spam Spam</p>
50      <button id="close" class="button"
        onclick="win.close();">CLOSE
        </button>
51      <button id="min" class="button"
        onclick="win.minimize();">MIN
        </button>
52      <button id="max" class="button"
        onclick="win.maximize();">MAX
        </button>
53  </body>
54  </html>
```

For this example, I'll just be using HTML buttons (**Figure 6.15**). I want them to be formatted somewhat so they stand out. They should also be absolutely positioned, so the user reliably knows where to find them (conventionally, such buttons are at the top of the window).

5. Within the HTML block, add the three buttons:

```
<button id="close" class="button"
→ onclick="win.close();">CLOSE
→ </button>

<button id="min" class="button"
→ onclick="win.minimize();">MIN
→ </button>

<button id="max" class="button"
→ onclick="win.maximize();">MAX
→ </button>
```

For each, a simple HTML button is used with a `class` of *button* and an `id` value matching those used in the CSS. When the *CLOSE* button is clicked, the `win.close()` function is invoked; when *MAX* is clicked, `win.maximize()` is invoked; and when *MIN* is clicked, `win.minimize()` is called. And that's all there is to it!

6. Save, test, debug, and run the completed application.

Most important, the three buttons should work as expected.

✔ Tips

■ If you're more graphically skilled than I am (which includes pretty much everyone), you could just as easily use images for the window background and for the three buttons.

■ The AIR application, even when using your chrome, will still create scrollbars as necessary (**Figure 6.16**).

■ The `close()` method does not necessarily quit the application. If multiple windows are open, `close()` only applies to the one window. Once the last window is closed, the application will terminate.

■ A window closed using the `close()` method cannot be reopened. If your application has a window that might be closed and then reopened, you should just change its visibility instead (to hide and then reveal it).

Figure 6.15 The application's main window without the system chrome but with custom close, minimize, and maximize buttons.

Figure 6.16 Regardless of the chrome being used, scrollbars are still automatically added when the page's content will not fit within the window.

Moving and Resizing Windows

If you played around with the previous example, you may have noticed that there are two items still missing. Not only does the system chrome provide you with a way to close, minimize, and maximize a window, but it also makes it possible to move and resize it. Without the system chrome, you also need to provide for this functionality.

Supporting movement is simple: Just create an area where the user would click to "grab" the window and invoke the startMove() method when the user clicks (and holds) on that grab area. To allow for dynamic resizing of the window, again an area or button must exist where the user would click and drag from. At that time, the startResize() method should be called. The difference here is that this function takes one argument: the location where the resizing starts.

The location is represented by a constant. For example, if the resizing is done by clicking and dragging on the top-right corner, the *where* value would be air. NativeWindowResize.TOP_RIGHT. To resize using the left side of the window (so the window is widened but not made taller), use air.NativeWindowResize.LEFT. There are nine values in all: TOP, BOTTOM, LEFT, RIGHT, TOP_LEFT, TOP_RIGHT, BOTTOM_LEFT, BOTTOM_RIGHT, and NONE (which is equivalent to BOTTOM_RIGHT).

Let's quickly update the previous example to add this functionality.

Script 6.10 The ability to move and resize the window has been added in this version of the application, thanks to two text labels and the requisite JavaScript.

```
1   <html><!-- Script 6.10 -->
2       <head>
3           <script src="AIRAliases.js" type=
            "text/javascript"></script>
4           <script type="text/javascript">
5
6           var win = window.nativeWindow;
7
8           </script>
9           <style type="text/css">
10          body {
11              background: #FC0;
12              color: #666
13          }
14
15          .button {
16              position: absolute;
17              top: 5px;
18              font-family: monospace;
19              color: #900;
20              font-size: 12px;
21          }
22
23          #close {
24              width: 50px;
25              right: 5px;
26          }
27
28          #min {
29              width: 40px;
30              right: 55px;
31          }
32
33          #max {
34              width: 40px;
35              right: 95px;
36          }
37
```

(script continues on next page)

Script 6.10 *continued*

```
38      .label {
39          position: absolute;
40          bottom: 5px;
41          font-family: monospace;
42          background-color:#CCC;
43          border: 1px dashed #666;
44          color: #000;
45          font-size: 12px;
46          padding:2px;
47      }
48
49      #move {
50          right: 60px;
51      }
52
53      #resize {
54          right: 7px;
55      }
56
57      </style>
58      <title>Custom Chrome</title>
59  </head>
60  <body>
61      <p>Spam Spam Spam Spam Spam</p>
62      <p>Spam Spam Spam Spam Spam</p>
63      <p>Spam Spam Spam Spam Spam</p>
64      <button id="close" class="button"
        onclick="win.close();">CLOSE
        </button>
65      <button id="min" class="button"
        onclick="win.minimize();">MIN
        </button>
66      <button id="max" class="button"
        onclick="win.maximize();">MAX
        </button>
67      <span id="move" class="label"
        onmousedown="win.startMove();">
        MOVE</span>
68      <span id="resize" class="label"
        onmousedown="win.startResize(air.
        NativeWindowResize.BOTTOM_RIGHT);">
        RESIZE</span>
69
70  </body>
71  </html>
```

To move and resize windows:

1. Open Script 6.9 in your text editor or IDE, if it is not already.

2. In the CSS section, add some new definitions (**Script 6.10**):

```
.label {
    position: absolute;
    bottom: 5px;
    font-family: monospace;
    background-color:#CCC;
    border: 1px dashed #666;
    color: #000;
    font-size: 12px;
    padding:2px;
}
#move {
    right: 60px;
}
#resize {
    right: 7px;
}
```

continues on next page

Similar to what I did with the buttons, I'll specially format and position the move and resize widgets (**Figure 6.17**). Both will appear in the lower-right corner.

3. Within the HTML block, add text representing these two new features:

```
<span id="move" class="label"
→ onmousedown="win.startMove();">
→ MOVE</span>

<span id="resize" class="label"
→ onmousedown="win.startResize
→ (air.NativeWindowResize.
→ BOTTOM_RIGHT);">RESIZE</span>
```

Instead of using buttons, these two new items will be simple text blocks. Each is placed within its own span with a class and id value to match the CSS definitions. For the *MOVE* text, when the mouse is clicked on it, the win.startMove() method is called. For the *RESIZE* text, when the mouse is clicked on it, the win.startResize() method is called, sending it the value air.NativeWindowResize.BOTTOM_RIGHT.

4. Save, test, debug, and run the completed application.

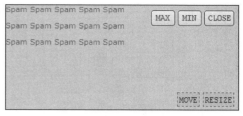

Figure 6.17 In the lower-right corner of the window, two more pieces of common functionality are added.

Working with Multiple Screens

One last window-related topic to discuss in this chapter is screens. If a user's computer has more than one screen connected, your application can take advantage of the screens available. All of the information about the screens in use can be accessed through the Screen class.

The two most important attributes of Screen are Screen.screens and Screen.mainScreen. The former returns an array of Screen objects: one object for each screen in use. The latter returns an object representing the primary screen.

CREATING MENUS

7

Menus are a common feature in almost every application. They provide access to application functionality without cluttering the main program window (although it is possible, and sometimes normal, to duplicate some functionality in menus and utility windows). Creating all sorts of menus in your AIR application is straightforward enough, and you'll learn everything you need to know in this chapter.

The chapter begins with a discussion of the basic terminology, which is mostly a matter of the types of menus that exist. You'll learn how to create menus, and then how to tie events to the menu items (so that selecting an option does something). Part of the point of AIR is to generate cross-platform applications, so you'll also find the code you need to make appropriate menus for both Windows and Mac OS X. The chapter concludes with secondary topics, like creating keyboard equivalents to menu items, adding mnemonics, and changing other menu item properties.

Menu Terminology

Before getting into the actual code, it's best to go through some of the terms used with menus. To start, there are several types of menus that a graphical program can contain.

Application menus exist on Mac OS X and appear at the top of the screen (**Figure 7.1**). A basic application menu is automatically created by the operating system, but you can replace it with your own.

Windows menus are a Windows operating system convention. These menus are associated with an individual window (**Figure 7.2**). Note that the application window must use the system chrome (see Chapter 6, "Making Windows") in order to have a windows menu.

Contextual menus only appear when the user right-clicks, Command-clicks, or Ctrl-clicks, depending on the operating system and its configuration (**Figure 7.3**). Pop-up menus are like contextual menus but can be invoked anywhere within a window (whereas contextual menus are applied to selected text, an image, etc.).

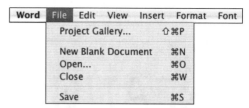

Figure 7.1 Part of the application menu for the Microsoft Word program running on Mac OS X.

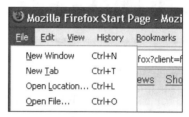

Figure 7.2 Programs on Windows, like Firefox here, have a *windows menu* that appears at the top of an open window.

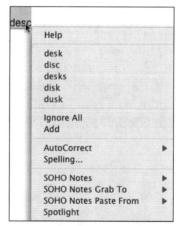

Figure 7.3 The contextual menu that appears after right-clicking on high-lighted text in Word (on Mac OS X).

Figure 7.4 Firefox's Dock menu for Mac OS X. The options in the menu change depending on whether the application is currently open or not.

Figure 7.5 The system tray menu for a program on Windows.

Dock and system tray menus appear when a user clicks on a representation of a program. On Mac OS X, all active and some inactive programs are represented in the Dock (**Figure 7.4**). As with the application menus, Dock menus start with some standard options, to which you can add options; however, unlike application menus, which can be completely overridden, you cannot remove the standard options from Dock menus. On Windows, some programs are represented in the system tray (**Figure 7.5**).

To create menus, you'll use two Adobe AIR classes: NativeMenu and NativeMenuItem. The first creates the actual menu; the second creates the items within the menu.

✔ Tips

- You can also create custom menus using ActionScript, MXML (an XML-based markup language associated with ActionScript), or JavaScript. But doing so is beyond the scope of this chapter, which instead focuses on native menus.

- You can create contextual menus using standard JavaScript or the AIR NativeMenu class. Again, the focus here is on native menus.

- One key distinction between Mac OS X and Windows is in applications versus windows. On Windows, each window is essentially an instance of the application. If you close the window, you close that instance of the application. On Mac OS X, an application can be open without any windows being open, and multiple windows can be open within the same (the only) instance of the application. This is why Macs have application menus but Windows uses window menus.

Creating a Menu

The first class you'll use for creating menus is, appropriately enough, `NativeMenu`. To start, you'll always want to create the root, or base, menu. The code to use is

```
var rootMenu = new air.NativeMenu();
```

For contextual and pop-up menus, the root menu may contain any combination of submenus, individual menu items, and separator lines. If you want to create the more common application or windows menu, you can only place submenus within this root menu.

To add a submenu, start by creating another `NativeMenu` object:

```
var fileMenu = new air.NativeMenu();
```

Next, create items to be added to the submenu:

```
var open = new
→ air.NativeMenuItem('Open');
var close = new
→ air.NativeMenuItem('Close');
```

The argument to this method is the label the item will have (i.e., the text that will appear in the running application). To add an item to a menu, use the menu object's `addItem()` method:

```
fileMenu.addItem(open);
fileMenu.addItem(close);
```

The items will appear in the menu in the order in which they are added.

To create a separator line, use `NativeMenuItem`, providing it with any label (which won't be shown) or none at all, but also add a second argument with a value of `true`:

```
var sep = new
→ air.NativeMenuItem('', true);
fileMenu.addItem(sep);
```

When the submenu is done, you can add it to the root menu:

```
rootMenu.addSubmenu(fileMenu, 'File');
```

The first argument is the `NativeMenu` object; the second is the label the submenu should have.

If you execute the lines of code to this point, `rootMenu` will be a menu containing one submenu whose label is *File*. That submenu will have three items: the first with a label of *Open*, the second with a label of *Close*, and the third being a separator line. Separators don't do anything, they just visually break up a menu (as the last item in this menu, the separator doesn't even do that, but that's irrelevant for now).

Figure 7.6 The window menu created by the instructional code.

Figure 7.7 The same menu as in Figure 7.6 but is now being used as an application menu on Mac OS X.

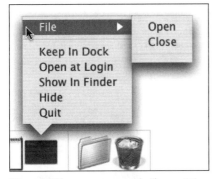

Figure 7.8 The same menu as in Figures 7.6 and 7.7 but is now added to the application's Dock menu.

After you've completely defined the menu, you'll need to set its type. To create a new window menu for Windows, use (**Figure 7.6**):

```
window.nativeWindow.menu = rootMenu;
```

To create a system tray icon menu for Windows, use:

```
air.NativeApplication.nativeApplication.
→ icon.menu = rootMenu;
```

To create an application menu for Mac OS X, use (**Figure 7.7**):

```
air.NativeApplication.nativeApplication.
→ menu = rootMenu;
```

As a reminder, setting a new application menu will replace the standard menu created by the operating system.

To create a Dock icon menu for Mac OS X, use:

```
air.NativeApplication.nativeApplication.
→ icon.menu = rootMenu;
```

As with the application menu, Mac OS X will provide a default set of menu options for the Dock menu. Unlike the application menu, by defining a new Dock menu, your menu items will be added to the existing Dock menu (**Figure 7.8**). You cannot modify the operating system-provided Dock menu items.

CREATING A MENU

To create a menu:

1. In your project's primary HTML file, create a new native menu (**Script 7.1**):

   `var rootMenu = new air.NativeMenu();`

   This object will be the root menu. Every submenu will be added to it.

   If you'd rather, you have the option of putting this and all the subsequent code within a function that's called once the page has loaded. I'm choosing not to, just to keep things simple.

2. Add a submenu:

   `var fileMenu = new air.NativeMenu();`

   This application's main menu (**Figures 7.9** and **7.10**) will have two submenus: *File* and *Help*. The code for the file menu will be written first.

Figure 7.9 The File menu, with its one menu item, as part of the application menu on Mac OS X.

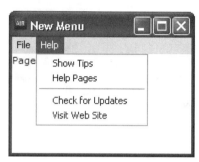

Figure 7.10 The Help menu with its four menu items (plus a separator) as part of the window menu on Windows.

Script 7.1 In this application, a menu with two submenus is created. You'll need to remove the backslashes (//) before one of the two last lines of JavaScript to create the menus for your operating system.

```
1    <html><!-- Script 7.1 -->
2        <head>
3            <title>New Menu</title>
4            <script type="text/javascript" src="AIRAliases.js"></script>
5            <script type="text/javascript">
6
7            // Root menu:
8            var rootMenu = new air.NativeMenu();
9
10           // Add a submenu:
11           var fileMenu = new air.NativeMenu();
12
13           // Add an item to the submenu:
14           var exit = new air.NativeMenuItem('Exit');
15           fileMenu.addItem(exit);
16
17           // Add another submenu:
18           var helpMenu = new air.NativeMenu();
19
20           // Add items to the submenu:
21           var showTips = new air.NativeMenuItem('Show Tips');
22           helpMenu.addItem(showTips);
23           var helpPages = new air.NativeMenuItem('Help Pages');
24           helpMenu.addItem(helpPages);
```

(script continues on next page)

3. Add an *Exit* option to the File menu:

```
var exit = new
→ air.NativeMenuItem('Exit');
fileMenu.addItem(exit);
```

To add an item to a menu, first create a new NativeMenuItem and provide that constructor the label value to use. Then call the parent menu's addItem() method. (As a reminder, a *constructor* is the default method automatically called when a new object of that type is created).

4. Add another submenu:

```
var helpMenu = new air.NativeMenu();
var showTips = new
→ air.NativeMenuItem('Show Tips');
helpMenu.addItem(showTips);
var helpPages = new
→ air.NativeMenuItem('Help Pages');
helpMenu.addItem(helpPages);
var separator = new
→ air.NativeMenuItem('', true);
helpMenu.addItem(separator);
var checkForUpdates = new air.
→ NativeMenuItem('Check for Updates');
helpMenu.addItem(checkForUpdates);
var visitWebSite = new air.
→ NativeMenuItem('Visit Web Site');
helpMenu.addItem(visitWebSite);
```

These lines duplicate the same processes as found in steps 2 and 3. This second menu will contain two items, a separator, and then two more items (see Figure 7.10).

continues on next page

Script 7.1 *continued*

```
⊖ ⊙ ⊙                              📄 Script
25        var separator = new air.NativeMenuItem('', true);
26        helpMenu.addItem(separator);
27        var checkForUpdates = new air.NativeMenuItem('Check for Updates');
28        helpMenu.addItem(checkForUpdates);
29        var visitWebSite = new air.NativeMenuItem('Visit Web Site');
30        helpMenu.addItem(visitWebSite);
31
32        // Add the submenus to the root menu:
33        rootMenu.addSubmenu(fileMenu, 'File');
34        rootMenu.addSubmenu(helpMenu, 'Help');
35
36        // Add the menu to the program...
37
38        // Un-comment to run on Windows:
39  //    window.nativeWindow.menu = rootMenu;
40
41        // Un-comment to run on Mac OS X:
42  //    air.NativeApplication.nativeApplication.menu = rootMenu;
43
44      </script>
45    </head>
46
47    <body>
48        <p>Page Content</p>
49    </body>
50  </html>
```

CREATING A MENU

5. Add the submenus to the root menu:

```
rootMenu.addSubmenu(fileMenu,
→ 'File');

rootMenu.addSubmenu(helpMenu,
→ 'Help');
```

The order in which the submenus are added dictates their order in the final menu.

6. Add the menu to the program.

If you're testing and running this on Windows, add this line:

```
window.nativeWindow.menu = rootMenu;
```

If you're testing and running this on Mac OS X, add:

```
air.NativeApplication.
→ nativeApplication.menu = rootMenu;
```

Script 7.1 shows both of these lines, but they are commented out (i.e., rendered inert). In the next section of this chapter you'll learn how to do this dynamically.

7. Save, test, debug, and run the completed application.

One thing you'll likely notice is that none of the menus items actually do anything.

In fact, there's no common way to exit the application because the Exit (or Quit, on Mac OS X) functionality provided by the operating system has been replaced. Keep reading for the solution. But in the meantime, just close the window to terminate the application.

✔ Tips

- In terms of debugging, if any of the menu creation syntax is wrong, the end result will almost always be a running application with the default menus or none at all. In such cases, check the console for any errors that might have occurred.

- Instead of creating menu items in the order in which you'd like them to appear, you can specify their index (order in the listing) using the addItemAt() method. Its first argument is the item being added, the second is its desired indexed position (starting at 0):

```
var sep = new air.NativeMenuItem('',
→ true);

fileMenu.addItemAt(sep, 2);
```

Handling Menu Events

One crucial step is missing in the previous example: The menu items don't actually do anything. As with most functionality in Adobe AIR applications, creating an object is only half the process; the other half is tying the object to an action. This means using events.

Two events are pertinent to menus: *displaying* and *select*. A displaying event is triggered just before a menu appears (in the nanosecond between the time a user clicks on it and when it's displayed). The most obvious example of when you might use this event would be to update a list of recently opened files each time that menu is viewed.

A select event occurs when a user selects a menu item (except for a submenu or a separator, neither of which can be selected). To perform an action when a menu item is selected, add an event listener:

```
var fullScreen = new
→ air.NativeMenuItem('Full Screen');
fullScreen.addEventListener(air.Event.
→ SELECT, makeFullScreen);
viewMenu.addItem(fullScreen);
```

This code tells the program that when the select event is triggered on the `fullScreen` menu item, the `makeFullScreen()` function (which would need to be defined) should be called. For more information on event listeners, see Chapter 4, "Basic Concepts and Code." To practice this, let's add a couple of event listeners to the menus already created.

To handle menu events:

1. Open Script 7.1 in your text editor or IDE, if it is not already.

   Throughout this entire chapter you'll continue to build on this one example until it's fully functional (or reasonably so).

2. Anywhere within the JavaScript, define a function that should be called when the user selects File > Exit (**Script 7.2**):

```
function doExit(e) {
    air.NativeApplication.
→ nativeApplication.exit();
}
```

continues on page 113

Script 7.2 Two event handlers are added to the application so that selection of File > Exit or Help > Help Pages causes something to happen (namely, termination of the program and the display of an alert box, respectively).

```
1   <html><!-- Script 7.2 -->
2       <head>
3           <title>Menu Events</title>
4           <script type="text/javascript" src="AIRAliases.js"></script>
5           <script type="text/javascript">
6
7           // Function for handling the Exit menu item selection:
8           function doExit(e) {
9               air.NativeApplication.nativeApplication.exit();
10          }
11
12          // Function for handling the Help Pages menu item selection:
13          function showHelp(e) {
14              alert('This is when the Help window would appear.');
15          }
16
```

(script continues on next page)

Script 7.2 *continued*

```
○ ○ ○                              📄 Script
17        // Root menu:
18        var rootMenu = new air.NativeMenu();
19
20        // Add a submenu:
21        var fileMenu = new air.NativeMenu();
22
23        // Add an item to the submenu:
24        var exit = new air.NativeMenuItem('Exit');
25        exit.addEventListener(air.Event.SELECT, doExit);
26        fileMenu.addItem(exit);
27
28        // Add another submenu:
29        var helpMenu = new air.NativeMenu();
30
31        // Add items to the submenu:
32        var showTips = new air.NativeMenuItem('Show Tips');
33        helpMenu.addItem(showTips);
34        var helpPages = new air.NativeMenuItem('Help Pages');
35
36        // Add the helpPages event listener:
37        helpPages.addEventListener(air.Event.SELECT, showHelp);
38
39        // Continue adding items:
40        helpMenu.addItem(helpPages);
41        var separator = new air.NativeMenuItem('', true);
42        helpMenu.addItem(separator);
43        var checkForUpdates = new air.NativeMenuItem('Check for Updates');
44        helpMenu.addItem(checkForUpdates);
45        var visitWebSite = new air.NativeMenuItem('Visit Web Site');
46        helpMenu.addItem(visitWebSite);
47
48        // Add the submenus to the root menu:
49        rootMenu.addSubmenu(fileMenu, 'File');
50        rootMenu.addSubmenu(helpMenu, 'Help');
51
52        // Add the menu to the program:
53  //    window.nativeWindow.menu = rootMenu;
54  //    air.NativeApplication.nativeApplication.menu = rootMenu;
55
56        </script>
57     </head>
58
59     <body>
60        <p>Page Content</p>
61     </body>
62  </html>
```

This function takes one argument, which will be an Event object. Although it won't be used within the function, it's still a good idea to accept that parameter. As for the function itself, it terminates the running application by invoking the exit() method of the NativeApplication object.

It really doesn't matter where within the JavaScript block you define this function, but I'll add mine to the top to keep it separate from the rest of the menu code.

3. Add another function to handle the selection of the Help > Help Pages menu item:

```
function showHelp(e) {
    alert('This is when the Help
    → window would appear.');
}
```

Logically, when users select this particular menu item, they should be shown the Help files for this application. You can easily use some of the code from Chapter 6 to have a new window pop up with that information. But since there is no Help documentation as of yet, an alert dialog will be created instead (**Figure 7.11**).

4. After creating the exit object, add an event listener to it:

```
exit.addEventListener(air.Event.
→ SELECT, doExit);
```

The event listener is added to the exit object, which is a menu item. The event being watched is air.Event.SELECT. When that event occurs, the doExit() function will be called (defined in step 2). You can place this code anywhere within the JavaScript after the exit object is created and before the rootMenu is turned into an application or windows menu.

5. After creating the helpPages object, add an event listener to it:

```
helpPages.addEventListener(air.
→ Event.SELECT, showHelp);
```

Most of this code is the same as the code in step 4; even the same event is being listened for. For this menu item, the function to be called is showHelp(), defined in step 3.

6. Save, test, debug, and run the completed application.

There's no cosmetic difference in the program, but now selecting Help > Help Pages creates the alert box (Figure 7.11) and selecting File > Exit terminates the application, as it should.

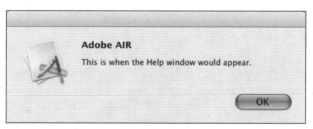

Figure 7.11 The stand-in for the Help Pages window. This appears when the user selects Help > Help Pages.

Event Bubbling

Menu events "bubble" up to the top, which is to say that if you have a Help menu with a Show Tips item in it, selection of that item triggers events for both Show Tips and Help. This knowledge is useful when you have a menu with a list of possible options of which the user would select one. For example, say you have a menu called *Window Size* whose items are possible values: *200x200*, *300x300*, *400x400*, and so on.

In this case, the easiest way to handle the selection is to add an event listener to the parent menu instead of adding one to each item:

```
windowSize.addEventListener(air.Event.SELECT, changeWindowSize);
```

(As already mentioned, the submenu cannot be selected, so it will never actually trigger the select event. But it can listen to events triggered by its menu items.)

The handling function should be written so that it accepts the event as an argument:

```
function changeWindowSize(e) {…
```

Now, within that function, `e.target` refers to the specific menu item that was selected. Its `label` attribute is the label of the selected item. Continuing this function, you might use a conditional to compare the label of the selected item against possible values and react accordingly:

```
var which = e.target;
if (which.label == '200x200') {
    // Resize to 200 x 200.
} else if (which.label == '300x300') {
    // Resize to 300 x 300.
}…
```

Instead of using a long `if-else-if` conditional, you might want to use a `switch`. In any case, if you find you are creating a menu where all the menu items perform subtle variations of the same behavior, that's probably a good opportunity to take advantage of how menu events bubble up to the surface.

OS-specific Menus

In the example that I've been developing throughout this chapter, I instructed you to use this line:

```
window.nativeWindow.menu = rootMenu;
```

to create a windows menu for Windows and this version:

```
air.NativeApplication.nativeApplication.
→ menu = rootMenu;
```

to create that same menu as an application menu on Mac OS X. But AIR applications are supposed to be cross-platform in nature. Although you could build and distribute two different versions of each program, you really don't have to. Instead, you can programmatically check if a menu type is supported and only create those that are.

A windows menu in Windows is added through a *native window* object. To confirm that the program is running on Windows, prior to adding such a menu, use:

```
if (air.NativeWindow.supportsMenu) {…
```

Conversely, an application menu on Mac OS X is added through a *native application* object.

To confirm that the program is running on Mac OS X, prior to adding such a menu, use:

```
if (air.NativeApplication.supportsMenu) {
```

(Technically, these conditionals aren't confirming that the program is running on Windows or Mac OS X but just that the associated menu type is supported.) Let's update the application with this in mind.

To create platform-specific menus:

1. Open Script 7.2 in your text editor or IDE, if it is not already.

2. Replace the line where the menu is added to the program with (**Script 7.3**):

    ```
    if (air.NativeWindow.supportsMenu) {
        window.nativeWindow.menu =
        → rootMenu;
    } else if (air.NativeApplication.
    → supportsMenu) {
        air.NativeApplication.
        → nativeApplication.menu =
        → rootMenu;
    }
    ```

    These two conditions were explained earlier. Here, they've just been put into an if-else if conditional.

continues on page 117

Script 7.3 By using a conditional to check what kinds of menus the current operating system supports, this application can automatically create operating system-specific menus. For Mac OS X, it also changes the label for the File › Exit menu item to *Quit*.

```
1    <html><!-- Script 7.3 -->
2      <head>
3        <title>OS-Specific Menus</title>
4        <script type="text/javascript" src="AIRAliases.js"></script>
5        <script type="text/javascript">
6
7          // Function for handling the Exit menu item selection:
8          function doExit(e) {
9            air.NativeApplication.nativeApplication.exit();
10         }
11
```

(script continues on next page)

Script 7.3 *continued*

```
 12        // Function for handling the Help Pages menu item selection:
 13        function showHelp(e) {
 14            alert('This is when the Help window would appear.');
 15        }
 16
 17        // Root menu:
 18        var rootMenu = new air.NativeMenu();
 19
 20        // Add a submenu:
 21        var fileMenu = new air.NativeMenu();
 22
 23        // Add an item to the submenu:
 24        var exit = new air.NativeMenuItem('Exit');
 25        exit.addEventListener(air.Event.SELECT, doExit);
 26        fileMenu.addItem(exit);
 27
 28        // Add another submenu:
 29        var helpMenu = new air.NativeMenu();
 30
 31        // Add items to the submenu:
 32        var showTips = new air.NativeMenuItem('Show Tips');
 33        helpMenu.addItem(showTips);
 34        var helpPages = new air.NativeMenuItem('Help Pages');
 35
 36        // Add the helpPages event listener:
 37        helpPages.addEventListener(air.Event.SELECT, showHelp);
 38
 39        // Continue adding items:
 40        helpMenu.addItem(helpPages);
 41        var separator = new air.NativeMenuItem('', true);
 42        helpMenu.addItem(separator);
 43        var checkForUpdates = new air.NativeMenuItem('Check for Updates');
 44        helpMenu.addItem(checkForUpdates);
 45        var visitWebSite = new air.NativeMenuItem('Visit Web Site');
 46        helpMenu.addItem(visitWebSite);
 47
 48        // Add the submenus to the root menu:
 49        rootMenu.addSubmenu(fileMenu, 'File');
 50        rootMenu.addSubmenu(helpMenu, 'Help');
 51
 52        // Add the menu to the program:
 53        if (air.NativeWindow.supportsMenu) { // Windows
 54            window.nativeWindow.menu = rootMenu;
 55        } else if (air.NativeApplication.supportsMenu) { // Mac
 56            exit.label = 'Quit';
 57            air.NativeApplication.nativeApplication.menu = rootMenu;
 58        }
 59
 60        </script>
 61    </head>
 62
 63    <body>
 64        <p>Page Content</p>
 65    </body>
 66 </html>
```

OS-SPECIFIC MENUS

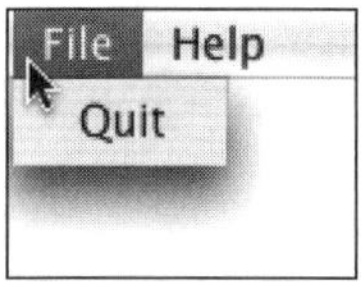

Figure 7.12 On Mac OS X, the File menu's one item is now labeled *Quit* instead of *Exit* (to better match Mac conventions).

3. Before the line that creates the Mac menu, change the label for the exit menu item:

```
exit.label = 'Quit';
```

As a convention, Macs use the word *Quit* instead of *Exit*. So to make this program even more operating system savvy, let's change that value. You can do so by assigning the `label` attribute of the menu item a new value. All the other functionality (namely, calling the `doExit()` function when selected) will remain the same.

4. Save, test, debug, and run the completed application.

The only apparent difference will be the change in the name of the item in the File menu when running the program on Mac OS X (**Figure 7.12**). But more important, you can now distribute and run this same program on both operating systems without further modification.

✔ Tips

■ Because window menus on Windows can only be created within windows that use the system chrome, you can check that condition, too:

```
if (air.NativeWindow.supportsMenu
→ && (air.nativeWindow.systemChrome
→ != air.NativeWindowSystemChrome.
→ NONE) ) {…
```

That being said, you, as the program's developer, should know whether you've created a window with the system chrome or not, so this check shouldn't be necessary.

■ Applications on Mac OS X normally have a menu whose name is the same as the application. You can create this by simply using:

```
rootMenu.addSubmenu(appMenu,
→ 'Application Name');
```

Obviously, you'd need to fill in the actual application's name.

Adding Keyboard Equivalents

Often, items in a menu have a *keyboard equivalent*, also called a *keyboard shortcut* or an *accelerator*. Keyboard equivalents consist of the key and the modifier or modifier keys. Of course, you're already familiar with this concept: Ctrl+C (Windows) or Command+C (Mac OS X) copies the currently selected item to the clipboard.

To add a keyboard equivalent to your AIR application, you start with the menu item:

```
var print = new
→ air.NativeMenuItem('Print');
```

Then set the item's keyEquivalent property to the primary key:

```
print.keyEquivalent = 'p';
```

Note that you should use a lowercase letter, because an uppercase letter assumes the use of the Shift key, which is one of the modifiers. Speaking of which, you also need to list the modifier or modifiers that go with the key. Obviously, you don't want to just use a single key because, using this example, every time I type the word *plié*, I'll trigger the menu item, and that would be maddening. Modifiers are set in an item's keyEquivalentModifiers property. It always takes an array of values, even if only one modifier is being set:

```
item.keyEquivalentModifiers = [modifiers];
```

The modifier values are AIR constants and are defined within the Keyboard class. Most are what you'd expect them to be (**Table 7.1**).

When defining keyboard equivalents, keep a few details in mind. Every keyboard equivalent must be unique for the application. In addition, you should try to make them consistent with the operating system: On Windows, Ctrl+O is used to open a file from within an application, so your program should use that shortcut too (if it has that functionality).

Also, understand that if you replace the application or windows menu, you'll lose all the standard operating system keyboard equivalents because you've eliminated those menus. So the program you create will not recognize Ctrl+P or Command+P for Print unless you make that explicit. Further, take into account that the different operating systems do not have the same modifier keys (Windows uses Shift, Ctrl, and Alt; Mac OS X uses Shift, Control, Option, and Command).

All that being said, one advantage of using keyboard equivalents is that when the user invokes that combination, a select event will be triggered on the corresponding menu item. No extra steps need to be taken in that regard.

Let's apply this knowledge to the running example by adding some keyboard equivalents: one for the Help Pages menu item and another for Exit/Quit.

Table 7.1 Each key on the keyboard is represented in AIR by a constant, which is found within the Keyboard class. Here is a sampling.

Keyboard Constants	
CONSTANT	KEY
ALTERNATE	Alt/Option
BACKSPACE	Backspace
DOWN	Down arrow
F13	F13
NUMBER_7	7
PAGE_UP	Page Up
SPACE	Spacebar

To assign keyboard equivalents:

1. Open Script 7.3 in your text editor or IDE, if it is not already.

2. Within the Windows section of the conditional, add an equivalent for the Help Pages menu item (**Script 7.4**):

   `helpPages.keyEquivalent = 'f1';`

   Sometimes you'll be able to create universal keyboard shortcuts (i.e., ones that are correct for any operating system), but not always. Since this file already has a conditional that essentially determines if the program is running on Windows or Mac, the keyboard shortcuts can easily be defined in a platform-conscience way. To start, a shortcut for Help Pages will be added. Although not universally supported, the first function key is frequently used for application or Windows help. It's used without a modifier.

   Note, again, that you should use the lowercase version of the letter: *f1*, not *F1*.

continues on page 121

Script 7.4 The application has been updated by adding keyboard equivalents to two menu items (one in each submenu). These keyboard shortcuts are also operating system-specific.

```
1    <html><!-- Script 7.4 -->
2        <head>
3            <title>Menu Keyboard Equivalents</title>
4            <script type="text/javascript" src="AIRAliases.js"></script>
5            <script type="text/javascript">
6
7            // Function for handling the Exit menu item selection:
8            function doExit(e) {
9                air.NativeApplication.nativeApplication.exit();
10           }
11
12           // Function for handling the Help Pages menu item selection:
13           function showHelp(e) {
14               alert('This is when the Help window would appear.');
15           }
16
17           // Root menu:
18           var rootMenu = new air.NativeMenu();
19
20           // Add a submenu:
21           var fileMenu = new air.NativeMenu();
22
23           // Add an item to the submenu:
24           var exit = new air.NativeMenuItem('Exit');
25           exit.addEventListener(air.Event.SELECT, doExit);
26           fileMenu.addItem(exit);
27
28           // Add another submenu:
29           var helpMenu = new air.NativeMenu();
30
31           // Add items to the submenu:
32           var showTips = new air.NativeMenuItem('Show Tips');
```

(script continues on next page)

Script 7.4 *continued*

```
33      helpMenu.addItem(showTips);
34      var helpPages = new air.NativeMenuItem('Help Pages');
35
36      // Add the helpPages event listener:
37      helpPages.addEventListener(air.Event.SELECT, showHelp);
38
39      // Continue adding items:
40      helpMenu.addItem(helpPages);
41      var separator = new air.NativeMenuItem('', true);
42      helpMenu.addItem(separator);
43      var checkForUpdates = new air.NativeMenuItem('Check for Updates');
44      helpMenu.addItem(checkForUpdates);
45      var visitWebSite = new air.NativeMenuItem('Visit Web Site');
46      helpMenu.addItem(visitWebSite);
47
48      // Add the submenus to the root menu:
49      rootMenu.addSubmenu(fileMenu, 'File');
50      rootMenu.addSubmenu(helpMenu, 'Help');
51
52      // Add the menu to the program:
53      if (air.NativeWindow.supportsMenu) { // Windows
54
55          // Add keyboard equivalents:
56          helpPages.keyEquivalent = 'f1';
57
58          exit.keyEquivalent = 'f4';
59          exit.keyEquivalentModifiers = [air.Keyboard.ALTERNATE];
60
61          window.nativeWindow.menu = rootMenu;
62
63      } else if (air.NativeApplication.supportsMenu) { // Mac
64
65          // Add keyboard equivalents:
66          helpPages.keyEquivalent = '?';
67          helpPages.keyEquivalentModifiers = [air.Keyboard.COMMAND];
68
69          exit.keyEquivalent = 'q';
70          exit.keyEquivalentModifiers = [air.Keyboard.COMMAND];
71
72          exit.label = 'Quit';
73
74          air.NativeApplication.nativeApplication.menu = rootMenu;
75
76      }
77
78      </script>
79    </head>
80
81    <body>
82        <p>Page Content</p>
83    </body>
84  </html>
```

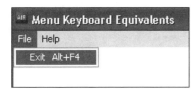

Figure 7.13 The File menu on Windows now shows that ALT + F4 is the keyboard equivalent for Exit.

Figure 7.14 The Help menu on Mac OS X reveals Command+? to be the keyboard equivalent for the Help Pages item.

3. Within the same conditional, add a Windows keyboard equivalent for Exit:

```
exit.keyEquivalent = 'f4';
exit.keyEquivalentModifiers =
→ [air.Keyboard.ALTERNATE];
```

The combination of Alt+F4 is used to close most applications on Windows.

4. Within the Mac section of the conditional, define the Help Pages and Quit keyboard equivalents:

```
helpPages.keyEquivalent = '?';
helpPages.keyEquivalentModifiers =
→ [air.Keyboard.COMMAND];
exit.keyEquivalent = 'q';
exit.keyEquivalentModifiers =
→ [air.Keyboard.COMMAND];
```

Macs use Command+? for Help and Command+Q to quit in every application.

5. Save, test, debug, and run the completed application (**Figures 7.13** and **7.14**).

As you can see in the figures, the keyboard equivalents are automatically listed next to the menu items.

Unfortunately, at the time of this writing, some of the keyboard equivalents are not implemented successfully in the 1.0 release of AIR. For example, the proper Help shortcut on Mac OS X is Command+?, but an equivalent defined as such doesn't work. You can instead define the shortcut using:

```
helpPages.keyEquivalent = '/';
helpPages.keyEquivalentModifiers =
→ [air.Keyboard.COMMAND,
→ air.Keyboard.SHIFT];
```

continues on next page

ADDING KEYBOARD EQUIVALENTS

In terms of the keys the user presses, this is the same as Command+?, and this combination will work; however, the menu item lists the shortcut as Command+Shift+/. It's a minor distinction, but one that other programs are able to get right.

Similarly, I have found using the function keys on Windows to be unreliable. Presumably these things will be worked out in future versions of AIR.

✔ Tips

■ To use multiple modifier keys, separate them by commas:

```
item.KeyEquivalentModifiers =
→ [air.Keyboard.SHIFT,
→ air.Keyboard.OPTION];
```

It does not matter in what order you list the keys.

■ You can add a key equivalent to a menu item in any type of menu, but they'll only work for application and window menus. They'll still appear in contextual menus, but they won't function.

■ Instead of the F1 key, you can set the keyboard equivalent for the Help Pages menu item to the Help key, which exists on many keyboards:

```
helpPages.keyboardEquivalent =
→ air.Keyboard.KEYNAME_HELP;
```

Establishing Mnemonics

Whereas keyboard equivalents are key combinations (used outside of any menu) that trigger menu events, *mnemonics* are meaningful keys used within menus. For example, on Windows, menu items often include a single underlined letter. Pressing that key (with the menu open) is the same as selecting that item and pressing Enter. On Windows and Mac OS X, by default the first character in a menu item's label is automatically a mnemonic (but not marked), but you can override this in AIR.

To add a mnemonic to a menu item, set its `mnemonicIndex` property. The assigned value should be the indexed position of the target character in the menu label. For example, in this code the letter G will be used as the mnemonic (uppercase or lowercase, it makes no difference):

```
var item = new
→ air.NativeMenuItem("Find Again");

item.mnemonicIndex = 6;
```

As with most lists in most programming languages, indexing begins at 0, so the first item has an index of 0, the second has an index of 1, and so on. In this example, G is the seventh item, so it's indexed at 6.

Changing a Menu Item's State

Along with keyboard equivalents and mnemonics, any item in a menu can have two states, which you can think of as just extra attributes. Commonly, some menu items are only usable when an action within the application has occurred. For example, you can only invoke Copy after you've made a selection. To add this quality to a menu item, set its enabled property. It takes a Boolean value:

```
var copy = new
→ air.NativeMenuItem('Copy');
copy.enabled = false;
if (/* something has been selected */) {
    copy.enabled = true;
}
```

Any menu item whose enabled property is false will be disabled and shown as grayed-out in the menu list (**Figure 7.15**).

The second state a menu item might have is checked. Some menu items, when selected, place a checkmark next to them, indicating their status (**Figure 7.16**). Again, this property takes a Boolean value, but unlike the enabled property, subsequent selections of the same menu item should toggle its checked value (from checked to unchecked or from unchecked to checked). The code in this next example demonstrates this.

To adjust the menu states:

1. Open Script 7.4 in your text editor or IDE, if it is not already.

2. After the existing two functions, add a third (**Script 7.5**):

```
function showHideTips(e) {
    if (showTips.checked == false) {
        showTips.checked = true;
    } else {
        showTips.checked = false;
    }
}
```

continues on page 126

Undo Typing	⌘Z
Repeat Typing	⌘Y
Cut	⌘X
Copy	⌘C
Copy to Scrapbook	
Paste	⌘V
Paste from Scrapbook	⇧⌘V
Paste Special...	
Paste as Hyperlink	
Clear	▶
Select All	⌘A
Find...	⌘F
Replace...	⇧⌘H
Go To...	⌘G
Links...	
Object	

Figure 7.15 Several items in this Edit menu are disabled and therefore not selectable.

Toolbars	▶
Firebug	F12
✔ Status Bar	
Sidebar	▶
Stop	Esc
Reload	Ctrl+R
Text Size	▶
Page Style	▶
Character Encoding	▶
Page Source	Ctrl+U
Full Screen	F11

Figure 7.16 The Status Bar item in Firefox's View menu has a checked state.

Script 7.5 To round out the functionality of the menus, the Show Tips item gets an event handler that calls a function that toggles its checked state. Secondarily, another menu item is disabled.

(script continues on next page)

```
1    <html><!-- Script 7.5 -->
2      <head>
3        <title>Menu States</title>
4        <script type="text/javascript" src="AIRAliases.js"></script>
5        <script type="text/javascript">
6
7        // Function for handling the Exit menu item selection:
8        function doExit(e) {
9          air.NativeApplication.nativeApplication.exit();
10        }
11
12        // Function for handling the Help Pages menu item selection:
13        function showHelp(e) {
14          alert('This is when the Help window would appear.');
15        }
16
17        // Function for handling the Show Tips menu item selection:
18        function showHideTips(e) {
19
20          // Toggle the value of showTips.checked:
21          if (showTips.checked == false) {
22            showTips.checked = true;
23          } else {
24            showTips.checked = false;
25          }
26
27        } // End of the showHideTips() function.
28
29        // Root menu:
30        var rootMenu = new air.NativeMenu();
31
32        // Add a submenu:
33        var fileMenu = new air.NativeMenu();
34
35        // Add an item to the submenu:
36        var exit = new air.NativeMenuItem('Exit');
37        exit.addEventListener(air.Event.SELECT, doExit);
38        fileMenu.addItem(exit);
39
40        // Add another submenu:
41        var helpMenu = new air.NativeMenu();
42
43        // Add items to the submenu:
44        var showTips = new air.NativeMenuItem('Show Tips');
45
46        // Add the showTips event listener:
47        showTips.addEventListener(air.Event.SELECT, showHideTips);
48        helpMenu.addItem(showTips);
49
50        var helpPages = new air.NativeMenuItem('Help Pages');
51
```

Script 7.5 *continued*

```
                                          📄 Script
52        // Add the helpPages event listener:
53        helpPages.addEventListener(air.Event.SELECT, showHelp);
54
55        // Continue adding items:
56        helpMenu.addItem(helpPages);
57        var separator = new air.NativeMenuItem('', true);
58        helpMenu.addItem(separator);
59        var checkForUpdates = new air.NativeMenuItem('Check for Updates');
60
61        // Disable the 'Check for Updates' option:
62        checkForUpdates.enabled = false;
63
64        helpMenu.addItem(checkForUpdates);
65        var visitWebSite = new air.NativeMenuItem('Visit Web Site');
66        helpMenu.addItem(visitWebSite);
67
68        // Add the submenus to the root menu:
69        rootMenu.addSubmenu(fileMenu, 'File');
70        rootMenu.addSubmenu(helpMenu, 'Help');
71
72        // Add the menu to the program:
73        if (air.NativeWindow.supportsMenu) { // Windows
74
75            // Add keyboard equivalents:
76            helpPages.keyboardEquivalent = 'f1';
77
78            exit.keyEquivalent = 'f4';
79            exit.keyEquivalentModifiers = [air.Keyboard.ALTERNATE];
80
81            window.nativeWindow.menu = rootMenu;
82
83        } else if (air.NativeApplication.supportsMenu) { // Mac
84
85            // Add keyboard equivalents:
86            helpPages.keyEquivalent = '?';
87            helpPages.keyEquivalentModifiers = [air.Keyboard.COMMAND];
88
89            exit.keyEquivalent = 'q';
90            exit.keyEquivalentModifiers = [air.Keyboard.COMMAND];
91
92            exit.label = 'Quit';
93
94            air.NativeApplication.nativeApplication.menu = rootMenu;
95
96        }
97
98        </script>
99    </head>
100
101    <body>
102        <p>Page Content</p>
103    </body>
104 </html>
```

This function will be called whenever the Show Tips menu option is selected. Within the function, a conditional checks if the current value of showTips.checked is *false* (you can refer to showTips within this function because it's a global variable). If that value is *false*, it'll be set to *true*. Otherwise, the value is *true* and should be set to *false*.

In a complete program you'd also include the code here that turns on and turns off the actual show tips feature.

3. After defining the showTips object (a few lines down in the script), add an event listener to it:

```
showTips.addEventListener(air.Event.
→ SELECT, showHideTips);
```

If you don't include this step, the selection of the menu item will never invoke the showHideTips() function.

4. Disable the Check for Updates menu item.

```
checkForUpdates.enabled = false;
```

Arbitrarily, I'll disable this just to demonstrate how that works. Again, in a standard program, there would be some condition that dictates when an object's enabled state would be set to true or false.

5. Save, test, debug, and run the completed application (**Figures 7.17** and **7.18**).

Figure 7.17 The updated Help menu with the disabled Check for Updates item. By selecting the Show Tips item, ...

Figure 7.18 ...it will then be marked as checked.

IMPORTING AND EXPORTING DATA

A key feature of many desktop applications is the ability to use the computer's clipboard. This means that a user should be able to select data in a program and place it on the clipboard (by either copying or cutting). The program should also be able to insert into a document data that is already in the clipboard (aka, pasting). Related to the use of the clipboard is support for dragging and dropping. The premise is the same as using the clipboard, but this process is mouse driven: The user selects something in one program and drags it to another window or program, or vice versa.

All this functionality is supported in any HTML-based AIR application by default, thanks to the WebKit rendering engine. In other words, without taking any extra steps, users will be able to copy application content or drag it out of the program. Also, in editable elements like text inputs and textareas, a user can cut content, paste new content in, and drag new content in. The purpose of this chapter is to demonstrate how you can use Adobe AIR to discreetly control how and where the user edits or copies an application's content. As an application's developer, this is part of the power you have (but don't let it go to your head).

Copying

As mentioned in the introduction to this chapter, the WebKit rendering engine provides all the functionality required to handle copying and other clipboard-related user activity. But you do have the option of overriding the default behavior. The first step in that process is to identify the function to be called when the user invokes the Copy command (either through an Edit menu, a mouse gesture, or a keyboard shortcut). This is done within the body tag:

```
<body oncopy="doCopy(event);">
```

That line specifies that when content—images, text, and so on—within the application's body is copied, the doCopy() function should be called, passing it the event that occurred.

The next step is to define the JavaScript function that will be called. It starts by accepting one argument, which will be the event:

```
function doCopy(e) {
}
```

Because the function will be replacing the default copy behavior, that default behavior needs to be prevented:

```
e.preventDefault();
```

The preventDefault() method can be used to prevent the default application action from being taken on any given event. For this copying example, it prevents the application from copying the data to the clipboard.

The next step that a copy function should always do is clear out all of the clipboard's existing content. The clipboard is accessible through the event's clipboardData property. To wipe it clean, call its clearData() method:

```
e.clipboardData.clearData();
```

This is recommended because the data to be copied there may not entirely overwrite its existing data (because the clipboard can store the same piece of data in many formats; see the "How the Clipboard Works" sidebar). Executing this one line will help to prevent bugs.

Assuming that the intent is to still allow the copy to work, the function will need to copy the selected content to the clipboard. The first step in doing so is to retrieve the selected content:

```
var data = window.getSelection();
```

Second, call the event's clipboardData.setData() method to place the selection onto the clipboard. Its first argument is a MIME type indicating the kind of data being copied there. MIME types are listed in **Table 8.1**. The second argument is the actual data. So to copy just plain text to the clipboard, you would write:

```
e.clipboardData.setData('text/plain',
→ data);
```

Table 8.1 These MIME types are used to identify the format of data to be stored in, or retrieved from, the clipboard.

Clipboard Data Formats	
MIME TYPE	MEANING
image/x-vnd.adobe.air.bitmap	BitmapData Object
application/x-vnd.adobe.air.file-list	an array of File objects
text/html	HTML-formatted text
text/plain	plain text
text/uri-list	a URL

COPYING

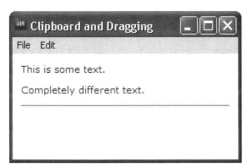

Figure 8.1 This very simple application will be used to demonstrate copying, cutting, pasting, dragging, and dropping.

How the Clipboard Works

It's important to understand that the clipboard doesn't just store one piece of information. The clipboard can actually store the same piece of information in multiple formats. For example, a chunk of formatted text copied from a Word document can be stored as the formatted text and as a plain text version (so that pasting that text into a plain text editor works without a problem).

It's important that you keep this multilayered clipboard structure in mind. When copying data to the clipboard, your AIR application needs to provide not just the data to be copied, but the application also needs to indicate the data's format. If they don't match (e.g., an image stored as plain text), the copy won't work. Similarly, when you retrieve data from the clipboard, the application indicates the format of the data it wants and will receive whatever data is stored in that format.

Because the clipboard can store the same piece of data in multiple formats, the doCopy() function can make that happen. Say, for example, the user selects a URL in the application. The doCopy() function can copy that to the clipboard as plain text, as HTML, and as a URL:

```
function doCopy(e) {
    var data = window.getSelection();
    var html =  '<a href="' + data
    + '">' + data + '</a>';
    e.clipboardData.setData('text/
    plain', data);
    e.clipboardData.setData('text/html',
    html);
    e.clipboardData.setData('text/
    uri-list', data);
}
```

To practice this and the other ideas in this chapter, let's create an application that has some text and a horizontal rule (**Figure 8.1**). The text at the top of the window can be copied, and later in the chapter, pasted into the bottom of the window. To keep things tidy, I'll break up the code into separate files.

COPYING

To copy data to the clipboard:

1. In your project's primary HTML file, include one separate JavaScript file (**Script 8.1**):

   ```
   <script type="text/javascript"
   → src="editFunctions.js"></script>
   ```

   Along with `AIRAliases.js`, which you'll want to include in pretty much every AIR project you create, this application will use one other separate JavaScript file. That script will define the functions that handle copying, cutting, and pasting.

2. In the body tag, associate an `oncopy` event with a function called `doCopy`:

   ```
   <body style="margin:10px"
   → oncopy="doCopy(event);">
   ```

   I'm also adding a bit of CSS styling to pad the page (so that text and such aren't butting up against the edges of the application window).

3. Add some text and a horizontal rule to the page:

   ```
   <p>This is some text.</p>
   <p>Completely different text.</p>
   <hr />
   ```

   The two text blocks will give the user two different items that can be copied. The horizontal rule will divide the page so that new content—pasted or dragged in—will appear below the provided content.

4. Save the file as `index.html`.

Script 8.1 The application's primary HTML file starts with just two blocks of text and a horizontal rule. It includes one new JavaScript file that defines all of the important functionality.

```
1    <html><!-- Script 8.1 -->
2       <head>
3          <title>Clipboard and Dragging</title>
4          <script type="text/javascript" src="AIRAliases.js"></script>
5          <script type="text/javascript" src="editFunctions.js"></script>
6       </head>
7
8    <body style="margin:10px" oncopy="doCopy(event);">
9
10      <p>This is some text.</p>
11
12      <p>Completely different text.</p>
13
14      <hr />
15
16   </body>
17   </html>
```

COPYING

Script 8.2 The editFunctions.js script defines the function called when the user copies selected content.

```
1   /* Script 8.2 - editFunctions.js
2    * This script defines the JavaScript
     function used to Copy.
3    */
4
5   // Function for copying data to the
     clipboard.
6   // Takes one argument: an event.
7   function doCopy(e) {
8
9       // Prevent the default behavior:
10      e.preventDefault();
11
12      // Clear the clipboard:
13      e.clipboardData.clearData();
14
15      // Get the selection:
16      var data = window.getSelection();
17
18      // Add the text to the clipboard:
19      e.clipboardData.setData('text/plain',
        data);
20
21  } // End of doCopy() function.
```

5. In a new JavaScript file, define the doCopy() function (**Script 8.2**):

```
function doCopy(e) {
    e.preventDefault();
    e.clipboardData.clearData();
    var data = window.getSelection();
    e.clipboardData.setData('text/
    → plain', data);
} // End of doCopy() function.
```

Thanks to the body's oncopy event listener, this function will be called when the user selects Edit > Copy or invokes the keyboard equivalent. This function receives one argument—the event. Within the function, you first need to prevent the default behavior and clear the current contents of the clipboard.

Next, identify the data the user selected. To find that value, refer to window.getSelection(). The selected text is then added to the clipboard. To accomplish that, the first argument in the setData() method should be the MIME type that represents plain text. The second argument is the data to be stored.

6. Save the file as editFunctions.js.

You'll need to save it in the project's directory, along with index.html (Script 8.1). If you want to place the JavaScript files within a subdirectory, you'll need to change the code in step 1 to match.

continues on next page

COPYING

7. Save, test, debug, and run the completed application.

When you go to test and build the program, make sure you include the JavaScript files (AIRAliases.js and editFunctions.js). In the running program, select any portion of text, and then choose Edit > Copy or press the keyboard equivalent. You can confirm that the copy worked by pasting the clipboard's content into another application's document (like a Word, Notepad, or TextEdit file).

Windows also provides the ClipBook Viewer (**Figure 8.2**), whereas Mac OS X has an Edit > Show Clipboard option in the Finder (**Figure 8.3**) for viewing what's stored in the clipboard.

✔ Tips

■ Whether the user invokes the copy command through a keyboard shortcut, a mouse event, or the Edit menu, the code in this example will work. If you define your own Edit menu, however (see Chapter 7, "Creating Menus"), you'll need to tie the selection of the Copy menu item to the doCopy() function using an event listener:

```
copy.addEventListener(air.Event.
→ SELECT, doCopy);
```

■ The Adobe Integrated Runtime provides an alternative way to use the clipboard for copying and pasting. However, the HTML-based techniques taught in this chapter are easier to use and don't have the same security restrictions. On the other hand, the AIR API methods for using the clipboard can support different data formats, like files and objects, and has other extra features.

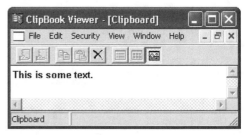

Figure 8.2 The ClipBook Viewer program on Windows shows the current contents of the clipboard. (If you don't know how to find the ClipBook Viewer, search the Web for instructions.)

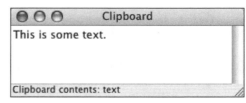

Figure 8.3 Within the Mac Finder, the Edit > Show Clipboard option brings up this window, which shows the clipboard's current contents. It also shows the data format at the bottom of the window.

COPYING

Cutting

Now that you've seen how to implement copy functionality in an AIR application, the next logical action to address is cutting. Cutting is simply copying the selected content and removing it.

Start by getting a reference to the selection:

```
var data = window.getSelection();
```

Then you'll want to make sure that the selection has been copied to the clipboard before you remove it:

```
e.preventDefault();
e.clipboardData.clearData();
e.clipboardData.setData('text/plain',
→ data);
```

Just to be clear, all this code would be placed within the function that's called when an HTML oncut event occurs, just as doCopy() is called when an oncopy event occurs.

In HTML there are a few different ways you can remove content from the page. The one I'll use here involves using a JavaScript Range object. A Range is a reference to any part of the HTML page. This next line creates a Range object called r, which represents the user selection:

```
var r = data.getRangeAt(0);
```

(You'll always want to call the getRangeAt() function like this, but in case you're curious, the 0 value specifies that the returned range should begin with the first element that the user selected.)

Once you have the Range object, removing the selection is simply a matter of calling its deleteContents() method:

```
r.deleteContents();
```

Before applying this code to the existing example, there's one more concept to mention. The WebKit rendering engine adds several of its own CSS style attributes. For the purposes of this chapter, I'll highlight -webkit-user-select. This attribute dictates what a user can select. Its default value of *auto* means the user can select anything. If given a value of *none*, the associated content cannot be selected:

```
<p style="-webkit-user-select: none">
→ The user cannot select this text!</p>
```

The third possible value is *text*, which means that the user can only select the text part of a given element:

```
<p style="-webkit-user-select: text">
→ The user cannot select the image.
→ <img src="file.png" /></p>
```

I mention this now because controlling what the user can select in an application is one way of controlling what the user can copy, cut, or drag out.

With this in mind, let's update the example to handle the cutting of page content.

To cut application content:

1. Open Script 8.1 in your text editor or IDE, if it is not already.

2. Add code to the body tag so that the doCut() function is called when the user invokes Edit > Cut (**Script 8.3**):

   ```
   <body style="margin:10px"
   → oncopy="doCopy(event);"
   → oncut="doCut(event);">
   ```

   The added code specifies that when a cut event happens, the doCut() function should be called.

3. Add some text that cannot be selected:

   ```
   <p style="-webkit-user-select:
   → none">The user cannot select
   → this text!</p>
   ```

   So you can see this in action, a new block of text that the user cannot select, copy, or cut is added to the page.

Script 8.3 The main HTML page is updated so that the doCut() function is called when the user attempts to cut any content. Another block of text, which the user cannot select, is also added to the page.

```
1    <html><!-- Script 8.3 (update of Script 8.1) -->
2        <head>
3            <title>Clipboard and Dragging</title>
4            <script type="text/javascript" src="AIRAliases.js"></script>
5            <script type="text/javascript" src="editFunctions.js"></script>
6        </head>
7
8    <body style="margin:10px" oncopy="doCopy(event);" oncut="doCut(event);">
9
10       <p>This is some text.</p>
11
12       <p>Completely different text.</p>
13
14       <p style="-webkit-user-select: none">The user cannot select this text!</p>
15
16       <hr />
17
18   </body>
19   </html>
```

Script 8.4 The revised version of `editFunctions.js` (see Script 8.2) now defines a `doCut()` function. It calls `doCopy()`, and then removes the user selection from the page. (I also removed some comments and blank lines in the existing content to save space.)

```
1    /* Script 8.4 - editFunctions.js (updated)
2     * This script defines the JavaScript
     functions used to Copy and Cut.
3     */
4
5    // Function for copying data to the
     clipboard.
6    // Takes one argument: an event.
7    function doCopy(e) {
8        e.preventDefault();
9        e.clipboardData.clearData();
10       var data = window.getSelection();
11       e.clipboardData.setData('text/plain',
         data);
12   } // End of doCopy() function.
13
14   // Function for cutting data.
15   // Takes one argument: an event.
16   function doCut(e){
17
18       doCopy(e);
19
20       // Remove the content from the page:
21       var data = window.getSelection();
22       var r = data.getRangeAt(0);
23       r.deleteContents();
24
25   } // End of doCut() function.
```

4. Save the updated file.

5. Open `editFunctions.js` (Script 8.2) in your text editor or IDE, if it is not already.

6. Begin defining the `doCut()` function (**Script 8.4**):

```
function doCut(e){
    doCopy(e);
```

As with `doCopy()`, this function takes one argument: the event. The first thing this function needs to do is replicate the functionality of the `doCopy()` function. Instead of doing that here, the `doCopy()` function will just be called, passing it the event object.

7. Remove the content from the page and complete the function:

```
    var data = window.getSelection();
    var r = data.getRangeAt(0);
    r.deleteContents();
} // End of doCut() function.
```

This code is explained in the introduction to these steps. Although the `doCopy()` function also created a reference to the user selection, this function still needs to take that step because it doesn't have access to the `data` variable defined in `doCopy()`.

continues on next page

CUTTING

8. Save, test, debug, and run the completed application (**Figures 8.4**, **8.5**, and **8.6**).

You can now copy or cut text from the top half of the window and then paste it into other applications.

✔ Tip

■ The -webkit-user-select style attribute is not foolproof. Even though the new block of text has a value of *none*, it's still possible for the user to copy that text, but it just won't appear as selected.

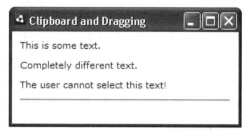

Figure 8.4 The application as it looks when it first runs.

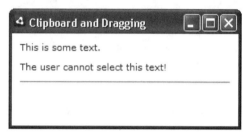

Figure 8.5 The second sentence (see Figure 8.4) has been cut from the application.

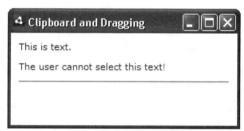

Figure 8.6 The word *some* in the first sentence has been cut from the application (compare with Figures 8.4 and 8.5).

CUTTING

Pasting

The third clipboard-related HTML event that an application can override is pasting. As with copying and cutting, start by telling the application to use a different function to handle such events:

```
<body onpaste="doPaste(event);">
```

The defined function then needs to accept an event as its lone argument:

```
function doPaste(e) {
    // Handle the pasting.
}
```

The specifics of what this function does will depend on the application, but the basic idea is that it will retrieve the data stored in the clipboard and add it to the application window.

Just as data is added to the clipboard by invoking the `setData()` method, data is retrieved using `getData()`. This method takes one argument, the format of the data to be retrieved:

```
var text = e.clipboardData.
→ getData('text/plain');
```

The format value should again be a MIME type, matching what's stored in the clipboard. This also means your application can select the format of the data being pasted if multiple formats are available. For example, if content was added to the clipboard using

```
e.clipboardData.setData('text/plain',
→ data);
e.clipboardData.setData('text/html',
→ html);
e.clipboardData.setData('text/uri-list',
→ data);
```

then the pasting function can access the data stored in any of those formats.

To confirm that the clipboard contains data in a given format, prior to retrieving it, call the `hasFormat()` method:

```
if(e.clipboardData.hasFormat('text/
→ html')){ …
```

To use this new information, let's update the example so that new pasted text is added to the window within a new DIV (**Figure 8.7**). This change will involve defining the `doPaste()` function and adding another one.

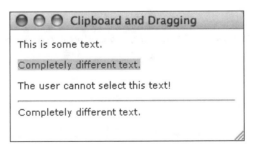

Figure 8.7 Text pasted within this application gets added below the horizontal rule as a new DIV.

To copy data to the clipboard:

1. Open Script 8.3 in your text editor or IDE, if it is not already.

2. Add a clause to the body tag so that the doPaste() function is called when the user invokes Edit > Paste (**Script 8.5**):

   ```
   <body style="margin:10px"
   → oncopy="doCopy(event);"
   → oncut="doCut(event);"
   → onpaste="doPaste(event);">
   ```

   The added code specifies that when a paste event happens, the doPaste() function should be called.

3. Save the updated file.

4. Open editFunctions.js (Script 8.4) in your text editor or IDE, if it is not already.

Script 8.5 The main HTML page is updated so that a user-defined doPaste() function is called when a paste event happens.

```
1    <html><!-- Script 8.5 (update of Script 8.3) -->
2       <head>
3          <title>Clipboard and Dragging</title>
4          <script type="text/javascript" src="AIRAliases.js"></script>
5          <script type="text/javascript" src="editFunctions.js"></script>
6       </head>
7
8    <body style="margin:10px" oncopy="doCopy(event);" oncut="doCut(event);" onpaste="doPaste(event);">
9
10      <p>This is some text.</p>
11
12      <p>Completely different text.</p>
13
14      <p style="-webkit-user-select: none">The user cannot select this text!</p>
15
16      <hr />
17
18   </body>
19   </html>
```

Script 8.6 Two new functions are added to the editFunctions.js file. One provides the paste functionality, the other adds new DIVs to the page.

```
1    /* Script 8.6 - editFunctions.js (updated)
2     * This script defines the JavaScript
     functions used to Copy, Cut, and Paste.
3     */
4
5    // Function for copying data to the
     clipboard.
6    // Takes one argument: an event.
7    function doCopy(e) {
8        e.preventDefault();
9        e.clipboardData.clearData();
10       var data = window.getSelection();
11       e.clipboardData.setData('text/plain',
         data);
12   } // End of doCopy() function.
13
14   // Function for cutting data.
15   // Takes one argument: an event.
16   function doCut(e){
17       doCopy(e);
18       var data = window.getSelection();
19       var r = data.getRangeAt(0);
20       r.deleteContents();
21   } // End of doCut() function.
22
23   // Function for pasting data from the
     clipboard.
24   // Takes one argument: an event.
25   function doPaste(e) {
26
27       // Paste text as a new DIV:
28       if (e.clipboardData.getData('text/
         plain')) {
29
30           addDiv( e.clipboardData.
             getData('text/plain') );
31
32       } else {
33
34           alert('Data type not yet supported!');
35
36       }
37
38   } // End of doPaste() function.
39
```

(script continues)

5. Define the doPaste() function (**Script 8.6**):

```
function doPaste(e) {
    if (e.clipboardData.getData('text/
    →plain')) {
        addDiv( e.clipboardData.
        →getData('text/plain') );
    } else {
        alert('Data type not yet
        →supported!');
    }
} // End of doPaste() function.
```

The first conditional checks to see if the clipboard contains plain text. If it does, then that text should be added to the application as a new DIV. This will be accomplished using another function called addDiv() that takes the clipboard's contents as an argument. To access those contents, refer to e.clipboardData. getData('text/plain').

continues on next page

Script 8.6 *continued*

```
40   // Function for adding new content in a DIV.
41   // Takes one argument: the content to be
     added.
42   function addDiv(content) {
43
44       // Create a new DIV:
45       var d = document.createElement('div');
46
47       // Add the content to the DIV:
48       d.innerText = content;
49
50       // Add the DIV to the page:
51       document.body.appendChild(d);
52
53       // Add a break:
54       document.body.appendChild(document.
         createElement('br'));
55
56   } // End of addDiv() function.
```

139

If the first conditional isn't true, the user is trying to paste nontext into the application. For now, the program will just cough up an alert (**Figure 8.8**).

6. Define a function that creates new DIV elements:

```
function addDiv(content) {
    var d = document.
    → createElement('div');
    d.innerText = content;
    document.body.appendChild(d);
    document.body.appendChild(document.
    → createElement('br'));
}
```

This function takes one argument: the content to be added to the page. Then, within the function, a new element of type DIV is created. Its innerText attribute—the text that goes between the opening and closing DIV tags—is assigned the value of the content. Then the DIV is added to the page, along with a break tag (for extra spacing).

7. Save, test, debug, and run the completed application (**Figures 8.9** and **8.10**).

You can copy text from the top half of the window and then paste it (Figure 8.9) or copy text from another application and paste it into this one (Figure 8.10).

✔ Tips

- You can see what formats are currently stored in the clipboard by referring to e.clipboardData.types. This will be a string of values like *text/html,text/plain,image/x-vnd.adobe.air.bitmap*.

- For security reasons, the clipboardData.getData() function can only be called within a function that handles paste events.

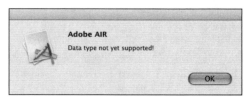

Figure 8.8 If the user attempts to paste data that isn't text, this alert will appear.

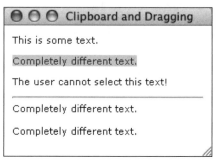

Figure 8.9 The same text has been pasted twice.

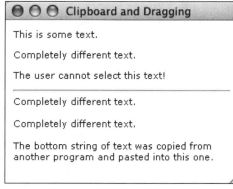

Figure 8.10 The bottom string of text was copied from another program and pasted into this one.

Working with Different Formats

The first three examples in this chapter show how relatively easy it is to copy text to the clipboard and to paste text back into an application. But AIR applications support many data formats:

◆ Text

◆ URLs

◆ Bitmaps (images)

◆ Files

◆ Objects

When working with any of these formats, the first change you'd make to your code is which MIME type (from Table 8.1) you'd use in your setData() and getData() calls. The second, and more important change, is what data you'd actually place in the clipboard or how you'd place the clipboard data in your application. For example, you can store an array of files in the clipboard, but you wouldn't place an array of files in an application's window (the list of file names, yes, or links to those files, but not the actual files).

To demonstrate how you might handle other data types in an AIR application, let's update the program so that it allows the user to select an image that can be copied to the clipboard (**Figure 8.11**). When the user pastes that clipboard content, or any other image, back into this application, it will be added to the lower section of the window (**Figure 8.12**).

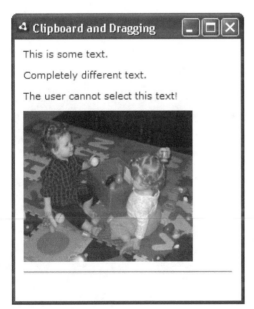

Figure 8.11 The application content now includes one JPEG image.

Figure 8.12 The application now supports the ability to paste both text and images into it.

To use files with the clipboard:

1. Open `index.html` (Script 8.5) in your text editor or IDE, if it is not already.

2. Add an image to the body of the page (**Script 8.7**):

```
<p><img src="kids.jpg" width="200"
→ height="173" /></p>
```

To add another element (besides the text) that the user can cut or copy, an image is added. You can download this image from the book's corresponding Web site—www.DMCInsights.com/air/, see the Extras page—or provide your own, changing the code accordingly. The image will need to be placed within the project's directory and be included in the build, too.

3. Save the updated file.

Script 8.7 The application's main page is updated to include an image that can be copied, cut, and pasted back.

```
1   <html><!-- Script 8.7 (update of Script 8.5) -->
2      <head>
3         <title>Clipboard and Dragging</title>
4         <script type="text/javascript" src="AIRAliases.js"></script>
5         <script type="text/javascript" src="editFunctions.js"></script>
6      </head>
7
8   <body style="margin:10px" oncopy="doCopy(event);" oncut="doCut(event);" onpaste="doPaste(event);">
9
10     <p>This is some text.</p>
11
12     <p>Completely different text.</p>
13
14     <p style="-webkit-user-select: none">The user cannot select this text!</p>
15
16     <p><img src="kids.jpg" width="200" height="173" /></p>
17
18     <hr />
19
20  </body>
21  </html>
```

4. In the editFunctions.js page (Script 8.6), after clearing the clipboard within the doCopy() function, check if the selection being copied is an image (**Script 8.8**):

```
if (e.target instanceof
→ HTMLImageElement) {
```

This may seem a bit like voodoo, so I'll explain this line in detail. The application contains both text and an image. When either is copied or cut, the doCopy() function will need to call the setData() method and provide it either *text/plain* or *image/x-vnd.adobe.air.bitmap* as the MIME type of the content. To know which MIME type to use, the script has to find out if the selection is text or an image, which is what this conditional does.

The e.target property is a reference to the user selection. It returns an object. If the user selected the image to copy (or cut), the object will be of type HTMLImageElement. If the user selected text, e.target will be an object of type HTMLParagraphElement. So this conditional checks to see if e.target is an object of type (i.e., an *instance of*) HTMLImageElement.

continues on page 145

Script 8.8 To support both text and image data types, the doCopy() and doPaste() functions are updated to handle different MIME types.

```
1    /* Script 8.8 - editFunctions.js (updated)
2     * This script defines the JavaScript functions used to Copy, Cut, and Paste.
3     */
4
5    // Function for copying data to the clipboard.
6    // Takes one argument: an event.
7    function doCopy(e) {
8        e.preventDefault();
9        e.clipboardData.clearData();
10
11       // Is the selection an image?
12       if (e.target instanceof HTMLImageElement) {
13
14           // Add the image to the clipboard:
15           e.clipboardData.setData('image/x-vnd.adobe.air.bitmap', e.target);
16
17       } else { // Text!
18
19           // Get the selection:
20           var data = window.getSelection();
21
22           // Add the text to the clipboard:
23           e.clipboardData.setData('text/plain', data);
24
25       }
26
27   } // End of doCopy() function.
28
```

(script continues on next page)

Script 8.8 *continued*

```
29   // Function for cutting data.
30   // Takes one argument: an event.
31   function doCut(e){
32       doCopy(e);
33       var data = window.getSelection();
34       var r = data.getRangeAt(0);
35       r.deleteContents();
36   } // End of doCut() function.
37
38   // Function for pasting data from the clipboard.
39   // Takes one argument: an event.
40   function doPaste(e) {
41
42       // Paste text as a new DIV:
43       if (e.clipboardData.getData('text/plain')) {
44
45           addDiv( e.clipboardData.getData('text/plain') );
46
47       } else if (e.clipboardData.getData('image/x-vnd.adobe.air.bitmap')) { // Image!
48
49           var image = e.clipboardData.getData('image/x-vnd.adobe.air.bitmap');
50
51           // Create a new DIV:
52           var d = document.createElement('div');
53
54           document.body.appendChild(image);
55           // Add the DIV to the page:
56           document.body.appendChild(d);
57
58           // Add a break:
59           document.body.appendChild(document.createElement('br'));
60
61       } else {
62
63           alert('Data type not yet supported!');
64
65       }
66
67   } // End of doPaste() function.
68
69   // Function for adding new content in a DIV.
70   // Takes one argument: the content to be added.
71   function addDiv(content) {
72       var d = document.createElement('div');
73       d.innerText = content;
74       document.body.appendChild(d);
75       document.body.appendChild(document.createElement('br'));
76   } // End of addDiv() function.
```

WORKING WITH DIFFERENT FORMATS

5. Copy the image to the clipboard:

```
e.clipboardData.setData('image/
→ x-vnd.adobe.air.bitmap', e.target);
```

If the conditional in step 4 is true, the selection is an image and it needs to be placed on the clipboard. To do so, call the setData() method using *image/x-vnd. adobe.air.bitmap* as the MIME type and e.target as the data (remember that e.target is a reference to the selected element so using it as the data value will work).

6. Complete the conditional begun in step 4:

```
} else {
    var data = window.getSelection();
    e.clipboardData.setData('text/
    → plain', data);
}
```

If the selection isn't an image (if e.target is not an instance of the HTMLImageElement class), the standard method for copying text to the clipboard is used. These middle two lines of code were already in the doCopy() function, and now they're within an else clause.

7. Add an else if clause to the conditional in the doPaste() function.

```
} else if (e.clipboardData.
→ getData('image/x-vnd.adobe.air.
→ bitmap')) {
    var image = e.clipboardData.
    → getData('image/x-vnd.adobe.air.
    → bitmap');
```

Figure 8.13 Attempting to paste an unsupported data type into the application results in this error message.

```
    var d = document.
    → createElement('div');
    document.body.appendChild(image);
    document.body.appendChild(d);
    document.body.appendChild(document.
    → createElement('br'));
```

The original conditional in the doPaste() function was a simple if else. Now it has a second condition that checks if the clipboard contains data in the *image/x-vnd.adobe.air.bitmap* format. If so, the clipboard contents are assigned to the image variable. Then a new DIV is created, the image is appended to it, and the DIV, plus a break, is added to the page. Unfortunately the addDiv() function can't be used here because it expects a string of text as an argument, not an image or other element.

8. Save, test, debug, and run the completed application (**Figure 8.13**).

✔ Tips

- Because of the way the clipboard works, you might be surprised at how difficult it is to paste content into this application that's not allowed. On Mac OS X, if I copied a file and pasted it, the file's name would be added as text; if I copied a video and pasted it, a still image from the video would be added. Windows wasn't quite as forgiving but was still pretty generous.

- You can define and use your own clipboard formats. By doing so, you won't be limited to storing data using just the formats listed in Table 8.1. But if the data is being pasted into another application that doesn't recognize the provided format type, the pasting won't work.

Drag and Drop In

Dragging and dropping is a mouse-driven process that emulates clipboard functionality without ever using the clipboard. The process starts by selecting something—text, an image, a file—in one application, clicking on it, and dragging that item into another location within the same application or even into another program. This is a feature provided by the operating system and supported by most programs. Naturally, your AIR applications can support dragging and dropping, too. Let's start by looking at the process of dragging something into an AIR application.

As with the copy, cut, and paste functionality, handling a drag and drop action is a matter of watching for events. **Table 8.2** lists the seven events related to dragging and dropping. When an application is receiving data being dragged into it, the most important events are ondragover and ondrop. You'll want the application to call a function when these events occur, so add code like this to the body of your HTML page:

```
<body ondragover="onDragFunction(event);"
→ ondrop="onDropFunction(event);">
```

Next, define the two associated functions. Each should be written to accept an event as an argument. The function called while something is being dragged into the application has a simple role: to prevent the default event behavior:

```
function onDragFunction(e) {
    e.preventDefault();
}
```

As with the copy example earlier in the chapter, it's sometimes best to have the application dictate what happens when the user drags content in. By default, content can only be dragged into editable areas, like text inputs and textareas. In this chapter's example, the user will be able to drag content into the application window.

The onDropFunction() needs to place the introduced data onto the page. To access that data, refer to the event's dataTransfer object. Its getData() method returns the data being transferred in:

eventName.dataTransfer.getData(*format*);

The data formats that can be dragged and dropped are the same MIME types as used for copying and pasting. So the onDropFunction(), which is called when the user releases the mouse button after dragging something into the application, would start like this:

```
function onDropFunction(e) {
    var data = e.dataTransfer.
    → getData('text/plain');

    // Do whatever with data.
}
```

In the next series of steps, the ongoing example will be updated to support the dragging in of text or images.

Table 8.2 These seven HTML events come into play when dragging content into or out of an application.

Drag Events	
EVENT	SENT BY
ondragstart	originator
ondrag	originator
ondragend	originator
ondragenter	target
ondragover	target
ondragleave	target
ondrop	target

To support drag and drop in:

1. Open index.html (Script 8.7) in your text editor or IDE, if it is not already.

2. Within the body tag, identify the functions to be called for two drag events (**Script 8.9**):

```
<body style="margin:10px" oncopy=
→ "doCopy(event);" oncut=
→ "doCut(event);" onpaste=
→ "doPaste(event);" ondragover=
→ "doDragOver(event);" ondrop=
→ "doDrop(event);">
```

Very similar to the code already discussed, this indicates to the program that when something is dragged into the application window, the doDragOver() function should be called. When something is dropped onto the application window, the doDrop() function should be called. Both are passed the actual event.

3. Create a new section for JavaScript:

```
<script type="text/javascript">
</script>
```

I'll add the JavaScript code for handling drag and drop events to the main HTML page rather than use a separate file as I did with the edit-related functions.

4. Define the doDragOver() function:

```
function doDragOver(e) {
    e.preventDefault();
}
```

This function just needs to ignore the default event behavior, as already explained.

5. Begin defining the doDrop() function:

```
function doDrop(e) {
```

This function takes one argument—the event assigned to the variable e.

continues on page 149

Script 8.9 In this updated version of the application, the user can now drag in text or images from other applications. New content will be added to the DOM.

```
1    <html><!-- Script 8.9 (update of Script 8.7) -->
2        <head>
3            <title>Clipboard and Dragging</title>
4            <script type="text/javascript" src="AIRAliases.js"></script>
5            <script type="text/javascript" src="editFunctions.js"></script>
6            <script type="text/javascript">
7            // Drag and drop functions are defined here!
8
9            // Function that's called while the user is dragging
10           // something into this application.
11           function doDragOver(e) {
12
13               // Prevent the default behavior:
14               e.preventDefault();
15
16           } // End of doDragOver() function.
17
```

(script continues on next page)

Script 8.9 *continued*

```
18      // Function that's called when the user drops
19      // whatever they've been dragging (onto the application).
20      function doDrop(e) {
21
22          // Handle the different types of data:
23          if (e.dataTransfer.getData('text/plain')) { // Text
24
25              // Add the text as a new DIV:
26              addDiv(e.dataTransfer.getData('text/plain'));
27
28          } else if (e.dataTransfer.getData('image/x-vnd.adobe.air.bitmap')) { // Image
29
30              var image = e.dataTransfer.getData('image/x-vnd.adobe.air.bitmap');
31
32              // Create a new DIV:
33              var d = document.createElement('div');
34
35              document.body.appendChild(image);
36              // Add the DIV to the page:
37              document.body.appendChild(d);
38
39              // Add a break:
40              document.body.appendChild(document.createElement('br'));
41
42          } else { // Other type of data
43              alert('Data type not yet supported!');
44          }
45
46      } // End of doDrop() function.
47      </script>
48  </head>
49
50  <body style="margin:10px" oncopy="doCopy(event);" oncut="doCut(event);" onpaste="doPaste(event);"
    ondragover="doDragOver(event);" ondrop="doDrop(event);">
51
52      <p>This is some text.</p>
53
54      <p>Completely different text.</p>
55
56      <p style="-webkit-user-select: none">The user cannot select this text!</p>
57
58      <p><img src="kids.jpg" width="200" height="173" /></p>
59
60      <hr />
61
62  </body>
63  </html>
```

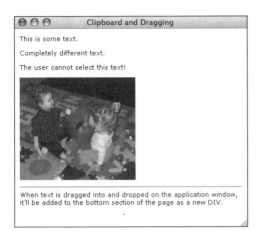

Figure 8.14 When text is dragged into and dropped on the application window, it'll be added to the bottom section of the page as a new DIV.

Figure 8.15 When an image is dragged into and dropped on the application window, it'll also be added to the bottom of the page.

6. If the data is in plain text format, add it to the page as a new DIV:

```
if (e.dataTransfer.getData('text/
→ plain')) {
    addDiv(e.dataTransfer.
    → getData('text/plain'));
```

The conditional will be true if there's plain text data being transferred in. If so, that data will be added as a new DIV in the page (**Figure 8.14**) using the same function created earlier for pasting text. In fact, most of this function will be like the doPaste() function except this one will refer to e.dataTransfer.getData() instead of e.clipboardData.getData().

7. If the data is in bitmap format, add it to the page as is:

```
} else if (e.dataTransfer.getData
→ ('image/x-vnd.adobe.air.bitmap')) {
    var image = e.dataTransfer.
    getData('image/x-vnd.adobe.air.
    → bitmap');
    var d = document.
    → createElement('div');
    document.body.appendChild(image);
    document.body.appendChild(d);
    document.body.appendChild(document.
    → createElement('br'));
```

Using the MIME type associated with bitmap images, the condition first checks if such data exists. Then the data is fetched and assigned to the image variable. This object is then appended to the page within a DIV followed by a break (**Figure 8.15**).

continues on next page

DRAG AND DROP IN

8. Complete the function:

```
    } else {
        alert('Data type not yet
        → supported!');
    }
} // End of doDrop() function.
```

This application will only support the drag and drop in of two data types: plain text and images. Anything else, like trying to drop a document into the application, merits an alert (**Figure 8.16**).

9. Save, test, debug, and run the completed application.

To test the application, drag any kind of data from any other application into this one. You'll see one of the three results (Figures 8.14, 8.15, and 8.16).

✔ Tip

- It's kind of tricky in any application to drag text, because clicking on it also starts the selection process. To pull this off, select some text, and then click and hold on it without moving the mouse. After a second or two you should then be able to move the mouse (while still holding down the button) to successfully drag the selected text.

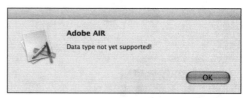

Figure 8.16 If the user attempts to drag into the application content that's not either plain text or an image, the user will see this message.

Table 8.3 An application can dictate what the user can do with content being dragged out of it by specifying the allowed drag effect.

Drag Effects Allowed	
VALUE	MEANING
none	No dragging allowed.
copy	The data should be copied.
link	The data should be linked to this application.
move	The data should be moved from this application.
copyLink	The data can be copied or linked.
copyMove	The data can be copied or moved.
linkMove	The data can be linked or moved.
all	Anything—copying, linking, or moving—can be done with the data.

Drag and Drop Out

Along with support for dragging content into an application's window, you can also choose to support a user's ability to drag application content into other programs. The net effect is the same as being able to copy or cut content within the application, and then paste it elsewhere.

Looking back at Table 8.2, the event to be watched for here is `ondragstart`. That event occurs when the user selects something, clicks on it, and then starts moving the cursor. The nice thing is that no special steps need to be taken to allow dragging content out of the application. However, if you'd like to prevent the user from doing this, you can cancel the drag using:

```
function cancelDrag(e) {
    e.cancelDefault();
}
<body ondragstart="cancelDrag(event);">
```

Alternatively, you can limit what the user can and cannot do with the data being dragged by assigning a value to the event's `dataTransfer.effectAllowed` property. **Table 8.3** lists the possible values.

As an example, if you want to let a user copy or link to something in your application, you would use this code:

```
function cancelDrag(e) {
    e.dataTransfer.effectAllowed =
    → 'copyLink';
}
<body ondragstart="cancelDrag(event);">
```

To use this information, let's regulate drag out functionality in the example program.

To support drag and drop in:

1. Open index.html (Script 8.9) in your text editor or IDE, if it is not already.

2. Within the body tag, identify the function to be called on when dragging begins (**Script 8.10**):

```
<body style="margin:10px" oncopy=
→ "doCopy(event);" oncut=
→ "doCut(event);" onpaste=
→ "doPaste(event);" ondragover=
→ "doDragOver(event);"
→ ondrop="doDrop(event);"
→ ondragstart="doDrag(event);">
```

Added is the association of the doDrag() function with the beginning of a dragging action.

Script 8.10 In this final version of the application, a JavaScript function dictates what can be done with content being dragged out of the program.

```
1   <html><!-- Script 8.10 (update of Script 8.9) -->
2     <head>
3       <title>Clipboard and Dragging</title>
4       <script type="text/javascript" src="AIRAliases.js"></script>
5       <script type="text/javascript" src="editFunctions.js"></script>
6       <script type="text/javascript">
7       // Drag and drop functions are defined here!
8
9       // Function that's called while the user is dragging
10      // something into this application.
11      function doDragOver(e) {
12          e.preventDefault();
13      }
14
15      // Function that's called when the user drops
16      // whatever they've been dragging (onto the application).
17      function doDrop(e) {
18          if (e.dataTransfer.getData('text/plain')) { // Text
19              addDiv(e.dataTransfer.getData('text/plain'));
20          } else if (e.dataTransfer.getData('image/x-vnd.adobe.air.bitmap')) { // Image
21              var image = e.dataTransfer.getData('image/x-vnd.adobe.air.bitmap');
22              var d = document.createElement('div');
23              document.body.appendChild(image);
24              document.body.appendChild(d);
25              document.body.appendChild(document.createElement('br'));
```

(script continues on next page

3. In the JavaScript section, define the doDrag() function:

```
function doDrag(e) {
    e.dataTransfer.effectAllowed =
    → 'copy';
}
```

That's all this function needs to do. It specifies that any content being dragged out can be copied (but nothing else is allowed).

continues on next page

Script 8.10 *continued*

```
26              } else { // Other type of data
27                  alert('Data type not yet supported!');
28              }
29          } // End of doDrop() function.
30
31          // Function for dragging content
32          // out of the application.
33          function doDrag(e) {
34
35              // Establish what's allowed:
36              e.dataTransfer.effectAllowed = 'copy';
37
38          } // End of doDrag() function.
39
40          </script>
41      </head>
42
43  <body style="margin:10px" oncopy="doCopy(event);" oncut="doCut(event);" onpaste="doPaste(event);"
    ondragover="doDragOver(event);" ondrop="doDrop(event);" ondragstart="doDrag(event);">
44
45      <p>This is some text.</p>
46
47      <p>Completely different text.</p>
48
49      <p style="-webkit-user-select: none">The user cannot select this text!</p>
50
51      <p><img src="kids.jpg" width="200" height="173" /></p>
52
53      <hr />
54
55  </body>
56  </html>
```

DRAG AND DROP OUT

4. Save, test, debug, and run the completed application (**Figures 8.17** and **8.18**).

You can test this application by selecting some text and dragging it either to the bottom section of the window (Figure 8.17) or to another application. Likewise, you can do the same with the image (Figure 8.18).

✔ Tips

■ Content being dragged from one editable region to another (for example, between textareas) will be performed as a move by default. You can override this behavior using your own ondrag handler.

■ Using the same values from Table 8.3, functions that handle the drag and drop in-related events can set the *eventName*.

dataTransfer.dropEffect property to dictate what kind of effect—copy, move, link—transpires.

■ The drag out function—doDrag() in this example—can use the *eventName*. dataTransfer.setData() method to make the content being dragged available in different formats.

Figure 8.17 Text selected in the top of the application window was dragged into the bottom part, thereby adding it to the page's content.

Figure 8.18 Dragging the same image from within the application to itself, results in a copy of the image being added to the page.

FILES AND DIRECTORIES

9

An application's ability to work with the files and directories on a user's computer is a basic necessity. Fortunately, doing so in an AIR application is generally one of the easiest things you'll ever implement. AIR provides three simple to use classes that offer all the file and directory-related functionality you'll ever need. In fact, there's so much information to be covered in this area that I've broken it down into two separate chapters.

In this chapter you'll learn about the fundamentals of working with files and directories. This includes allowing users to select a file or directory on their computer, accessing basic file information (its name, size, creation date, and so forth), and listing the contents of a directory. Examples will also demonstrate how to create, copy, move, delete, and trash directories and files. In Chapter 10, "Working with File Content," you'll learn how to write to and read from a file in different ways.

Fundamentals

As I've done in some other chapters, I'll begin by covering some of the basic information you'll need before working with files and directories. You should read these three topics before moving on to the actual examples.

AIR classes involved

When it comes to working with files and directories, there are three defined classes of note:

◆ `File`

◆ `FileStream`

◆ `FileMode`

Of these, `File` is by far the most important. You'll use a `File` object to refer to a file or a directory on the user's computer. Once you have a `File` object, you can create new files and directories, move them, delete them, copy them, list their contents (for directories), and so forth. Everything is done with at least one `File` object.

To create a `File` object, you would write

```
var file = new air.File();
```

But `File` objects will sometimes be created without the new keyword, depending on the circumstance. You'll see examples like this:

```
var file = air.File.desktopDirectory;
```

The next topic discusses what this particular line of code means, but for now just understand that when it comes to creating a `File` object, you use new when referring to just `air.File()` and you omit new when referring to `air.File.something`.

The `FileStream` object is used to read from or write to a file. The `FileMode` object contains definitions for four constants that will be used with the `FileStream` object. Both of these classes will be demonstrated in Chapter 10.

Paths and directories

You can reference files and directories on a user's computer in two ways. The first is through its *native path*, which is an operating-system specific absolute reference. A valid native path value on Windows might be `C:\Documents and Settings\`*username*`\Desktop\`*filename*. On Mac, it might be `/Users/`*username* `/Desktop/`*filename* (replacing *username* with an actual username for that computer).

So if you want to explicitly state where a file is when creating a `File` object, you would do this:

```
var file = new air.File();
file.nativePath = '/path/to/file';
```

That code is the same as using this:

```
var file = new air.File('/path/to/file');
```

In both cases, */path/to/file* would be replaced with the actual path: for example, `C:\Documents and Settings...` or `/Users/`*username* .... Still, the fact is you won't often use this method of identifying a file because */path/to/file* will inevitably be operating-system-specific, thereby making your application less universal. A better way of referring to a file is to use an associated shortcut and the `resolvePath()` method.

When using native paths, there are five associated shortcuts for common locations that an application often references. The first three are user-related:

◆ *userDirectory* (`C:\Documents and Settings\`*username* on Windows; `/Users/`*username* on Mac OS X)

◆ *documentsDirectory* (`C:\Documents and Settings\`*username*`\My Documents` on Windows; `/Users/`*username*`/Documents` on Mac OS X)

FUNDAMENTALS

- *desktopDirectory* (`C:\Documents and Settings\`*username*`\Desktop` on Windows; `/Users/`*username*`/Desktop` on Mac OS X)

Each AIR application also has two associated shortcuts. The first is *applicationStorageDirectory*, which points to the application's storage directory (naturally). Where, exactly, this is on the computer depends on many conditions, but it would likely be within the `C:\Documents and Settings\`*username*`\Application Data` directory on Windows and within `/Users/`*username*`/Library/Preferences` on Mac OS X.

The second application-related reference is to the directory where the program is installed: *applicationDirectory*. Note that while you might read data from the application directory (i.e., data and files that were installed with the program), you likely don't want to write new data there. That's what the application storage directory is for, after all.

As an example of this information, to create a `File` object that points to where the application was installed, use

```
var file = air.File.applicationDirectory;
```

To create a `File` object that points to the user's home directory regardless of operating system, use

```
var file = air.File.userDirectory;
```

To refer to a file located within one of these locations, use the `resolvePath()` method. Provide it with the name of a file or directory that is the final destination, and it will return the full, absolute path to it. For example, to point to `file.txt`, which is on the user's desktop, you would use

```
var file = air.File.desktopDirectory.
→ resolvePath('file.txt');
```

That line of code will be the same as assigning `C:\Documents and Settings\`*username*`\Desktop\file.txt` to `file.nativePath` on Windows and assigning `/Users/`*username*`/Desktop/file.txt` to `file.nativePath` on Mac OS X. But by using the shortcut and the `resolvePath()` method, your application will work on both operating systems without any tweaks.

As already stated, referring to an item's *native path* is the first—and probably preferred—way to refer to a file or directory. The second way is to use a URL. Chapter 4 discusses the important URL schemes. For files and directories, there are three important schemes: *file*, *app-storage*, and *app*. The URL `app-storage:/prefs.xml` provides the same reference as `air.File.applicationStorageDirectory.resolvePath('prefs.xml')`; similarly `app:/data.xml` equates to `air.File.applicationDirectory.resolvePath('data.xml')`.

The `file.txt` document on the user's desktop could also be found using `file:///Documents and Settings/`*username*`/Desktop/file.txt` and `file:///Users/`*username*`/Desktop/file.txt`. (The three slashes after *file:* are actually two slashes—`file://`—followed by an implied host value of *localhost*, followed by the next slash; this is the same as `file://localhost/Documents and Settings`.)

Keep in mind that because of the differences among the various operating systems, a *file* reference will only be valid on a single platform (e.g., `file:///Documents and Settings/`*username*`/...` only works for Windows). Conversely, *app* and *app-storage* will work on all operating systems.

For the most part, you'll use a `File` object and its native path value when working with files and directories. You will find the occasional situation in which some other function expects to receive a URL value for a file or directory, in which case you'll make use of its URL scheme value.

✔ Tips

- It's not a problem to have spaces in your file and path names. AIR will convert those to the URL-encoded equivalent—%20—as needed.

- Having a `File` object represent a file or directory that does not yet exist won't generate errors. In fact, this is a common thing to do for applications that create files and directories. You will, however, see errors if an application attempts to read from, move, or delete files or directories that don't exist.

- Windows uses the backslash (\ ) to separate folders in a path, whereas Mac OS X uses the forward slash (/). You can refer to `air.File.separator` in an application to fetch the current operating system's correct slash.

- Since the backslash character has a special role in JavaScript (it's used to escape characters to create other meanings, like \n which equates to a newline), you must use two backslashes to define a path on Windows:

```
var file = air.File.
→ applicationDirectory.
→ resolvePath('resources\\data.xml');
```

- The `getRelativePath()` method of the `File` object will return the relative path between two files.

Synchronicity

The third concept that you must comprehend for working with files and directories is *synchronicity*. Transactions, like the writing of data to a file, can be done in either *synchronous* or *asynchronous* modes. In synchronous mode, the application performs the transaction all in one burst, meaning that other tasks the application may do have to wait until the transaction is complete. In asynchronous mode, the transaction goes on behind the scenes, and the program or the user can continue to do other tasks. As an example, most Ajax processes in Web pages (or AIR applications) are asynchronous: The user can continue to scroll through the page, enter text into a form, and so on while the JavaScript is making a behind the scenes request.

In your AIR programming, you'll need to choose between these two modes. Doing so normally involves using a different method for a task. For example, the `moveToTrash()` method sends the referenced file to the user's trash. That's the synchronous version of the method; there's also the asynchronous `moveToTrashAsync()`. The most important distinction between these two modes from a programming standpoint is that the asynchronous methods require the use of event listeners that do whatever needs to be done when the transaction is occurring or completed.

So, in short, synchronous transactions are easier to program for and are perfectly fine for tasks that will take but a moment (like reading a small amount of text in from a text file). Asynchronous transactions require more programming but will result in a more polished experience for the end user when it comes to more intensive tasks. To most easily demonstrate these concepts, this chapter primarily uses the synchronous methods. Asynchronous alternatives will be discussed here and there, and in more detail in the next chapter.

FUNDAMENTALS

File and Directory Browsing

Commonplace in most applications is the ability for users to select a file or directory from their computer. For example, users might choose a file to edit or select a directory where a file should be saved. Creating a browse for file (**Figure 9.1**) or browse for directory (**Figure 9.2**) prompt in AIR is easy. Start by creating an object of File type (in either case):

```
var selection = new air.File();
```

If you want to start the user off in a given location, use the appropriate shortcut reference without the new keyword:

```
var selection = air.File.userDirectory;
```

To create the browse for file prompt, call that method:

```
file.browseForFile('Prompt text');
```

To create the browse for directory prompt, call that method:

```
file.browseForDirectory('Prompt text');
```

In both cases the argument provided is the text that appears in title bar of the dialog window (see Figures 9.1 and 9.2).

Both of these methods are asynchronous (there are no synchronous alternatives). This means that event handlers must be assigned to them prior to calling browseForFile() or browseForDirectory(). The event to be watched for is SELECT:

```
file.addEventListener(air.Event.SELECT,
→ selectFunction);
function selectFunction(e) {
    // Do whatever.
}
```

To practice using these methods, let's create an application that starts by letting users select a file or a directory, and then reiterates to them what they selected.

Figure 9.1 The browse for file dialog on Windows.

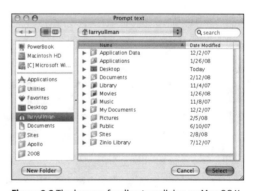

Figure 9.2 The browse for directory dialog on Mac OS X.

To allow a user to select a file or directory:

1. In your project's primary HTML file, create a new `File` object (**Script 9.1**):

```
var file = new air.File();
```

That's all there is to it unless you'd rather start the user off in a set directory, in which case you might use

```
var file = air.File.userDirectory;
```

or

```
var file = air.File.
→ documentsDirectory;
```

or

```
var file = air.File.desktopDirectory;
```

Just to be clear, this example is being created from scratch. My assumption is that you already know how to create the `application.xml` file and the primary HTML page (if not, see Chapter 2, "Creating an HTML Application," and Chapter 3, "AIR Development Tools").

continues on page 162

Using Filters

The `File` object's `browseForOpen()` and `browseForOpenMultiple()` methods take an optional second argument, which is an array of file filters. You can use this to restrict the kinds of files the user can select. To start, create a new `FileFilter` object. The first argument is descriptive text, and the second is a list of allowed extensions:

```
var filter = new air.FileFilter('Images', '*.jpg;*.jpeg;*.gif;*.png');
```

Note that each extension starts with the wildcard character (*, which means that any file name is allowed) followed by the extension. Each item is separated by a semicolon.

This `filter` object can only be provided to `browseForOpen()` as an array. You must therefore use this code in your `browseForOpen()` call:

```
file.browseForOpen('Prompt', new window.runtime.Array(filter));
```

Alternatively, you can formally create an array, and then add the filter as an element, but I like the simplicity of the one-step approach. In the next chapter, you'll see an example of how a filter is used to allow the user to only open plain text files.

Script 9.1 This simple program reports back to users what file or directory they selected.

```
1    <html><!-- Script 9.1 -->
2        <head>
3            <title>User Browsing</title>
4            <script type="text/javascript" src="AIRAliases.js"></script>
5            <script type="text/javascript">
6
7            // Create an object of File type:
8            var file = new air.File();
9
10           // Add the event listener:
11           file.addEventListener(air.Event.SELECT, itemWasSelected);
12
13           // Function that will be called
14           // when the event occurs.
15           function itemWasSelected(e) {
16
17               // Use an alert to print the selected item's name:
18               alert ('You selected: ' + file.nativePath);
19
20           } // End of itemWasSelected() function.
21
22           // Function called when the user clicks the
23           // 'Select a File' button.
24           function selectFile() {
25
26               // Create the Open prompt:
27               file.browseForOpen('Choose a file:');
28
29           }
30
31           // Function called when the user clicks the
32           // 'Select a Directory' button.
33           function selectDirectory() {
34
35               // Create the Open prompt:
36               file.browseForDirectory('Choose a directory:');
37
38           }
39
40           </script>
41       </head>
42
43   <body>
44
45       <button onclick="selectFile();">Select a File</button>
46
47       <button onclick="selectDirectory();">Select a Directory</button>
48
49   </body>
50   </html>
```

2. Add the event listener.

```
file.addEventListener(air.Event.
→ SELECT, itemWasSelected);
```

The event to be listened for is `air.Event.SELECT`. When that event occurs for this object, the `itemWasSelected()` function will be called.

3. Define the `itemWasSelected()` function:

```
function itemWasSelected(e) {
  alert ('You selected: ' +
  → file.nativePath);
}
```

This function will use an alert to report the selected item's native path value.

4. Define a function that prompts the user to select a file:

```
function selectFile() {
  file.browseForOpen('Choose a
  → file:');
}
```

The application will have just two buttons (**Figure 9.3**). Clicking the *Select a File* button will call this function, which in turn calls the `browseForOpen()` method.

5. Define a function that prompts the user to select a directory:

```
function selectDirectory() {
  file.browseForDirectory('Choose
  → a directory:');
}
```

The other application button calls this function, which calls the `browseForDirectory()` method, using a different prompt as well (**Figure 9.4**). Other than that, allowing the user to select a file or a directory is the same process.

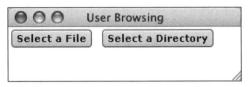

Figure 9.3 The barebones application with two buttons. One will prompt the user to select a file, the other to select a directory.

Figure 9.4 The prompt for selecting a directory.

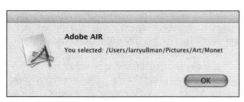

Figure 9.5 The native path value of the selected directory is printed using an alert.

6. Create the two buttons:

```
<button onclick="selectFile();">
→ Select a File</button>
<button onclick="selectDirectory();">
→ Select a Directory</button>
```

In a real program, you'd likely call the `selectFile()` function using a File > Open command, but for this example, a simple button is fine.

7. Save, test, debug, and run the completed application (**Figure 9.5**).

✔ Tips

■ The `browseForOpenMultiple()` method allows the user to select multiple files. The event to be listened for when using this method is `air.FileListEvent. SELECT_MULTIPLE`. In the event handling function, the `file` variable (or whatever you name it) would actually be an array of `File` objects.

■ The `canonicalize()` method of the `File` object formats the `nativePath` value using the correct case. For example, you can likely get away with referring to the file `C:\Documents and Settings\ Username\FileName` as `C:\documents and settings\username\FILENAME`, but this method will correct the reference. It also expands shortened names on Windows to their full length.

Accessing File Information

The File object has more than two dozen properties, some of which are listed in **Table 9.1**. Each property provides information about the referenced file or directory. For example, as Script 9.1 shows, you can get a file's native path (i.e., absolute path) using file.nativePath. Let's use the information in Table 9.1 to update the last example so that it tells a little bit more about the selected item.

To use a file's information:

1. Open Script 9.1 in your text editor or IDE, if it is not already.

2. Remove the alert() line from the itemWasSelected() function (**Script 9.2**).

continues on page 166

Table 9.1 These file and directory attributes provide common information about the item. Note that packages only exist on Mac OS X (but can be treated like directories), symbolic links are not the same as aliases or shortcuts (they're primarily used on Unix, Linux, and Mac OS X), and the parent attribute returns a File object representing the parent folder.

File Object Properties	
creationDate	When it was created
exists	If it exists
extension	What a file's extension is
isDirectory	If it is a directory
isHidden	If it is hidden
isPackage	If it is a package (Mac OS X)
isSymbolicLink	If it is a symbolic link
modificationDate	When it was last modified
name	Its name
nativePath	Its full name and path
parent	Its parent folder
size	Its size in bytes
url	Its URL scheme value

Script 9.2 Some of the selected file or directory's information will be printed by this updated version of Script 9.1.

```
1    <html><!-- Script 9.2 -->
2      <head>
3        <title>File Information</title>
4        <script type="text/javascript" src="AIRAliases.js"></script>
5        <script type="text/javascript">
6
7        // Create an object of File type:
8        var file = new air.File();
9
10       // Add the event listener:
11       file.addEventListener(air.Event.SELECT, itemWasSelected);
12
13       // Function that will be called
14       // when the event occurs.
15       function itemWasSelected(e) {
16
17           // Add the information to a variable:
18           var message = 'You selected ' + file.name;
19           message += ', located within the ' + file.parent.name + ' folder. ';
20           message += 'It was created on ' + file.creationDate;
21           message += '. It was last modified on ' + file.modificationDate + '.';
22
```

(script continues on next page)

Script 9.2 *continued*

```
23          // If it's not a directory, add the file's size:
24          if (!file.isDirectory) {
25              message += ' It is ' + Math.ceil(file.size/1024) + 'KB in size.';
26          }
27
28          // Place the message on the page:
29          var p = document.createElement('p');
30          p.innerText = message;
31          document.body.appendChild(p);
32
33      } // End of itemWasSelected() function.
34
35      // Function called when the user clicks the
36      // 'Select a File' button.
37      function selectFile() {
38
39          // Create the Open prompt:
40          file.browseForOpen('Choose a file:');
41
42      }
43
44      // Function called when the user clicks the
45      // 'Select a Directory' button.
46      function selectDirectory() {
47
48          // Create the Open prompt:
49          file.browseForDirectory('Choose a directory:');
50
51      }
52
53      </script>
54  </head>
55
56  <body>
57
58      <button onclick="selectFile();">Select a File</button>
59
60      <button onclick="selectDirectory();">Select a Directory</button>
61
62  </body>
63  </html>
```

Instead of using an alert dialog, this version of the application will print out a bunch of information by adding a paragraph to the Document Object Model (**Figure 9.6**).

3. Create a message variable, starting with the item's name:

```
var message = 'You selected ' +
→ file.name;
```

Unlike the `nativePath` property, which stores the absolute path to a file, the `name` property contains just the file or directory name. It'll be assigned to a string variable, along with some literal text, that will later be added to the DOM.

4. Add the item's parent folder, creation date, and modification date to the message:

```
message += ', located within the ' +
→ file.parent.name + ' folder. ';
message += 'It was created on ' +
→ file.creationDate;
message += '. It was last modified
→ on ' + file.modificationDate + '.';
```

Three more strings—combinations of literal text and file attributes—are concatenated to the `message` variable. Because the `parent` property returns a `File` object that points to the parent directory, its `name` attribute is what should be added to the string (if you add just `file.parent` to the message string, the value *object File* will be displayed).

Figure 9.6 The program now prints out the name, dates, and other information about the selected file or directory.

5. Add the file's size to the message:

```
if (!file.isDirectory) {
  message += ' It is ' + Math.ceil
  → (file.size/1024) + 'KB in size.';
}
```

The size attribute only has a value for nondirectories (getting a directory's size requires adding up all of its file sizes). For this reason, a conditional first checks that the file isn't a directory. If that is true, the file's size in kilobytes is determined by dividing its size value (which is in bytes) by 1024, and then rounding this up to the next highest integer (so that a file smaller than one kilobyte doesn't appear as being 0KB in size).

6. Add the message to a paragraph on the page:

```
var p = document.createElement('p');

p.innerText = message;

document.body.appendChild(p);
```

First a new element of type p is created. Next, its innerText value is assigned the message variable (innerText is what goes between the opening and closing tags). Then this paragraph is appended to the document body.

7. Save, test, debug, and run the completed application (**Figure 9.7**).

✔ Tips

■ If a file or folder is in the root directory, its parent attribute will be that root directory. The name of that parent folder will therefore be / on Mac OS X and C: (or whatever drive) on Windows.

■ If the user selects his or her root directory, file.parent.name will not have a value. To account for this possibility, you could use a conditional that prints the parent folder's name only if it is not null.

Figure 9.7 The information for a file and a directory. Because a selected item's information is displayed by adding a paragraph to the DOM, the page will continue to list every selected file or directory.

Reading Directories

Although you can provide your AIR application with a specific directory or filename to use, or you can allow the user to select one, sometimes it's necessary for an application to find a file on its own. For example, iTunes has the ability to look for music files on your computer.

The `File` object's `getDirectoryListing()` and `getDirectoryListingAsync()` methods can be used to retrieve every file and folder within a given directory. This function returns an array of `File` objects, one for each item in the directory. To use it, start by creating a `File` object and provide it with the directory to read. You could use

```
var dir = new air.File('/path/to/dir');
```

Or, more likely, start with a common reference:

```
var dir = air.File.userDirectory;
```

Of course, you can also use code as in the previous example that allows the user to select a directory.

Next, call the `getDirectoryListing()` (or `getDirectoryListingAsync()`) method and assign the result to another variable:

```
var stuff = dir.getDirectoryListing();
```

Now `stuff` is an array; you can iterate through it as you would any other array:

```
for (i = 0; i < stuff.length; i++) {
    // Do whatever with stuff[i].
}
```

For this next example, the contents of a directory will be displayed in an unordered list (**Figure 9.8**).

To read a directory:

1. In your project's primary HTML file, begin a new JavaScript function (**Script 9.3**):

```
window.onload = function() {

}
```

I'll start by creating a new project with its own root HTML page. Within it an anonymous function will be defined that is automatically called once the window has loaded. This is necessary because the page will add elements to the DOM, and the document's body will only exist after the page has loaded.

2. Within the anonymous function, get the contents of a directory:

```
var dir = air.File.desktopDirectory;

var contents =
→ dir.getDirectoryListing();
```

These two lines, already explained, are all that's required. For this example, the target directory will be the user's desktop. Now the `contents` variable is an array of `File` objects.

Figure 9.8 This application shows the files and folders that exist on the user's desktop. This image was taken while the program was running on Windows.

READING DIRECTORIES

3. If the directory isn't empty, create an unordered list:

```
if (contents.length > 0) {
    var ul = document.
createElement('ul');
    var li = Array();
```

This conditional checks that there is at least one item in the array (i.e., in the directory). If so, a new element of type ul is created, along with an array called li. This array will be used to add each item in the directory to the unordered list.

4. Add all visible items to the list:

```
for (i = 0; i < contents.length; i++) {
    if (!contents[i].isHidden) {
        li[i] = document.
→ createElement('li');
        li[i].innerText =
→ contents[i].name;
        ul.appendChild(li[i]);
    } // End of isHidden IF.
} // End of FOR loop.
```

continues on next page

Script 9.3 This program lists the visible files and folders found on the user's desktop.

```
          ● ● ●                        Script
1     <html><!-- Script 9.3 -->
2         <head>
3         <title>Directory Listing</title>
4         <script type="text/javascript" src="AIRAliases.js"></script>
5         <script type="text/javascript">
6
7         // Create an object of File type,
8         // pointing to the user's desktop.
9         var dir = air.File.desktopDirectory;
10
11        // Once the page has loaded, call this function:
12        window.onload = makeList;
13
14        // Function for creating the directory listing.
15        function makeList() {
16
17            // Get the directory's contents:
18            var contents = dir.getDirectoryListing();
19
20            // Check that it's not empty:
21            if (contents.length > 0) {
22
23                // Make an unordered list:
24                var ul = document.createElement('ul');
25                var li = Array();
26
27                // Loop through the contents:
28                for (i = 0; i < contents.length; i++) {
29
30                    // Print only visible items:
31                    if (!contents[i].isHidden) {
32
```

(script continues on next page)

READING DIRECTORIES

This basic for loop construct will access every element within the contents array. Within the loop, a conditional checks that the current item—accessed via contents[i]—isn't hidden. This is an optional step, but because the getDirectoryListing() method returns hidden files, showing them here could be confusing to the viewer.

To add the item to the list, a new element of type li is added to the li array. Its innerText value will be the name of the file. This element is then appended to the unordered list. Using an array to create and add list items is necessary because reusing the same li element over and over won't work.

5. Add the list to the page:

```
document.body.appendChild(ul);
```

6. Complete the main conditional:

```
} else {
    var p = document.
    → createElement('p');
    p.innerHTML = 'The directory
    → is empty.';
    document.body.appendChild(p);
}
```

Script 9.3 *continued*

```
33              // Create a list item:
34              li[i] = document.createElement('li');
35              li[i].innerText = contents[i].name;
36              ul.appendChild(li[i]);
37
38          } // End of isHidden IF.
39
40      } // End of FOR loop.
41
42      // Add the UL to the page:
43      document.body.appendChild(ul);
44
45  } else { // Nothing there!
46
47      // Make a paragraph:
48      var p = document.createElement('p');
49      p.innerHTML = 'The directory is empty.';
50      document.body.appendChild(p);
51
52  }
53
54 } // End of makeList() function.
55
56 </script>
57 </head>
58
59 <body>
60
61 <h3>What's on your Desktop?</h3>
62
63 </body>
64 </html>
```

```
● ● ●        Directory Listing
What's in your Documents Folder?

   ● AdobeStockPhotos
   ● By Application
   ● Clients
   ● DMCI
   ● Icons
   ● Maptacular
   ● Microsoft User Data
   ● Other Documents
   ● Other Web
   ● Personal Finance
   ● Programming
   ● QuickBooks
   ● Roxio Converted Items
   ● Signet
   ● Updater
   ● Web Templates
   ● Work - Other
   ● Writing
```

Figure 9.9 The listing of my documents directory (on Mac OS X). The heading has also been changed to match the directory in use.

If the conditional in step 3 is false, the directory is empty. In that case, a paragraph is added to the page saying as much.

7. If you want, create a heading within the page's body:

   `<h3>What's on your Desktop?</h3>`

8. Save, test, debug, and run the completed application.

   If you'd like, change the directory (to `documentsDirectory` or something else) and rerun the program (**Figure 9.9**).

✔ Tips

■ One way you could expand this example would be to add a check box indicating whether or not hidden files should be revealed. Then the conditional in the loop would read something like

```
if (!contents[i].isHidden &&
→ (document.getElementById
→ ('showHidden').checked == false)) {
```

You would also need to add a function that removes the unordered list and redraws it when the box is checked or unchecked. The next example shows how to recreate a list of items.

■ To use the asynchronous version of the `getDirectoryListing()` method, you'll need to add an event listener to the `File` object. The event to be watched is `FileListEvent.DIRECTORY_LISTING`. Sample code for this would be:

```
var dir = air.File.userDirectory;
dir.getDirectoryListingAsync();
dir.addEventListener(air.
→ FileListEvent.DIRECTORY_LISTING,
→ doList);
function doList(e) {
   var contents = e.files;
   // FOR loop…
}
```

Deleting Files and Directories

Files and directories can be deleted using the deleteFile() and deleteDirectory() methods (or the deleteFileAsync() and deleteDirectoryAsync() versions).

```
var file = air.File.documentsDirectory.
→ resolvePath('somefile');
file.deleteFile();
var dir = air.File.userDirectory.
→ resolvePath('Some Dir');
dir.deleteDirectory();
```

By default, the delete directory methods will only get rid of empty directories. To delete a directory that may have some files or subdirectories in it, pass the method an argument with the value true:

```
dir.deleteDirectory(true);
```

If you'd rather take less drastic steps, you can move the file or directory to the trash. That way the item won't be officially removed until the user empties the trash (or Recycle Bin on Windows). The moveToTrash() and moveToTrashAsync() functions do this:

```
var file = air.File.documentsDirectory.
→ resolvePath('somefile');
file.moveToTrash();
var dir = air.File.userDirectory.
→ resolvePath('Some Dir');
dir.moveToTrash();
```

To test this new knowledge, let's add links to the previous application that give the user the option of deleting a file or folder.

To delete a file or directory:

1. Open Script 9.3 in your text editor or IDE, if it is not already.

2. Within the makeList() function, after creating the ul object, add an id attribute to it (**Script 9.4**):

   ```
   ul.setAttribute('id', 'contents');
   ```

   To have the application reflect any changes, the program will need to be able to remove and re-create the unordered list. One way of removing a document element is to refer to its ID, so one is being added to the list here.

3. Within the for loop, after creating the li element, add an onclick event handler to it:

   ```
   li[i].setAttribute('onclick',
   → 'deleteItem("' + contents[i].
   → nativePath + '");');
   ```

   The user will be able to delete an item simple by clicking on its name. To add that functionality, onclick event handlers are added to each list item. When the item is clicked on, the deleteItem() function will be called. This function will be passed the nativePath value of the item to be deleted (so that the function knows what to get rid of).

4. Begin a new function called *deleteItem*:

   ```
   function deleteItem(which) {
   ```

   This is the function that will be called when the user clicks on an item. It's passed the item's nativePath value, which is an absolute reference to the item on the user's computer.

continues on page 175

Script 9.4 This update of Script 9.3 adds `onclick` event handlers to the list of items so that clicking on one will move it to the trash.

```
1    <html><!-- Script 9.4 -->
2        <head>
3        <title>Directory Listing</title>
4        <script type="text/javascript" src="AIRAliases.js"></script>
5        <script type="text/javascript">
6
7        // Create an object of File type,
8        // pointing to the user's desktop.
9        var dir = air.File.desktopDirectory;
10
11       // Once the page has loaded, call this function:
12       window.onload = makeList;
13
14       // Function for creating the directory listing.
15       function makeList() {
16
17           // Get the directory's contents:
18           var contents = dir.getDirectoryListing();
19
20           // Check that it's not empty:
21           if (contents.length > 0) {
22
23               // Make an unordered list:
24               var ul = document.createElement('ul');
25
26               // Give the ul an ID:
27               ul.setAttribute('id', 'contents');
28
29               var li = Array();
30
31               // Loop through the contents:
32               for (i = 0; i < contents.length; i++) {
33
34                   // Print only visible items:
35                   if (!contents[i].isHidden) {
36
37                       // Create a list item:
38                       li[i] = document.createElement('li');
39                       li[i].innerText = contents[i].name;
40
41                       // Add an onclick event handler:
42                       li[i].setAttribute('onclick', 'deleteItem("' + contents[i].nativePath + '");');
43
44                       ul.appendChild(li[i]);
45
46                   } // End of isHidden IF.
47
48               } // End of FOR loop.
49
```

(script continues on next page)

173

Script 9.4 *continued*

```
                                            Script
50          // Add the UL to the page:
51          document.body.appendChild(ul);
52
53      } else { // Nothing there!
54
55          // Make a paragraph:
56          var p = document.createElement('p');
57          p.innerHTML = 'The directory is empty.';
58          document.body.appendChild(p);
59
60      }
61
62  } // End of makeList() function.
63
64
65  // Function for deleting an item.
66  // Takes one argument: the native path of the item.
67  function deleteItem(which) {
68
69      // Confirm with the user prior to deleting:
70      if (confirm('Delete ' + which + '?')) {
71
72          // Get a reference to the item:
73          var trash = new air.File();
74          trash.nativePath = which;
75
76          // Delete it:
77          trash.moveToTrash();
78
79          // Remake the list:
80          document.body.removeChild(document.getElementById('contents'));
81          makeList();
82
83      } // End of confirm IF.
84
85  } // End of deleteItem() function.
86
87  </script>
88  </head>
89
90  <body>
91
92  <h3>What's on your Desktop?</h3>
93  <p>Click on an item's name to delete it.</p>
94
95  </body>
96  </html>
```

Figure 9.10 This confirmation dialog makes it clear to the user what has been selected for removal and provides one last opportunity to prevent the deletion.

5. If the user definitely wants to delete the file, get rid of it:

```
if (confirm('Delete ' + which + '?')) {
    var trash = new air.File();
    trash.nativePath = which;
    trash.moveToTrash();
```

Rather than just immediately deleting the item, the user must click OK in a confirmation dialog (**Figure 9.10**). If the user clicks OK, a reference to the item is created by declaring a new File object and assigning it the provided nativePath value. Finally, the item is moved to the trash. Although I've been saying this script demonstrates deleting items, I'm playing it safe and just trashing each item.

continues on next page

Creating Directories and Files

To create a directory, use the aptly named createDirectory() method of the File object. Provide it with the name and location of the directory you'd like to create:

```
var file = air.File.documentsDirectory('My App');
```

That line creates a File object that references a directory called *My App*, which is found within the user's documents directory. Presumably, at this point, that directory does not exist.

Next, call the createDirectory() method:

```
file.createDirectory();
```

This function will create the named directory if it can and do nothing if it cannot.

If you only need to create a temporary directory, use createTempDirectory(). It will create a new, unique directory. You should delete the directory when exiting the program if it is no longer needed (it will not be automatically deleted).

The createTempFile() function creates a temporary file on the user's computer. It could be used, for example, to store data that only needs to exist for the life of the running program. If necessary, it can be made permanent by moving it elsewhere on the computer.

Creating files is done differently than creating directories because they need content, which must be written to the file. See the next chapter for details.

DELETING FILES AND DIRECTORIES

In a real application, I might be inclined to add a check that the item exists, prior to attempting to delete it:

```
if (trash.exists) {…
```

6. Re-create the unordered list:

```
document.body.removeChild(document.
→ getElementById('contents'));
makeList();
```

If you don't re-create the unordered list, it will continue to show the removed items. To rebuild it, start by deleting the existing list, which is accomplished by using the `removeChild()` method, and then passing it the element to be removed, which is returned by `getElementById()`. Then call the `makeList()` function.

7. Complete the `deleteItem()` function:

```
    } // End of confirm IF.

} // End of deleteItem() function.
```

8. Add instructions for the user to the body of the page:

```
<p>Click on an item's name to
→ delete it.</p>
```

9. Save, test, debug, and run the completed application (**Figures 9.11** and **9.12**).

✔ Tips

- If you'd rather not play it safe by moving an item to the trash, you can use this code instead:

```
if (trash.isDirectory) {
    trash.deleteDirectory(true);
} else {
    trash.deleteFile();
}
```

- If you're using the asynchronous versions of the delete functions—`deleteDirectoryAsync()` and `deleteFileAsync()`—the event to be watched for is `air.Event.COMPLETE`. If you add an event listener for that event, when the directory has been completely deleted, your handling function will be called.

Figure 9.11 The original list.

Figure 9.12 The redrawn list after deleting an item (`testing.txt`).

Copying and Moving

Directories and files can be copied on the user's computer or moved from one location to another. Copying uses the `copyTo()` method and two valid `File` objects: One represents the original name and location, the second is the destination name and location. Even if you want to create a copy of a file or directory in the same directory as the original, you'll still need two `File` objects (and the second will need a new name, or else you won't get a copy).

```
var source = air.File.
→ userDirectory('file.txt');
var dest = air.File.
→ desktopDirectory('file.txt');
source.copyTo(dest);
```

The above code will copy `file.txt`, located in the user's home directory, to the user's desktop (keeping the name `file.txt`).

The `copyTo()` method takes an optional second argument, indicating whether or not an overwrite should be allowed. Assuming you have the same `source` and `dest` objects from above, this line will replace an existing `file.txt` on the user's desktop:

```
source.copyTo(dest, true);
```

Moving a file is exactly the same as copying—requiring two objects with different native paths—but involves the `moveTo()` method:

```
var source = air.File.
→ userDirectory('file.txt');
var dest = air.File.
→ desktopDirectory('file.txt');
source.moveTo(dest);
```

That code moves `file.txt` from the user's home directory to the user's desktop. The `moveTo()` method also takes an optional second argument. If provided with a value of `true`, it will overwrite any existing item with the same name.

As a demonstration of this, the next example allows the user to select a file, select a directory, and then either copy or move the file to that directory (**Figure 9.13**).

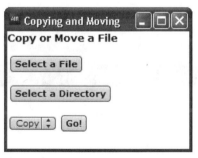

Figure 9.13 The application when the user first loads it.

To copy or move a file:

1. In your project's primary HTML file, create two File objects (**Script 9.5**).

```
var file = new air.File();

var dir = new air.File();
```

Again, I'm starting from scratch with a new project.

2. Create two flag variables:

```
var fileSelected = false;

var dirSelected = false;
```

To ensure that the copying or moving isn't attempted until both a file and a directory have been selected, these two flag variables will track their statuses.

3. Add event listeners to the two File objects:

```
file.addEventListener(air.Event.
→ SELECT, fileWasSelected);

dir.addEventListener(air.Event.
→ SELECT, dirWasSelected);
```

For both objects, the event to be watched for is air.Event.SELECT. Each object has its own associated function to be called when that event happens.

4. Define the fileWasSelected() function:

```
function fileWasSelected(e) {

    document.getElementById
    → ('fileName').innerText =
    → file.nativePath;

    fileSelected = true;

}
```

This function will be called when the user selects a file from the hard drive. It then shows the selected file next to the corresponding button on the page (**Figure 9.14**). The associated flag variable is also set to true.

5. Define the dirWasSelected() function:

```
function dirWasSelected(e) {

    document.getElementById
    → ('dirName').innerText =
    → dir.nativePath;

    dirSelected = true;

}
```

This is just a slight variation on the dirWasSelected() function. The directory's native path value will be displayed next to that button, and the matching flag variable gets set to true.

continues on page 181

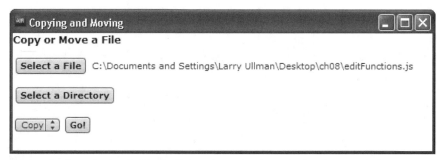

Figure 9.14 After selecting the file, the file's native path value is displayed next to the button.

COPYING AND MOVING

Script 9.5 This application will move or copy a selected file to a new directory.

```
1    <html><!-- Script 9.5 -->
2      <head>
3        <title>Copying and Moving</title>
4        <script type="text/javascript" src="AIRAliases.js"></script>
5        <script type="text/javascript">
6
7        // Create two File objects:
8        var file = new air.File();
9        var dir = new air.File();
10
11       // Flag variables:
12       var fileSelected = false;
13       var dirSelected = false;
14
15       // Add the event listeners:
16       file.addEventListener(air.Event.SELECT, fileWasSelected);
17       dir.addEventListener(air.Event.SELECT, dirWasSelected);
18
19       // Function called when the file is selected.
20       function fileWasSelected(e) {
21
22          document.getElementById('fileName').innerText = file.nativePath;
23          fileSelected = true;
24
25       } // End of fileWasSelected() function.
26
27       // Function called when the directory is selected.
28       function dirWasSelected(e) {
29
30          document.getElementById('dirName').innerText = dir.nativePath;
31          dirSelected = true;
32
33       } // End of dirWasSelected() function.
34
35       // Function called when the user clicks the
36       // 'Select a File' button.
37       function selectFile() {
38
39          // Create the Open prompt:
40          file.browseForOpen('Choose a file:');
41
42       }
43
44       // Function called when the user clicks the
45       // 'Select a Directory' button.
46       function selectDirectory() {
47
```

(script continues on next page)

Script 9.5 *continued*

```
     000                                    Script
48              // Create the Open prompt:
49              dir.browseForDirectory('Choose a directory:');
50
51         }
52
53         // Function called when the user clicks Go!
54         function doCopyMove() {
55
56             // Make sure that both items have been selected:
57             if (fileSelected && dirSelected) {
58
59                 // Determine the destination:
60                 var dest = new air.File();
61                 dest.nativePath = dir.nativePath + air.File.separator + file.name;
62
63                 // Copy or move:
64                 if (document.getElementById('copyMove').value == 'copy') {
65                     file.copyTo(dest);
66                     alert('The file has been copied!');
67                 } else {
68                     file.moveTo(dest);
69                     alert('The file has been moved!');
70                     fileSelected = false;
71                 }
72
73             } else { // Missing something!
74                 alert('You must select a file and a directory first!');
75             }
76
77         } // End of doCopyMove() function.
78
79         </script>
80     </head>
81
82  <body>
83
84     <h3>Copy or Move a File</h3>
85
86     <p><button onclick="selectFile();">Select a File</button> <span id="fileName"></span></p>
87
88     <p><button onclick="selectDirectory();">Select a Directory</button> <span id="dirName">
        </span></p>
89
90     <p><select id="copyMove"><option value="copy">Copy</option><option value="move">Move
        </option></select><button onclick="doCopyMove();">Go!</button></p>
91
92  </body>
93  </html>
```

6. Define a function for selecting a file:

```
function selectFile() {
    file.browseForOpen('Choose a
→ file:');
}
```

This function will be called when the user clicks the *Select a File* button. It generates the browse for open dialog (see Figure 9.1).

7. Define a function for selecting a directory:

```
function selectDirectory() {
    dir.browseForDirectory('Choose a
→ directory:');
}
```

This function will be called when the user clicks this *Select a Directory* button. It generates the browse for directory dialog (as in Figure 9.2).

8. Begin the doCopyMove() function:

```
function doCopyMove() {
    if (fileSelected && dirSelected) {
```

This is the most important function, because it performs the actual copying or moving. The function will be called when the user clicks the *Go!* button (see Figures 9.13 and 9.14). Within the function, a conditional confirms that both the file and directory have been selected (by referring to the flag variables).

9. Identify the destination for the file:

```
var dest = new air.File();
dest.nativePath = dir.nativePath +
air.File.separator + file.name;
```

One more File object is necessary to identify the destination. That native path value will be the nativePath of the selected directory, plus the operating-system-specific separator (a forward or backward slash), plus the selected file's name.

10. If appropriate, copy the file:

```
if (document.getElementById
→ ('copyMove').value == 'copy') {
    file.copyTo(dest);
    alert('The file has been copied!');
```

The user can indicate the action to be performed—copy or move—using the select menu. If the user chooses copy (the default option), the copyTo() method is called and an alert informs the user of the action (**Figure 9.15**).

11. Otherwise, move the file:

```
} else {
    file.moveTo(dest);
    alert('The file has been moved!');
    fileSelected = false;
}
```

continues on next page

Figure 9.15 The result after copying the file to the destination.

COPYING AND MOVING

Besides using the `moveTo()` function, instead of `copyTo()`, the other significant alteration here is the resetting of the `fileSelected` variable's value to `false`. This is necessary because the file no longer exists in the same location after a move, so its reference is inaccurate. By setting `fileSelected` to `false`, the user will need to select a new file (even if that means the same file in its new location) prior to copying or moving again.

12. Complete the `doCopyMove()` function:

```
    } else { // Missing something!
      alert('You must select a file
      → and a directory first!');
    }
  } // End of doCopyMove() function.
```

If the user clicks *Go!* before selecting both a file and a directory, the use will see this alert (**Figure 9.16**).

13. Within the body of the page, create the necessary buttons:

```
<p><button onclick="selectFile();">
→ Select a File</button> <span
→ id="fileName"></span></p>

<p><button onclick=
→ "selectDirectory();">Select a
→ Directory</button> <span
→ id="dirName"></span></p>
```

The first button invokes the `selectFile()` function; the second, the `selectDirectory()` function.

14. Add the select menu and the *Go!* button:

```
<p><select id="copyMove"><option
→ value="copy">Copy</option><option
→ value="move">Move</option>
→ </select><button onclick=
→ "doCopyMove();">Go!</button></p>
```

15. Save, test, debug, and run the completed application.

✔ Tips

■ Note that this application will not perform the move if a file with the same name already exists in that destination. To account for that possibility, you could add an event listener that watches for an `IOError` or call the `moveTo()` method within a `try…catch` block.

■ The `clone()` method duplicates the existing `File` object, giving you two references to the same file:

```
var file = air.File.
→ userDirectory('file.txt');
var file2 = file.clone();
```

■ To rename a file, use the `moveTo()` method, but leave the directory the same and change the name value:

```
var source = air.File.
→ userDirectory('file.txt');
var dest = air.File.
→ userDirectory('newname.txt');
source.moveTo(dest);
```

COPYING AND MOVING

Figure 9.16 This alert is shown if the user tries to copy or move a file without having selected both a file and a directory.

WORKING WITH FILE CONTENT

10

Chapter 9, "Files and Directories," covers the basics of working with files and directories in Adobe AIR. This chapter extends that information and discusses reading from and writing to files. Both are important techniques to use in an application and neither is hard to accomplish, but you must keep two details in mind: whether the transactions will be synchronous or asynchronous and the format of the file to be read from or written to.

The topic of synchronicity was introduced in the first section of the previous chapter. When reading in and writing out small amounts of data, using synchronous transactions will work well, so I'll start by showing you how to perform synchronous reads and writes. With more data, you'll want to take the asynchronous route, so you'll see an example of that, too.

As for the format, a distinction needs to be made between working with plain text and binary data. To start, you'll learn how to handle plain text files; there'll be a binary example at the end.

I'll also add that while the code here will be somewhat simple, some of the concepts can be confusing, particularly if you've never done anything like this before. You'll see terms like *encoding, character set*, and *Unicode* and have to understand that a character is not the same as a byte (you'll read and write *bytes* of data, even to a plain text file; one character may require more than one byte). If this section's references to these terms and related concepts aren't sufficient for you, search the Web for some basic tutorials on Unicode, character encodings, and so forth.

Reading from Files

Reading from and writing to files requires a `File` object and a `FileStream` object. As always, the `File` object is a reference to a file on the user's computer (existing or to be created):

```
var file = air.File.applicationDirectory.
→ resolvePath('data.txt');
```

That line associates `file` with `data.txt`, which is found in the directory where the application was installed.

Next, create an object of type `FileStream`:

```
var stream = new air.FileStream();
```

Then open the file for reading and/or writing, using the `stream.open()` method. It takes two arguments. The first is the `File` object and the second is the mode:

```
stream.open(file, mode).
```

The mode is represented by a constant (**Table 10.1**) and dictates what can be done with the file. So to simply read from a file, you would use

```
stream.open(file, air.FileMode.READ);
```

How you read in the actual data depends on the format it's in. UTF-encoded text, which is text in a Unicode format, can be read using `readUTFBytes()`. This function takes one argument—the number of bytes to read in—and returns a string. To indicate how many bytes to read, you can refer to `stream.bytesAvailable`.

```
var data = stream.readUTFBytes(stream.
→ bytesAvailable);
```

In synchronous mode, that line will read in an entire file and assign the results to the `data` variable.

When you're done using the file, be certain to close the stream:

```
stream.close();
```

Table 10.1 These four constants, all defined within the `FileMode` class, are used as the second argument to the `FileStream` class's `open()` method.

FileMode Constants	
CONSTANT	OPENS THE FILE FOR…
READ	Reading only
WRITE	Writing, creating the file if it doesn't exist, erasing any existing data if it does.
APPEND	Writing, creating the file if it doesn't exist, appending new data to the existing data if it does.
UPDATE	Reading and writing, creating the file if it doesn't exist, keeping existing data.

Reading via Ajax

A second way an application can read text data from a file is to use Ajax. Chapter 4, "Basic Concepts and Code," has an example of this. Performing an `XMLHttpRequest` on a text file is the same as reading its contents (because the contents of the file will be the "response" of the request). If the data to be read in is fairly short, you may want to consider taking the Ajax route instead of using `File` and `FileStream` objects.

If the file being read contains just XML data (which itself is merely marked-up plain text), it'd be much better to perform a simple `XMLHttpRequest` on that file, reading in the `responseXML`. That way you'll end up with usable XML. If you use the `File` and `FileStream` combination on an XML file, turning the file contents into usable XML data will require extra steps.

READING FROM FILES

Doing so makes the file available to other applications.

To practice reading from (and next, writing to) text files, let's create a simple text editor that allows the user to open any plain text file and edit its contents. In the next section of the chapter, you'll expand this application so that you can also create a new text file from scratch.

To read from a text file:

1. In the JavaScript section of the main HTML file, create the required objects (**Script 10.1**):

   ```
   var file = new air.File();
   var stream = new air.FileStream();
   ```

continues on next page

Script 10.1 This application displays the contents of a selected text file.

```
1    <html><!-- Script 10.1 -->
2    <head>
3    <title>Text Editor</title>
4    <script type="text/javascript" src="AIRAliases.js"></script>
5    <script type="text/javascript">
6
7    // Create the objects:
8    var file = new air.File();
9    var stream = new air.FileStream();
10
11   // Need an event listener for selecting the file:
12   file.addEventListener(air.Event.SELECT, fileWasSelected);
13
14   // Define a function that will be called
15   // when the selection event occurs:
16   function fileWasSelected(e) {
17
18       // Open the file for reading:
19       stream.open(file, air.FileMode.READ);
20
21       // Get the contents:
22       var data = stream.readUTFBytes(stream.bytesAvailable);
23
24       // Close the file:
25       stream.close();
26
27       // Place the contents on the page:
28       document.getElementById('theText').value = data;
29
30   } // End of fileWasSelected() function.
31
32   // Function called to browse for the file:
33   function doOpen() {
34
35       // Limit what kinds of files can be opened:
36       var filter = new air.FileFilter('Text', '*.txt;*.html;*.css;*.js');
37
```

(script continues on next page)

2. Add an event listener to the `File` object:

`file.addEventListener(air.Event.`
`→ SELECT, fileWasSelected);`

This application starts with nothing but an Open button (**Figure 10.1**). When the user clicks the button, a prompt appears to select a file from the computer. After a file is selected, the `SELECT` event is triggered and the `fileWasSelected()` function is called. It reads in the text file.

3. Begin defining the `fileWasSelected()` function:

`function fileWasSelected(e) {`

Like functions associated with an event, this one takes a single argument: the event.

4. Read in the file's contents:

`stream.open(file, air.FileMode.READ);`

`var data = stream.readUTFBytes(stream.`
`→ bytesAvailable);`

`stream.close();`

The first line opens the file for reading. The second reads in its contents, assigning the contents to `data`. The third line closes the file. And that's it.

Figure 10.1 The program when first started.

Script 10.1 *continued*

```
38      // Create the dialog:
39      file.browseForOpen('Choose a file:', [filter]);
40
41  } // End of doOpen() function.
42
43  </script>
44
45  <style>
46      textarea { border: none;}
47  </style>
48
49  </head>
50  <body>
51
52  <button id="btnOpen" onclick="doOpen();">Open</button><hr />
53  <textarea cols="60" rows="40" id="theText"></textarea>
54
55  </body>
56  </html>
```

5. Display the contents on the page and complete the function:

```
document.getElementById('theText')
→ .value = data;

} // End of fileWasSelected()
→ function.
```

To display the file's contents with the intent of being able to edit them (that functionality will be added in the next example), they'll be placed within an HTML textarea whose ID value is *theText*. Note that you need to assign `data` to the textarea's `value` attribute; using `innerText` will cause problems.

6. Define a function that creates the browse for open dialog (**Figure 10.2**):

```
function doOpen() {
   var filter = new air.
   → FileFilter('Text', '*.txt;
   → *.html;*.css;*.js');
   file.browseForOpen('Choose a
   → file:', [filter]);
}
```

This function will be called when the user clicks the Open button. Because the application will only expect plain text files, the dialog will use a filter to limit what kinds of files—by extension—can be selected. This concept is covered in the "Using Filters" sidebar in Chapter 9. Obviously, you could expand the list of acceptable extensions.

On Windows, files that don't match the filter won't be revealed in the browse for open dialog. On Mac OS X, files that don't match the filter will be visible but not selectable.

7. If you want, add some CSS to make the textarea less apparent:

```
<style>textarea {
border: none;
}</style>
```

I'll get rid of the textarea's traditional border so that the place where the user edits text looks more like a Word document or other application (**Figure 10.3**).

continues on next page

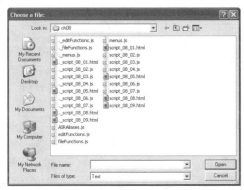

Figure 10.2 The dialog in which the user can select a plain text file for viewing or editing.

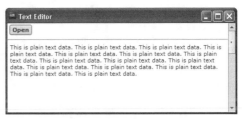

Figure 10.3 A file's contents are displayed on the page seamlessly (i.e., without the standard textarea border).

READING FROM FILES

8. Within the body, add a button and a textarea:

```
<button id="btnOpen" onclick=
→ "doOpen();">Open</button><hr />
<textarea cols="60" rows="40"
→ id="theText"></textarea>
```

The button needs to call doOpen() when the user clicks it. The textarea needs to have an ID value of *theText*.

9. Save, test, debug, and run the completed application.

You should be able to open any file with a .txt, .html, .css, or .js extension. Click Open again to view a different file (**Figure 10.4**).

✔ Tips

■ One nice addition to this program would be to indicate the document being viewed. You could display it in the title bar by setting document.title to file.name.

■ This program doesn't have overt "close" functionality because the opening of any text file replaces the previously viewed contents of a different file. To add "close" functionality, just clear out the contents of the textarea when the user clicks a button:

```
function doClose() {
   document.getElementById('theText')
   → .innerText = '';
}

<button id="btnClose" onclick=
→ "doClose();">Close</button>
```

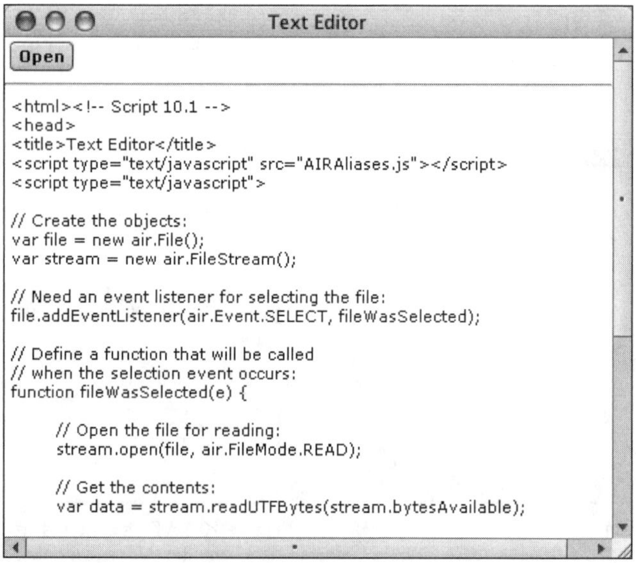

READING FROM FILES

```
⬤ ⬤ ⬤                    Text Editor
┌──────┐
│ Open │
└──────┘
<html><!-- Script 10.1 -->
<head>
<title>Text Editor</title>
<script type="text/javascript" src="AIRAliases.js"></script>
<script type="text/javascript">

// Create the objects:
var file = new air.File();
var stream = new air.FileStream();

// Need an event listener for selecting the file:
file.addEventListener(air.Event.SELECT, fileWasSelected);

// Define a function that will be called
// when the selection event occurs:
function fileWasSelected(e) {

     // Open the file for reading:
     stream.open(file, air.FileMode.READ);

     // Get the contents:
     var data = stream.readUTFBytes(stream.bytesAvailable);
```

Figure 10.4 The contents of another text file, viewed within the application.

Writing to Files

The previous example showed how to read in plain text data. Now let's expand on that and write plain text data to a file. You still need to create File and FileStream objects:

```
var file = air.File.
→ applicationStorageDirectory.
→ resolvePath('data.txt');
var stream = new air.FileStream();
```

Then open the file using one of the three modes that allow for writing (see Table 10.1):

```
stream.open(file, air.FileMode.WRITE);
```

To write plain text to the file, use writeUTFBytes():

```
stream.writeUTFBytes('text to be
→ written');
```

After all the data has been written, close the file:

```
stream.close();
```

And that's all there is to writing plain text to a file! However, adding this functionality to the existing text editor (Script 10.1) is a little complicated because the application will need to respond differently to the two possible triggers of a SELECT event.

◆ When the user selects a file to open, the file's data needs to be read in and displayed. When the user selects a file to be saved, the application needs to write the current text data to that file. Both user selections trigger the same AIR event, but the application responses are opposite.

◆ Adding slightly to the complication, if the user clicks Save when no file has been opened, the user needs to be prompted as to where the file should be saved (**Figure 10.5**). If the user clicks Save after a file has been selected, the application should just write the data to that file.

The solution to these issues is to rewrite the logic a bit and use a couple of extra variables to track what's going on.

Figure 10.5 This dialog asks the user to indicate where a file should be saved, including what its name should be.

To write to a file:

1. Open Script 10.1 in your text editor or IDE, if it is not already.

2. Add two variables (**Script 10.2**).

   ```
   var filename = null;
   var mode = null;
   ```

   The first variable will store the name of the file. This could be the file just opened or the file to which the user wants to write the data. By using this variable, the program will know if the user is editing an existing document or creating a new one (in which case, the program should prompt the user for where to save data).

   The second variable will track what mode—open or save—the program is in. This is necessary so that the program knows how to respond to the selection event.

3. Change the name of the `fileWasSelected()` function to `readData()`.

   The `fileWasSelected()` function is called when the user selects a file. Originally, that function read in the data from that file. Now the `fileWasSelected()` function will need to read in the data if the user just opened a file but write out the data if the user just selected where the file should be saved. For simplicity sake, I'll just rename the old `fileWasSelected()` function—because it contains the entire `readData()` code—and create a new `fileWasSelected()`.

4. Within the `doOpen()` function, assign a value to `mode`:

   ```
   mode = 'open';
   ```

   Step 2 discusses the point of the `mode` variable. The `doOpen()` function was defined in Script 10.1 and is invoked when the user clicks the Open button.

The function still creates the browse for open dialog, but now it also records the fact that the application is in open mode.

5. Begin the `writeData()` function:

   ```
   function writeData() {
       var data = document.getElementById
       → ('theText').value;
       data = data.replace(/\n/g, air.File.
       → lineEnding);
   ```

   This function will contain the code already explained for writing text data to a file. The text to be written is the value of the *theText* textarea, so that needs to be retrieved first.

   The third line here is necessary because of a little catch involving line endings. When a user presses Enter/Return within a textarea, a newline (\n) is added to the text. Mac OS X uses the same character to terminate a line in a file, so on that platform, data from a textarea directly written to a file will maintain the same line breaks. However, Windows uses a combination of the carriage return (\r) and the newline to mark line breaks. So to make this application more universal, this last line takes the `data` string and calls the `replace()` function on it, replacing every instance of \n (the /\n/g is a quick way of doing a global replace) with the system-used line endings. That value can be found in `air.File.lineEnding`.

6. Complete the `writeData()` function:

   ```
   stream.open(file, air.FileMode.
   → WRITE);
   stream.writeUTFBytes(data);
   stream.close();
   } // End of writeData() function.
   ```

   Finally, the file is opened for writing, the data is written there, and the file is closed.

continues on page 193

Script 10.2 The text editing application is updated so it allows the user to save new or edited text to a file. The functionality is rather simple, but the logic takes a little work.

```
1    <html><!-- Script 10.2 -->
2    <head>
3    <title>Text Editor</title>
4    <script type="text/javascript" src="AIRAliases.js"></script>
5    <script type="text/javascript">
6
7    // Flag variables:
8    var filename = null;
9    var mode = null;
10
11   // Create the objects:
12   var file = new air.File();
13   var stream = new air.FileStream();
14
15   // Need an event listener for selecting the file:
16   file.addEventListener(air.Event.SELECT, fileWasSelected);
17
18   // Function that reads in the data.
19   function readData() {
20
21       stream.open(file, air.FileMode.READ);
22       var data = stream.readUTFBytes(stream.bytesAvailable);
23       stream.close();
24       document.getElementById('theText').value = data;
25
26   } // End of readData() function.
27
28   // Function called to browse for the file:
29   function doOpen() {
30
31       // Update the mode:
32       mode = 'open';
33
34       // Limit what kinds of files can be opened:
35       var filter = new air.FileFilter('Text', '*.txt;*.html;*.css;*.js');
36
37       // Create the dialog:
38       file.browseForOpen('Choose a file:', [filter]);
39
40   } // End of doOpen() function.
41
42   // Function that writes the data to the file.
43   function writeData() {
44
45       // Get the text and convert line endings:
46       var data = document.getElementById('theText').value;
47       data = data.replace(/\n/g, air.File.lineEnding);
48
49       // Open the file for writing:
50       stream.open(file, air.FileMode.WRITE);
51
```

(script continues on next page)

WRITING TO FILES

Script 10.2 *continued*

```
52      // Write the data:
53      stream.writeUTFBytes(data);
54
55      // Close the file:
56      stream.close();
57
58   } // End of writeData() function.
59
60   // Define a function that will be called
61   // when the selection event occurs:
62   function fileWasSelected(e) {
63
64      // Assign the selection to filename:
65      filename = file.nativePath;
66
67      // Call the right function depending upon the mode:
68      if (mode == 'open') {
69         readData();
70      } else if (mode == 'save') {
71         writeData();
72      }
73
74   } // End of fileWasSelected() function.
75
76   // Function to be called when the user clicks Save:
77   function doSave() {
78
79      // Set the mode:
80      mode = 'save';
81
82      // Either write the data or prompt the user first:
83      if (filename) {
84         writeData();
85      } else {
86         file.browseForSave('Save');
87      }
88
89   } // End of doSave() function.
90
91   </script>
92
93   <style>
94      textarea { border: none;}
95   </style>
96
97   </head>
98   <body>
99
100  <button id="btnOpen" onclick="doOpen();">Open</button> <button id="btnSave"
     onclick="doSave();">Save</button><hr />
101  <textarea cols="60" rows="40" id="theText"></textarea>
102
103  </body>
104  </html>
```

7. Begin a new `fileWasSelected()` function:

```
function fileWasSelected(e) {
    filename = file.nativePath;
```

This new version of the function will still be called when the user selects a file (because the event listener specifies that's what should happen). But, as I mention in step 3, this version does things a bit differently. To start, it assigns to the `filename` variable the `nativePath` value of the selected file. This will be used later in the script, but it is necessary to have two different references to the file (one in `filename` and one in `file`).

8. Call the appropriate function, depending on the mode:

```
if (mode == 'open') {
    readData();
} else if (mode == 'save') {
    writeData();
}
```

The `mode` variable is necessary because there's no other way of knowing in this function if the event that just occurred is the selection of the file for reading or for writing. But the function that starts either process—`doOpen()` and `doSave()`—will assign the right value to `mode` to make that distinction. All that's left to do is call the corresponding function that does the actual work: `readData()` or `writeData()`.

9. Complete the `fileWasSelected()` function.

```
} // End of fileWasSelected()
→ function.
```

10. Begin the `doSave()` function.

```
function doSave() {
    mode = 'save';
```

This function is called when the user clicks the Save button. It first assigns a value to the `mode` variable.

continues on next page

Random Access

This chapter's examples perform sequential actions: reading or writing from the beginning of a file straight through to the end. But AIR applications have the option of randomly accessing files, both for reading or writing.

The `FileStream` object has a property called *position*. This attribute stores the current location in the file where the next read or write will begin. This value is an integer, representing bytes.

For any read operation, `position` is initially 0. The same is true when a file is opened for writing. From there on, unless explicitly changed, position will be updated to reflect the latest read or write. So if you open a new file and read in 200 bytes, `position` will then be 200 (because 200 bytes starting at 0 were read). When a file is opened for appending new data, the `position` value is irrelevant: New data will always be added at the end of the file.

The stream's `position` attribute is most important when using the UPDATE mode or performing asynchronous transactions.

To change a file's position, assign it a new value:

```
stream.position = 234;
```

You can do this after a stream has been opened using either `open()` or `openAsync()`. The next read or write call after the assignment will begin at that position.

WRITING TO FILES

11. Add an if-else conditional:

```
if (filename) {
  writeData();
} else {
  file.browseForSave('Save');
}
```

The user could click Save under two circumstances: to save the edits just made to an existing file or to save the data as a new file. In the first case, the only thing that needs to happen is a call to the writeData() function. In the second case, the user needs to select where the data should be saved (i.e., the file's name and location). **Figure 10.6** illustrates the application's complete logic.

12. Complete the doSave() function:

```
} // End of doSave() function.
```

13. Add a Save button to the page:

```
<button id="btnSave" onclick=
→ "doSave();">Save</button>
```

This button needs to call the doSave() function when clicked.

14. Save, test, debug, and run the completed application.

If you start by opening a file for reading, clicking Save updates that file with any changes. If you start by typing text in a blank textarea, clicking Save prompts you to choose where to save the file and what it should be called (Figure 10.5). Subsequent clicks on Save write all the data to the file without reprompting the user.

✔ Tips

- The open and save functionality would normally be invoked using menu items and/or keyboard equivalents. To save space, I've omitted this information here, but see Chapter 7, "Creating Menus," for instructions.

- If you open a text file in any application and all of the text is bunched together, this is likely because the line breaks are not being handled properly.

- The UPDATE mode can be used to randomly read from or write to a file. If you write 100 bytes of data to the middle of the file, it will replace the 100 bytes already there without affecting any data before or after.

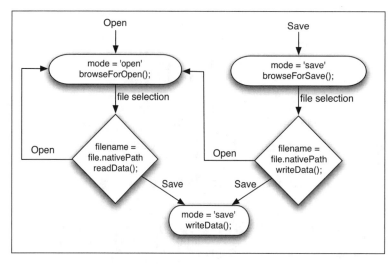

Figure 10.6 This diagram shows how the Save button can have two different outcomes, depending on whether a file is currently open or not. Also, a file selection can be followed by two different actions (reading from it or writing to it).

WRITING TO FILES

An Asynchronous Example

The text editor example developed thus far (Scripts 10.1 and 10.2) performs synchronous transactions. This means that after a request to read from or write to a file, nothing else happens until that reading or writing is completed. When dealing with small amounts of data, this isn't a problem. With more data, the wait may be apparent to the end user, which is never a good thing.

Performing asynchronous transactions isn't hard, but it does require more code. You'll need to create event listeners for relevant events (because the program continues to do other tasks while the transaction goes on).

For performing an asynchronous read, the events to be watched are `ProgressEvent.PROGRESS` and `Event.COMPLETE`. While a read is taking place, `PROGRESS` events will repeatedly be triggered. After the entire file has been read in, the `COMPLETE` event happens. You'll want to identify these event listeners before the stream is opened:

```
var file = air.File.applicationDirectory.
➝ resolvePath('data.txt');
var stream = new air.FileStream();
stream.addEventListener(air.Event.
➝ COMPLETE, readComplete);
stream.addEventListener(air.
➝ ProgressEvent.PROGRESS,
➝ readInProgress);
stream.openAsync(file, air.FileMode.
➝ READ);
```

Notice, as well, that the `openAsync()` function is used to open the stream instead of just `open()`.

With synchronous reads, the `readUTFBytes()` method is used, but you shouldn't use it for performing asynchronous reads. I'll explain why: If you have a file that's, say, 1 KB in size, the synchronous read grabs all 1,024 bytes at once. With an asynchronous read, 75 bytes might be read, then the next 224, then the next 103, and so forth until all the data has been fetched. Some characters that will be read from the text file will require more than one byte to represent them. If you use `readUTFBytes()`, it's possible that a read will only grab part of a character's bytes, and the read function will then interpret this as a different character. The solution is to use the `readMultiByte()` method. This function takes the number of bytes to read as its first argument and the character set as its second. You can name a character set as a string (like *iso-8859-1* in quotes) or assume that the file uses the operating system's default character set. That value is represented by `air.File.systemCharset`.

A similar concern involves what to do with the data as it's being read in. With a synchronous read, the entire file will be read in at once and can be assigned to a variable, put on the page, whatever. With an asynchronous read, the file will be read incrementally. Instead of just assigning the read data to a variable, you'll want to *append* it so the existing data is not replaced by the next read.

With these two considerations in mind, this next bit of code performs the asynchronous reading of a file, storing all the contents in the `data` variable:

```
var data = '';
function readInProgress(e) {
    data += stream.readMultiByte(stream.
    ➝ bytesAvailable, air.File.
    ➝ systemCharset);
}
```

Note that you don't have to do anything to start the read. As soon as the stream is opened some amount of data will be read into the *buffer* (a section of memory that stores input and output). That will trigger the PROGRESS event, which will call the readInProgress() function, which will call readMultiByte(). That function actually retrieves the data from the buffer, not the file. After it's done that, the buffer is cleared of its existing data and more data is read from the text file and stored in the buffer. This triggers the PROGRESS event, and the process continues until the entire file has been read.

Finally, the readComplete() function should do something with the read in data and close the file.

```
function readComplete(e) {
    // Do something with data.
    stream.close();
}
```

To perform asynchronous writing, you'll still call the openAsync() method, but you don't actually need to use event listeners. The writing may take some time (relatively speaking), but it will happen behind the scenes. Think of it like playing fetch with your dog: There's nothing you have to watch for or do while you're waiting for the dog to go get the stick or ball.

To perform asynchronous writing, you don't want to use writeUTFBytes(), instead use writeMultiByte(). It takes the data to be written as its first argument and the character set of the data as its second. The complete asynchronous code for writing data is therefore just:

```
var file = air.File.applicationDirectory.
→ resolvePath('data.txt');
var stream = new air.FileStream();
stream.openAsync(file, air.FileMode.
→ WRITE);
stream.writeMultiByte('text',
→ air.File.systemCharset);
stream.close();
```

And in case it crossed your mind, rest assured that the file won't be closed until the data is completely is written. Although asynchronous transactions allow for multiple tasks to happen at once, it doesn't mean that sequentially dependent code will be executed improperly.

To apply this new knowledge, let's update the text editor to perform both asynchronous reads and writes.

Handling Errors

When performing asynchronous reads and writes, you have the option of watching for error events, specifically an IOErrorEvent.IO_ERROR. If you add to the FileStream object a listener for that event, the associated function will be called should an input or output error occur.

```
stream.addEventListener(air.IOErrorEvent.IO_ERROR, errorHandler);
function errorHandler(e) {
    alert(e.text);
}
```

The text attribute of the triggered event will represent the error message.

The most common errors would be attempting to access a file that doesn't exist, issues related to permissions, and attempts to overwrite files and directories that already exist.

To perform asynchronous transactions:

1. Open Script 10.2 in your text editor or IDE, if it is not already.

2. At the top of the JavaScript code, create a new global variable (**Script 10.3**):

   ```
   var data = '';
   ```

   This variable will store the data being read in from a file. Because it'll be used inside of two functions, I'm creating it as a global variable here.

3. Add two event listeners:

   ```
   stream.addEventListener(air.
   → ProgressEvent.PROGRESS,
   → readInProgress);
   stream.addEventListener(air.Event.
   → COMPLETE, readComplete);
   ```

   The first event listener specifies that the readInProgress() function should be called when the PROGRESS event (defined in the ProgressEvent class) happens. The second line adds an event listener to the COMPLETE event, calling the readComplete() at that time. Both event listeners are added to the FileStream object.

continues on page 199

Script 10.3 This third and final version of the text editor performs asynchronous reading and writing, which should result in a better experience for the user when handling large text files.

```
1   <html><!-- Script 10.3 -->
2   <head>
3   <title>Text Editor</title>
4   <script type="text/javascript" src="AIRAliases.js"></script>
5   <script type="text/javascript">
6
7   // For the data to be read in:
8   var data = '';
9
10  // Flag variables:
11  var filename = null;
12  var mode = null;
13
14  // Create the objects:
15  var file = new air.File();
16  var stream = new air.FileStream();
17
18  // Need an event listener for selecting the file:
19  file.addEventListener(air.Event.SELECT, fileWasSelected);
20
21  // Add asynchronous event listeners:
22  stream.addEventListener(air.ProgressEvent.PROGRESS, readInProgress);
23  stream.addEventListener(air.Event.COMPLETE, readComplete);
24
25  // Function that reads in the data.
26  function readData() {
27
28      // Open the file for reading:
29      stream.openAsync(file, air.FileMode.READ);
30
31  } // End of readData() function.
32
```

(script continues on next page)

Script 10.3 *continued*

```
                                    Script
33    // Function called to browse for the file:
34    function doOpen() {
35        mode = 'open';
36        var filter = new air.FileFilter('Text', '*.txt;*.html;*.css;*.js');
37        file.browseForOpen('Choose a file:', [filter]);
38    } // End of doOpen() function.
39
40    // Function that writes the data to the file.
41    function writeData() {
42
43        // Get the text and convert line endings:
44        var data = document.getElementById('theText').value;
45        data = data.replace(/\n/g, air.File.lineEnding);
46
47        // Open the file for writing:
48        stream.openAsync(file, air.FileMode.WRITE);
49
50        // Write the data:
51        stream.writeMultiByte(data, air.File.systemCharset);
52
53        // Close the file:
54        stream.close();
55
56    } // End of writeData() function.
57
58    // Define a function that will be called
59    // when the selection event occurs:
60    function fileWasSelected(e) {
61        filename = file.nativePath;
62        if (mode == 'open') {
63            readData();
64        } else if (mode == 'save') {
65            writeData();
66        }
67    } // End of fileWasSelected() function.
68
69    // Function to be called when the user clicks Save:
70    function doSave() {
71        mode = 'save';
72        if (filename) {
73            writeData();
74        } else {
75            file.browseForSave('Save');
76        }
77    } // End of doSave() function.
78
79    // Function for asynchronous read progress.
80    function readInProgress(e) {
81
82        // Append the data to the variable:
83        data += stream.readMultiByte(stream.bytesAvailable, air.File.systemCharset);
84
85    } // End of readInProgress() function.
86
```

(script continues on next page)

AN ASYNCHRONOUS EXAMPLE

4. Change the `readData()` function so that it only calls the `openAsync()` method:

```
stream.openAsync(file,
→ air.FileMode.READ);
```

The previous version of this text editor used asynchronous reading, so the opening, reading, and closing of a file can take place all within this one function. Now this function just begins the reading process. The `readInProgress()` and `readComplete()` functions will finish the job.

5. Define the `readInProgress()` function:

```
function readInProgress(e) {
    data += stream.readMultiByte
    → (stream.bytesAvailable,
    → air.File.systemCharset);
}
```

This function reads in the available bytes and appends them to `data` using the concatenation assignment operator (`+=`).

6. Define the `readComplete()` function:

```
function readComplete(e) {
    document.getElementById('theText')
    → .value = data;
    stream.close();
    data = '';
}
```

This function will be called when all the data has been read in. It does three things. First, it places the read in data on the page by assigning it to the `value` attribute of the `textarea` (as the synchronous example had). Second, it closes the

continues on next page

Script 10.3 *continued*

```
87   // Function for when reading is done.
88   function readComplete(e) {
89
90       // Place the contents on the page:
91       document.getElementById('theText').value = data;
92
93       // Close the file:
94       stream.close();
95
96       // Clear the contents of data:
97       data = '';
98
99   } // End of readComplete() function.
100
101  </script>
102
103  <style>
104      textarea { border: none;}
105  </style>
106
107  </head>
108  <body>
109
110  <button id="btnOpen" onclick="doOpen();">Open</button> <button id="btnSave"
     onclick="doSave();">Save</button><hr />
111  <textarea cols="60" rows="40" id="theText"></textarea>
112
113  </body>
114  </html>
```

AN ASYNCHRONOUS EXAMPLE

file. Third, it clears out the value of `data` by assigning to it an empty string. This is necessary in case the user opens a second file during the same session.

7. Change the `writeData()` function to be asynchronous.

   To do so, change the first two of the three lines within the function to

   ```
   stream.openAsync(file,
   → air.FileMode.WRITE);
   ```

   ```
   stream.writeMultiByte(data,
   → air.File.systemCharset);
   ```

   The first change is to use `openAsync()` instead of `open()`. The second is to

use `writeMultiByte()` instead of `writeUTFBytes()`.

8. Save, test, debug, and run the completed application (**Figures 10.7** and **10.8**).

✔ Tips

- Although you don't normally need to attend to them, when it comes to asynchronous write events, the important ones to watch for are `OutputProgressEvent.OUTPUT_PROGRESS` and `Event.COMPLETE`.

- The `bytesAvailable` property refers to the number of bytes available in the buffer.

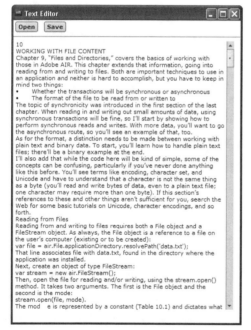

Figure 10.7 To test the asynchronous version of the text editor, I pasted in (as plain text), and saved as a new file, the 5,500 words in this chapter.

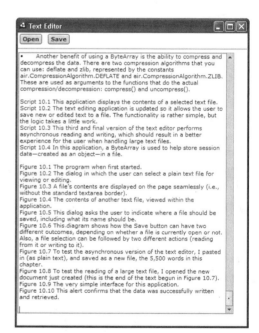

Figure 10.8 To test the reading of a large text file, I opened the new document just created (this is the end of the text begun in Figure 10.7).

Using Binary Data

The first three examples all involve plain text files. A plain text file normally has an extension like .txt, .html, .css, .js, .php, and so forth. You'll also hear these referred to as ASCII files. In them you'll only find characters that you can type (or insert) and no formatting or graphics. Pretty much everything else on a computer is a binary file: images, MP3s, Word documents, RTF (Rich Text Format) files, and so on.

To work with binary data, you'll use the ByteArray class defined in Adobe AIR:

```
var ba = new air.ByteArray();
```

Now, ba is an object of type ByteArray that can store binary data. Interestingly, you can treat a ByteArray just like a file stream. You can write data to and read data from it. You can see how long it is (in bytes) by referring to its length. You can navigate through it randomly by referencing its position attribute. You can see how much data there is between the current position and its length by referring to its bytesAvailable.

This code writes some text to a ByteArray, and then reads it back in:

```
ba.writeUTFBytes('text string');
ba.position = 0;
var data = ba.readUTFBytes(ba.
  ⇢ bytesAvailable);
```

You can write any type of data to a byte array (using the same FileStream functions), read any type of data from it, randomly access its contents, and you don't even need to open and close the ByteArray. More important, you can write a ByteArray to a file, thereby creating a binary file. To do so, use the stream's writeBytes() function, passing it the ByteArray as its first argument:

```
var file = air.File.documentsDirectory
  ⇢ ('data');
var stream = new air.FileStream();
stream.open(file, air.FileMode.WRITE);
stream.writeBytes(ba);
stream.close();
```

continues on next page

Big Endian, Little Endian

Binary data is trickier than plain text because of the "big endian, little endian" problem. Some text characters and all numbers require multiple bytes to be represented. On some computer systems, the important byte is stored first, followed by the less important bytes (this is *big endian* ordering). On other computer systems, the important bytes are left to last (*little endian*). If data is stored using big endian but read as if it was in little endian (or vice versa), the result will be a mess.

You can specify the endian order using constants in the Endian class. The appropriate values are air.Endian.BIG_ENDIAN and air.Endian.LITTLE_ENDIAN. To establish the endian setting, you can refer to the FileStream's endian property (for files) or the ByteArray's endian property (for ByteArray objects).

The ByteArray class is used when working with the encrypted local store option, which is a way to securely store data on the user's computer. This is discussed in Chapter 15, "Security Techniques." You'll also use it when working with various types of media—images, sound files, PDFs, and the like—or when sending data to, or downloading data from, networked computers. In this next example, just to keep things clear and simple, some session data will be written to a binary file using a ByteArray. It will then be retrieved back into a ByteArray.

To work with binary data:

1. In your project's primary HTML file, create the required objects (**Script 10.4**):

   ```
   var file = air.File.createTempFile();
   var stream = new air.FileStream();
   ```

   This program will store some session data (the kind of data that an application might track while the user is running it) in a temporary file. The createTempFile() method takes care of identifying and creating a file for this purpose.

2. Begin a function that will write some data to a file:

   ```
   function doWrite() {
       var input = new air.ByteArray();
   ```

   The application has just two buttons (**Figure 10.9**). When the Write button is clicked, this function will be called. Its role is to store some binary data in a file. It begins by creating a new ByteArray object.

3. Create some imaginary session data:

   ```
   var session = new Object();
   session.firstName = 'Larry';
   session.lastName = 'Ullman';
   session.age = 12;
   ```

Script 10.4 In this application, a ByteArray is used to help store session data—created as an object—in a file.

```
1   <html><!-- Script 10.4 -->
2   <head>
3   <title>ByteArray</title>
4   <script type="text/javascript"
    src="AIRAliases.js"></script>
5   <script type="text/javascript">
6
7   // Create the objects:
8   var file = air.File.createTempFile();
9   var stream = new air.FileStream();
10
11  // Function that writes the data to a file.
12  function doWrite() {
13
14      // Create a ByteArray object:
15      var input = new air.ByteArray();
16
17      // Store some data in an object:
18      var session = new Object();
19      session.firstName = 'Larry';
20      session.lastName = 'Ullman';
21      session.age = 12;
22
23      // Write the object to the ByteArray:
24      input.writeObject(session);
25
26      // Write the data to the file:
27      stream.open(file, air.FileMode.WRITE);
28      stream.writeBytes(input);
29      stream.close();
30
31      // Tell the user what happened:
32      alert('The data has been written.');
33
34  } // End of doWrite() function.
35
36  // Function that reads the data from the
    file.
37  function doRead() {
38
39      // Create a ByteArray object:
40      var output = new air.ByteArray();
41
42      // Read the data from the file:
43      stream.open(file, air.FileMode.READ);
44      stream.readBytes(output);
45      stream.close();
46
```

(script continues on next page)

Script 10.4 *continued*

```
47      // Assign the object to a variable:
48      var info = output.readObject();
49
50      // Confirm that it worked:
51      alert('info.firstName: ' + info.
        firstName);
52
53   } // End of doRead() function.
54
55   </script>
56   </head>
57
58   <body>
59
60   <button id="btnWrite" onclick="doWrite();">
     Write</button> <button id="btnRead"
     onclick="doRead();">Read</button>
61
62   </body>
63   </html>
```

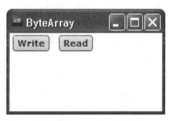

Figure 10.9 The very simple interface for this application.

Applications, like Web sites, that store session data normally do so as a series of *name=value* pairs. In JavaScript, this can be accomplished by creating a new object, where the object's attributes are the names and their values are (obviously) the values. Here, three pieces of data are represented.

4. Store the object in the `ByteArray`:

`input.writeObject(session);`

The `writeObject()` method takes an object as its first argument and writes that to the `ByteArray`. Now the session data is stored in a binary data variable that can be written to a file.

5. Write the `ByteArray` to the file:

```
stream.open(file, air.FileMode.
→ WRITE);
```

`stream.writeBytes(input);`

`stream.close();`

The `writeBytes()` method will do the trick here. Now the file contains binary data, which represents the session object.

In truth, you can write an object directly to a file by using the `writeObject()` method of the stream. However, I wanted to play with the `ByteArray` class a little, so that it's familiar to you in later chapters when you'll use it more legitimately.

6. Complete the `doWrite()` function:

```
alert('The data has been
→ written.');
```

`} // End of doWrite() function.`

The alert provides a simple way of indicating to the user that something has happened.

continues on next page

USING BINARY DATA

7. Begin a function for reading in the data:

```
function doRead() {
  var output = new air.ByteArray();
```

This function will be called when the Read button is clicked (see Figure 10.9). It starts by creating a new `ByteArray` object.

8. Read the file data into the `ByteArray`:

```
stream.open(file, air.FileMode.READ);
stream.readBytes(output);
stream.close();
```

The `readBytes()` method reads in raw bytes of data, assigning them to the `ByteArray` object provided as the first argument to the function.

9. Access and report on the stored data:

```
var info = output.readObject();
alert('info.firstName: ' + info.
→ firstName);
```

The `output` object contains binary data (specifically, an object in a serialized format). To get the data to a usable format again, the `readObject()` method is called, assigning the results to the `info` variable. Then one piece of the session data is reported using an alert (**Figure 10.10**).

10. Complete the `doWrite()` function.

```
} // End of doWrite() function.
```

11. Add two buttons to the page:

```
<button id="btnWrite" onclick="do
→ Write();">Write</button> <button
→ id="btnRead" onclick="doRead();">
→ Read</button>
```

Each button calls the corresponding function.

12. Save, test, debug, and run the completed application.

✔ Tips

- Windows makes a distinction between plain text and binary files. On Mac OS X and Unix, there is no difference between them: A plain text file can also be treated as a binary file.

- Binary files often contain a Byte Order Mark (BOM) that indicates whether the big endian or little endian ordering was used.

- Another benefit of using a `ByteArray` is the ability to compress and decompress the data. There are two compression algorithms that you can use: deflate and zlib, represented by the constants `air.CompressionAlgorithm.DEFLATE` and `air.CompressionAlgorithm.ZLIB`. These are used as arguments to the functions that do the actual compression/decompression: `compress()` and `uncompress()`.

Figure 10.10 This alert confirms that the data was successfully written and retrieved.

Working with Databases

The Adobe AIR software comes with the open source (and most excellent) SQLite database application built in. This is a lightweight tool that's easy to use and has more than enough features for most programs. Thanks to the inclusion of SQLite, your AIR applications have a smart and simple way to store and retrieve data.

In this chapter you'll learn the basics of working with an SQLite database from an AIR application. Although the chapter doesn't assume experience with SQLite specifically, it will help if you're familiar with using relational databases in general and have already utilized SQL (Structured Query Language, which is used to communicate with pretty much every database application). For more information on SQLite, see `www.sqlite.org`. For more on SQL, see my book *MySQL, 2nd Edition: Visual QuickStart Guide* (Peachpit Press, 2006) or any other reference you have available.

The fundamentals of using a database will be demonstrated in this chapter by creating a task-management application. In the next chapter you'll learn some best practices and other techniques for incorporating a database into an AIR program. Before getting into the code, let me add that, like working with files and directories, you can use both synchronous and asynchronous functions. The first two examples are done synchronously, whereas the rest take the asynchronous route, which is generally better. Finally, note that some database-related debugging tips are at the end of the next chapter. If you have any problems with this chapter's code, see the debugging tips for help in solving those problems.

Connecting to a Database

Interacting with an SQLite database starts with the SQLConnection class. However, an SQLite database is just a file on the computer, so you'll need a File object as well (see Chapter 9, "Files and Directories," for the basics on working with files).

```
var conn = new air.SQLConnection();
var db = air.File.
→ applicationStorageDirectory.
→ resolvePath('something.db');
```

This second line creates a new object of File type. This object represents the file called something.db, which is located within the AIR application's storage directory. This is a logical place for an application's database (see Chapter 9 and Chapter 4, "Basic Concepts and Code," for more on this directory). Note that it doesn't matter what extension you use, if any, for the database file, although .db is a logical choice.

To work with a database synchronously, you can just call the open() method, passing it the File object as the first argument:

```
conn.open(db);
```

If you'd like the referenced file to be created if it doesn't exist (e.g., when you go to create the database for the first time), pass this function a second argument with the value air.SQLMode.CREATE.

```
conn.open(db, air.SQLMode.CREATE);
```

At this point you're ready to run queries on the database: to create tables, to populate them (insert records), to update tables, to retrieve data, and so forth. The rest of the chapter explains those steps. When the application is done doing whatever needs to be done, close the database connection:

```
conn.close();
```

There's not much in terms of functionality in the information provided thus far, but let's run it in an application anyway, just to make sure it works before making the code more useful and more complicated.

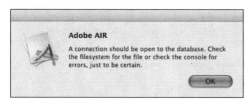

Figure 11.1 The result of running the first application.

Script 11.1 This first simple script just tests the basics of connecting to an SQLite database.

```
1   <html><!-- Script 11.1 -->
2   <head>
3   <title>Databases</title>
4   <script type="text/javascript"
    src="AIRAliases.js"></script>
5   <script type="text/javascript">
6
7   // Create the objects:
8   var conn = new air.SQLConnection();
9   var db = air.File.
    applicationStorageDirectory.
    resolvePath('ch11.db');
10
11  // Open the database:
12  conn.open(db, air.SQLMode.CREATE);
13
14  // Alert the user:
15  alert('A connection should be open to
    the database. Check the filesystem for the
    file or check the console for errors, just
    to be certain.');
16
17  // Close the database:
18  conn.close();
19
20  </script>
21  </head>
22  <body>
23  </body>
24  </html>
```

To connect to a database:

1. In your project's primary HTML file, create two new objects (**Script 11.1**).

```
var conn = new air.SQLConnection();
var db = air.File.
→ applicationStorageDirectory.
→ resolvePath('ch11.db');
```

The first line creates the object of type `SQLConnection`. The second line creates a `File` object that refers to a file named `ch11.db`, which is found within this application's storage directory.

2. Open the database connection:

```
conn.open(db, air.SQLMode.CREATE);
```

The database should now be open and will be created if the file doesn't already exist.

3. Notify the user:

```
alert('A connection should be
→ open to the database. Check the
→ filesystem for the file or check
→ the console for errors, just to
→ be certain.');
```

So that the application does something, this alert is used.

4. Close the database connection:

```
conn.close();
```

As with files, you should close the connection to a database when the application is done using it.

5. Save, test, debug, and run the completed application (**Figure 11.1**).

Note that if any errors occur, they should be displayed in the console.

continues on next page

6. Check your application's storage directory for the creation of the database file (**Figure 11.2**).

The application storage directory is another folder on the computer—besides the folder where the application exists—dedicated to this program. On Mac OS X, this will be /Users/*username*/Library/Preferences/*appID.publisherID*/Local Store. On Windows, this will be something like C:\Documents and Settings*username*\Application Data*appID.publisherID*\Local Store. Note that, in both cases, *username* would be replaced with your actual username for the computer and *appID* would be replaced with the id value from the application's XML descriptor file. The *.publisherID* value comes from the signing certificate used when building the application. It'll be a string of random-looking characters that uniquely identifies the application's associated creator. When running the application using the adl (i.e., without formally installing it), there will be no *.publisherID* value.

On my Mac my username is *Larry* and the application.xml file for this program contains this line—

<id>ToDoList</id>

—so I can find the created database in /Users/Larry/Library/Preferences/ToDoList/Local Store during the testing process (when there is no *publisherID* value).

✔ Tips

- If you don't provide a File object when calling open() (or for asynchronous transactions, openAysnc()), SQLite will create the database in memory:

  conn.open(null, air.SQLMode.CREATE);

- Since an SQLite database is just a file on the computer, it—and its contents—are accessible by other applications. SQLite, while great, doesn't have the same security protections that other database applications possess. If the data being stored should not be accessible by other applications, use an EncryptedLocalStore instead (see Chapter 15, "Security Techniques."

- An application's use of its storage directory is just one reason you need to give your AIR applications a unique id value. If two programs have the same application ID and publisher ID, they'll both read and write data from the same directory.

Figure 11.2 The database file, newly created by the application, is found in its storage directory.

CONNECTING TO A DATABASE

Creating a Database

Any application should only need to create a database (which is to say create the tables in a database) once. In the next chapter you'll learn how to distribute an application with the database already made, but here you'll learn how to have the application create it from scratch.

Creating a table in a database is a matter of running the proper SQL command: `CREATE TABLE tablename`... To run any SQL command on SQLite, start with your `SQLConnection` object, which points to the database file:

```
var conn = new air.SQLConnection();
var db = air.File.
→ applicationStorageDirectory.
→ resolvePath('something.db');
conn.open(db, air.SQLMode.CREATE);
```

Next, you'll need an object of type `SQLStatement`:

```
var sql = new air.SQLStatement();
```

Assign the `SQLConnection` object to its `sqlConnection` property:

```
sql.sqlConnection = conn;
```

To run the query on the database, it must first be assigned to the `SQLStatement` object's `text` property. The following command creates a table with two columns:

```
sql.text = 'CREATE TABLE testing (id
→ INTEGER PRIMARY KEY AUTOINCREMENT,
→ something TEXT)';
```

Finally, execute the SQL command:

```
sql.execute();
```

Note that these instructions are particular to synchronous procedures. When interfacing with SQLite asynchronously (discussed throughout the rest of the chapter), you'll need to establish and use event listeners. Those instructions are in the next section of the chapter.

As mentioned in the introduction, there's not enough room in the book to cover SQL in detail, but the language is pretty easy to follow. If you've never used SQLite before, **Table 11.1** lists the available types you can use for table columns and the "Intro to SQLite" sidebar provides a brief introduction to the software as a whole.

Table 11.1 These are the four data types supported by SQLite. Although there is no formal date or time type, such values can be stored in a text column.

SQLite Data Types	
NAME	**STORES**
INTEGER	A signed (plus/minus) integer
REAL	A floating-point number
TEXT	Any string
BLOB	Binary data

To create a database:

1. Open Script 11.1 in your text editor or IDE, if it is not already.

2. Create an SQLStatement object (**Script 11.2**).

   ```
   var sql = new air.SQLStatement();
   ```

3. After opening the database connection but before closing it, link the connection object to the statement object:

   ```
   sql.sqlConnection = conn;
   ```

   This tells the statement object through which connection the queries should be executed.

Script 11.2 This application actually creates a table in an SQLite database. The table made here is used in the rest of the chapter's examples.

```
1    <html><!-- Script 11.2 -->
2    <head>
3    <title>Databases</title>
4    <script type="text/javascript" src="AIRAliases.js"></script>
5    <script type="text/javascript">
6
7    // Create the objects:
8    var conn = new air.SQLConnection();
9    var db = air.File.applicationStorageDirectory.resolvePath('ch11.db');
10   var sql = new air.SQLStatement();
11
12   // Open the database:
13   conn.open(db, air.SQLMode.CREATE);
14
15   // Associate the statement with the connection:
16   sql.sqlConnection = conn;
17
18   // Define the query:
19   sql.text = 'CREATE TABLE todo (id INTEGER PRIMARY KEY AUTOINCREMENT, item TEXT NOT NULL, added
     TEXT DEFAULT CURRENT_TIMESTAMP, completed TEXT DEFAULT NULL)';
20
21   // Execute the query:
22   sql.execute();
23
24   // Alert the user:
25   alert('The table has been created.');
26
27   // Close the database:
28   conn.close();
29
30   </script>
31   </head>
32   <body>
33   </body>
34   </html>
```

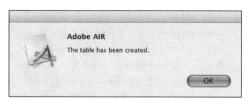

Figure 11.3 The alert generated when this application runs.

Intro to SQLite

SQLite is an extremely popular database that many people may not even know they've used before. It's present in Mac OS X (used by many applications), the Firefox Web browser, the PHP scripting language, and in literally millions of portable devices. Its widespread use is due to its very small size and open-source license. It also dispenses with many advanced and administrative features, making it easy to use.

From a technical standpoint, SQLite differs from the best known database applications (Oracle, MySQL, SQL Server, etc.) in many ways. One big difference is that SQLite only supports four data types: It has no date or time type, and it doesn't constrain data by type (meaning that it'll let you store a string in a column defined as a real number). SQLite also has no system for managing users and permissions: A database is a file on the computer and all the data is readable and writable by any user or application (depending on the operating system's permissions on that file).

SQLite mostly adheres to the SQL92 standard and has a minimum of built-in functions. You can do pretty much whatever you normally do in other database applications with a few exceptions: support for triggers, ALTER TABLE commands, views, and joins are incomplete. There are also no foreign key constraints. But for most database needs, SQLite will do just fine.

4. Define the CREATE TABLE query:

```
sql.text = 'CREATE TABLE todo (id
INTEGER PRIMARY KEY AUTOINCREMENT,
→ item TEXT NOT NULL, added TEXT
→ DEFAULT CURRENT_TIMESTAMP,
→ completed TEXT DEFAULT NULL)';
```

This command will create a table containing four columns. The first is named *id* and will be an automatically incremented primary key. Basically the id column will be a unique way to refer to every record in the column (if you're not familiar with primary keys, search the Web or see one of my books about SQL). As an automatically incremented integer, the first record inserted will have an id value of 1, the next 2, and so on.

The second column, *item*, will be the actual task in the user's to-do list. It must always have a value (it cannot be null). The third and fourth columns will store textual representations of a point in time. The first will reflect when the item was added. Its default value will be the current timestamp (i.e., the moment the record is added to the table). The other column will be updated when a task is completed. If a task has no completed value, that means it still needs to be done. When it has been completed, this column will register the time that the task was marked as completed. Doing it this way is better than just deleting completed tasks, because the user would then have no record as to what has been accomplished.

5. Execute the query:

```
sql.execute();
```

6. Change the alert to reflect the updates to the script:

```
alert('The table has been created.');
```

7. Save, test, debug, and run the completed application (**Figure 11.3**).

continues on next page

✔ Tips

- The SQLConnection object has two properties that affect the size and behavior of a database that is created: autoCompact and pageSize. If you don't know what these properties mean or how they are used, you can search online for details. These values can only be adjusted prior to creating a database.

- Your table names cannot begin with *sqlite_*, because that prefix is reserved for SQLite's use.

- You can confirm the creation of the table by opening the database file in any application that can read SQLite databases (**Figure 11.4**). Search the Web for a program that will run on your operating system (one of the best seems to be Sqliteman at www.sqliteman.com).

- The data types supported by SQLite are tricky. So it's a subject that I'm glossing over here. If you'll be using SQLite a lot, I recommend you read its simple manual, but with respect to data types, check out the pages on *column affinity* for more information.

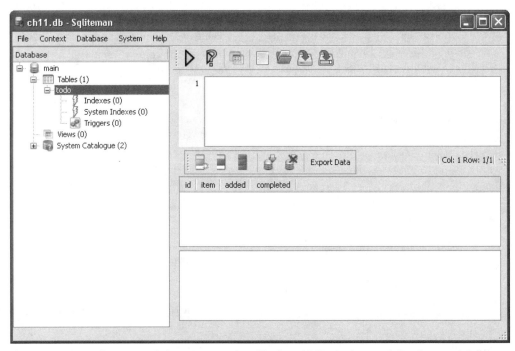

Figure 11.4 Using Sqliteman on Windows, I can see the tables in an SQLite database and view the records in it.

CREATING A DATABASE

Inserting Records

When you have a complete and working database, you can start doing what's important: storing data in it. This is accomplished using an INSERT query. The process of running an INSERT query is the same as that used to run a CREATE query: create the SQLConnection, File, and SQLStatement objects, open the connection, associate the connection with the statement, assign the SQL command to the SQLStatement's text property, and then execute the statement. I could walk you through this, but it's time to start performing asynchronous communications instead of the synchronous ones used thus far. When a program does activities that take more time to complete (like inserting, selecting, updating, and deleting records), using asynchronous communications will result in a more professional application.

You start by opening the database using openAsync(), but you'll need to set up event listeners before doing so. The first event to watch for is air.SQLEvent.OPEN:

```
var conn = new air.SQLConnection();
var db = air.File.
→ applicationStorageDirectory.
→ resolvePath('something.db');
conn.addEventListener(air.SQLEvent.OPEN,
→ dbOpen);
conn.openAsync(db, air.SQLMode.CREATE);
```

Figure 11.5 The complete to-do list application, to be written over the course of this chapter.

What the corresponding handling function—doOpen() in this case—does depends on the application. If the application retrieves some information from the database when launched, the code that does that would be called after opening the connection.

The next steps would be to create the SQLStatement object and assign to it the connection:

```
var sql = new air.SQLStatement();
sql.sqlConnection = conn;
```

To this statement object you'll want to add an event listener, watching for SQLEvent.RESULT. Such an event is triggered when a positive result is returned by the database:

```
sql.addEventListener(air.SQLEvent.
→ RESULT, sqlResult);
```

Now you can assign the query to the SQL statement and execute it:

```
sql.text = 'INSERT INTO testing
→ (something) VALUES ("This is some
→ text.")';
sql.execute();
```

In the next example, I'll start building a to-do list management application (**Figure 11.5**). By the end of the chapter, the application will allow the user to add new list items, mark them as completed, and delete them. This example will be started from scratch here with the assumption that the database has already been created using the previous application. Because the database should already exist, the openAsync() method will use a second argument of air.SQLMode. UPDATE instead of air.SQLMode.CREATE. This value indicates that the database should be opened for reading or writing but should not be created if it doesn't exist.

Before running through these steps, there's one other important item to note. For simplicity sake, the value a user enters into a text input will be used as-is in the SQL INSERT command. This is a potential security hole that allows the user to break the database. In the next chapter you'll see a preferred but slightly more complicated way to integrate user-supplied values into a query.

To insert records:

1. In your project's primary HTML file, create the necessary objects (**Script 11.3**):

   ```
   var conn = new air.SQLConnection();
   var db = air.File.
   → applicationStorageDirectory.
   → resolvePath('ch11.db');
   var insert = new air.SQLStatement();
   ```

Script 11.3 To start creating a to-do list manager, this program offers the user a way to add items to the database.

```
1   <html><!-- Script 11.3 -->
2   <head>
3   <title>To-Do List</title>
4   <script type="text/javascript" src="AIRAliases.js"></script>
5   <script type="text/javascript">
6
7   // Create the objects:
8   var conn = new air.SQLConnection();
9   var db = air.File.applicationStorageDirectory.resolvePath('ch11.db');
10  var insert = new air.SQLStatement();
11
12  // Do the prep work after the application has loaded:
13  window.onload = function() {
14
15      // Disable the Add Item button until we're ready for it:
16      document.getElementById('btnAddItem').disabled = true;
17
18      // Add the event handlers:
19      conn.addEventListener(air.SQLEvent.OPEN, dbOpen);
20      insert.addEventListener(air.SQLEvent.RESULT, insertResult);
21
22      // Open the database:
23      conn.openAsync(db, air.SQLMode.UPDATE);
24
25  } // End of anonymous function.
26
27  // When the application has closed, close the database connection:
28  window.onbeforeunload = function() {
29      conn.close();
30  }
31
32  // Function called when the database is opened.
33  function dbOpen() {
34
35      // Associate the connection with the SQLStatement:
36      insert.sqlConnection = conn;
37
```

(script continues on next page)

Script 11.3 *continued*

```
      ⚫ ⚫ ⚫               📄 Script
38        // Enable the 'Add Item' button:
39        document.getElementById('btnAddItem').
          disabled = false;
40
41    } // End of dbOpen() function.
42
43    // Function called when the user clicks
      'Add Item'.
44    function addItem() {
45
46        // Get the value:
47        var item = document.
          getElementById('item').value;
48
49        if (item.length > 0) { // Make sure
          there's something there!
50
51            // Escape any apostrophes:
52            item = item.replace(/'/g, "''");
53
54            // Insert the item:
55            insert.text = "INSERT INTO todo
              (item) VALUES ('" + item + "')";
56            insert.execute();
57
58        } // End of item.length IF.
59
60    } // End of addItem() function.
61
62    // Function called when an INSERT works.
63    function insertResult() {
64        alert ('The item has been added.');
65        document.getElementById('item').value =
          null;
66    }
67
68    </script>
69
70    <style>
71    body {margin:10px;}
72    p {font-size: 16px;}
73    </style>
74
75    </head>
76
77    <body>
78
79    <h3>To-Do List</h3>
80
81    <input type="text" id="item" /> <button
      id="btnAddItem" onclick="addItem()">Add
      Item</button><hr />
82
83    </body>
84    </html>
```

There's nothing new here, but I'll point out two details. First, I'm calling the SQLStatement object *insert*, because it'll be used to insert records into the database. Second, although the name of this database is still ch11.db (as in the previous two examples), the program will only work if it uses the same application ID and publisher ID values as the previous example. If that's not the case, the applicationStorageDirectory location will be different, and this program won't have a database to use!

2. Define a function to be called after the application loads:

   ```
   window.onload = function() {
       document.getElementById
       → ('btnAddItem').disabled = true;
   } // End of anonymous function.
   ```

   This anonymous function will be automatically called once the application (or window, technically) has loaded. It starts by disabling the Add Item button, so that the user can't even attempt to add any items until this program knows that the database connection is open.

3. Add the event listeners and open the connection:

   ```
   conn.addEventListener(air.SQLEvent.
   → OPEN, dbOpen);
   insert.addEventListener(air.
   → SQLEvent.RESULT, insertResult);
   conn.openAsync(db, air.SQLMode.
   → UPDATE);
   ```

continues on next page

The first event listener watches for an OPEN event on the connection object. When that happens, the dbOpen() function will be called. The second event listener watches for a RESULT event on the statement object. When the statement query successfully runs on the database, this event will occur, thereby calling the insertResult() function.

Notice that when opening the database, the second argument is air.SQLMode.UPDATE, which means that the database must already exist and it's now being opened for just reading and writing.

4. Create a function that closes the database connection:

```
window.onbeforeunload = function() {
    conn.close();
}
```

The database connection needs to remain open while the program is running (because the user may continue to add items to it). But it also should be closed before the application quits. To accomplish that, an anonymous function will be called right before the window unloads (i.e., closes). Within the anonymous function, the connection's close() method is called.

5. Define the dbOpen() function:

```
function dbOpen() {
    insert.sqlConnection = conn;
    document.getElementById
    → ('btnAddItem').disabled = false;
} // End of dbOpen() function.
```

This function is called after the connection has been made to the database. It needs to do two things: associate the connection with the insert statement and enable the Add Item button so the user can begin adding tasks.

6. Begin defining the addItem() function:

```
function addItem() {
    var item = document.
    → getElementById('item').value;
    if (item.length > 0) {
```

This function will be called when the user clicks the Add Item button (see Figure 11.5). The function starts by retrieving what the user entered into the text input, whose id value is *item*. Next, a conditional confirms that something was entered into the input. This prevents insertions from being made before the user has even typed anything.

7. Escape any apostrophes in the item's value:

```
item = item.replace(/'/g, "''");
```

The to-do item's value will be part of a query that looks like this:

```
INSERT INTO todo (item) VALUE ('The
→ actual item value here.')
```

Because the value is wrapped within single quotation marks, any apostrophes within the value will break the query. To prevent that, the replace() method is applied to the value, globally replacing any occurrence of a single apostrophe with two apostrophes. This is how you *escape* the apostrophe to make it usable in a query.

If you haven't used regular expressions before, this code might not mean much to you. The slashes mark the beginning and end of the pattern being matched. The pattern here is just a single apostrophe. The *g* after the second slash means that a global replace should be made (i.e., every apostrophe should be replaced, not just the first one encountered).

8. Define and run the INSERT query:

```
insert.text = "INSERT INTO todo
→ (item) VALUES ('" + item + "')";
insert.execute();
```

Step 7 shows the composed query with the value in place. With respect to the table, the id column doesn't need to be provided with a value, because it will be automatically assigned. The same goes for *added*, which will automatically be assigned the current timestamp. The fourth column also doesn't need a value because it will be null until the task is actually done.

9. Complete the addItem() function:

```
} // End of item.length IF.
} // End of addItem() function.
```

10. Define the insertResult() function:

```
function insertResult() {
  alert ('The item has been added.');
  document.getElementById('item').
→ value = null;
}
```

This function will be called if the insert statement successfully runs on the database. It should notify the user that the item was added and clear the current value from the text input.

11. Within the body of the page, add a text input and a button:

```
<input type="text" id="item" />
→ <button id="btnAddItem"
→ onclick="addItem()">Add Item
→ </button><hr />
```

The text input needs to have an id of *item*, matching the code in addItem(). The button can have any name but needs to call the addItem() function when clicked.

I've also add a small section of CSS (see the script), just to make things a bit neater.

12. Save, test, debug, and run the completed application (**Figures 11.6** and **11.7**).

✔ Tips

- To retrieve the value of the automatically incremented primary key, you would do this in this example's insertResult() function:

```
var result = insert.getResult();
var pk = result.lastInsertRowID;
```

- SQLite does not support the syntax for inserting multiple records using one query:

```
INSERT INTO todo (item) VALUES
→ ('Something'), ('Something Else'),
→ ('A 3rd Thing')
```

This is possible within the popular MySQL database but is not part of the SQL standard.

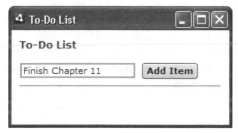

Figure 11.6 To add an item to the to-do list, enter the text in the box, and then click the button.

Figure 11.7 The application reports on the results.

INSERTING RECORDS

Handling Errors

A key difference between average and professional applications is how errors are handled. In a poorly written program, no consideration is made for errors, so it seems as if the expectation is they'll never occur. A complete program addresses every possible error, no matter how much extra code it takes. When interacting with databases, errors are rather common (particularly during the development stage), so you should account for them.

To properly handle errors that occur, add an event listener to every SQL-related object:

```
var conn = new air.SQLConnection();
conn.addEventListener(air.SQLErrorEvent.
→ ERROR, dbError);
var sql = new air.SQLStatement();
sql.addEventListener(air.SQLErrorEvent.
→ ERROR, dbError);
```

The error to be watched for is SQLErrorEvent.ERROR. Whether the error occurred during the connection process or while executing a command, an SQLErrorEvent.Error will be raised. (This is true when performing asynchronous communications; synchronous errors are found within SQLError not SQLErrorEvent). Notice that you'll need to add event listeners to both the SQLConnection and SQLStatement objects, but it's acceptable if they both invoke the same function.

The error handling function should take an event as its argument. Within the function, the error message can be found in the event's *errorName*.error.message property. More details will be in its *errorName*.error.details property. An associated error ID will be in *errorName*.error.errorID. The *errorName*. error.operation property reflects what was

happening when the error occurred. With this in mind, to simply report when an error occurred, you would use:

```
function dbError(e) {
    alert('The following error occurred: '
    → + e.error.message);
}
```

Let's apply this to the application so that any errors that occur will be handled in some way. As a reminder, Chapter 12, "Database Techniques," has a section devoted to debugging applications that interact with an SQLite database.

To handle errors:

1. Open Script 11.3 in your text editor or IDE, if it is not already.

2. Within the first anonymous function, add two more event listeners (**Script 11.4**):
   ```
   conn.addEventListener(air.
   → SQLErrorEvent.ERROR, dbError);
   insert.addEventListener(air.
   → SQLErrorEvent.ERROR, dbError);
   ```

3. Define the dbError() function:
   ```
   function dbError(e) {
       alert("The following error
       → occurred: " + e.error.message +
       → "\nDetails: " + e.error.details
       → + "\nOperation: " + e.error.
       → operation);
   }
   ```
   This function will report the error message in some detail to the end user. To do so, some literal text plus the values of e.error.message, e.error.details, and e.error.operation will be alerted. Newlines (\n) are added so that the message is printed over several lines.

continues page 220

Script 11.4 For a more professional result, the application has been updated to handle (at least, acknowledge) any errors that might occur. (I've also cleaned out some comments and blank lines in the existing code, just to tighten up the length of the script.)

```
1    <html><!-- Script 11.4 -->
2    <head>
3    <title>To-Do List</title>
4    <script type="text/javascript" src="AIRAliases.js"></script>
5    <script type="text/javascript">
6
7    // Create the objects:
8    var conn = new air.SQLConnection();
9    var db = air.File.applicationStorageDirectory.resolvePath('ch11.db');
10   var insert = new air.SQLStatement();
11
12   // Do the prep work after the application has loaded:
13   window.onload = function() {
14       document.getElementById('btnAddItem').disabled = true;
15
16       // Add the event handlers:
17       conn.addEventListener(air.SQLEvent.OPEN, dbOpen);
18       conn.addEventListener(air.SQLErrorEvent.ERROR, dbError);
19       insert.addEventListener(air.SQLEvent.RESULT, insertResult);
20       insert.addEventListener(air.SQLErrorEvent.ERROR, dbError);
21
22       conn.openAsync(db, air.SQLMode.UPDATE);
23   } // End of anonymous function.
24
25   // When the application has closed, close the database connection:
26   window.onbeforeunload = function() {
27       conn.close();
28   }
29
30   // Function called when the database is opened.
31   function dbOpen() {
32       insert.sqlConnection = conn;
33       document.getElementById('btnAddItem').disabled = false;
34   } // End of dbOpen() function.
35
36   // Function for reporting errors.
37   function dbError(e) {
38       alert("The following error occurred: " + e.error.message + "\nDetails: " + e.error.details +
         "\nOperation: " + e.error.operation);
39   }
40
41   // Function called when the user clicks 'Add Item'.
42   function addItem() {
43       var item = document.getElementById('item').value;
44       if (item.length > 0) {
45           item = item.replace(/'/g, "''");
46           insert.text = "INSERT INTO todo (item) VALUES ('" + item + "')";
47           insert.execute();
48       } // End of item.length IF.
49   } // End of addItem() function.
50
```

(script continues on next page)

HANDLING ERRORS

You wouldn't want to do this with a real application (with few exceptions, showing end users detailed and complex error messages isn't appropriate), but it will be useful debugging information for you as you write and test the application.

4. Save, test, debug, and run the completed application.

To see the effect of this updated example, you'll need to already have a problem, or introduce one here (**Figures 11.8** and **11.9**).

✔ Tips

■ Another very useful piece of information for debugging purposes is the value of the exact query being executed. You can display this value by referring to the SQLStatement's text attribute (e.g., insert.text).

■ To handle the errors that occur while performing synchronous communications, use a try...catch or try...catch... finally structure.

Script 11.4 *continued*

```
51   // Function called when an INSERT works.
52   function insertResult() {
53       alert ('The item has been added.');
54       document.getElementById('item').value =
         null;
55   }
56
57   </script>
58
59   <style>
60   body {margin:10px;}
61   p {font-size: 16px;}
62   </style>
63
64   </head>
65
66   <body>
67
68   <h3>To-Do List</h3>
69
70   <input type="text" id="item" />
     <button id="btnAddItem" onclick="addItem()">
     Add Item</button><hr />
71
72   </body>
73   </html>
```

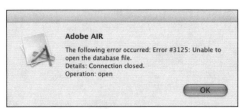

Figure 11.8 The application spits out this error message if there is a problem connecting to the database. (I removed the database file to make this error happen.)

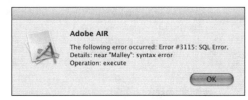

Figure 11.9 If the application didn't safeguard against using apostrophes in values, the task *Buy O'Malley Wedding Gift* would create this error.

Selecting Records

The next logical step when working with a database is to retrieve stored data from it. This is accomplished using a SELECT query, and it begins just like the CREATE and INSERT queries. Assuming you've already created the SQLConnection and File objects (conn and db, respectively), then added the event listeners and opened the database, the next steps would be:

```
var sql = new air.SQLStatement();
sql.sqlConnection = conn;
sql.addEventListener(air.SQLErrorEvent.
→ ERROR, dbError);
sql.addEventListener(air.SQLEvent.
→ RESULT, sqlResult);
sql.text = 'SELECT * FROM testing';
sql.execute();
```

Select queries differ from INSERT (and CREATE, UPDATE, and DELETE) queries in that they return a result set—the stored data that matched the query—that must be handled. That process would be accomplished within the function that handles the air.SQLEvent. RESULT event. To start, fetch the results:

```
var results = sql.getResult();
```

You should then confirm that the results aren't empty (which would be the case if the SELECT query ran successfully but didn't return any matches):

```
if (results.data != null) {
```

Assuming that the result set isn't empty, you can access every returned row using a loop:

```
for (var i = 0; i < results.data.length;
→ i++) {
    // Do something with results.data[i].
}
```

In this loop, results.data is an array, where each element of that array represents one returned row. Within each element or row (results.data[i]), you have another array: the columns selected. Using the testing table example, where the table has two columns—id and something, you would therefore refer to results.data[i].id and results.data[i].something.

To apply this knowledge to the to-do list application, the list of existing events will be pulled from the database and displayed (**Figure 11.10**).

Figure 11.10 The list of to-do items is displayed in the bottom section of the application window.

To select records:

1. Open Script 11.4 in your text editor or IDE, if it is not already.

2. Create a second SQLStatement object (**Script 11.5**):

   ```
   var select = new air.SQLStatement();
   ```

   Although you could reuse the insert SQLStatement object for the SELECT query, it's actually better if you don't (see the debugging tips at the end of the next chapter). So a new SQLStatement is declared and is called select.

3. Add two new event listeners:

   ```
   select.addEventListener(air.
   → SQLEvent.RESULT, listItems);
   select.addEventListener(air.
   → SQLErrorEvent.ERROR, dbError);
   ```

   The select object will use the same error handling function as the other two objects but have its own SQLEvent.RESULT function called *listItems*.

4. Within the dbOpen() function, associate the new SQLStatement object with conn, and then call the showItems() function:

   ```
   select.sqlConnection = conn;
   showItems();
   ```

continues on page 225

Script 11.5 Now the application will display the current to-do list by selecting those records from the database.

```
   ⬤ ⬤ ⬤                                    Script
1    <html><!-- Script 11.5 -->
2    <head>
3    <title>To-Do List</title>
4    <script type="text/javascript" src="AIRAliases.js"></script>
5    <script type="text/javascript">
6
7    // Create the objects:
8    var conn = new air.SQLConnection();
9    var db = air.File.applicationStorageDirectory.resolvePath('ch11.db');
10   var insert = new air.SQLStatement();
11   var select = new air.SQLStatement();
12
13   // Do the prep work after the application has loaded:
14   window.onload = function() {
15       document.getElementById('btnAddItem').disabled = true;
16
17       // Add the event handlers:
18       conn.addEventListener(air.SQLEvent.OPEN, dbOpen);
19       conn.addEventListener(air.SQLErrorEvent.ERROR, dbError);
20       insert.addEventListener(air.SQLEvent.RESULT, insertResult);
21       insert.addEventListener(air.SQLErrorEvent.ERROR, dbError);
22
23       select.addEventListener(air.SQLEvent.RESULT, listItems);
24       select.addEventListener(air.SQLErrorEvent.ERROR, dbError);
25
26       conn.openAsync(db, air.SQLMode.UPDATE);
27   } // End of anonymous function.
28
```

(script continues on next page)

Script 11.5 *continued*

```
29    // When the application has closed, close the database connection:
30    window.onbeforeunload = function() {
31        conn.close();
32    }
33
34    // Function called when the database is opened.
35    function dbOpen() {
36
37        // Associate the connection with the SQLStatements:
38        insert.sqlConnection = conn;
39        select.sqlConnection = conn;
40
41        // Show the current list of items:
42        showItems();
43
44        document.getElementById('btnAddItem').disabled = false;
45    } // End of dbOpen() function.
46
47    // Function for reporting errors.
48    function dbError(e) {
49        alert("The following error occurred: " + e.error.message + "\nDetails: " + e.error.details +
              "\nOperation: " + e.error.operation);
50    }
51
52    // Function called when the user clicks 'Add Item'.
53    function addItem() {
54        var item = document.getElementById('item').value;
55        if (item.length > 0) {
56            item = item.replace(/'/g, "'''");
57            insert.text = "INSERT INTO todo (item) VALUES ('" + item + "')";
58            insert.execute();
59        } // End of item.length IF.
60    } // End of addItem() function.
61
62    // Function called when an INSERT works.
63    function insertResult() {
64        alert ('The item has been added.');
65        document.getElementById('item').value = null;
66
67        // Update the list:
68        showItems();
69
70    } // End of insertResult() function.
71
72    // Function that selects all the items.
73    function showItems() {
74        select.text = 'SELECT id, item FROM todo ORDER BY added ASC';
75        select.execute();
76    } // End of showItems() function.
77
78    // Function that adds the items to the page.
79    function listItems() {
80
```

(script continues on next page)

Script 11.5 *continued*

```
81      // If the list already exists, remove it:
82      if (document.getElementById( 'list' )) {
83          document.body.removeChild( document.getElementById('list') );
84      }
85
86      // Create a DIV:
87      var div = document.createElement('div');
88      div.setAttribute('id', 'list');
89
90      // Variable used to add elements:
91      var p = null;
92
93      // Get the results of the query:
94      var results = select.getResult();
95      if (results.data != null) { // Some records returned!
96
97          // Loop through the results:
98          for (var i = 0; i < results.data.length; i++) {
99
100             p = document.createElement('p');
101
102             // Show the item:
103             p.innerText = results.data[i].item;
104
105             // Add to the DIV:
106             div.appendChild(p);
107
108         } // End of FOR loop.
109
110     } else { // No records returned!
111         div.innerText = 'There are currently no to-do items.';
112     }
113
114     // Add the DIV to the page:
115     document.body.appendChild(div);
116
117 } // End of listItems() function.
118
119 </script>
120
121 <style>
122 body {margin:10px;}
123 p {font-size: 16px;}
124 </style>
125
126 </head>
127
128 <body>
129
130 <h3>To-Do List</h3>
131
132 <input type="text" id="item" /> <button id="btnAddItem" onclick="addItem()">Add Item</button><hr />
133
134 </body>
135 </html>
```

When using asynchronous functions and event listeners, the logic of an application can become muddled. In step 3 it was established that the `listItems()` function will be called when the SELECT query returns a positive result. But the query still needs to be defined and executed. That will take place within the `showItems()` function. Essentially, it starts the process of showing the list of to-do items, so it's called within the `doOpen()` function.

5. Define the `showItems()` function:

```
function showItems() {
    select.text = 'SELECT id, item
    ↪ FROM todo ORDER BY added ASC';
    select.execute();
}
```

This function does two things: It defines the query to be run and then calls the `execute()` method. The function selects two values from each row in the `todo` table in the order in which they were added.

6. Begin defining the `listItems()` function:

```
function listItems() {
    if (document.
    ↪ getElementById( 'list' )) {
        document.body.
        ↪ removeChild( document.
        ↪ getElementById( 'list' ) );
    }
    var div = document.
    ↪ createElement('div');
    div.setAttribute('id', 'list');
    var p = null;
```

As stated, this function will be called once the SELECT query has returned a result. Its role is to fetch those results and display them. Doing that requires adding elements to the Document Object Model (DOM). Every item will be placed within a paragraph that's part of a DIV whose id attribute will have a value of *list*.

This function starts by checking if such an element already exists. If so, it should be removed. This would be the case after a user has added another item, at which time the list needs to be updated (i.e., removed and re-created). This function then starts the process of creating the necessary elements and variables.

7. Fetch and validate the query results:

```
var results = select.getResult();
if (results.data != null) {
    for (var i = 0; i < results.data.
    ↪ length; i++) {
```

First, the results are fetched by calling the `getResult()` method of the SQLStatement object. Second, a check ensures that the results aren't empty, meaning that some records were returned. Third, a for loop is defined that will be used to access every returned record.

8. Within the for loop, add the item to the page:

```
p = document.createElement('p');
p.innerText = results.data[i].item;
div.appendChild(p);
```

First, a new item of type paragraph is created. Then its innerText attribute—the value between the opening and closing tags—is set to the value of the item column in the current row.

Finally, the paragraph is added to the DIV.

continues on next page

9. Complete the `for` loop and the `if` conditional:

```
} // End of FOR loop.
} else { // No records returned!
  div.innerText = 'There are
  → currently no to-do items.';
}
```

If the user doesn't have any current to-do items, a message is added to the DIV instead of a series of paragraphs (**Figure 11.11**).

10. Complete the `listItems()` function:

```
document.body.appendChild(div);
} // End of listItems() function.
```

The function just needs to add the DIV to the page.

11. Call the `showItems()` function within the `insertResult()` function:

```
showItems();
```

The `showItems()` function, which starts the process of displaying the to-do list, is called by the anonymous function that runs after the page has loaded. But it needs to be called again here after a user has added a new item. If that step wasn't taken, the just-added task wouldn't show in the list until the user reran the application (and that just won't do).

12. Save, test, debug, and run the completed application.

✔ Tips

■ If you have an application that only needs to select records from a database and will never alter its contents (via updates or deletions), you can open the database in `air.SQLMode.READ` mode.

■ There is a series of SQL classes and functionality defined in Adobe AIR for accessing a database's *schema*. The schema represents information about a database: what tables it contains, what columns are in those tables, and so forth. One possible use for this information would be if you wanted to create an Adobe AIR application for managing SQLite databases. See the AIR documentation for details on these classes.

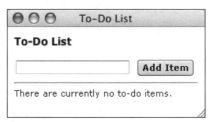

Figure 11.11 If the user doesn't have any tasks to be done (which is to say that the todo table is empty), the user will see a message at the bottom of the window.

SELECTING RECORDS

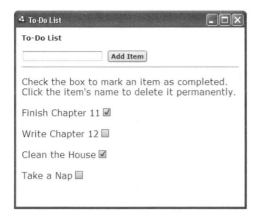

Figure 11.12 Another look at the complete application (similar to what's shown on Mac OS X in Figure 11.5).

Updating and Deleting Records

Thus far you've learned how to execute CREATE, INSERT, and SELECT queries. These are the most important three, but two more still need to be covered: UPDATE and DELETE. Both are executed just like every other query but handling the results is much more like an INSERT than a SELECT, because no records will be returned by them.

Code that both updates and deletes records in a table would look like this (without error handling and creating the requisite user-defined functions):

```
var conn = new air.SQLConnection();
var db = air.File.
→ applicationStorageDirectory.
→ resolvePath('something.db');
conn.addEventListener(air.SQLEvent.OPEN,
→ dbOpen);
conn.openAsync(db, air.SQLMode.UPDATE);
var update = new air.SQLStatement();
update.sqlConnection = conn;
var delete = new air.SQLStatement();
delete.sqlConnection = conn;
update.addEventListener(air.SQLEvent.
→ RESULT, updateResult);
delete.addEventListener(air.SQLEvent.
→ RESULT, deleteResult);
update.text = 'UPDATE testing SET
→ something="new value" WHERE id=23';
update.execute();
delete.text = 'DELETE FROM testing WHERE
→ id=7482';
delete.execute();
```

With this in mind, the application will be expanded one last time, providing the user a check box to indicate if a task is completed or not and the ability to delete a task by clicking on its name (**Figure 11.12**).

To update and delete records:

1. Open Script 11.5 in your text editor or IDE, if it is not already.

2. Add two more SQLStatement objects (**Script 11.6**).

   ```
   var update = new air.SQLStatement();
   var del = new air.SQLStatement();
   ```

   It may seem like overkill for this application to contain four different SQLStatement objects (one for each query type), but it really is best to do it this way. The result will be better performance and a less likelihood of bugs.

3. Within the first anonymous function, add event listeners for the new objects:

   ```
   update.addEventListener(air.
   → SQLErrorEvent.ERROR, dbError);
   del.addEventListener(air.SQLEvent.
   → RESULT, deleteResult);
   del.addEventListener(air.
   → SQLErrorEvent.ERROR, dbError);
   ```

   Both objects will have error event listeners but only the delete object gets a result event listener. That's because the update will be triggered by the user clicking the check box (see Figure 11.12), so an effect of the user's action (i.e., the box being marked checked or unchecked) will already be apparent to the user.

4. Within the dbOpen() method, associate the new objects with the connection:

   ```
   update.sqlConnection = conn;
   del.sqlConnection = conn;
   ```

5. Within the showItems() function, change the SELECT query so that it also retrieves the completed value from the database:

   ```
   select.text = 'SELECT id, item,
   → completed FROM todo ORDER BY
   → added ASC';
   ```

The check box next to each item (see Figure 11.12) will indicate if a task has been completed or not. To know this, the completed value for each item also must be fetched from the database.

6. Within the listItems() function, declare two more variables:

   ```
   var p, c, span = null;
   ```

   This function will need a bit more work. Originally, it created a new paragraph for each item, and then added the paragraph to the DIV. Now each item needs to have the item text and a check box as separate components within the paragraph, so more elements are needed. The desired end result is that each item will be added to the DOM in a format like this:

   ```
   <p><span id="#" onclick=
   → "deleteItem();">Item text.
   → </span><input type="checkbox"
   → id="#" onclick="updateItem()"></p>
   ```

   That's the target HTML to create, replacing both instances of # with the item's actual ID value from the database.

7. Remove the existing three lines from the for loop (see Script 11.5) and start by adding these lines:

   ```
   p = document.createElement('p');
   span = document.createElement('span');
   c = document.createElement('input');
   c.setAttribute('type', 'checkbox');
   ```

   Rather than trying to tell you what changes to make to the existing list-Items() code, just remove the existing three lines and start writing the for loop's body from scratch. It begins by creating three elements, making the input element a type of *checkbox*.

continues on page 232

Script 11.6 By adding check boxes, the user can mark a to-do list item as completed or not. Another addition to the to-do list management application is the ability to permanently delete any item by clicking its name.

```
1    <html><!-- Script 11.6 -->
2    <head>
3    <title>To-Do List</title>
4    <script type="text/javascript" src="AIRAliases.js"></script>
5    <script type="text/javascript">
6
7    // Create the objects:
8    var conn = new air.SQLConnection();
9    var db = air.File.applicationStorageDirectory.resolvePath('ch11.db');
10   var insert = new air.SQLStatement();
11   var select = new air.SQLStatement();
12   var update = new air.SQLStatement();
13   var del = new air.SQLStatement();
14
15   // Do the prep work after the application has loaded:
16   window.onload = function() {
17       document.getElementById('btnAddItem').disabled = true;
18
19       // Add the event handlers:
20       conn.addEventListener(air.SQLEvent.OPEN, dbOpen);
21       conn.addEventListener(air.SQLErrorEvent.ERROR, dbError);
22       insert.addEventListener(air.SQLEvent.RESULT, insertResult);
23       insert.addEventListener(air.SQLErrorEvent.ERROR, dbError);
24       select.addEventListener(air.SQLEvent.RESULT, listItems);
25       select.addEventListener(air.SQLErrorEvent.ERROR, dbError);
26
27       update.addEventListener(air.SQLErrorEvent.ERROR, dbError);
28
29       del.addEventListener(air.SQLEvent.RESULT, deleteResult);
30       del.addEventListener(air.SQLErrorEvent.ERROR, dbError);
31
32       conn.openAsync(db, air.SQLMode.UPDATE);
33   } // End of anonymous function.
34
35   // When the application has closed, close the database connection:
36   window.onbeforeunload = function() {
37       conn.close();
38   }
39
40   // Function called when the database is opened.
41   function dbOpen() {
42
43       // Associate the connection with the SQLStatements:
44       insert.sqlConnection = conn;
45       select.sqlConnection = conn;
46       update.sqlConnection = conn;
47       del.sqlConnection = conn;
48
49       showItems();
50       document.getElementById('btnAddItem').disabled = false;
51   } // End of dbOpen() function.
52
```

(script continues on next page)

UPDATING AND DELETING RECORDS

Script 11.6 *continued*

```
53     // Function for reporting errors.
54     function dbError(e) {
55         alert("The following error occurred: " + e.error.message + "\nDetails: " + e.error.details +
           "\nOperation: " + e.error.operation);
56     }
57
58     // Function called when the user clicks 'Add Item'.
59     function addItem() {
60         var item = document.getElementById('item').value;
61         if (item.length > 0) {
62             item = item.replace(/'/g, "'''");
63             insert.text = "INSERT INTO todo (item) VALUES ('" + item + "')";
64             insert.execute();
65             showItems();
66         } // End of item.length IF.
67     } // End of addItem() function.
68
69     // Function called when an INSERT works.
70     function insertResult() {
71         alert ('The item has been added.');
72         document.getElementById('item').value = null;
73         showItems();
74     } // End of insertResult() function.
75
76     // Function that selects all the items.
77     function showItems() {
78         select.text = 'SELECT id, item, completed FROM todo ORDER BY added ASC';
79         select.execute();
80     } // End of showItems() function.
81
82     // Function that adds the items to the page.
83     function listItems() {
84
85         // If the list already exists, remove it:
86         if (document.getElementById('list')) {
87             document.body.removeChild(document.getElementById('list'));
88         }
89
90         // Create a DIV:
91         var div = document.createElement('div');
92         div.setAttribute('id', 'list');
93
94         // Variables used to add elements:
95         var p, c, span = null;
96
97         // Get the results of the query:
98         var results = select.getResult();
99         if (results.data != null) { // Some records returned!
100            // Loop through the results:
101            for (var i = 0; i < results.data.length; i++) {
102
103                // Create the elements:
104                p = document.createElement('p');
105                span = document.createElement('span');
106                c = document.createElement('input');
107                c.setAttribute('type', 'checkbox');
108
```

(script continues on next page)

Script 11.6 *continued*

```
                                                    Script
109         // Mark completed items as checked:
110         if (results.data[i].completed != null) {
111             c.setAttribute('checked', 'checked');
112         }
113
114         // Each ID attribute is its database ID:
115         c.setAttribute('id', results.data[i].id);
116         span.setAttribute('id', results.data[i].id);
117
118         // Show the item:
119         span.innerText = results.data[i].item;
120
121         // Add event listeners:
122         c.addEventListener('click', updateItem, false);
123         span.addEventListener('click', deleteItem, false);
124
125         // Add to the DIV:
126         p.appendChild(span);
127         p.appendChild(c);
128         div.appendChild(p);
129
130      } // End of FOR loop.
131   } else { // No records returned!
132      div.innerText = 'There are currently no to-do items.';
133   }
134   // Add the DIV to the page:
135   document.body.appendChild(div);
136 } // End of listItems() function.
137
138 // Function called when a DELETE works.
139 function deleteResult() {
140    alert ('The item has been deleted.');
141    showItems();
142 } // End of deleteResult() function.
143
144 // Function for deleting items.
145 function deleteItem(which) {
146
147    // Get the item's info:
148    var id = which.target.id;
149    var item = which.target.innerText;
150
151    // Confirm with the user prior to deleting:
152    if (confirm('Delete "' + item + '"?')) {
153
154        del.text = 'DELETE FROM todo WHERE id='+ id;
155        del.execute();
156
157    } // End of confirm IF.
158
159 } // End of deleteItem() function.
160
161 // Function for marking items as completed.
162 function updateItem(which) {
163
```

(script continues on next page)

8. If the item is complete, check the box:

```
if (results.data[i].completed
→ != null) {
  c.setAttribute('checked',
  → 'checked');
}
```

The results.data[i].completed variable refers to the returned completed value from the database for the currently accessed item. This column will either contain a date/time value or null. If it's not null, the box should be checked, indicating that the user had previously marked the task as completed.

9. Add id attributes to the span and check box, and then add the item text to the span.

```
c.setAttribute('id', results.
→ data[i].id);
span.setAttribute('id', results.
→ data[i].id);
span.innerText = results.data[i].
→ item;
```

The span and the check box will be the elements that the user clicks on to make something happen: delete the item and mark it as completed, respectively. For this reason, each of these elements on the page needs to have an id attribute whose value matches the item's database ID. That's what the first two lines do.

10. Add event listeners to the span and the check box:

```
c.addEventListener('click',
→ updateItem, false);
span.addEventListener('click',
→ deleteItem, false);
```

Script 11.6 *continued*

```
164    // Get the item's ID:
165    var id = which.target.id;
166
167    // Make the query:
168    update.text = 'UPDATE todo SET
       completed=';
169    if (which.target.checked) {
170      update.text += 'CURRENT_TIMESTAMP';
171    } else {
172      update.text += 'NULL';
173    }
174    update.text += ' WHERE id='+ id;
175
176    update.execute();
177
178 } // End of updateItem() function.
179
180 </script>
181
182 <style>
183 body {margin:10px;}
184 p {font-size: 16px;}
185 </style>
186
187 </head>
188
189 <body>
190
191 <h3>To-Do List</h3>
192
193 <input type="text" id="item" />
    <button id="btnAddItem" onclick="addItem()">
    Add Item</button><hr />
194 <p>Check the box to mark an item as
    completed. Click the item's name to
    delete it permanently.</p>
195
196 </body>
197 </html>
```

If this application performed synchronous communications with SQLite, I would simply add onclick attributes to both items, like so:

```
c.setAttribute('onclick',
→'updateItem(' + results.data[i].
→id + ');');
```

However, because the program performs asynchronous communication, I must formally add JavaScript event listeners to the objects using this code.

11. Add the items to the DIV:

```
p.appendChild(span);
p.appendChild(c);
div.appendChild(p);
```

12. Create the deleteResult() function:

```
function deleteResult() {
  alert ('The item has been
  →deleted.');
  showItems();
}
```

This function will be called when the delete object returns a positive result. It should alert the user that the item was deleted, and then refresh the list by calling showItems().

13. Begin the deleteItem() function:

```
function deleteItem(which) {
  var id = which.target.id;
  var item = which.target.innerText;
```

Figure 11.13 The act of deleting a task is confirmed before being executed on the database.

This function will be called when the user clicks on a task's name in the list. At that time, this function will be passed an event, which I'm assigning to a variable called *which*.

The function needs to run a DELETE query on the table using the task's primary key in a WHERE clause. To get that value for the clicked on item, refer to which.target.id. The *which.target* part refers to the object that was the recipient of the action (the clicking). Its id attribute represents the associated database ID. The delete alert will confirm, by name, that the user wants to delete the task (**Figure 11.13**). To do that, the item's innerText value, which is the actual task, is needed.

14. Complete the deleteItem() function:

```
  if (confirm('Delete "' + item
  →+ '"?')) {
    del.text = 'DELETE FROM todo
    →WHERE id='+ id;
    del.execute();
  } // End of confirm IF.
} // End of deleteItem() function.
```

The confirmation prompt (see Figure 11.13) is a nice little safety check. Then the query is defined and executed.

15. Begin the updateItem() function:

```
function updateItem(which) {
  var id = which.target.id;
  update.text = 'UPDATE todo SET
  →completed=';
```

This function is very similar to deleteItem(). It first determines the id value of the item that was checked, and then it defines and runs an UPDATE query on the database.

continues on next page

UPDATING AND DELETING RECORDS

16. Complete the `updateItem()` function:

```
if (which.target.checked) {
    update.text +=
    → 'CURRENT_TIMESTAMP';
} else {
    update.text += 'NULL';
}
update.text += ' WHERE id='+ id;
update.execute();
} // End of updateItem() function.
```

This function could be called under two conditions. In the first, the user checked a box, meaning that the item should be marked as completed by setting its `completed` value in the table to the current date and time. In the second condition, the user unchecks a previously checked box, in which case the `completed` value in the table should be set back to `null`. The query is therefore defined based on the current value of `which.target.checked`.

17. Within the body, add some instructions for the user.

```
<p>Check the box to mark an item as
→ completed. Click the item's name
→ to delete it permanently.</p>
```

18. Save, test, debug, and run the completed application (**Figures 11.14** and **11.15**).

✔ Tips

■ Technically, the value of the `id` attribute in HTML can't begin with a number. But that kind of restriction is more applicable to HTML run in a Web browser that may be formally validated. But if this choice bothers you, you could change each value to *item#* (where # represents the database ID value), and then chop off the *item* part in the functions to get to the ID.

■ Clicking on an item's name to delete it really isn't the best or most logical interface, but I wanted to do something simple in that regard. Alternatively, you could create a delete button or image that when clicked passes the item's ID to the `deleteItem()` function.

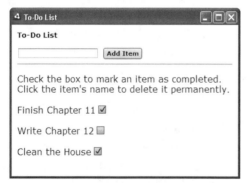

Figure 11.14 The result after clicking OK in the confirmation prompt (see Figure 11.13 for the prompt and compare the list with that in Figure 11.12).

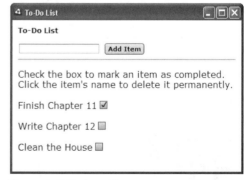

Figure 11.15 The house became messy again, so I unchecked the *Clean the House* task.

UPDATING AND DELETING RECORDS

DATABASE TECHNIQUES

Chapter 11, "Working with Databases," covers all the basics for using an SQLite database in your Adobe AIR applications. Every interaction with a database that you'll ever perform will use that information. But there are some other concepts and general techniques that you should also be aware of, and that's the focus here.

This chapter teaches some new, more advanced ideas, as well as demonstrates a handful of best practices. To start, you'll learn how to distribute a database with an application rather than having the application create it from scratch. The next three topics—prepared statements, fetching SELECT results in groups, and using transactions—can be used to improve the efficiency and security of your programs. The chapter concludes with more recommendations for improving performance, as well as a bunch of tips to aid you in debugging the inevitable database-related glitch.

Distributing Databases

The second example in the previous chapter includes the code for creating a new database. Your applications are obviously capable of doing that, but it actually doesn't make much sense to include all that functionality in an application when the database only ever needs to be created once. A better solution is to create the database when you write the application, package the database with it, and then have the application copy the database to its final destination when the user runs the program for the first time. This is possible with SQLite databases, because the same database file can be transferred from one operating system to the next without complication (another reason for SQLite's popularity).

In the next sequence of steps, you'll learn how you can distribute databases with the programs you create. The specific database to be created will be for banking-like transactions and will be used in the rest of the examples in this chapter. Before getting into the steps, I should explain one fact: computers are tricky when it comes to working with numbers. As an example, if I stored the value 23.50 in an SQLite column defined as REAL, and then added 1 to this value, the result may end up as 24.4999999. Often these little quirks aren't a problem, but when dealing with money, you can't be too careful. The solution in this example will be to represent all dollar amounts (or whatever currency you want to work worth) in cents. So 23.50 will be stored as 2350.

To distribute databases:

1. Define the SQL commands necessary to create the database.

   Database design is a big but very important topic, and I cover it in some of my other books (you can also find some

tutorials online by searching for *database design* and *database normalization*). The following SQL commands are what I devised for creating the database to be used throughout the rest of the chapter:

```
CREATE TABLE accounts (id INTEGER
→ PRIMARY KEY AUTOINCREMENT, name
→ TEXT NOT NULL, balance INTEGER
→ NOT NULL CHECK( (typeof(balance) =
→ 'integer') AND (balance > 0) ) )
```

and

```
CREATE TABLE transfers (id INTEGER
→ PRIMARY KEY AUTOINCREMENT, from_id
→ INTEGER NOT NULL, to_id INTEGER
→ NOT NULL, amount INTEGER
→ CHECK( (typeof(amount) =
→ 'integer') AND (amount > 0) ) )
```

The first table is the most important: It contains an ID column (the primary key), a column to store a person's name, and a column to store the person's account balance. In a real application, the person's name would be divided into two (or three) columns, but I'm simplifying this a bit here.

The second table will record the history of all transactions. For this chapter's examples, this means the transfers between accounts. The accounts table will always be updated to reflect current balances, but it's good to have another record of what has occurred. This second table has one column for the transfer ID, one for the person from whom the money is coming, and another for the person to whom the money is going. A fourth column reflects the amount being transferred. Fully fleshed out, I would likely also add a column that stores the date and time of each transaction.

Note as well that in these two tables I use *constraints* for added data integrity. This topic is discussed in the "Adding Constraints" sidebar.

2. Create the application's database on your own computer.

You can create an SQL database by writing an AIR application that does it for you (use Script 11.2 as an example, but you'll need to assign each CREATE TABLE command to an SQLStatement object, and then execute each). You can also create the database using the command-line sqlite3 client that comes with the software (if you've formally installed SQLite on your computer). A third option is to download and use one of the many third-party applications that exist for creating and managing SQLite databases.

If you don't want to go through the steps of creating the database yourself, you can download it from this book's corresponding Web site at www.DMCInsights.com/air/ (see the Downloads page).

3. Copy the database file to the project's directory.

For the purposes of this chapter, the name of the database created in step 2 is *ch12.db*.

4. In your project's primary HTML file, begin a new JavaScript function (**Script 12.1**):

```
window.onload = function() {
}
```

continues on next page

Script 12.1 This script simply demonstrates the code that you would use to distribute a database with an application.

```
1   <html><!-- Script 12.1 -->
2   <head>
3   <title>Chapter 12</title>
4   <script type="text/javascript" src="AIRAliases.js"></script>
5   <script type="text/javascript">
6
7   // Function to be called when the application loads.
8   window.onload = function() {
9
10      // Database file:
11      var db = air.File.applicationStorageDirectory.resolvePath('ch12.db');
12
13      // Copy the database file to the storage
14      // directory if it's not already there.
15      if (!db.exists) {
16          var original = air.File.applicationDirectory.resolvePath('ch12.db');
17          original.copyTo(db);
18      }
19
20  }
21
22  </script>
23  </head>
24  <body>
25  </body>
26  </html>
```

The premise of the steps for distributing databases is that the database file will be bundled with the application, so it doesn't need to be created on the user's machine. After the program has been installed, the database will be in the application's directory. That's not where you want the database to be when the application starts writing data to it. Instead, the database needs to be moved to the application's *storage* directory. That's what will happen within this anonymous function.

5. Create a reference to the database file:

```
var db = air.File.
→ applicationStorageDirectory.
→ resolvePath('ch12.db');
```

Every application that uses a database also needs a `File` object that refers to it. As mentioned in step 3, the database that the running application uses needs to be in the application's storage directory and, in this case, called *ch12.db*.

6. If the file doesn't exist, copy it from the application's directory to the application's storage directory:

```
if (!db.exists) {
    var original = air.File.
    → applicationDirectory.
    → resolvePath('ch12.db');
    original.copyTo(db);
}
```

DISTRIBUTING DATABASES

Adding Constraints

As explained in Chapter 11, SQLite is very lenient when it comes to working with data types. Only four types are supported by the database, but you can actually store data of one type, like a string, in a column of another type, like a real number (with very few exceptions). SQLite allows you to define columns using more specific data types, like `CHAR(10)` instead of `TEXT`, but SQLite won't enforce the implied restrictions.

One thing you can do is add *constraints* to columns when creating the table. Constraints are just part of a column's definition that restrict what values can be stored in that column. Although they've been present in SQLite for a while, they haven't been enforced until version 3.3.0.

One constraint is `UNIQUE`, which means that no two rows can have the exact same value for that column or combination of columns. You can also define a column as `NOT NULL`, meaning that every row must contain a value for that column. Columns can also be given a `DEFAULT` value, which will be used when no value is provided for that column. Finally, as in this chapter's example, you can add a `CHECK` constraint. To do so, follow the column's type with *CHECK*, followed by an expression in parentheses. In this chapter's two tables, `CHECK` constraints ensure that the account balances and transaction amounts are positive integers. To do so, two clauses are part of the expression, joined by an `AND`. The first clause—`typeof(col) = 'integer'`—specifies that the type of the value being inserted must be an integer. The second clause—`col > 0`—simply specifies that the value must be greater than 0. These two checks will help protect the integrity of the data being stored.

In all cases, if the values used in an `INSERT` or `UPDATE` query fail to pass a constraint, the query won't take effect and an error will be raised (which will need to be handled by your program).

To end up with the database in the application's storage directory, when the program runs, it should check for the presence of the database file in its final destination. If the database isn't found there, the original should be copied from the application's directory.

That's all there is to it. The rest of the application can use the database normally.

7. Be certain to include the database file when you package the final application (**Figure 12.1**).

✔ Tips

■ Using this method of distributing a database with an application has an added benefit: If the program has a "reinstall" or "clear database" functionality, all that would be necessary would be to replace the current database (in the application storage directory) with the distributed one (from the application directory).

■ You can create backups of an application's data (if stored in a database) by simply copying the database file to another location.

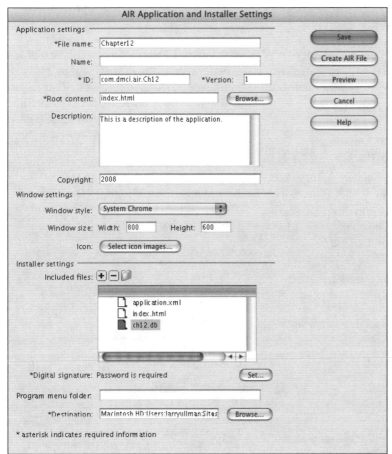

Figure 12.1 To distribute a database with an application, place it in your project's directory, and then include that file when building the actual .air file. Here, using Dreamweaver CS3 with the Adobe AIR Extension, you can see the database listed in the included files.

Using Prepared Statements

In the INSERT example in the previous chapter, it was noted that an admitted security hole was present. Namely, the user's input was being added to the query without taking extra precautions. This allows for *SQL injection attacks*, where the user purposefully enters malicious text in an attempt to break, damage, or simply learn something about the database. With some database applications, SQL injection attacks can be prevented by using an escaping function that sanctifies the submitted text. That's not an option with SQLite, but there is another solution.

Most database applications support *prepared statements*, and SQLite is no exception. The premise behind a prepared statement is that the query to be executed is defined using placeholders for specific data:

```
var sql = new air.SQLStatement();
sql.sqlConnection = conn;
sql.text = 'INSERT INTO testing
→ (something) VALUES (?)';
```

The question mark represents the actual value to be used in the query. Note that even though the value to be used in this particular case will be a text string, no quotation marks are placed around the question mark.

The next step is to associate values with the placeholders. When using question marks, which is to say *unnamed placeholders*, assign values to them by using the SQLStatement's parameters attribute. It's an indexed array, beginning at 0:

```
sql.parameters[0] = 'text to be
→ inserted';
```

Then execute the query:

```
sql.execute();
```

The end result of these steps is the same as literally executing INSERT INTO testing (something) VALUES ('text to be inserted').

Instead of using question marks for placeholders, you can name the parameters, starting with either a colon or @, followed by a simple identifier:

```
sql.text = 'INSERT INTO users (username,
→ email, password) VALUES (@un, @e, @p)';
sql.parameters['@un'] = 'troutster';
sql.parameters['@e'] = 'd@example.com';
sql.parameters['@p'] = 'somepass';
sql.execute();
```

Whether you use named or unnamed parameters is really up to you. For simple queries, I prefer to go the unnamed route.

There are two benefits to using prepared statements. The first is the improved security: Data used in a query is separated from the actual query and aren't vulnerable to SQL injection attacks. The second benefit is performance: The query is sent to the database and parsed (checked for syntax and validity) only once. Multiple executions of the same query with different values will go more quickly than repeatedly executing literal queries.

To practice this, let's create an application for adding accounts to the database created in the previous section of the chapter (**Figure 12.2**).

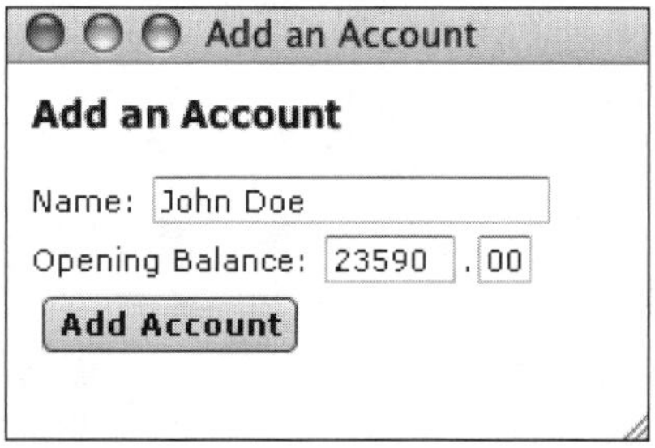

Figure 12.2 This program provides a way to add new accounts. The data entered here will be inserted into the database using prepared statements (see Script 12.2).

To use prepared statements:

1. In your project's primary HTML file, create the required objects (**Script 12.2**):

   ```
   var conn = new air.SQLConnection();
   var db = air.File.
   → applicationStorageDirectory.
   → resolvePath('ch12.db');
   var insert = new air.SQLStatement();
   ```

   This application will use three objects. The first is of type SQLConnection, which is required to connect to a database. The second is of type File, representing the actual database file. The third is a SQLStatement object, which will represent the query to be executed.

2. Create an anonymous function that does the prep work:

   ```
   window.onload = function() {
      conn.addEventListener(air.
      → SQLEvent.OPEN, dbOpen);
      conn.addEventListener(air.
      → SQLErrorEvent.ERROR, dbError);
      insert.addEventListener(air.
      → SQLEvent.RESULT, insertResult);
      insert.addEventListener(air.
      → SQLErrorEvent.ERROR, dbError);
      conn.openAsync(db, air.SQLMode.
      → UPDATE);
   }
   ```

   After the application has loaded, this function will be called, performing the necessary setup (see the previous chapter for explanations on these lines).

   continues on page 243

Script 12.2 This program uses prepared statements with its INSERT query for improved security and performance.

```
 1   <html><!-- Script 12.2 -->
 2   <head>
 3   <title>Add an Account</title>
 4   <script type="text/javascript" src="AIRAliases.js"></script>
 5   <script type="text/javascript">
 6
 7   // Create the objects:
 8   var conn = new air.SQLConnection();
 9   var db = air.File.applicationStorageDirectory.resolvePath('ch12.db');
10   var insert = new air.SQLStatement();
11
12   // Do the prep work after the application has loaded:
13   window.onload = function() {
14
15      // Add the event handlers:
16      conn.addEventListener(air.SQLEvent.OPEN, dbOpen);
17      conn.addEventListener(air.SQLErrorEvent.ERROR, dbError);
18      insert.addEventListener(air.SQLEvent.RESULT, insertResult);
19      insert.addEventListener(air.SQLErrorEvent.ERROR, dbError);
20
21      // Open the database:
22      conn.openAsync(db, air.SQLMode.UPDATE);
23
24   } // End of anonymous function.
25
```

(script continues on next page)

Script 12.2 *continued*

```
⊜ ⊖ ⊜                                    📄 Script
26   // When the application has closed, close the database connection:
27   window.onbeforeunload = function() {
28       conn.close();
29   }
30
31   // Function for reporting errors.
32   function dbError(e) {
33       alert('An error occurred.');
34   }
35
36   // Function called when the database is opened.
37   function dbOpen() {
38       insert.sqlConnection = conn;
39   }
40
41   // Function called when the user clicks 'Add Item'.
42   function addAccount() {
43
44       // Insert the item:
45       insert.text = 'INSERT INTO accounts (name, balance) VALUES (?, ?)';
46       insert.parameters[0] = document.getElementById('name').value;
47       insert.parameters[1] = +(document.getElementById('dollars').value + document.
         getElementById('cents').value);
48       insert.execute();
49
50   } // End of addItem() function.
51
52   // Function called when an INSERT works.
53   function insertResult() {
54
55       // Notify the user:
56       alert ('The account has been added.');
57
58       // Reset the inputs:
59       document.getElementById('name').value = null;
60       document.getElementById('dollars').value = null;
61       document.getElementById('cents').value = '00';
62
63   } // End of the insertResult() function.
64
65   </script>
66
67   </head>
68
69   <body style="margin:10px;">
70
71   <h3>Add an Account</h3>
72
73   Name: <input type="text" id="name"><br>Opening Balance:  <input type="text" id="dollars"
     size="6">.<input type="text" id="cents" value="00" size="2" maxlength="2"><br><button onclick=
     "addAccount()">Add Account</button>
74
75   </body>
76   </html>
```

USING PREPARED STATEMENTS

3. Create a second anonymous function:

```
window.onbeforeunload = function() {
    conn.close();
}
```

This anonymous function will be called right before the application quits. Its sole purpose is to close the database connection.

4. Create an error handling function:

```
function dbError(e) {
    alert('An error occurred.');
}
```

Per the event listeners added in step 2, this function will be called when a connection or query error happens. In this example, not much is done, but see code in the "Handling Errors" section of the previous chapter for suggestions as to what information you could include in the alert (or see the debugging section at the end of this chapter).

5. Create the dbOpen() function.

```
function dbOpen() {
    insert.sqlConnection = conn;
}
```

Once the database connection is made, this function will be called. It associates the connection with the SQLStatement object. If you want, you could do what the example in the previous chapter did: disable the Add Account button in the anonymous function, and then reenable it here after the database connection has been established.

6. Define the addAccount() function:

```
function addAccount() {
    insert.text = 'INSERT INTO
 → accounts (name, balance) VALUES
 → (?, ?)';
```

```
    insert.parameters[0] = document.
 → getElementById('name').value;
    insert.parameters[1] = +(document.
 → getElementById('dollars').value
 → + document.getElementById
 → ('cents').value);
    insert.execute();
}
```

The application contains three text inputs and a button. When the user clicks the button, this function will be called. It defines and executes the query.

The query is first defined as a simple INSERT, populating two of the three columns in the accounts table (the id column will be automatically assigned a value). Placeholders are used in the query to represent the values to be used. Then the values are assigned to the insert. parameters attribute. Finally, the command is executed.

For the account balance, the value to be used will be the cents amount concatenated to the dollars amount (so 4390 and 35 become 439035; see the explanation before the "Distributing Databases" set of steps as to why this is necessary). Unfortunately, if you were to assign just that as the parameter value, the query would fail the constraint check because the value type would be a string, not an integer. The solution is to forcibly cast the value to a number by applying the unary plus operator to it. This is just a little trick that guarantees the value will be a number (alternatively, you could add 0 to the value to achieve the same result, although that wouldn't have the secondary benefit of guaranteeing that the number is positive).

continues on next page

To shorten the example, I omitted code that checks that all three form values aren't empty, but you should do that in a real application. You could also include JavaScript code that confirms that the entered balance is a positive integer (which the database will also check) instead of forcing it to be, and you could check that the cents input is two characters long.

7. Create the insertResult() function:

```
function insertResult() {
    alert ('The account has been
    ⇥ added.');
    document.getElementById('name').
    ⇥ value = null;
    document.getElementById('dollars')
    ⇥ .value = null;
    document.getElementById('cents').
    ⇥ value = '00';
}
```

This function will be called when the INSERT query returns a positive result (thanks to the event listener created in step 2). It alerts the user that the account was added (**Figure 12.3**), and then resets the values in the form (**Figure 12.4**). As you can also see in Figures 12.2 and 12.4, the cents input will be given a default value of *00*.

8. Within the body of the page, add three text inputs and a button:

```
Name: <input type="text"
⇥ id="name"><br>Opening Balance:
⇥ <input type="text" id="dollars"
⇥ size="6">.<input type="text"
⇥ id="cents" value="00" size="2"
⇥ maxlength="2"><br><button
⇥ onclick="addAccount()">Add
⇥ Account</button>
```

9. Save, test, debug, and run the completed application (**Figure 12.5**).

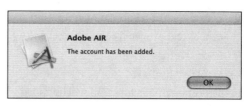

Figure 12.3 If the INSERT query works, the user will see this alert.

Figure 12.4 After an INSERT query works, the form is reset (the cents input has a default value of *00*).

Figure 12.5 Attempts to add an account without a positive balance (which would also happen if a nonnumber was entered, as in this figure) will result in an error because the INSERT query will be rejected by the constraints on the balance column.

✔ Tip

■ The prepared statements discussed here are also known as *inbound parameters*: Placeholders are used to represent values going into a database. SQLite does not support *outbound named parameters* (the association of values returned by a SELECT query with variables) like Oracle does.

USING PREPARED STATEMENTS

Fetching Records in Groups

In Chapter 11, the SELECT query used retrieved and displayed every returned record in one series of actions. If your query returns a lot of records, that methodology can lead to some application delays and choppiness, even when performing asynchronous database communications. As an alternative, you can fetch the results of a SELECT query in groups.

The execute() method of the SQLStatement object takes an optional first argument, which is the number of records to fetch:

```
sql.execute(10);
```

Figure 12.6 The list of every account stored in the database.

That command would return the first ten records matched by the SELECT query. Then the function associated with the air.Event. SQLResult event would be called. Within it you should make sure that some results were returned and handle those. This process is the same as using execute() normally:

```
function selectResult() {
    var results = sql.getResult();
    if (results.data != null) {
        // Handle the results.
    }
```

To fetch more of the records matched by the query, you then call the next() method, providing it with the maximum number of records to return. Before doing this, you should make sure that the application hasn't already fetched every returned record. With both these ideas in mind, the rest of the selectResult() function would look like this:

```
    if (!result.complete) {
        sql.next(10);
    }
} // End of selectResult() function.
```

If there are more records to fetch, the next ten will be requested, resulting in this function being called again. Those ten records will be handled, and then, if the result set hasn't been completely fetched, the next ten. This process will be repeated until all the records have been returned.

To demonstrate this, let's create an application that retrieves and displays every account entered into the ch12.db database (**Figure 12.6**). This will be written as a separate program from Script 12.2, but you could easily apply the knowledge and code demonstrated in Chapter 11 to put the INSERT and SELECT functionality within the same application.

To fetch results in groups:

1. In your project's primary HTML file, create the required objects (**Script 12.3**).

```
var conn = new air.SQLConnection();

var db = air.File.
→ applicationStorageDirectory.
→ resolvePath('ch12.db');

var select = new air.SQLStatement();
```

This program uses the same database populated by Script 12.2. Keep in mind that for this to work, both scripts must have the same application ID value (in the XML descriptor file) and publisher ID value (which comes from the certificate used to sign the .air file; this is not applicable if you are running the examples using the adl utility).

Script 12.3 By changing the way the execute() method is called, this application fetches the results of the SELECT statement in smaller groups.

```
1    <html><!-- Script 12.3 -->
2    <head>
3    <title>View All Accounts</title>
4    <script type="text/javascript" src="AIRAliases.js"></script>
5    <script type="text/javascript">
6
7    // Create the objects:
8    var conn = new air.SQLConnection();
9    var db = air.File.applicationStorageDirectory.resolvePath('ch12.db');
10   var select = new air.SQLStatement();
11
12   // Do the prep work after the application has loaded:
13   window.onload = function() {
14
15       // Add the event handlers:
16       conn.addEventListener(air.SQLEvent.OPEN, dbOpen);
17       conn.addEventListener(air.SQLErrorEvent.ERROR, dbError);
18       select.addEventListener(air.SQLEvent.RESULT, listAccounts);
19       select.addEventListener(air.SQLErrorEvent.ERROR, dbError);
20
21       // Open the database:
22       conn.openAsync(db, air.SQLMode.READ);
23
24   } // End of anonymous function.
25
26   // When the application has closed, close the database connection:
27   window.onbeforeunload = function() {
28       conn.close();
29   }
30
31   // Function for reporting errors.
32   function dbError(e) {
33       alert('An error occurred.');
34   }
35
36   // Function called when the database is opened.
37   function dbOpen() {
38
39       // Associate the connection with the SQLStatement:
40       select.sqlConnection = conn;
41
```

(script continues on next page)

Script 12.3 *continued*

```
42    // Get all the accounts:
43    select.text = 'SELECT name, balance FROM
      accounts ORDER BY name ASC';
44    select.execute(3);
45
46    } // End of dbOpen() function.
47
48    // Function that adds the items to the page.
49    function listAccounts() {
50
51        // Variables used to add elements:
52        var div = document.getElementById('list');
53        var p, acct = null;
54
55        // Get the results of the query:
56        var results = select.getResult();
57
58        if (results.data != null) { // Some
          records returned!
59
60            // Loop through the results:
61            for (var i = 0; i < results.data.
              length; i++) {
62
63                // Create what should be displayed:
64                acct = results.data[i].name + ' $'
                  + (results.data[i].balance/100);
65
66                // Create the elements:
67                p = document.createElement('p');
68                p.innerText = acct;
69
70                // Add to the DIV:
71                div.appendChild(p);
72
73            } // End of FOR loop.
74
75            // Get more if more exist:
76            if (!results.complete) {
77                select.next(3);
78            }
79
80        } // End of results.data != null IF.
81
82    } // End of listAccounts() function.
83
84    </script>
85
86    </head>
87
88    <body style="margin:10px;">
89
90    <h3>List of Accounts</h3>
91
92    <div id="list"></div>
93
94    </body>
95    </html>
```

FETCHING RECORDS IN GROUPS

2. Create an anonymous function that does the prep work:

```
window.onload = function() {
  conn.addEventListener(air.
    SQLEvent.OPEN, dbOpen);
  conn.addEventListener(air.
    SQLErrorEvent.ERROR, dbError);
  select.addEventListener(air.
    SQLEvent.RESULT, listAccounts);
  select.addEventListener(air.
    SQLErrorEvent.ERROR, dbError);
  conn.openAsync(db, air.SQLMode.
    READ);
}
```

This code should be pretty familiar to you by now. When the SELECT query returns a positive result, the listAccounts() function will be called. I'll also point out that the database is opened in just read mode, because that's all this program will do.

3. Create a second anonymous function and the error handling function:

```
window.onbeforeunload = function() {
  conn.close();
}
function dbError(e) {
  alert('An error occurred.');
}
```

4. Create the dbOpen() function:

```
function dbOpen() {
  select.sqlConnection = conn;
  select.text = 'SELECT name,
    balance FROM accounts ORDER BY
    name ASC';
  select.execute(3);
}
```

continues on next page

When the database connection is made, this function will be called. It associates the connection with the SQLStatement object, then defines the SELECT query, and executes it. Notice that I'm having the execute statement only return a fairly small number of records (three). This is because there aren't that many records in the database. When you have a more populated database, you'll want to change this value to 10 or 20 or 30.

5. Begin the listAccounts() function:

```
function listAccounts() {
    var div = document.
    → getElementById('list');
    var p, acct = null;
    var results = select.getResult();
    if (results.data != null) {
```

The function begins by getting an association for the place on the page where all of the accounts will be listed. This will be within a DIV whose id value is *list*. To this DIV, one paragraph will be added for each record (you could also list the accounts within a table if you'd rather). Then the results are fetched and a conditional makes sure the results are not empty. That conditional would be false if the query didn't return any records.

6. Add each account to the page:

```
for (var i = 0; i < results.data.
→ length; i++) {
    acct = results.data[i].name + ' $'
    → + (results.data[i].balance/100);
    p = document.createElement('p');
    p.innerText = acct;
    div.appendChild(p);
}
```

The loop goes through each fetched record. Within the loop, the acct variable is assigned the value of the account holder's name, plus a space, plus a dollar sign, plus their balance (divided by 100 to turn the integer cents value into a decimal dollar value: e.g., 117 to 1.17). Then a new paragraph element is created, given the acct value, and appended to the DIV.

7. Complete the listAccounts() function:

```
        if (!results.complete) {
            select.next(3);
        }
    } // End of results.data != null IF.
} // End of listAccounts() function.
```

After the for loop, a check needs to be made to see if there are more results to be fetched. This can be done by checking the value of results.complete. If results.complete is not true, there are more records to be returned, so select.next() is called and fetches three more records.

8. Within the body of the page, add a DIV with an id of *list*:

```
<div id="list"></div>
```

9. Save, test, debug, and run the completed application.

✔ Tip

■ One modification you could make to this and the next example would be to format the account balances as currency. This would mean separating thousands by commas and ensuring that there are always exactly two numbers after the decimal point. If you search online using *JavaScript format currency*, you'll find sample code that does all this.

Performing Transactions

Transactions are a different way of executing database queries. With the standard method used in this and the previous chapter, a query is run as soon as its execute() method is called. More important, its effects are permanent: There is no way of undoing an executed query. An alternative method is to run queries within a *transaction*. By doing so, you can create checks that guarantee everything worked as expected. Then you can either make the queries permanent or undo their collective effects, depending on the overall result.

To use transactions in your Adobe AIR application, you use three SQLConnection methods. To start a transaction, call begin():

```
conn.begin();
```

From that point onward, every query will only have a temporary impact until the commit() method is called:

```
conn.commit();
```

The other option would be to undo all the queries by calling the rollback() method:

```
conn.rollback();
```

From a programming perspective, using these functions is really straightforward. The trick is being able to determine when it's appropriate to commit a transaction and when it should be rolled back. This next application, which allows a user to transfer funds from one account to another (**Figure 12.7**), will demonstrate the logic underlying transactions. In this particular case, keep in mind that the transfer involves three steps:

1. Updating the "from" account to subtract the amount being transferred from the balance.

2. Updating the "to" account to add the amount being transferred to the balance.

3. Recording the transaction in the transfers table.

If any one of these three steps fail, the entire transaction should be undone.

Figure 12.7 To transfer funds from one account to another, the accounts are selected using the pull-down menus, and the transfer amount is entered into the text boxes.

To perform transactions:

1. In your project's primary HTML file, create the necessary objects (**Script 12.4**):

```
var conn = new air.SQLConnection();

var db = air.File.
→ applicationStorageDirectory.
→ resolvePath('ch12.db');

var select = new air.SQLStatement();

var update = new air.SQLStatement();

var insert = new air.SQLStatement();
```

Transferring funds from one account to another will require one SELECT query (to get all the account information), one UPDATE query (to update the balances), and one INSERT query (to record the transaction). One SQLStatement object for each of these is created, plus the SQLConnection and File objects.

continues on page 253

Script 12.4 This program uses transactions to guarantee that a series of queries works completely. If not, all the potential effects are undone.

```
 1   <html><!-- Script 12.4 -->
 2   <head>
 3   <title>Transfer Funds</title>
 4   <script type="text/javascript" src="AIRAliases.js"></script>
 5   <script type="text/javascript">
 6
 7   // Create the objects:
 8   var conn = new air.SQLConnection();
 9   var db = air.File.applicationStorageDirectory.resolvePath('ch12.db');
10   var select = new air.SQLStatement();
11   var update = new air.SQLStatement();
12   var insert = new air.SQLStatement();
13
14   // Needed global variables:
15   var count, amount, to, from = 0;
16
17   // Do the prep work after the application has loaded:
18   window.onload = function() {
19       conn.addEventListener(air.SQLEvent.OPEN, dbOpen);
20       conn.addEventListener(air.SQLErrorEvent.ERROR, dbError);
21       select.addEventListener(air.SQLEvent.RESULT, listAccounts);
22       select.addEventListener(air.SQLErrorEvent.ERROR, dbError);
23       update.addEventListener(air.SQLEvent.RESULT, updateResult);
24       update.addEventListener(air.SQLErrorEvent.ERROR, transactionError);
25       insert.addEventListener(air.SQLEvent.RESULT, insertResult);
26       insert.addEventListener(air.SQLErrorEvent.ERROR, transactionError);
27
28       conn.openAsync(db, air.SQLMode.UPDATE);
29   } // End of anonymous function.
30
31   // When the application has closed, close the database connection:
32   window.onbeforeunload = function() {
33       conn.close();
34   }
35
```

(script continues on next page)

Script 12.4 *continued*

```
  ┌──────────────────────────────────────────────────────────────────────┐
  │ ⊖ ⊖ ⊖                        📄 Script                                 │
  ├──────────────────────────────────────────────────────────────────────┤
36   // Function for reporting regular errors.
37   function dbError(e) {
38      alert('An error occurred.');
39   }
40
41   // Function for reporting transaction errors.
42   function transactionError(e) {
43
44      // Alert the user:
45      alert('The transfer could not be made because an error occurred.');
46
47      // Undo the effects:
48      conn.rollback();
49
50      // Cancel any outstanding queries:
51      conn.cancel();
52
53   } // End of transactionError() function.
54
55   // Function called when the database is opened.
56   function dbOpen() {
57      select.sqlConnection = conn;
58      update.sqlConnection = conn;
59      insert.sqlConnection = conn;
60      getAccounts();
61   } // End of dbOpen() function.
62
63   // Function that runs the SELECT query.
64   function getAccounts() {
65      select.text = 'SELECT id, name, balance FROM accounts ORDER BY name ASC';
66      select.execute();
67   }
68
69   // Function that adds the items to the page.
70   function listAccounts() {
71
72      // Clear existing values:
73      removeChildren('fromMenu');
74      removeChildren('toMenu');
75
76      var o, acct = null;
77      var results = select.getResult();
78      for (var i = 0; i < results.data.length; i++) {
79         acct = results.data[i].name + ' $' + (results.data[i].balance/100);
80
81         // Create the elements:
82         o = document.createElement('option');
83         o.setAttribute('value', results.data[i].id);
84         o.innerText = acct;
85         document.getElementById('fromMenu').appendChild(o);
86         document.getElementById('toMenu').appendChild(o.cloneNode(true));
87
88      } // End of FOR loop.
89   } // End of listAccounts() function.
90
```

(script continues on next page)

PERFORMING TRANSACTIONS

Script 12.4 *continued*

```
 91    // Function for clearing nodes.
 92    function removeChildren(which) {
 93       var parent = document.getElementById(which);
 94       while (parent.hasChildNodes()) {
 95          parent.removeChild( parent.lastChild );
 96       }
 97    }
 98
 99    // Function that starts the transfer process.
100    function transfer() {
101
102       // Reset the counter:
103       count = 0;
104
105       // Get the form data:
106       amount = +(document.getElementById('dollars').value + document.getElementById('cents').value);
107       to = document.getElementById('toMenu').value;
108       from = document.getElementById('fromMenu').value;
109
110       // Start a transaction:
111       conn.begin();
112
113       // Update the "from" account:
114       update.text = 'UPDATE accounts SET balance = balance + ? WHERE id = ?';
115       update.parameters[0] = -amount;
116       update.parameters[1] = from;
117       update.execute();
118
119    } // End of transfer() function.
120
121    // Function called when an UPDATE returns a positive result.
122    function updateResult() {
123
124       // Increment the counter:
125       count++;
126
127       // See what stage we're at:
128       if (count == 1) { // Run the second update:
129
130          update.parameters[0] = amount;
131          update.parameters[1] = to;
132          update.execute();
133
134       } else if (count == 2) { // Run the insert.
135
136          insert.text = 'INSERT INTO transfers (from_id, to_id, amount) VALUES (?, ?, ?)';
137          insert.parameters[0] = from;
138          insert.parameters[1] = to;
139          insert.parameters[2] = amount;
140          insert.execute();
141
142       } else { // Problem!
143
```

(script continues on next page)

PERFORMING TRANSACTIONS

Script 12.4 *continued*

```
           ⊖ ⊖ ⊖                    📄 Script
144              alert('The transfer could not be
                 made because an error occurred.');
145              conn.rollback();
146              conn.cancel();
147
148          } // End of if-else if.
149
150      } // End of updateResult() function.
151
152      // Function called when an INSERT works.
153      function insertResult() {
154
155          // Check the count to verify success:
156          if (count == 2) { // Good!
157              alert('Transfer made!');
158              conn.commit();
159              getAccounts();
160          } else { // Bad!
161              alert('The transfer could not be
                 made because an error occurred.');
162              conn.rollback();
163              conn.cancel();
164          }
165
166      } // End of insertResult() function.
167
168      </script>
169
170      </head>
171
172      <body style="margin:10px;">
173
174      <h3>Transfer Funds</h3>
175
176      From: <select id="fromMenu"><option>
         From Account</option></select> To:
         <select id="toMenu"><option>To Account
         </option></select><br>Amount: <input
         type="text" id="dollars" size="6">.<input
         type="text" id="cents" value="00" size="2"
         maxlength="2"><br><button onclick=
         "transfer()">Transfer</button>
177
178      </body>
179      </html>
```

2. Create the necessary global objects:

```
var count, amount, to, from = 0;
```

Because this program will go in and out of several functions, some global variables will be necessary. One, count, will be used to track the success of the transaction. The other three all represent values used in the transaction. All four variables are initially given a value of 0.

3. Create an onload anonymous function:

```
window.onload = function() {
    conn.addEventListener(air.
      → SQLEvent.OPEN, dbOpen);
    conn.addEventListener(air.
      → SQLErrorEvent.ERROR, dbError);
    select.addEventListener(air.
      → SQLEvent.RESULT, listAccounts);
    select.addEventListener(air.
      → SQLErrorEvent.ERROR, dbError);
    update.addEventListener(air.
      → SQLEvent.RESULT, updateResult);
    update.addEventListener(air.
      → SQLErrorEvent.ERROR,
      → transactionError);
    insert.addEventListener(air.
      → SQLEvent.RESULT, insertResult);
    insert.addEventListener(air.
      → SQLErrorEvent.ERROR,
      → transactionError);
    conn.openAsync(db, air.SQLMode.
      → UPDATE);
}
```

continues on next page

PERFORMING TRANSACTIONS

For the most part, this should all be familiar territory. However, this code uses two different functions for handling the errors that might occur. The connection and SELECT object errors will be handled by dbError(). The UPDATE and INSERT objects, both of which will be used in the transaction, have their errors handled by transactionError(). That function will take some extra steps that dbError() will not.

4. Define the onbeforeunload and dbError() functions:

```
window.onbeforeunload = function() {
   conn.close();
}
function dbError(e) {
   alert('An error occurred.');
}
```

This second function is the generic error handling function and is associated with the conn and select objects.

5. Define the transactionError() function:

```
function transactionError(e) {
   alert('The transfer could not be
   → made because an error occurred.');
   conn.rollback();
   conn.cancel();
}
```

If an error occurs during the transaction, this function will be called. Its duty is to report the problem to the user (**Figure 12.8**), and then rollback any changes made. A call to the cancel() method cancels any other queries that might be queued for execution on the database.

6. Define the dbOpen() method:

```
function dbOpen() {
   select.sqlConnection = conn;
   update.sqlConnection = conn;
   insert.sqlConnection = conn;
   getAccounts();
}
```

Along with associating the statements with the connection object, this function calls getAccounts(), which executes the SELECT query that populates the pull-down menus.

7. Define the getAccounts() function:

```
function getAccounts() {
   select.text = 'SELECT id, name,
   → balance FROM accounts ORDER BY
   → name ASC';
   select.execute();
}
```

This function defines and executes the SELECT query. It returns every record in the accounts table.

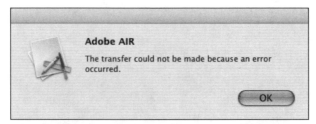

Figure 12.8 When an error occurs during the funds transfer transaction, the user will see this error and no permanent account changes will be made.

8. Begin defining the `listAccounts()` table:

```
function listAccounts() {
    removeChildren('fromMenu');
    removeChildren('toMenu');
```

This function's purpose is to populate the two pull-down menus (see Figure 12.7). That will occur when the program first loads and after each transfer (so that the menus reflect the changes). In this second situation, the function needs to start by getting rid of the current options in both menus. To do so, another function named *removeChildren* is called, passing that function the `id` value of the element to be cleared of subelements (this will be explained more in step 12).

9. Retrieve the query results:

```
var o, acct = null;
var results = select.getResult();
for (var i = 0; i < results.data.
→ length; i++) {
    acct = results.data[i].name + ' $'
    → + (results.data[i].balance/100);
```

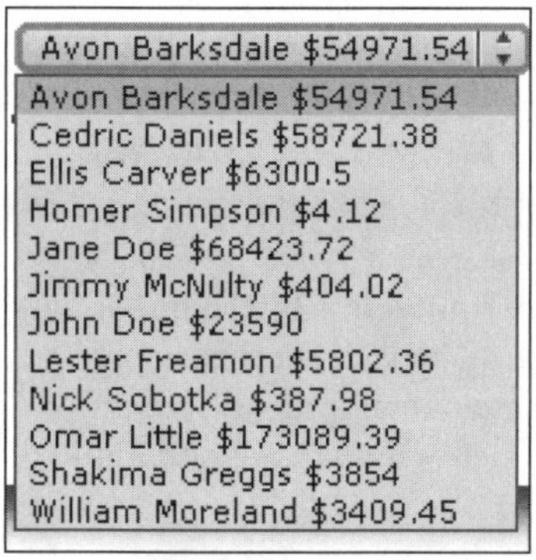

```
Avon Barksdale $54971.54  ▲▼
Avon Barksdale $54971.54
Cedric Daniels $58721.38
Ellis Carver $6300.5
Homer Simpson $4.12
Jane Doe $68423.72
Jimmy McNulty $404.02
John Doe $23590
Lester Freamon $5802.36
Nick Sobotka $387.98
Omar Little $173089.39
Shakima Greggs $3854
William Moreland $3409.45
```

Figure 12.9 The dynamically generated pull-down menu of accounts. Both menus (see Figure 12.7) will contain the same options in the same order.

Two variables will be needed to create the pull-down menu options. Those are declared first. Then the results are fetched and a loop is written to access them all (to save space, I've omitted the check to see that `results.data` is not equal to null). Within the loop, the `acct` variable is assigned a value of the person's name, followed by a space, followed by a dollar sign, followed by the balance divided by 100. The same thing was done with the query results in Script 12.3.

10. Add each record as a pull-down menu option:

```
o = document.
→ createElement('option');
o.setAttribute('value', results.
→ data[i].id);
o.innerText = acct;
document.getElementById
→ ('fromMenu').appendChild(o);
document.getElementById('toMenu').
→ appendChild(o.cloneNode(true));
```

Still within the `for` loop, a new element of type `option` is created. It's assigned an attribute called *value* with a value of the record's ID. The `innerText` attribute of this option will be the `acct` variable, which is assigned a value in step 9. The end result will be this HTML code for each record in the table:

```
<option value="1">John Doe $23590
→ </option>
```

The element is first added to the "from" account menu, and then added to the "to" account menu by appending to that element a clone of the original object (**Figure 12.9**).

continues on next page

11. Complete the `listAccounts()` function:

```
  } // End of FOR loop.
} // End of listAccounts() function.
```

12. Define the `removeChildren()` function:

```
function removeChildren(which) {
  var parent = document.
→ getElementById(which);
  while (parent.hasChildNodes()) {
    parent.removeChild( parent.
    → lastChild );
  }
}
```

This function is called—twice—by `listAccounts()`. It's needed to get rid of all the existing options in each pull-down menu. That will be necessary prior to repopulating the pull-down menus with the updated values after a transfer. To clear out the existing options, the function removes every existing node (i.e., child) of a given element.

This function is passed the *id* value of the element to be cleared of children. This will be either *toMenu* or *fromMenu*. The function then gets a reference for the parent element. Then a loop gets rid of each node, one at a time, for as long as the parent element has nodes.

13. Begin defining the `transfer()` function:

```
function transfer() {
  count = 0;
  amount = +(document.getElementById
  → ('dollars').value + document.
  → getElementById('cents').value);
  to = document.getElementById
  → ('toMenu').value;
  from = document.getElementById
  → ('fromMenu').value;
```

The other functions to this point handle the prep work and error handling; this one starts the application's primary purpose. It will be called when the user clicks the Transfer button (see Figure 12.7). Within this function, the global count variable is assigned a value of 0. This variable will be used to track the success of the transaction. Then the three pertinent values—the amount being transferred, the ID of the user from whom that amount is coming, and the ID of the user to whom that amount is going—are assigned to global variables. To guarantee that the amount value is an integer, the unary plus sign operator is applied to its value (this little trick is briefly discussed in step 6 of "Using Prepared Statements").

14. Complete the `transfer()` function:

```
conn.begin();
update.text = 'UPDATE accounts
→ SET balance = balance + ?
→ WHERE id = ?';
update.parameters[0] = -amount;
update.parameters[1] = from;
update.execute();
} // End of transfer() function.
```

As I said, this function begins the transfer process, which means it needs to begin the transaction by calling begin(). Then the query is defined using prepared statements. Ordinarily, the two update queries used in this situation would be:

```
UPDATE accounts SET balance =
→ balance - amount WHERE id = fromID
```
and
```
UPDATE accounts SET balance =
→ balance + amount WHERE id = toID
```

However, the performance of the application will be improved if the query is the same for both. To make that possible, the "from" account will have the negation of the transfer amount added to that person's balance (which is equivalent to just subtracting it).

15. Begin defining the updateResult() function:

```
function updateResult() {
  count++;
  if (count == 1) {
    update.parameters[0] = amount;
    update.parameters[1] = to;
    update.execute();
```

Per the code in step 3, this function will be called when an UPDATE query runs successfully. That should be the case twice: when the query executed in the transfer() function works and when the second update query (executed here) works. To know which specific update event just happened, the count variable will be used in a conditional, so the first thing this function does is increment the value of count. After the first UPDATE query runs, count will have a value of 1, and this function will know to execute the second UPDATE query. To do that, the parameters are assigned new values using the global variables (you don't need to reassign a query to update.text, because it already has the right value), and then the execute() method is called.

16. Add an else if clause to the updateResult() function:

```
} else if (count == 2) {
  insert.text = 'INSERT INTO
→ transfers (from_id, to_id,
→ amount) VALUES (?, ?, ?)';
  insert.parameters[0] = from;
  insert.parameters[1] = to;
  insert.parameters[2] = amount;
  insert.execute();
```

If count has a value of 2, then both UPDATE queries worked and it's time to record the transaction in the transfers table. This query also uses prepared statements.

17. Complete the updateResult() function:

```
} else { // Problem!
  alert('The transfer could
→ not be made because an error
→ occurred.');
  conn.rollback();
  conn.cancel();
} // End of if-else if.
} // End of updateResult() function.
```

The else clause will only ever be applied if this function is called but count does not have a value of 1 or 2. That should never happen, but just to be safe, if it does, the transaction is rolled back and any other queries waiting to be executed are cancelled (the same as if a database error occurred during the transaction).

continues on next page

18. Define the `insertResult()` function:

```
function insertResult() {
  if (count == 2) {
    alert('Transfer made!');
    conn.commit();
    getAccounts();
  } else {
    alert('The transfer could
    → not be made because an error
    → occurred.');
    conn.rollback();
    conn.cancel();
  }
}
```

Per the code in step 3, this function will be called when the INSERT query returns a positive result. If you follow the logic of this application (**Figure 12.10**), this should only be the case after both UPDATE queries worked, meaning that count has a value of 2. If that's the case, the user will be alerted (**Figure 12.11**), the transaction committed, and the pull-down menus updated (by calling the getAccounts() function). If you want, you could also reset the form elements at this point.

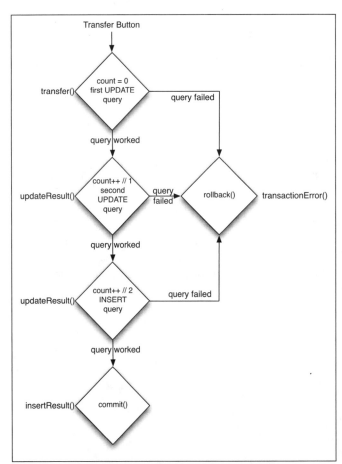

Figure 12.10 This flowchart shows how the success or failure of each query is handled by the application.

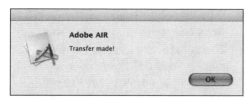

Figure 12.11 If everything works, the user will see this result, and the values in the pull-down menus will be updated.

If, for some reason, count does not equal 2, the user will be notified, the transaction rolled back, and any remaining queries canceled (again, as if a database error had occurred).

19. Within the page body, add the necessary inputs:

```
From: <select id="fromMenu">
→ <option>From Account</option>
→ </select> To:<select id="toMenu">
→ <option>To Account</option>
→ </select><br>Amount: <input
→ type="text" id="dollars"
→ size="6">.<input type="text"
→ id="cents" value="00" size="2"
→ maxlength="2"><br><button
→ onclick="transfer()">Transfer
→ </button>
```

20. Save, test, debug, and run the completed application.

To see what would happen when a transfer fails, attempt to transfer out of one person's account more money than is available.

✔ Tips

- You can only perform one transaction (aka group of queries) at a time.

- You can control how the database locking is handled during a transaction by passing an argument to the begin() method. Database locking refers to what other activities can and cannot be performed while a transaction is in progress. The various options are defined in the SQLTransactionLockType class.

PERFORMING TRANSACTIONS

Improving Performance

In the two chapters in which working with SQLite is discussed—Chapter 11 and this one, most of the examples focus on the rudimentary steps: how to execute an INSERT query, how to retrieve SELECT query results, how to use prepared statements, and so on. You'll also find occasional mention for improving your application's performance when it comes to working with databases, but I'll go ahead and list all the best practices I can offer here.

To improve an application's performance:

◆ Select only what's necessary from a database.

It's easy and common to use SELECT queries that retrieve every column or potentially every row of a table, even if all that information will never be used. Always limit which columns and rows you select. Doing so thereby restricts how much data is being transferred back and forth, as well as how much logic your application may need to handle it all.

◆ Have the database do as much work as possible.

If you know that you'll need to alter the selected data in any way, have your SQL query address that if it can, making the database do the heavy lifting. For example, in this chapter all dollar amounts have been stored in integer format, and then divided by 100 in the program to convert the values to dollars and cents. It would be best to have the query perform this math.

◆ Use prepared statements.

Prepared statements won't always be more efficient than standard queries, but if an application will run the same query multiple times (with variations on some of the data used in the query), then prepared statements are clearly the way to go.

◆ Only connect to a database if and when necessary.

This goes back to a mistake commonly made by Web developers: connecting to a database on every page in a site, even if there are pages that don't use the database. Obviously, having a program take steps that aren't necessary, like connecting to a database, will always hinder performance.

◆ Create the database connection before it's needed.

If an application will use a database, make sure it exists and establish the connection (i.e., open it) before it's time to execute queries on it. In the examples in this chapter, the database is opened after the window has loaded but before the user clicks any button that triggers some database actions.

◆ Use the asynchronous methods.

Besides providing for a smoother user experience, asynchronous database communications perform better than synchronous ones.

◆ Use transactions for related groups of queries.

Along with improving the database's integrity, transactions can improve the performance of an application when there are lots of queries being run together.

◆ Use separate SQLStatement objects for each query.

I've made a habit of abiding by this rule in these two chapters and for good reason. Your AIR application will optimize how queries are handled, making them execute as efficiently as possible. Reusing the same SQLStatement object for different queries will prevent such possible optimizations.

Debugging Techniques

Any time you have two technologies working together, the potential for errors increases exponentially. When using SQLite with an Adobe AIR application, problems could occur within your HTML page, your JavaScript code, the SQL syntax, or the SQLite database. Debugging such problems is first of all a matter of trying to hunt down where the true fault lies. The following list of tips cover everything you need to know and do to solve any database-related problem.

To debug database applications:

◆ Use alerts to confirm the values of variables, queries, results, and so on.

This is also a general debugging tip, but when a SQL query depends on data coming from a variable—and most will, take extra steps to confirm what the values of those variables and queries are.

◆ Use alerts to confirm which functions are called and when.

In more complicated programs, like Script 12.4, the execution will go in and out of lots of functions. To be certain which functions are called and when, use a simple alert like:

```
alert('Inside the selectResult()
→ function.');
```

◆ While developing a program, display as detailed an error message as possible.

Chapter 11 provides some code for displaying all the available error messages associated with a database problem. Use that to debug a problem, but don't use it in released applications (where a user could see it, although by that time the program should be error free).

◆ Validate all user-supplied input.

The examples in this chapter and Chapter 11 don't do a good job of this, but for what it's worth I do point out that shortfall. Chapter 15, "Security Techniques," has some specific recommendations as to how you can validate user-supplied input.

◆ Avoid making assumptions.

This is related to the previous bullet but also includes tasks like checking that a SELECT query returned some results prior to attempting to retrieve the results:

```
if (results.data != null) {…
```

Another check you might want to perform includes confirming that a database file exists prior to connecting to it.

◆ Pay attention to where the database file is located.

This is particularly important when storing the database file in the application's storage directory (which should often be the case). Where exactly on the user's computer that location is found depends in part on the application's ID and publisher ID. Be aware of these values when debugging problems (for example, if the database doesn't seem to have the right tables or data in it, your application may be looking at the wrong database).

◆ Run queries on, and confirm the structure and contents of, a database using a third-party application.

continues on next page

DEBUGGING TECHNIQUES

One of the absolute best debugging tips for any application (desktop or Web-based) that interacts with a database is to print out the query being run, and then run that query using another interface. By doing so, you'll be able to see the syntax of the query, see the results it produces, and even immediately see any errors that may be caused without the middleman, which is JavaScript and your AIR application. Taking these steps will most likely clarify whether the problem is with the query, the query results, or how those results are being handled by the application.

◆ Use prepared statements.

As stated in the corresponding section earlier in the chapter, prepared statements will make your application much more secure and less prone to bugs (because potentially problematic data won't cause SQL syntax errors).

◆ Use constraints in the database tables.

Constraints are added checks that the data being entered into a database is appropriate. Extra precautions are always a good idea.

◆ Normalize the database.

Database normalization is a huge topic but one you should become familiar with if you use databases frequently. A properly designed database will be more reliable than one hastily put together. And when it comes to databases, the reliability of the data is paramount.

◆ Explicitly name the columns to be populated in INSERT queries.

There are two syntaxes for an INSERT query:

INSERT INTO tablename VALUES (…)

and

INSERT INTO tablename (col1, col2,…) → VALUES (…)

The second format, although more wordy, is less likely to cause errors. Or, in a worst-case scenario, the errors that do arise will be more evident.

13

NETWORKING

Most of this book's content focuses on interactions between an application and the operating system as a whole. This includes making windows, creating menus for common tasks, interacting with the clipboard, and working with files, directories, and databases. Naturally, much of what an application does involves these tasks. But there's a whole different realm of interactions that can take place between an application and other computers: networking activities.

This chapter is dedicated to client-server communications, where the AIR application running on the user's computer is the client and another computer is the server. One of this chapter's examples will simply show how to confirm that a server is available for communications. Two examples will demonstrate how to send data to the server, and three will use server-provided content in the application.

The URLRequest Class

Of the various networking-related classes you'll use in an AIR application, `URLRequest` will be used the most. A `URLRequest` object only provides a reference to the resource to which your application should connect, so it doesn't do much but will be needed by the classes that do.

When you create a `URLRequest` object, you can provide it with the URL the application will use:

```
var url = new air.URLRequest
→ ('http://www.example.com');
```

A `URLRequest` object can use many different URL schemes: *http*, *https*, *file*, *app*, and *app-storage*. The last two, which point to items found within the application and application storage directories, can only be used in code running within the application security sandbox (see Chapter 15, "Security Techniques," if you don't understand what *application security sandbox* means). And although this chapter will use `URLRequest` objects to interact with other computers, they can be used in conjunction with `File`, `Sound`, and other object types.

As I said, the actual `URLRequest` object doesn't do much, so as an example of how it can be used, I'll turn to the `URLMonitor` class. It is defined in the `servicemonitor.swf` file that comes with the AIR SDK. The `URLMonitor` class can be used to literally monitor a URL— to see if this application on this computer can access a Web site.

When you create a `URLMonitor` object, you provide it with a `URLRequest` instance:

```
var monitor = new air.URLMonitor(url);
```

To the monitor you want to add an event listener that watches for status changes:

```
monitor.addEventListener(air.
→ StatusEvent.STATUS, statusChange);
```

Finally, start the monitor:

```
monitor.start();
```

You can find the status of the resource being monitored by referring to the monitor object's `available` property:

```
function statusChange(e) {
    alert(monitor.available);
}
```

If `monitor.available` has a value of `true`, the application can access that URL.

Let's run through all this again in a simple, sample application.

To monitor a URL:

1. In your project's primary HTML file, include the Shockwave file (**Script 13.1**):

   ```
   <script src="servicemonitor.swf"
   → type="application/x-shockwave-
   → flash"></script>
   ```

   To use the URLMonitor class, an application must include this file. For the type attribute, make sure you specify its value as *application/x-shockwave-flash*.

2. In a JavaScript block, create the two objects:

   ```
   var url = new air.URLRequest
   → ('http://www.example.com');
   var monitor = new air.URLMonitor(url);
   ```

   This code is pretty much the same as the code explained earlier. The URL *http://www.example.com* will work (it does actually exist), or you can use any other address here.

continues on next page

Script 13.1 This first example confirms the application's ability to access a particular Web site.

```
      ● ● ●                                   Script
1     <html><!-- Script 13.1 -->
2     <head>
3     <title>URLRequest and URLMonitor</title>
4     <script src="servicemonitor.swf" type="application/x-shockwave-flash"></script>
5     <script type="text/javascript" src="AIRAliases.js"></script>
6     <script type="text/javascript">
7
8     // Create the two objects:
9     var url = new air.URLRequest('http://www.example.com');
10    var monitor = new air.URLMonitor(url);
11
12    // Add the event listener:
13    monitor.addEventListener(air.StatusEvent.STATUS, statusChange);
14
15    // Start the monitor:
16    monitor.start();
17
18    // Function called whenever the monitor status changes.
19    function statusChange(e) {
20
21        // Find the document element:
22        var status = document.getElementById('status');
23
24        // Set the value based upon availability:
25        if (monitor.available) {
26            status.innerText = 'available';
27        } else {
28            status.innerText = 'not available';
29        }
30
31    } // End of statusChange() function.
32
33    </script>
34    </head>
35    <body>
36
37    <div>The resource is <strong id="status"></strong>.</div>
38
39    </body>
40    </html>
```

3. Add an event listener to the URLMonitor object:

```
monitor.addEventListener(air.
→ StatusEvent.STATUS, statusChange);
```

When the URLMonitor object's status changes—from available/connected to unavailable/unconnected or vice versa, the statusChange() function will be called.

4. Start the monitor:

```
monitor.start();
```

If you don't include this line, the application won't actually do anything.

5. Begin the statusChange() function:

```
function statusChange(e) {
    var status = document.getElementBy
    → Id('status');
```

The role of this function is to add some text to the application indicating whether the given resource is available or not. The specific document element that will be updated is called *status*, and a reference to that is created here.

Figure 13.1 If the application can access the URL, this will be the result.

6. Complete the statusChange() function:

```
    if (monitor.available) {
        status.innerText = 'available';
    } else {
        status.innerText = 'not
        → available';
    }
} // End of statusChange() function.
```

If the available property of the monitor object has a value of true, the status element will be assigned an innerText value of *available*. Otherwise it's assigned a value of *not available*.

7. Within the body of the page, create an area with an id of *status*:

```
<div>The resource is <strong
id="status"></strong>.</div>
```

Thanks to the conditional in the statusChange() function, this sentence will end up reading either *The resource is available.* (**Figure 13.1**) or *The resource is not available.* (**Figure 13.2**).

Figure 13.2 When the application cannot access the URL, either because the user's computer or the URL's server is not online, this will be the result.

8. Copy the servicemonitor.swf to the project directory.

   You'll find it in the AIR SDK's frameworks folder.

9. Save, test, debug, and run the completed application.

   Remember to include the Shockwave file when you build the actual .air file.

   As a quick way to test the application, while it's running, temporarily disable or enable your Internet connection.

✔ Tips

■ There are several other properties of the URLRequest class that I don't cover in this book. Most of them are only used for more advanced purposes, and some are only usable within application security sandbox content.

■ The URLRequestDefaults class is where you can set new default values for all URLRequest objects used by an application. It also has a setLoginCredentials-ForHost() method, which is used to set the hostname/username/password combination used to access restricted areas.

Opening a URL with a Browser

An AIR application can also open a URL using the computer's default Web browser. To do so, create a URLRequest object for the resource, and then call the air.navigateToURL() function:

```
var url = new air.URLRequest('http://www.example.com');
air.navigateToURL(url);
```

(Note that this function is not associated with any object you have to create.)

For security reasons, there are restrictions as to what resources can be requested from where. Content in the application sandbox can request *http*, *https*, *file*, *app*, and *app-storage* content (plus *mailto*, which will invoke the computer's default email application). Content loaded from the remote sandbox can only request *http*, *https*, and *mailto* resources. Content in the local sandbox will also only allow a subset of the URL schemes to be used, depending on the privileges and context.

THE URLREQUEST CLASS

Receiving Data

The first example in this chapter shows how easy it is to connect to a URL. That code can also confirm two things: that the user has a live network connection and that the named Web site is available. But you'll almost always want your applications to do more than just this; normally, they should either retrieve data from that URL or send data to it.

To retrieve data, start by creating the URLRequest object:

```
var url = new air.URLRequest
➝ ('http://www.example.com/page.txt');
```

From there, instead of using a URLMonitor object, which can only monitor the status of a URL, create an object of type URLLoader

```
var loader = new air.URLLoader();
```

This class is used to handle the data returned by a resource. The data the server sends back will not be available until all of it has been received, so the URLLoader needs an event listener for the load completion:

```
loader.addEventListener(air.Event.
➝ COMPLETE, loadComplete);
```

Finally, start the loading by invoking the load() method, passing it the URLRequest object:

```
loader.load(url);
```

The function that handles the COMPLETE event should be written to accept an event argument:

```
function loadComplete(e) {
}
```

Within the function, you can access the retrieved data by either referring to the event's target attribute or the original loader variable, if it's global. For either, refer to the data property:

```
alert(e.target.data);
```

or

```
alert(loader.data);
```

To see how this works in a real example, this next application will fetch a stock quote stored in an online text file.

To receive remote data:

1. In your project's primary HTML file, create the two required objects (**Script 13.2**):

   ```
   var url = new air.URLRequest
   → ('http://www.dmcinsights.com/
   → air/ch13data.txt');

   var loader = new air.URLLoader();
   ```

   The resource being requested—*www. dmcinsights.com/air/ch13data.txt*—is a plain text file that just contains a number.

   You can use this URL or change it to a page of your own creation.

2. Add an event listener to the URLLoader object:

   ```
   loader.addEventListener(air.Event.
   → COMPLETE, loadComplete);

   loader.load(url);
   ```

   When the object has completely downloaded the entire response, the load-Complete() function will be called. The second line begins the loading process.

   continues on next page

Script 13.2 This application reads in the data from a text file found online, and then places that content within the HTML page.

```
1   <html><!-- Script 13.2 -->
2   <head>
3   <title>Retrieving Data</title>
4   <script type="text/javascript" src="AIRAliases.js"></script>
5   <script type="text/javascript">
6
7   // Create the two objects:
8   var url = new air.URLRequest('http://www.dmcinsights.com/air/ch13data.txt');
9   var loader = new air.URLLoader();
10
11  // Add the event listener:
12  loader.addEventListener(air.Event.COMPLETE, loadComplete);
13
14  // Load the resource:
15  loader.load(url);
16
17  // Function that handles the complete loading of the resource.
18  function loadComplete(e) {
19
20      // Update the page:
21      document.getElementById('data').innerText = loader.data;
22
23  } // End of loadComplete() function.
24
25  </script>
26  </head>
27  <body>
28  <div>According to the remote server, the Adobe Systems Inc. (ADBE) stock price is $<span
    id="data"></span>.</div>
29  </body>
30  </html>
```

RECEIVING DATA

3. Define the `loadComplete()` function:

```
function loadComplete(e) {
    document.getElementById('data').
    → innerText = loader.data;
}
```

As with the previous example, this function will update an element on the page. This time the value retrieved from the resource, accessible in `loader.data`, is assigned to the span element with an id of *data*.

4. Within the body of the page, create the text and the span element:

```
<div>According to the remote server,
→ the Adobe Systems Inc. (ADBE)
→ stock price is $<span id="data">
→ </span>.</div>
```

The stock price, which is stored in the text file on the server, will be inserted into this sentence.

5. Save, test, debug, and run the completed application (**Figure 13.3**).

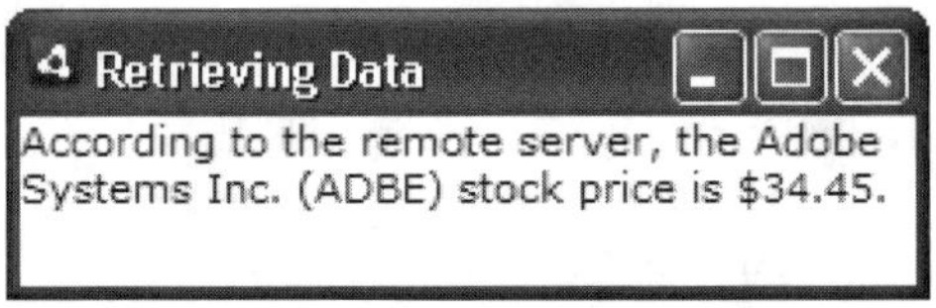

Figure 13.3 The contents of the online text file are inserted into the text of this application.

✔ Tips

■ Script 13.2 may seem like a trivial example, but if you had a server page that dynamically retrieved and printed a stock price, that could be invoked by this application, thereby providing a desktop application with up-to-date stock quotes.

■ For security reasons, you want to be especially careful with how external data—like that coming from an online server—is used by an application. It's much safer to use that data for an element's `innerText` and `value` attributes than for its `innerHTML` or `outerHTML` attributes. See Chapter 15 for more on security.

■ One AIR application can communicate with another AIR application running on the same computer by using the `LocalConnection` class.

Parsing Data

The previous example quickly demonstrated how simple it can be to retrieve content from an online resource and use it in a desktop application. Such functionality will often be at the heart of an Adobe AIR application, but the same concept can be used to better ends. In that example, one string of text was being read in; what if you wanted to retrieve more discrete bits of data? For example, what if instead of containing just a single stock price, the online file has the stock name, symbol, price, number of traded shares, and so forth?

One solution would be to store the information in XML format. That data could then be retrieved using a standard `XMLHttpRequest`. You could also still retrieve the content using the previous method, in which case, after retrieving the text string, you'd need to create a `DOMParser` object to turn the text into usable XML.

A simpler alternative to using XML is to represent the data as a series of *name=value* pairs like so: *name=Adobe%20Systems%20Inc.&symbol=ADBE&price=34.45...*

Each *name=value* pair is separated by an ampersand. The only trick to this format is that it needs to be properly URL-encoded: Spaces must be represented by *%20* (as in the above), ampersands by *%26*, the equals sign by *%3D*, and so forth. (You'll often see this in URLs in your Web browser; search the Web for more information.)

Once you have data in this format, you can tell the `URLLoader` object to expect it. By default, a `URLLoader` expects to receive plain text. It can also treat the received response as either binary data or as a `URLVariables` object. You don't actually need to know anything else about this object right now, except to understand that it will automatically parse the names and values out of the text string, making them easier to refer to.

To tell the `URLLoader` object what to expect, assign the appropriate constant to its `data` attribute:

```
var loader = new air.URLLoader();
loader.dataFormat = air.
→ URLLoaderDataFormat.VARIABLES;
```

The other two constants are `air.URLLoaderDataFormat.TEXT` (the default) and `air.URLLoaderDataFormat.BINARY`.

In the function that's called when the load is complete, `loader.data`, will now be an object of type `URLVariables`. Assuming the example line of *name=value* pairs, the function could refer to `loader.data.name`, `loader.data.symbol`, `loader.data.price`, and so on.

To test this out, let's create a new application, similar to the previous example, that retrieves more information from a different resource.

To parse remote data:

1. In your project's primary HTML file, create the two required objects (**Script 13.3**):

   ```
   var url = new air.URLRequest
   → ('http://www.dmcinsights.com/air/
   → ch13vars.txt');
   
   var loader = new air.URLLoader();
   ```

   Again, you can use this URL or create your own. This particular file contains just one line of text:

   close=34.45&change=0.32&date=3/20/2008

2. Change the expected data format:

   ```
   loader.dataFormat = air.
   → URLLoaderDataFormat.VARIABLES;
   ```

   Instead of just receiving some plain text, this line indicates that the data will be a string of *name=value* pairs to be parsed by a URLVariables object.

3. Add the event listener and load the URL:

   ```
   loader.addEventListener(air.Event.
   → COMPLETE, loadComplete);
   loader.load(url);
   ```

Script 13.3 By using the URLVariables class behind the scenes, the data read from the server can be easily parsed into individual variables.

```
1    <html><!-- Script 13.3 -->
2    <head>
3    <title>Parsing Data</title>
4    <script type="text/javascript" src="AIRAliases.js"></script>
5    <script type="text/javascript">
6
7    // Create the two objects:
8    var url = new air.URLRequest('http://www.dmcinsights.com/air/ch13vars.txt');
9    var loader = new air.URLLoader();
10
11   // Indicate the data format:
12   loader.dataFormat = air.URLLoaderDataFormat.VARIABLES;
13
14   // Add the event listener:
15   loader.addEventListener(air.Event.COMPLETE, loadComplete);
16
17   // Load the resource:
18   loader.load(url);
19
20   // Function that handles the complete loading of the resource.
21   function loadComplete(e) {
22
23       // Assign the closing price:
24       document.getElementById('close').innerText = loader.data.close;
25
26       // Retrieve the price change:
27       var change = loader.data.change;
28
29       // Update the element's class:
30       var changeElement = document.getElementById('change');
31       if (change < 0) {
32           changeElement.className = 'negative';
33       } else if (change > 0) {
34           changeElement.className = 'positive';
35       }
36
```

(script continues on next page)

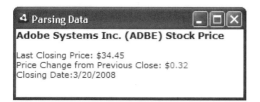

Figure 13.4 In this application, three separate pieces of information are read in from a file and placed in their proper places within the main page.

Script 13.3 *continued*

```
37      // Place the change on the page:
38      changeElement.innerText =
        Math.abs(change);
39
40      // Place the date on the page:
41      document.getElementById('date').
        innerText = loader.data.date;
42
43    } // End of loadComplete() function.
44
45    </script>
46
47    <style>
48    .negative { color: #C03; }
49    .positive { color: #060; }
50    </style>
51
52    </head>
53    <body>
54
55    <h3>Adobe Systems Inc. (ADBE) Stock
      Price</h3>
56    <div>Last Closing Price: $<span
      id="close"></span></div>
57    <div>Price Change from Previous Close:
      $<span id="change"></span></div>
58    <div>Closing Date:<span id="date">
      </span></div>
59
60    </body>
61    </html>
```

4. Begin defining the `loadComplete()` function:

```
function loadComplete(e) {
    document.getElementById('close').
    → innerText = loader.data.close;
```

The three pieces of information retrieved from the online file will be placed within some context in the HTML page (**Figure 13.4**). To start, the element with an `id` value of *close* will be provided with the *close* value from the text file.

5. Handle the price change:

```
var change = loader.data.change;
var changeElement = document.
→ getElementById('change');
if (change < 0) {
    changeElement.className =
    → 'negative';
} else if (change > 0) {
    changeElement.className =
    → 'positive';
}
changeElement.innerText =
→ Math.abs(change);
```

To make output a little more interesting, the price change (the difference between the most recent closing price and the previous closing price) will be formatted in the application page differently if it's positive or negative. To accomplish that, this first line grabs the change value from the retrieved data. Then a conditional checks if that value is less than or greater than 0. If it's negative, the associated element will be assigned a CSS class value of *negative*, meaning it'll be displayed in red font. If the change is positive, it'll be displayed in green, thanks to the *positive* CSS class definition. Finally, the absolute value of the change is added to the page (the negation symbol representing a price drop will no longer be necessary because the CSS indicates the downturn).

continues on next page

PARSING DATA

6. Complete the function:

```
document.getElementById('date').
→ innerText = loader.data.date;
} // End of loadComplete() function.
```

Finally, the date value retrieved from the server is added to the page.

7. Define two CSS classes:

```
<style>
.negative { color: #C03; }
.positive { color: #060; }
</style>
```

As stated in step 5, these two classes will be used to format the change value, making its font color either red or green.

8. Within the body of the page, add the requisite content and elements:

```
<h3>Adobe Systems Inc. (ADBE) Stock
→ Price</h3>
<div>Last Closing Price: $<span
→ id="close"></span></div>
<div>Price Change from Previous
→ Close: $<span id="change">
→ </span></div>
<div>Closing Date:<span id="date">
→ </span></div>
```

9. Save, test, debug, and run the completed application.

✔ Tips

- For many of these examples, you could take the code from Script 13.1 to test for a connection to the resource prior to attempting to interact with it.

- Instead of directly telling the URLLoader class to receive a URLVariables object, you could have it receive the response as text, and then do this in the handling function:

```
var vars = new air.
→ URLVariables(loader.data);
```

Then you would refer to vars.close, vars.change, and vars.date. I think it's easier to take the route demonstrated in Script 13.3.

Working with Sockets

Many computer users aren't familiar with the concept of a socket, even though they end up using them all the time. A socket is a way in which one computer can communicate with another. An important distinction of a socket is that it provides for persistent (i.e., open until closed) connections. (By comparison, a standard HTTP request involves the opening of a connection, the transfer of data, and then the quick closing of that connection.)

You could connect to a server through a socket for any number of reasons:

- To interact with an email service

- To communicate with a database

- To upload or download files over FTP

- To use IRC or a chat application like Jabber

In Adobe AIR applications you can monitor a socket connection using SocketMonitor, just as you use URLMonitor to monitor a URL. The SocketMonitor class is also defined in the servicemonitor.swf file.

To interact with a server via sockets, use the Socket or XMLSocket classes. The former works with binary data and the latter uses XML data. The online AIR documentation has examples for using both.

Transmitting Data

The previous two examples show how you can read data from a network resource into an Adobe AIR application, but data transfers can work the other way, too. AIR applications with access to a network connection can transmit data from the client to the server. An application might need to do this to request to update an online database, to submit user feedback, or to fetch more specific results from the server (for example, to indicate for which stock the price and other information should be returned).

To send data to a server, two URLRequest attributes are involved. The first is method. This property indicates the method used to request the URL page. The two most common methods are GET and POST, which are represented by the constants air.URLRequestMethod.GET and air.URLRequestMethod.POST (GET is the default value). If you're not familiar with these terms, you may be best served by doing a quick search online (e.g., the Wikipedia entry is helpful). In simplest terms, a GET request is the most common type made: When you load a bookmarked URL in your Web browser or click on a link in a page, that's GET. Such requests are normally used just to *retrieve information from* a server. POST requests are commonly used to *provide information to* a server, for example, when you submit a form.

To change the request type, do this:

```
var url = new air.URLRequest
→('http://www.example.com/page.jsp');
url.method = air.URLRequestMethod.POST;
```

The second attribute of the URLRequest object that you'll use is data. To this property you can assign a string of text, a ByteArray, or a URLVariables object. To use this last option, create a URLVariables object:

```
var appData = new air.URLVariables();
```

Then add *name=value* pairs to the object by treating the name as an attribute of the object:

```
appData.make = 'Toyota';
appData.model = 'Sienna';
appData.year = 2004;
```

Those lines add three *name=value* pairs to the appData object.

The final step in sending data to a server is to associate the data with the URLRequest object, and then load the resource:

```
url.data = data;
loader.load(url);
```

The data will be sent to the server when the request is performed through the URLLoader object.

To help you conceptualize this process using the above code, think of it as being similar to having a form on a Web site with inputs named *make*, *model*, and *year*. When the form is submitted, it would send the user-entered values—*Toyota*, *Sienna*, and *2004*—to *www.example.com/page.jsp*, which would handle the form data. This brings me to the last step in the process: The server resource needs to be written to accept data submission and respond in some way. You can do this using PHP, JSP (Java Server Pages), Ruby on Rails, ASP.NET, ColdFusion, and many other technologies.

For a real-world example of this concept, the next application will handle the entering of the application's license code. This process normally works as follows:

1. The user purchases an online a license for an application.

2. The application asks for the license information to unlock it. The user enters the values returned by step 1.

3. The application submits the user-supplied information to the server.

4. If the submitted license information is correct, the application is updated to reflect that it's been properly registered.

The following application will focus on steps 2 and 3 of this process.

To transmit data:

1. In your project's primary HTML file, create the form (**Script 13.4**):

```
<h3>Enter your license information:
→ </h3>
<p>Registered To: <input type="text"
→ id="name"></p>
<p>License Code: <input type="text"
→ id="license"></p>
<p><input type="submit" value="Submit"
→ onclick="checkLicense();"></p>
```

So that you can follow the logic more easily, I'll start by creating the form (**Figure 13.5**). It contains two text inputs and a button that calls the checkLicense() function when clicked.

2. Within the JavaScript code, create the three necessary objects:

```
var url = new air.URLRequest
→ ('http://www.dmcinsights.com/air/
→ ch13license.php');
var loader = new air.URLLoader();
var data = new air.URLVariables();
```

This application needs URLRequest and URLLoader objects, like the previous two examples, plus a URLVariables object.

As for the page being used by this example, it's a PHP script that expects to receive a name and a license value sent to it via the POST method. The script contains just:

```
<?php
if (isset($_POST['name'],
→ $_POST['license']) &&
   ($_POST['name'] == 'J. Doe') &&
   ($_POST['license'] == 'XYZ123') ) {
   echo 'Valid License Entered!'
} else {
   echo 'Invalid License Entered!';
}
?>
```

continues on page 278

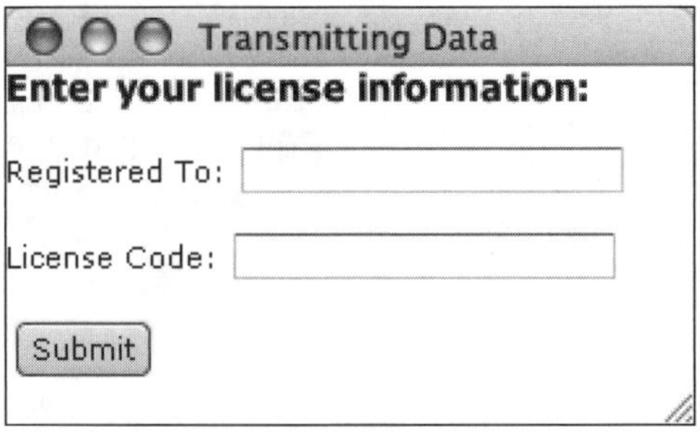

Figure 13.5 The form where a user enters the already purchased license information.

TRANSMITTING DATA

Script 13.4 This application simulates the process of authenticating a program's license by submitting user-entered values to a server.

```
1    <html><!-- Script 13.4 -->
2    <head>
3    <title>Transmitting Data</title>
4    <script type="text/javascript" src="AIRAliases.js"></script>
5    <script type="text/javascript">
6
7    // Create the objects:
8    var url = new air.URLRequest('http://www.dmcinsights.com/air/ch13license.php');
9    var loader = new air.URLLoader();
10   var data = new air.URLVariables();
11
12   // Change the method:
13   url.method = air.URLRequestMethod.POST;
14
15   // Add the event listener:
16   loader.addEventListener(air.Event.COMPLETE, loadComplete);
17
18   // Function that handles the complete loading of the resource.
19   function loadComplete(e) {
20
21       alert(loader.data);
22
23   } // End of loadComplete() function.
24
25   // Function called when the user clicks the Submit button.
26   function checkLicense() {
27
28       // Assign the data to the URLVariables object:
29       data.name = document.getElementById('name').value;
30       data.license = document.getElementById('license').value;
31
32       // Assign the URLVariables object to the URLRequest object:
33       url.data = data;
34
35       // Load the resource:
36       loader.load(url);
37
38   } // End of checkLicense() function.
39
40   </script>
41
42   </head>
43   <body>
44
45   <h3>Enter your license information:</h3>
46   <p>Registered To: <input type="text" id="name"></p>
47   <p>License Code: <input type="text" id="license"></p>
48   <p><input type="submit" value="Submit" onclick="checkLicense();"></p>
49
50   </body>
51   </html>
```

In case you're unfamiliar with PHP, I'll explain what this means. The conditional checks if the script receives name and license values (both posted to this page). It also confirms that *name* has a value of *J. Doe* and *license* has a value of *XYZ123*. If those three conditions are all true, the text *Valid License Entered!* is printed by this PHP script. If any of those conditions is false, *Invalid License Entered!* is printed. In an actual program, the PHP script should match the information against that provided when the user bought the license (likely stored in a database), but for testing purposes, this code will suffice.

3. Change the request method:

```
url.method = air.URLRequestMethod.
→ POST;
```

POST is the logical method type to use in situations like this, where data is being sent to a page for validation purposes.

4. Add an event listener to the URLLoader object:

```
loader.addEventListener(air.Event.
→ COMPLETE, loadComplete);
```

There will be two aspects to this application: the sending of the data to the server and the reading of the response back from the server. The loadComplete() function will handle the second part.

5. Define the loadComplete() function:

```
function loadComplete(e) {
    alert(loader.data);
} // End of loadComplete() function.
```

This function, which is called when the response from the server is completely loaded, will just print out the returned text using an alert dialog. The response of the server should be one of the two messages printed by the PHP page (see step 2). Note that for this reason, the PHP page doesn't include the basic HTML tags.

Working Offline

Although always-on Internet connections are prominent these days, applications cannot assume that users are always online. If they're not, applications that send data to or retrieve data from a networked resource will need to make adjustments. But fortunately, handling such contingencies is rather simple.

You'll first need to establish a monitor that detects the application's ability to connect to the resource. If it can't connect, most likely meaning either the user or the server is offline, the application would take alternate steps. For example, if the application downloads content, it might just indicate to the user that the feature can only run while the user is online.

If an application provides content to a server, there are two ways being offline might be handled. With the license example (Script 13.4), the program might again indicate that an Internet connection is required to perform that task. But take, for example, an application where a user enters transactions (like, say, purchase orders) that are then transmitted to an online server. In such a case, the data could be stored in a client-side text file or database, and then automatically transmitted when the user is online again. By writing an application this way, it will be usable at all times, with only some of the functionality dependent on an Internet connection.

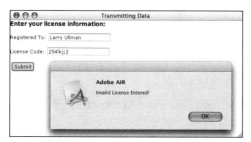

Figure 13.6 The result if incorrect license information is submitted, including none at all.

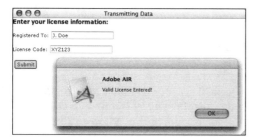

Figure 13.7 If the correct information (case sensitive) is entered into the form, the user is notified that a valid license was submitted.

6. Begin defining the checkLicense() function:

```
function checkLicense() {
    data.name = document.
getElementById('name').value;
    data.license = document.
    → getElementById('license').value;
```

This function needs to send the user-submitted data (from the form) to the server. It starts by adding *name=value* pairs to the URLVariables object.

7. Complete the checkLicense() function:

```
    url.data = data;
    loader.load(url);
} // End of checkLicense() function.
```

The final two steps are to associate the URLVariables object with the URLRequest object and to call the URLLoader's load() method to actually send the request and read in the response.

8. Save, test, debug, and run the completed application (**Figures 13.6** and **13.7**).

✔ Tips

■ The air.sendToUrl() function will make a request of a URL without acknowledging the server's response.

■ Most large Web sites like Google, Amazon, Flickr, YouTube, and eBay provide an API (Application Programming Interface) through which an application—desktop or online—can interact with their site. Normally, you create an account with the site, and then provide that information along with certain parameters—search terms, specific product ID, and so on—in an application request. Using these APIs along with the code in Script 13.4, you can incorporate the content those sites provide in your applications.

Downloading Files

Another way that a desktop application might interact with a server (besides accessing pages and reading in the response) is to download a file from it. The concept is the same, but the amount of data and what the application does with that data is different.

Start, of course, with a URLRequest object:

```
var url = new air.URLRequest
→ ('http://www.example.com/somefile');
```

From there, you could use the URLLoader class to download the file data, reading in the response as binary data. However, if you know you'll be handling binary data, the URLStream class provides a more basic tool for the job:

```
var urlStream = new air.URLStream();
```

To download small files, add an event listener that will be called when the download (aka, the server response) is complete:

```
urlStream.addEventListener(air.Event.
→ COMPLETE, saveFile);
```

(The next section discusses alternative code for downloading large files.)

To begin the download, call the load() method of the URLStream object:

```
urlStream.load(url);
```

When all of the file data has been downloaded, it's stored in the urlStream object.

To turn that into a file on the user's computer, you'll need to read it into a ByteArray object (see Chapter 10, "Working with File Content"), and then write the ByteArray object to a file:

```
var data = new air.ByteArray();
urlStream.readBytes(data, 0,
→ urlStream.bytesAvailable);
var file = air.File.desktopDirectory.
→ resolvePath('somefile');
var fileStream = new air.FileStream();
fileStream.open(file, air.FileMode.WRITE);
fileStream.writeBytes(data, 0,
→ data.length);
fileStream.close();
```

This next script will implement all of this code, downloading a file from a server (after the user clicks a button, **Figure 13.8**) and saving that file on the user's desktop.

To download a file:

1. In your project's primary HTML file, create the first two necessary objects (**Script 13.5**):

   ```
   var url = new air.URLRequest
   → ('http://www.dmcinsights.com/air/
   → ch13code.zip');
   var urlStream = new air.URLStream();
   ```

   For this example, the item to be downloaded will be the code for this chapter's examples. It's called *ch13code.zip* and is located at this book's corresponding Web site (www.DMCInsights.com/air/).

continues on page 282

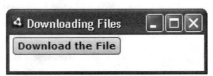

Figure 13.8 When the user clicks this button, a file from a server will be downloaded.

Script 13.5 To download a file from a server to the user's computer, this script reads the server response into a URLStream, then reads that data into a ByteArray, and finally writes the ByteArray to a file.

```
1    <html><!-- Script 13.5 -->
2    <head>
3    <title>Downloading Files</title>
4    <script type="text/javascript" src="AIRAliases.js"></script>
5    <script type="text/javascript">
6
7    // Create the objects:
8    var url = new air.URLRequest('http://www.dmcinsights.com/air/ch13code.zip');
9    var urlStream = new air.URLStream();
10
11   // Add the event listener:
12   urlStream.addEventListener(air.Event.COMPLETE, saveFile);
13
14   // Function called when the user clicks the button.
15   function downloadFile() {
16
17      // Start the download:
18      urlStream.load(url);
19
20   } // End of downloadFile() function.
21
22   // Function called when all of
23   // the data has been downloaded.
24   function saveFile(e) {
25
26      // Read the downloaded data into a ByteArray:
27      var data = new air.ByteArray();
28      urlStream.readBytes(data, 0, urlStream.bytesAvailable);
29
30      // Write the data to a file:
31      var file = air.File.desktopDirectory.resolvePath('ch13code.zip');
32      var fileStream = new air.FileStream();
33      fileStream.open(file, air.FileMode.WRITE);
34      fileStream.writeBytes(data, 0, data.length);
35      fileStream.close();
36
37      // Notify the user:
38      alert('The file has been downloaded!');
39
40   } // End of saveFile() function.
41
42   </script>
43   </head>
44   <body>
45
46   <button onclick="downloadFile();">Download the File</button>
47
48   </body>
49   </html>
```

DOWNLOADING FILES

281

2. Add an event listener to the URLStream object:

```
urlStream.addEventListener(air.
→ Event.COMPLETE, saveFile);
```

This line states that when the entire server response has been downloaded, the saveFile() function should be called.

3. Define the downloadFile() function:

```
function downloadFile() {
    urlStream.load(url);
}
```

This function will be called when the user clicks the button. It begins the downloading process by calling the load() method.

4. Begin defining the saveFile() function:

```
function saveFile(e) {
```

This function will be called when the file download is complete. It takes an event as an argument, although it won't be used.

5. Read the downloaded data into a ByteArray object:

```
var data = new air.ByteArray();
urlStream.readBytes(data, 0,
→ urlStream.bytesAvailable);
```

The urlStream object contains all the downloaded data. To access that data, it'll need to be assigned to a ByteArray object, so one is created first. Then the readBytes() method reads all of the data (from 0 to urlStream.bytesAvailable) into the ByteArray object. See Chapter 10 for more information on working with ByteArray objects.

6. Write the data to a file:

```
var file = air.File.desktopDirectory.
resolvePath('ch13code.zip');
var fileStream = new air.FileStream();
fileStream.open(file, air.FileMode.
→ WRITE);
fileStream.writeBytes(data, 0,
→ data.length);
fileStream.close();
```

A File object is created first and points to a file called *ch13code.zip*, which is located on the user's desktop. Then the file is opened for writing, the data is written there, and the file is closed.

7. Alert the user and complete the function:

```
    alert('The file has been
    downloaded!');
} // End of saveFile() function.
```

8. Within the body of the page, create a button that will start the process:

```
<button onclick="downloadFile();">
→ Download the File</button>
```

9. Save, test, debug, and run the completed application (**Figures 13.9** and **13.10**).

Figure 13.9 After the file has been written to the desktop, the user will see this alert.

Figure 13.10 The file on my desktop, as downloaded from a server.

DOWNLOADING FILES

Downloading Large Files

One of the benefits of using URLStream instead of URLLoader to download files is that the URLStream object can access the returned data incrementally (a URLLoader object can only use the full response). When downloading large files, you'll want to take advantage of this feature so as not to max out the computer's RAM (because the downloaded data is stored in the application's memory until its written to a file). To handle the download incrementally, add an event listener that responds to the download progress:

```
urlStream.addEventListener(air.
→ ProgressEvent.PROGRESS, writeToFile);
```

Downloading a file incrementally really means writing the downloaded data to the file on the user's computer incrementally. So, start by opening the file outside of the writeToFile() function (because the file should only be opened once and the write-ToFile() function will be called repeatedly):

```
var file = air.File.desktopDirectory.
→ resolvePath('largeFile');
var fileStream = new air.FileStream();
fileStream.open(file, air.FileMode.WRITE);
```

The writeToFile() function will still read the downloaded data into a ByteArray, and then write that ByteArray to the file:

```
var data = new air.ByteArray();
urlStream.readBytes(data, 0,
→ urlStream.bytesAvailable);
fileStream.writeBytes(data, 0,
→ data.length);
```

Here's how the writeToFile() function will work differently than the saveFile() function in Script 13.4: When the downloading begins, some of the online file's data will be placed into the URLStream object, and then the writeToFile() function will be called because progress has been made. The function will write all the data that's been downloaded thus far to the File object. Then that data will be automatically removed from the urlStream object and more will be downloaded into it, thus calling the writeToFile() function again. This loop will continue until all the data has been downloaded.

Let's modify the previous example to handle the download in this manner.

To download a large file:

1. Place a relatively large file on a server.

   Rather than overwhelming my server by having *X* number of readers all repeatedly download a large file, I'll leave it to you to find your own resource for this example. This can be any file of, say, 100 KB in size or greater that you place or find on a Web site. Make note of the file's URL.

2. Open Script 13.5 in your text editor or IDE, if it is not already.

continues on next page

3. Change the URLResource object's value to use the target file created (or found) in step 1 (**Script 13.6**):

```
var url = new air.URLRequest
→ ('http://www.example.com/
→ largeFile.pdf');
```

You'll need to replace the sample value here with the complete address of your target. For my own purposes, I'll download a large PDF file.

4. Move the lines that create the File and FileStream objects out of the saveFile() function so they come after the URLStream object that is created:

```
var file = air.File.desktopDirectory.
→ resolvePath('largeFile.pdf');

var fileStream = new air.FileStream();
```

Because these objects will be needed by multiple functions, they should be defined outside of any function to make them global in scope.

Script 13.6 This updated version of Script 13.5 writes the downloaded data to a file in increments instead of all at once.

```
1   <html><!-- Script 13.6 -->
2   <head>
3   <title>Downloading Large Files</title>
4   <script type="text/javascript" src="AIRAliases.js"></script>
5   <script type="text/javascript">
6
7   // Create the objects:
8   var url = new air.URLRequest('http://www.example.com/largeFile.pdf');
9   var urlStream = new air.URLStream();
10  var file = air.File.desktopDirectory.resolvePath('largeFile.pdf');
11  var fileStream = new air.FileStream();
12
13  // Add the event listeners:
14  urlStream.addEventListener(air.ProgressEvent.PROGRESS, writeToFile);
15  urlStream.addEventListener(air.Event.COMPLETE, saveFile);
16
17  // Function called when the user clicks the button.
18  function downloadFile() {
19
20      // Open the file:
21      fileStream.open(file, air.FileMode.WRITE);
22
23      // Start the download:
24      urlStream.load(url);
25
26  } // End of downloadFile() function.
27
28  // Function called when some of
29  // the data has been downloaded.
30  function writeToFile(e) {
31
```

(script continues on next page)

DOWNLOADING LARGE FILES

Script 13.6 *continued*

```
32    // Only write every 50KB or more:
33    if (urlStream.bytesAvailable > 51200) {
34        var data = new air.ByteArray();
35        urlStream.readBytes( data, 0,
          urlStream.bytesAvailable);
36        fileStream.writeBytes( data, 0,
          data.length);
37    }
38
39    } // End of writeToFile() function.
40
41    // Function called when all of
42    // the data has been downloaded.
43    function saveFile(e) {
44
45        // Write the remaining data to the file:
46        var data = new air.ByteArray();
47        urlStream.readBytes(data, 0,
          urlStream.bytesAvailable);
48        fileStream.writeBytes(data, 0,
          data.length);
49
50        // Close the file:
51        fileStream.close();
52
53        // Notify the user:
54        alert('The file has been downloaded!');
55
56    } // End of downloadComplete() function.
57
58    </script>
59    </head>
60    <body>
61
62    <button onclick="downloadFile();">Download
      the File</button>
63
64    </body>
65    </html>
```

5. Add a progress event listener to the URLStream object:

```
urlStream.addEventListener(air.
→ ProgressEvent.PROGRESS,
→ writeToFile);
```

When the download is complete, the saveFile() function will still be called, but other download progress will be handled by the writeToFile() function.

6. Move the opening of the file to within the downloadFile() function:

```
fileStream.open(file, air.FileMode.
→ WRITE);
```

Since the file needs to be opened outside of the writeToFile() function, this can logically be done within the downloadFile() function, which starts the download process.

7. Define the writeToFile() function:

```
function writeToFile(e) {
    if (urlStream.bytesAvailable >
    → 51200) {
        var data = new air.ByteArray();
        urlStream.readBytes( data, 0,
        → urlStream.bytesAvailable);
        fileStream.writeBytes( data, 0,
        → data.length);
    }
}
```

This function needs to write the down-loaded data to the file. However, it will be called repeatedly as the download progresses, and it shouldn't write the data every time it's called. If it did that, the application might just end up writing a couple of bytes at a time, which isn't very efficient. Instead, a conditional is used to dictate that the data should be written only after 50 KB has been downloaded.

continues on next page

DOWNLOADING LARGE FILES

8. Update the saveFile() function so it writes the last bit of data to the file, and then closes it:

```
function saveFile(e) {
  var data = new air.ByteArray();
  urlStream.readBytes(data, 0,
  → urlStream.bytesAvailable);
  fileStream.writeBytes(data, 0,
  → data.length);
  fileStream.close();
  alert('The file has been
  → downloaded!');
}
```

This function will be called when the download is complete. By that point, most of the file's data should have been written to the file. However, there's likely to be some data left in the URLStream because only every 50 KB or so is written to the file in writeToFile(). For example, if only the last 12 KB of the file is downloaded after the previous call to writeToFile(), that data will still be in urlStream. This function therefore writes the remaining data to the file prior to closing it.

9. Save, test, debug, and run the completed application (**Figures 13.11** and **13.12**).

✔ Tips

- If a file download fails because not all the file's content is properly written to the desktop file, the likely result will either be an inability to open the file or some of the file's content will be missing.

- Another way of understanding what happens in this example is to consider that a URLStream object works exactly like a FileStream object. Script 10.3, which shows how a FileStream is incrementally read, demonstrates the same basic concept being used here: incrementally accessing data.

Figure 13.11 This version of the application looks essentially the same as its predecessor (Figure 13.8).

Figure 13.12 The 572 KB PDF file downloaded by the application.

DOWNLOADING LARGE FILES

Uploading Files

The last topic to be covered in this chapter is how to upload a file to a server. There are a few different ways you could do this. One option would be to use the Socket class to FTP the document to a server. This is an excellent way to go, provided you know how to set up and use an FTP server.

A second method would be to read the file into a ByteArray, assign that to the URLRequest object's data attribute, and then use a URLLoader to request a page on the server, thereby sending it the file as well. This is similar to Script 13.4 but uses a ByteArray instead of a URLVariables object.

The third option, and the one I'll use here, is based upon the File class. The File class defines a method called upload(). This method performs an upload of the file to a server, as if the user had selected the file in a standard HTML form and then submitted that form. What's nice about using this method is that the file upload is performed asynchronously, meaning that the upload will happen in the background while the user can continue to perform other tasks within the application.

Assuming you have a File object that already refers to a file on the user's computer (for example, one the user has selected), the next steps would be to add event listeners to that object. The pertinent events are air.ProgressEvent.PROGRESS and air.Event.COMPLETE:

```
file.addEventListener(air.ProgressEvent.
→ PROGRESS, uploadProgress);
file.addEventListener(air.Event.COMPLETE,
→ uploadComplete).
```

The complete event is triggered once the file has been completely uploaded. The progress event is frequently triggered while the upload is happening. Within that handling function, you can refer to the event's bytes-Loaded attribute to see how much of the file has been uploaded. The event's bytesTotal attribute reflects the total file size (as does the File object's size attribute).

To call the upload() method, you need to provide it with a URLRequest object. That object should refer to the URL to which the file should be sent:

```
var url = new air.URLRequest
→ ('http://www.example.com/upload.php');
file.upload(url, 'aFile');
```

The second argument in this method is the name associated with the uploaded file. This isn't the file's actual name from the user's computer, but rather like the name given to a file input in an HTML form. This value provides the handling script with a reference to the uploaded file.

Handling file uploads using a server-side script is beyond the scope of this book, but this next example will demonstrate the AIR application code involved.

To upload a file:

1. In your project's primary HTML file, create two objects (**Script 13.7**):

   ```
   var file = new air.File();
   var url = new air.URLRequest
   → ('http://www.dmcinsights.com/air/
   → ch13upload.php');
   ```

   The URL referenced here is a dummy page on my site that won't do anything with the uploaded file but is still quite usable for demonstrating this technique.

2. Add event listeners to the File object:

   ```
   file.addEventListener(air.Event.
   → SELECT, fileWasSelected);
   file.addEventListener(air.Event.
   → COMPLETE, uploadComplete);
   ```

   Two separate events need to be attended to. The first is a SELECT event, which is triggered when the user has selected a file from the computer. The second is a COMPLETE event, which is triggered when the file has been uploaded.

3. Define the fileWasSelected() function:

   ```
   function fileWasSelected(e) {
       alert ('You selected: ' +
       → file.nativePath);
       file.upload(url, 'theFile');
   }
   ```

   This function does two things. First, it reports back to the user the file that the user selected (**Figure 13.13**). Second, it starts the file upload by calling the File object's upload() method.

4. Define the uploadComplete() function:

   ```
   function uploadComplete(e) {
       alert('The file has been
       → uploaded.');
   }
   ```

   This function lets the user know that the file was completely uploaded to the server (**Figure 13.14**). Because the upload happens asynchronously, the user can do other things in the application (if there were other things to do) while that file is being uploaded.

continues on page 290

Figure 13.13 After the user selects a file from the computer, its full path is displayed in an alert.

Figure 13.14 The result after the file upload is finished.

UPLOADING FILES

Script 13.7 This application uploads to a server a file that the user has selected.

```
1    <html><!-- Script 13.7 -->
2    <head>
3    <title>Uploading Files</title>
4    <script type="text/javascript" src="AIRAliases.js"></script>
5    <script type="text/javascript">
6
7    // Create the objects:
8    var file = new air.File();
9    var url = new air.URLRequest('http://www.dmcinsights.com/air/ch13upload.php');
10
11   // Add the event listeners:
12   file.addEventListener(air.Event.SELECT, fileWasSelected);
13   file.addEventListener(air.Event.COMPLETE, uploadComplete);
14
15   // Function that will be called
16   // when the File has been selected.
17   function fileWasSelected(e) {
18
19       // Use an alert to print the selected item's name:
20       alert ('You selected: ' + file.nativePath);
21
22       // Upload the file:
23       file.upload(url, 'theFile');
24
25   } // End of fileWasSelected() function.
26
27   // Function called when the upload is complete.
28   function uploadComplete(e) {
29       alert('The file has been uploaded.');
30   }
31
32   // Function called when the user clicks the
33   // 'Select a File' button.
34   function selectFile() {
35
36       // Create the Open prompt:
37       file.browseForOpen('Choose a file:');
38
39   }
40
41   </script>
42   </head>
43   <body>
44
45   <button onclick="selectFile();">Select a File to Upload</button>
46
47   </body>
48   </html>
```

UPLOADING FILES

5. Define the `selectFile()` function:

```
function selectFile() {
   file.browseForOpen('Choose a
   → file:');
}
```

This function is called when the user clicks the Select a File button (**Figure 13.15**). It generates the browse for open prompt (**Figure 13.16**).

6. Within the body of the page, create the button.

```
<button onclick="selectFile();">
→ Select a File to Upload</button>
```

7. Save, test, debug, and run the completed application.

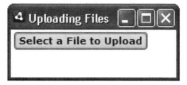

Figure 13.15 The simple application.

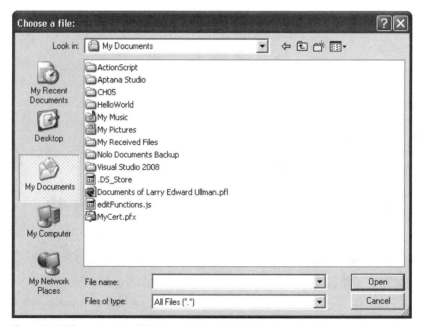

Figure 13.16 The prompt in which the user selects the file to be uploaded.

UPLOADING FILES

14

USING OTHER MEDIA

Desktop applications, like Web pages, rely on more than just text for their content. In this chapter you'll learn how to use three specific kinds of media in an AIR application: sounds, PDFs, and XML data.

The bulk of the chapter focuses on sounds, specifically MP3s. Using sounds in an AIR application isn't complicated, but there's lots that can be done with them, so you'll see four examples that illustrate the available options. Conversely, PDFs can be easily displayed but there's not much more to them than that, so one simple program will cover pretty much everything you need to know with respect to PDFs. XML data is a different kind of resource but one that hasn't been discussed in detail elsewhere and deserves some attention. The XML example that wraps up the chapter can be used by any AIR application you create.

Playing Sounds

AIR applications have the capability of playing MP3 files using the Sound class (AIR does not directly support playing other sound file types.) To start, you'll need to create a URLRequest object, which will be a reference to the sound file (the URLRequest class is discussed in more detail in Chapter 13, "Networking"). To create a URLRequest object, you provide its constructor (the method called when an object of that type is created) with a URL value. For a file on the user's computer, the URL would begin with *app-resource*, *app*, or *file*. For example, to reference a sound that was installed along with the application, you would use

```
var url = new air.URLRequest('app:/
→ sound.mp3');
```

As you might infer, because the Sound class uses a URLRequest object, it means your application can also play sounds found online:

```
var url = new air.URLRequest
→ ('http://www.example.com/sound.mp3');
```

Along with the URLRequest object, you'll need an object of class Sound:

```
var sound = new air.Sound();
```

Note that each Sound object can only reference one sound file. If an application needs to access multiple sound files, you'll need multiple Sound objects.

The final two steps are to load and play the MP3:

```
sound.load(url);
sound.play();
```

As an example of this information, the next script shows how an AIR application can play a sound as an effect after the user does something.

Script 14.1 This program plays a sound when the user clicks the button.

```
1   <html><!-- Script 14.1 -->
2     <head>
3       <title>Playing Sounds</title>
4       <script type="text/javascript"
        src="AIRAliases.js"></script>
5       <script type="text/javascript">
6
7       // Create the objects:
8       var url = new air.URLRequest
        ('app:/sounds/bell.mp3');
9       var sound = new air.Sound();
10
11      // Load the sound after the
        application has loaded:
12      window.onload = function() {
13
14        // Load the sound:
15        sound.load(url);
16
17      } // End of anonymous function.
18
19      // Function called when the user
        clicks the button.
20      function playSound() {
21        sound.play();
22      }
23
24      </script>
25    </head>
26    <body>
27    <button onclick="playSound();">Play the
      Sound</button>
28    </body>
29  </html>
```

To play sounds:

1. In your project's primary HTML file, create the necessary objects (**Script 14.1**):

```
var url = new air.URLRequest('app:/
→ sounds/bell.mp3');

var sound = new air.Sound();
```

The two requisite objects are defined here. The first is of type URLRequest and points to the bell.mp3 sound found within the application's sounds directory (**Figure 14.1**).

2. Create an anonymous function that loads the sound:

```
window.onload = function() {
    sound.load(url);
}
```

After the application (technically, the window) has loaded, this anonymous function will be called. It loads the sound file so that it's ready to play when appropriate.

3. Create a function that plays the sound:

```
function playSound() {
    sound.play();
}
```

Invoking the Sound object's play() method is all that's required.

4. Within the body, create a button that invokes the playSound() function:

```
<button onclick="playSound();">Play
→ the Sound</button>
```

5. Place the bell.mp3 file in your project's sounds directory.

You can download this file from the book's supporting Web site (www.DMCInsights.com/air/, see the Downloads page). Alternatively, you can use your own sound file. Just make sure that it's relatively short—not an entire song, for example—and change the code in the script to match that file's name.

6. Save, test, debug, and run the completed application (**Figure 14.2**).

✔ Tips

■ The ability to work with sounds found within a SWF file is defined in the SoundMixer class.

■ AIR applications can also access sound through a computer's microphone via the Microphone class. See the online documentation for more information.

Figure 14.1 This image of Aptana Studio's project directory shows the sound file required by the program.

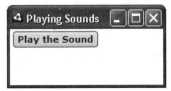

Figure 14.2 The application, which is more impressive aurally than it is visually.

Playing Long Sounds

For very short sounds, like interface effects associated with user actions, the code outlined in the previous section of the chapter will work just fine. For longer sounds, like songs, or sounds being played over the Internet, a different approach is necessary. In such cases, the sound file will take longer to load and attempts to play it before it's fully loaded could cause problems.

The most foolproof approach to playing long sounds successfully is to make sure a sound has completely loaded before playing it. This is accomplished by adding an event listener for the COMPLETE event:

```
sound.addEventListener( air.Event.
→ COMPLETE, loadComplete);
function loadComplete(e) {
    sound.play();
}
```

Another type of event that ought to be listened for is air.IOErrorEvent.IO_ERROR. Such an event will occur if the sound file can't be found or fully loaded:

```
sound.addEventListener( air.
→ IOErrorEvent.IO_ERROR, soundError);
function soundError(e) {
    // Do whatever.
}
```

To apply this new knowledge, the next example allows the user to select an MP3 from the user's computer, and then play it.

To play long sounds:

1. In your project's primary HTML file, create the necessary objects (**Script 14.2**):

   ```
   var url = null;
   var sound = new air.Sound();
   var file = new air.File();
   ```

   This application uses three kinds of objects: URLRequest, Sound, and File. The last two are created here; the URLRequest object will be created later in the script (after the user selects the file), but because that object needs to be a global variable, it's declared here.

2. Add the necessary event listeners:

   ```
   file.addEventListener(air.Event.
   → SELECT, fileWasSelected);
   sound.addEventListener(air.Event.
   → COMPLETE, loadComplete);
   sound.addEventListener(air.
   → IOErrorEvent.IO_ERROR, soundError);
   ```

   The File object needs to listen for a SELECT event, which is triggered when the user selects a file. The Sound object needs to listen to both a COMPLETE event (for when the sound has completely loaded) and an IO_ERROR event (in case of problems).

3. Create a function for selecting a file:

   ```
   window.onload = function() {
       var filter = new air.
       → FileFilter('MP3', '*.mp3');
       file.browseForOpen('Choose an
       → MP3:', [filter]);
   }
   ```

continues on page 296

Script 14.2 In this application, the user is first prompted to select an MP3 file from the computer. Then, once the sound has fully loaded, the user can play the selected sound.

```
1    <html><!-- Script 14.2 -->
2       <head>
3          <title>Playing Sounds</title>
4          <script type="text/javascript" src="AIRAliases.js"></script>
5          <script type="text/javascript">
6
7          // Create the objects:
8          var url = null;
9          var sound = new air.Sound();
10         var file = new air.File();
11
12         // Add the event listeners:
13         file.addEventListener(air.Event.SELECT, fileWasSelected);
14         sound.addEventListener(air.Event.COMPLETE, loadComplete);
15         sound.addEventListener(air.IOErrorEvent.IO_ERROR, soundError);
16
17         window.onload = function() {
18
19            // Limit what kinds of files can be opened:
20            var filter = new air.FileFilter('MP3', '*.mp3');
21
22            // Create the Open prompt:
23            file.browseForOpen('Choose an MP3:', [filter]);
24
25         } // End of anonymous function.
26
27         // Function that will be called
28         // when the file has been selected.
29         function fileWasSelected(e) {
30
31            // Associate the file with the URLRequest:
32            url = new air.URLRequest(file.url);
33
34            // Load the sound:
35            sound.load(url);
36
37         } // End of fileWasSelected() function.
38
39         // Function called when the sound has been loaded.
40         function loadComplete(e) {
41            document.getElementById('play').disabled = false;
42         }
43
44         // Function called when the user clicks the 'Play' button.
45         function playSound() {
46            sound.play();
47         }
48
49         // Function for handling sound errors.
50         function soundError(e) {
51            alert('An error occurred. The MP3 cannot be played');
52         }
53
54         </script>
55      </head>
56      <body>
57      <button id="play" onclick="playSound();" disabled>Play</button>
58      </body>
59   </html>
```

This anonymous function will be called as soon as the application opens. Its purpose is to get the user to select an MP3 file to play. It first creates a filter, limiting the type of file that the user can select to just those with an .mp3 extension. Then it creates the prompt in which the user selects the file (**Figure 14.3**). See Chapter 9, "Files and Directories," for more on this code.

4. Define the fileWasSelected() function:

```
function fileWasSelected(e) {
    url = new air.URLRequest(file.url)
    sound.load(url);
}
```

This function will automatically be called after the user has selected a file from the computer. This function's purpose is to load the sound file (in the previous example, that happened in an anonymous onload function). First, the url variable is declared an object of type URLRequest. For the object's value, use file.url. This will be something like *file:///Users/larry/Music/artist/album/songname.mp3*. Second, the sound file is loaded.

5. Define the loadComplete() function:

```
function loadComplete(e) {
    document.getElementById('play').
    → disabled = false;
}
```

Figure 14.3 The prompt in which a user can select an MP3 file located on their computer.

Figure 14.4 After the selected MP3 file has been loaded, the application's Play button will be enabled.

Per the event listener added to the sound object in step 2, this function will be called once the sound file has completely loaded. It enables the Play button so that the user can play the selected song (**Figure 14.4**).

6. Create a function that plays the sound:

```
function playSound() {
    sound.play();
}
```

This function will be called when the user clicks the Play button.

7. Define the soundError() function:

```
function soundError(e) {
    alert('An error occurred. The MP3
    → cannot be played');
}
```

8. Within the body of the page, create the Play button:

```
<button id="play" onclick=
→ "playSound()" disabled>Play
→ </button>
```

The button is initially disabled. It will be enabled—so that the user can play the selected sound—after the sound has completely loaded.

9. Save, test, debug, and run the completed application.

✔ Tips

- To know when a sound has finished playing, add an event listener that watches for the air.Event.SOUND_COMPLETE event.

- To start the browse for open prompt in a specific directory, change the way you create the File object. This line tells the prompt to begin looking in the user's home directory:

```
var file = new air.File.
→ userDirectory;
```

Playing Streaming Sounds

Sounds (and videos) played over the Internet are normally *streamed*—played simultaneously as the data is being loaded. When the "playhead" catches up to the data that has been loaded, the playing pauses until more data is loaded, at which point playback resumes. Certainly you've seen examples of this many times over.

AIR applications can handle streaming sounds, too, but the code and logic is a little different than that used to handle nonstreaming sounds. Start with your URLRequest and Sound objects:

```
var url = new air.URLRequest
→ ('http://www.example.com/song.mp3');
var sound = new air.Sound();
```

Next, create an object of type SoundLoaderContext. Its constructor takes two arguments:

```
var slc = new air.SoundLoaderContext
→ (buffer, check);
```

The first argument is the number of milliseconds of content that should be loaded before the sound starts playing. The default value is 1,000 milliseconds (or one second). The second argument is more complicated. This is a Boolean value that indicates whether or not the application should look for a "cross-domain policy file" from the server when it loads the sound file. For this example, using a value of false is fine, but the sidebar "The AIR Security Model" goes into more detail as to how the AIR security model applies to sound files.

In this next example, the user will enter the URL for a sound file to be played. The sound will then play as it's loading. At the same time, a counter will indicate how many bytes have been loaded (**Figure 14.5**). To accomplish that, an event listener will be added to the Sound object that watches for air. ProgressEvent.PROGRESS. In the function called as that event is repeatedly triggered, you can see how much of the file has been loaded by referring to the event's bytesLoaded property. The event's bytesTotal property stores the file's complete size.

Figure 14.5 The application shows how the loading of the streaming file is progressing as it plays the sound.

To stream sounds:

1. In your project's primary HTML file, create the necessary objects (**Script 14.3**):

   ```
   var url = null;
   var sound = new air.Sound();
   var slc = new air.SoundLoaderContext
   → (10000, false);
   ```

   This example uses three objects: one of type URLRequest, one of type Sound, and another of type SoundLoaderContent. Because the specific URL associated with the URLRequest object won't be known until the user enters that value into the form (see Figure 14.5), that variable is declared as null for now.

2. Create a counter:

   ```
   var count = 0;
   ```

   The program will show the progress as the sound loads. This variable will represent that progress and is initially set at 0 (because no progress has been made).

continues on next page

Script 14.3 This script demonstrates three new ideas. First, it allows the user to enter a URL of a sound to be played over the Internet. Second, it streams the sound (plays it while it's loading). Third, the program shows the loading progress as it's happening.

```
                                    Script
1    <html><!-- Script 14.3 -->
2        <head>
3            <title>Playing Sounds</title>
4            <script type="text/javascript" src="AIRAliases.js"></script>
5            <script type="text/javascript">
6
7            // Create the objects:
8            var url = null;
9            var sound = new air.Sound();
10           var slc = new air.SoundLoaderContext(10000, false);
11
12           // Add the event listeners:
13           sound.addEventListener(air.ProgressEvent.PROGRESS, loadProgress);
14           sound.addEventListener(air.IOErrorEvent.IO_ERROR, soundError);
15
16           // To count the load progress:
17           var count = 0;
18
19           // Function called when the user clicks 'Play'.
20           // It creates the URLRequest object and attempts to load the sound.
21           function getSound() {
22
23               // Get and test the input:
24               var input = document.getElementById('url').value;
25               if (input.length > 0) {
26
27                   document.getElementById( 'play' ).disabled = true;
28
29                   // Create the URLRequest object:
30                   url = new air.URLRequest(input);
31
32                   // Load the sound:
33                   sound.load(url, slc);
34                   sound.play();
35
```

(script continues on next page)

3. Begin defining the getSound() function:

```
function getSound() {
   var input = document.
   → getElementById('url').value;
   if (input.length > 0) {
      document.getElementById( 'play' )
      → .disabled = true;
```

This function will be called when the user clicks the Play button. It starts by performing minimal validation—that something was entered into the text input. Then it disables the Play button, so the user doesn't mess things up by clicking Play again while the sound is streaming.

4. Load and play the sound:

```
url = new air.URLRequest(input);
sound.load(url, slc);
sound.play();
```

Unlike the previous two examples, this time the load() method is provided with a second argument, which is an object of type SoundLoaderContext.

5. Complete the getSound() function:

```
   } else {
      alert('Please enter a valid URL
      → for an MP3 file.');
   }
} // End of getSound() function.
```

Script 14.3 *continued*

```
36          } else {
37             alert('Please enter a valid URL for an MP3 file.');
38          }
39
40       } // End of getSound() function.
41
42       // Function that gets called as the load progresses.
43       function loadProgress(e) {
44
45          // Update the counter every 100000+ bytes:
46          if ( e.bytesLoaded > (count + 100000) ) {
47             document.getElementById('report').innerText = e.bytesLoaded + ' of ' + e.bytesTotal
                + ' bytes loaded';
48             count = e.bytesLoaded;
49          } // End of IF.
50
51       } // End of loadProgress() function.
52
53       // Function for handling sound errors.
54       function soundError(e) {
55          alert('An error occurred. The MP3 cannot be played.');
56       }
57
58       </script>
59    </head>
60    <body>
61    URL: <input type="text" id="url"> <button id="play" onclick="getSound();">Play</button>
62    <div id="report"></div>
63    </body>
64 </html>
```

If the user didn't enter anything in the text box prior to clicking Play, the user sees this alert (**Figure 14.6**).

6. Begin defining the loadProgress() function:

```
function loadProgress(e) {
    if ( e.bytesLoaded > (count +
    → 100000) ) {
```

This function will be called repeatedly as the data is continually loaded. It will display the progress of the load (see Figure 14.6). Rather than updating the display every time the function is called, it'll only do so after every additional 100,000 bytes. To check that status, the conditional confirms that the current value of e.bytesLoaded is more than 100,000 greater than count (the count variable will store the previous bytesLoaded value).

7. Display the current number of bytes loaded:

```
document.getElementById('report').
→ innerText = e.bytesLoaded + ' of '
→ + e.bytesTotal + ' bytes loaded';
count = e.bytesLoaded;
```

To show in the application the number of bytes loaded, the innerText attribute of the *report* DIV will be repeatedly assigned a new value. The content itself will be in the syntax *X of Y bytes loaded*. The first value will be the number loaded, which is found in e.bytesLoaded. The second value will be the total number of bytes in the file, which is found in e.bytesTotal. Finally, the count variable is assigned the current e.bytesLoaded value so that the conditional created in step 6 will work.

8. Complete the loadProgress() function:

```
    } // End of IF.
} // End of loadProgress() function.
```

9. Define the soundError() function:

```
function soundError(e) {
    alert('An error occurred. The MP3
    → cannot be played.');
}
```

This function will be called should an IO_ERROR occur, for example, if the sound can't be loaded (**Figure 14.7**).

10. Within the body of the page, add a text input, a button, and a DIV:

```
URL: <input type="text" id="url">
→ <button id="play" onclick=
→ "getSound();">Play</button>
<div id="report"></div>
```

The user will type the URL in the text input, and then click the button, which in turn calls the getSound() function. The DIV will be used by the JavaScript to display the load progress message (see step 7).

continues on next page

Figure 14.6 Thanks to a little bit of validation, this alert appears if the user clicked the Play button without having entered a URL for the sound to be played.

Figure 14.7 This alert will be generated if the provided URL does not point to a sound file that the application can stream.

PLAYING STREAMING SOUNDS

301

11. Save, test, debug, and run the completed application (**Figure 14.8**).

✔ Tips

■ You may notice that the total number of bytes loaded sometimes differs from the stated number of total bytes. This can happen if the file doesn't communicate the correct total number of bytes it contains (and is not necessarily a problem).

■ To improve the security and reliability of this application, you could ensure that the user-submitted URL begins with *http://*, *https://*, or *ftp://* and that it ends with *.mp3*. The JavaScript substring() function can be used for these purposes.

■ You could also use the information from Chapter 13 to confirm that the application can access the provided URL prior to attempting to load the sound.

Figure 14.8 The application after the file has completely loaded (also see the first Tip).

The AIR Security Model

The AIR security model is based on sandboxes: the realms in which various elements "play." The sandbox that an HTML page, a Shockwave file, and so on are in dictates what they can and cannot do, as well as what they'll need the user's permission to do.

To start, there is the *application sandbox*, which is the content that is installed with the application (content found within the application's directory). Content in the application sandbox—for example, the application's primary HTML document—is the least restricted in terms of what it can do. Any content not found in the application's directory will either be part of the *local* (i.e., the user's computer) or *remote* (i.e., not the user's computer) sandbox. Both are more restricted because something found on the Internet shouldn't have the same power as an application the user installed on his or her computer.

With respect to sound files, content in the network sandbox can't load or play sounds found locally. Content in the local sandbox cannot load or play remote sounds without the user's permission. In cases where sounds can be loaded and played, if the sound file and the page attempting to access it are in different domains, the sound's other data is not accessible unless a "cross-domain policy file" is used. In other words, in some cases an AIR application cannot access a sound's ID3 information or use some of the SoundMixer and SoundTransform methods without checking the validity of the request.

All that being said, application sandbox content, like the examples in this chapter, don't have these restrictions, so you can provide a value of false for the second argument when creating a SoundLoaderContext object. Chapter 15, "Security Techniques," discusses application security in much greater detail.

Controlling Sounds

The examples thus far simply play selected songs. But AIR applications allow sound playback to be controlled in other ways, including:

◆ Pausing sounds

◆ Resuming playback of a paused sound

◆ Tracking the playback

◆ Adjusting the sound volume

◆ Adjusting the panning (left-right levels)

To perform these tasks, you'll need to use some new classes.

You first need to know that the play() method of the Sound object takes an optional first argument, which is the point, in milliseconds, at which the playing should begin. With that knowledge, you could easily start playing a sound at any random spot:

```
sound.play(60000); // Start 1 minute in.
```

This is good to know, because to pause a playing sound, you actually have to stop it and start it playing again at that same spot (there is no actual pause feature). To know where the playing was stopped, use a SoundChannel object. One is returned by the play() method:

```
var sc = sound.play();
```

The current playback position is available in the SoundChannel's position attribute. So you might have a pause button that calls this function:

```
var marker = 0;
function pause() {
    marker = sc.position;
    sc.stop();
}
```

Note that you call the SoundChannel object's stop() method to terminate playback (the Sound object doesn't have a stop() method).

To start the sound playing again at the point it was paused, you just need to provide the play() method with that marker value:

```
function play() {
    sound.play(marker);
}
```

A sound's volume and panning (how much sound is going to the left channel and how much is going to the right) are managed by the SoundTransform class. You can create an object of this type using

```
var st = new air.SoundTransform(vol,
→ pan);
```

The first attribute, representing the volume, is a number between 0 (muted) and 1 (full volume). The second attribute, representing the panning, is a number between -1 (entirely left channel) and 1 (entirely right channel), with 0 meaning the channels receive equal weight. To associate the object with the playing sound, add it as the third argument when calling the play() method:

```
sound.play(marker, 0, st);
```

The second argument, which I haven't mentioned before, is the number of times the sound should be looped. If you don't want to loop the sound, use the value 0.

Note that the volume and panning apply just to the associated sound. These values don't affect the volume or panning of the operating system as a whole or of other sounds that this same program may use. That functionality is handled by the SoundMixer class.

You can also adjust the volume and panning by assigning new values to the SoundTransform object's volume and pan attributes:

```
st.volume = 1; // Full volume
```

To make such changes take effect while a sound is playing, reassociate the SoundTransform object (with its updated values) with the SoundChannel object:

```
sc.soundTransform = st;
```

Let's take all this information and update Script 14.2 to add pause and volume control buttons to the application (**Figure 14.9**).

Figure 14.9 After selecting an MP3 file to play, the user can now play and pause the sound, as well as increase or decrease the sound's volume.

To control sounds:

1. Open Script 14.2 in your text editor or IDE.

2. After creating the initial three objects, create three new variables and one more object (**Script 14.4**):

```
var sc = null;
var marker = 0;
var vol = 0.5;
var st = new air.SoundTransform(vol,
→ 0);
```

continues on page 306

Script 14.4 This is an update of Script 14.2, which played a sound the user selected from the user's computer. This version allows the user to pause the sound, plus adds control over the sound's volume.

```
1    <html><!-- Script 14.4 -->
2       <head>
3          <title>Playing Sounds</title>
4          <script type="text/javascript" src="AIRAliases.js"></script>
5          <script type="text/javascript">
6
7          // Create the objects:
8          var url = null;
9          var sound = new air.Sound();
10         var file = new air.File();
11         var sc = null;
12         var marker = 0;
13         var vol = 0.5;
14         var st = new air.SoundTransform(vol, 0);
15
16         // Add the event listeners:
17         file.addEventListener(air.Event.SELECT, fileWasSelected);
18         sound.addEventListener(air.Event.COMPLETE, loadComplete);
19         sound.addEventListener(air.IOErrorEvent.IO_ERROR, soundError);
20
21         window.onload = function() {
22            var filter = new air.FileFilter('MP3', '*.mp3');
23            file.browseForOpen('Choose an MP3:', [filter]);
24         }
25
```

(script continues on next page)

Script 14.4 *continued*

```
26      // Function that will be called
27      // when the file has been selected.
28      function fileWasSelected(e) {
29          url = new air.URLRequest(file.url);
30          sound.load(url);
31      }
32
33      // Function called when the sound has been loaded.
34      function loadComplete(e) {
35          document.getElementById('play').disabled = false;
36          document.getElementById('pause').disabled = false;
37      }
38
39      // Function called when the user clicks the 'Play' button.
40      function playSound() {
41          sc = sound.play(marker, 0, st);
42      }
43
44      // Function called when the user clicks the 'Pause' button.
45      function pauseSound() {
46
47          // Get the current position:
48          marker = sc.position;
49
50          // Stop the playing:
51          sc.stop();
52
53      } // End of pauseSound() function.
54
55      // Function for adjusting the volume.
56      function adjustVolume(how) {
57
58          // Increasing or decreasing the volume?
59          if (how == 'up') {
60              if (vol < 1.0) vol += 0.1;
61          } else if (how == 'down') {
62              if (vol > 0.1) vol -= 0.1;
63          }
64
65          // Enact the changes:
66          st.volume = vol;
67          sc.soundTransform = st;
68
69      } // End of adjustVolume() function.
70
71      // Function for handling sound errors.
72      function soundError(e) {
73          alert('An error occurred. The MP3 cannot be played');
74      }
75
76      </script>
77
78  </head>
79  <body>
80      <button id="play" onclick="playSound()" disabled>Play</button>
81      <button id="pause" onclick="pauseSound()" disabled>Pause</button>
82      <button id="volUp" onclick="adjustVolume('up')">+</button>
83      <button id="volDown" onclick="adjustVolume('down')">-</button>
84  </body>
85  </html>
```

CONTROLLING SOUNDS

The `sc` variable will later be of SoundChannel type, which is used to control the playing of the sound. It needs to be a global variable, so is declared here. The `marker` global variable will be used for tracking where in the sound the virtual playhead currently is. The next two variables will be used to control the volume. First, `vol` is set as 0.5, which is to say half volume. Then a `SoundTransform` object is created, using this volume value and unadjusted panning.

3. In the `loadComplete()` function, enable the Pause button:

```
document.getElementById('pause').
→ disabled = false;
```

This function already enabled the Play button after the sound was loaded, now it will also enable the to-be-added Pause button. If you want to be extra precise, you could only enable Pause when the song is playing and only enable Play when the song is not playing.

4. Within the `playSound()` function, update the call of the `play()` method:

```
sc = sound.play(marker, 0, st);
```

The `play()` method will now use three arguments: `marker` (where to start playing), the loop value (0), and the `SoundTransform` object. The `SoundChannel` object returned by this method call will be assigned to the `sc` variable.

When the user first clicks play, `marker` will have a value of 0, so playback will begin at the start of the song.

5. Define the `pauseSound()` function:

```
function pauseSound() {
   marker = sc.position;
   sc.stop();
}
```

This function will be called when the user clicks the Pause button. It first gets the current playhead position, assigning that to the `marker` variable. Then it stops the playback. When the user clicks Play again, this new value for `marker` will be used to restart the sound at this same spot.

6. Begin defining the `adjustVolume()` function:

```
function adjustVolume(how) {
```

This function will be called when the user clicks on one of two volume-adjusting buttons. Each passes to this function a value, either *up* or *down*.

7. Use a conditional to appropriately adjust the value of the `vol` variable:

```
if (how == 'up') {
   if (vol < 1.0) vol += 0.1;
} else if (how == 'down') {
   if (vol > 0.1) vol -= 0.1;
}
```

If the user clicked the + button (see Figure 14.9), the volume should be increased by ten percent, as long as it's not already at the highest possible value of 1. Conversely, if the user clicked the - (minus) button, the volume should be decreased by ten percent, as long as it's not already at the lowest possible value of 0.

8. Complete the `adjustVolume()` function:

```
   st.volume = vol;
   sc.soundTransform = st;
} // End of adjustVolume() function.
```

To make the volume changes take effect on the playing sound, the new volume value needs to be assigned to the `SoundTransform` object's volume attribute. Then the updated `SoundTransform` object needs to be assigned to the `SoundChannel` object's `soundTransform` attribute.

9. Within the body of the page, add three more buttons:

```
<button id="pause" onclick=
→ "pauseSound()" disabled>Pause
→ </button>
<button id="volUp" onclick=
→ "adjustVolume('up')">+</button>
<button id="volDown" onclick="adjust
→ Volume('down')">-</button>
```

The new Pause button calls the pauseSound() function. Both volume buttons call the adjustVolume() function, passing it different values.

10. Save, test, debug, and run the completed application.

✔ Tip

■ If you call the stop() method of the SoundChannel object on a sound that's currently being streamed (i.e., is still being loaded), the sound won't stop playing. Instead, the sound will stop playing at that point, and then immediately restart at the beginning (because the sound is still streaming). The Sound object's close() method will stop the playing of a streaming sound and prevent it from continuing to load.

Viewing ID3 Information

The MP3 format uses ID3 metadata to store information about the sound file. Your AIR applications can read this data to find out the song's name, the artist, and so forth. Because not all MP3 files will necessarily contain the ID3 information, your application should only attempt to read in this data after an air.Event.ID3 event has occurred:

```
sound.addEventListener(air.Event.ID3, displayID3);
```

Within the handling function (here, displayID3()), the ID3 info is available within the Sound object's id3 attribute. For example, the song name is stored in s.id3.songName and the artist in s.id3.artist. There's also s.id3.album, s.id3.genre, s.id3.track, and s.id3.year (all of these assume that s is an object of Sound type). If you look up the formal description of the Sound class's id3 attribute, you'll see tables of other properties, like the sound's total time (s.id3.TIME), the recording date (s.id3.TRDA), and so forth.

The only thing to note is that the availability of the ID3 data (if it is present in the file) also depends on the security settings. If the application accessing the sound file and the sound file itself are in the same security sandbox, or if the sound file is in the application security sandbox, getting the ID3 data won't be a problem. Otherwise, getting the data depends on the use of the SoundLoaderContext object. See the "Playing Streaming Sounds" section of this chapter for more on this object.

Displaying PDFs

As you might expect, since both technologies come from Adobe, AIR applications support the viewing of PDF (Portable Document Format) files. To do so, the AIR application uses the Adobe Reader plug-in, as long as the user has version 8.1 or higher of that already installed. Your application can check the user's support for PDFs by referring to `air.HTMLLoader.PDFCapability`. Its value will be one of four constants: `STATUS_OK`, `ERROR_INSTALLED_READER_NOT_FOUND`, `ERROR_INSTALLED_READER_TOO_OLD`, and `ERROR_PREFERRED_READER_TOO_OLD`. The first constant is the value to watch for; the last three are frighteningly long but clear in their meanings (the final constant indicates that an acceptable version is installed but not set as the default).

PDFs can be displayed in an application using the same methods you'd use in an HTML page, primarily this means in objects or iframes. As a quick example of this, the next application will allow the user to view a PDF on the computer, provided that PDF support is enabled.

To display PDF content:

1. In your project's primary HTML file, create the necessary object (**Script 14.5**):

   ```
   var file = new air.File();
   file.addEventListener(air.Event.
   → SELECT, fileWasSelected);
   ```

   This application only requires one object, of type `File`. This object will be associated with the selected PDF. One event listener is added to the object and listens for a `SELECT` event. That will be triggered once the user has selected the file.

2. Create an anonymous function that checks for PDF support:

   ```
   window.onload = function() {
       if (air.HTMLLoader.pdfCapability
       → == air.HTMLPDFCapability.
       → STATUS_OK) {
   ```

   After the application (technically, the window) has loaded, this anonymous function will be called. It first checks to see if the user's computer will allow for displaying of PDFs within this AIR application.

continues on page 310

Script 14.5 This simple application displays a PDF that the user has selected, assuming that the user's computer supports PDFs in AIR applications.

```
1   <html><!-- Script 14.5 -->
2      <head>
3         <title>Displaying PDFs</title>
4         <script type="text/javascript" src="AIRAliases.js"></script>
5         <script type="text/javascript">
6
7         // Create the object:
8         var file = new air.File();
9         file.addEventListener(air.Event.SELECT, fileWasSelected);
10
11        // Function called when the window loads.
12        window.onload = function() {
13
14           // Check for support:
15           if (air.HTMLLoader.pdfCapability == air.HTMLPDFCapability.STATUS_OK) {
16
17              // Limit what kinds of files can be opened:
18              var filter = new air.FileFilter('PDF', '*.pdf');
19
20              // Create the Open prompt:
21              file.browseForOpen('Choose a PDF:', [filter]);
22
23           } else { // No support!
24              alert('Your computer does not support the display of PDFs in this application.
                 Please upgrade to the latest version of Adobe Reader.');
25           }
26
27        } // End of anonymous function.
28
29        // Function that will be called
30        // when the file has been selected.
31        function fileWasSelected(e) {
32
33           // Add the file to the page as an object:
34           var o = document.createElement('object');
35           o.setAttribute('width', '100%');
36           o.setAttribute('height', '100%');
37           o.setAttribute('data', file.url);
38           o.setAttribute('type', 'application/pdf');
39           document.body.appendChild(o);
40
41        } // End of fileWasSelected() function.
42
43        </script>
44     </head>
45     <body>
46
47     </body>
48  </html>
```

3. Prompt the user to select a PDF:

```
var filter = new air.
→ FileFilter('PDF', '*.pdf');
file.browseForOpen('Choose a PDF:',
→ [filter]);
```

Similar to the code in the first example of this chapter, a filter is established that only allows the user to select files with a .pdf extension. Then the browse for open prompt is created (**Figure 14.10**).

4. Complete the anonymous function:

```
    } else {
        alert('Your computer does not
→ support the display of PDFs in
→ this application. Please
→ upgrade to the latest version
→ of Adobe Reader.');
    }
} // End of anonymous function.
```

If the conditional begun in step 2 is false, this application can't display PDFs and the user is told as much (**Figure 14.11**).

5. Create the `fileWasSelected()` function:

```
function fileWasSelected(e) {
    var o = document.
→ createElement('object');
    o.setAttribute('width', '100%');
    o.setAttribute('height', '100%');
    o.setAttribute('data', file.url);
    o.setAttribute('type',
→ 'application/pdf');
    document.body.appendChild(o);
}
```

This is the function that is called after the user has selected the PDF file from the computer. Within the function, a new object element will be created and added to

Figure 14.10 The prompt in which the user selects a PDF file to view.

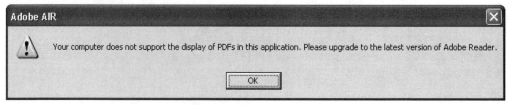

Figure 14.11 If the user does not have at least version 8.1 of Adobe Reader installed and enabled on the computer, this message appears when the user tries to run the application.

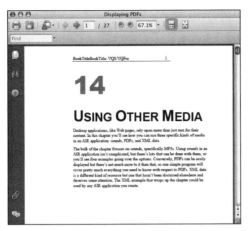

Figure 14.12 A PDF version of this chapter displayed in an AIR application.

Working with Other Media

This chapter demonstrates how to work with three specific mediums in an AIR application: sounds, PDFs, and XML data. I focus on these three because Adobe AIR's support and interactions with them is different than with other media, and they're commonly used in many programs.

AIR applications can use other media, too, like videos and images. There's nothing special as to how you'd use either: Use the same techniques as you would to place videos and images on an HTML page. AIR applications can also make extensive use of Flash content, naturally, either in HTML pages or by creating AIR applications with Flash as the foundation (a topic outside the scope of this book).

Adobe AIR also supports Digital Rights Management (DRM) for files. This can be used to control access to FLV (Flash video) and MP4 files (e.g., to paying customers). This feature is well covered in the online documentation.

the page. The result of this code will be the addition to the page's body of a line like

```
<object width="100%" height="100%"
→ data="file:///path/to/something.
→ pdf" type="application/pdf">
```

6. Save, test, debug, and run the completed application (**Figure 14.12**).

   Just like viewing a PDF in a Web browser, it will take a few seconds for the Reader plug-in to load the PDF file.

✔ Tips

- You cannot display PDFs in a transparent or fullscreen window.

- Because PDFs can contain JavaScript, you can use JavaScript to communicate between an Adobe AIR application and a PDF. See Adobe's online documentation for details.

DISPLAYING PDFS

Handling XML Data

Taking a slightly different approach, the last type of media I'll discuss in this chapter is XML data. While XML data is in fact just properly formatted plain text (like HTML), it needs to be handled differently than you would other plain text because the meaning is in the formatting.

The topic of XML is expansive and far beyond what I could discuss in this book, but I will provide some context for the next example. XML data has one root element (a made-up value) with one or more subelements within it:

```
<library>
<book></book>
<book></book>
</library>
```

Any element can have attributes:

```
<book isbn="0-321-52461-6"></book>
```

Element values go between the opening and closing tags:

```
<author>Larry Ullman</author>
```

Any element can also have subelements:

```
<book isbn="0-321-52461-6">
<title>Adobe AIR (Adobe Integrated
→ Runtime) with Ajax: Visual QuickPro
→ Guide</title>
<author>Larry Ullman</author>
</book>
```

XML is a popular format because it represents both the data being stored and the information about that data. With little or no other context, multiple applications can use the same XML data effectively.

A program can use XML data for any number of purposes. For example, iTunes stores information about the songs in your music library using an XML file. Another common use, which will be the basis of this next example (**Figure 14.13**), is to store a user's application preferences in XML format.

As mentioned earlier, the trick to using XML data is that although it is in fact plain text, it needs special treatment to be usable. Start by reading in the data as you would text stored in any file:

```
var file = air.File.
→ applicationStorageDirectory.
→ resolvePath('file.xml');
var stream = new air.FileStream();
stream.open(file, air.FileMode.READ);
var data = stream.readUTFBytes(stream.
→ bytesAvailable);
stream.close();
```

At this point, data is a string of text that happens to contain XML data. Next, you create a new object of type DOMParser (this is part of JavaScript, not something new to Adobe AIR):

```
var dp = new DOMParser();
```

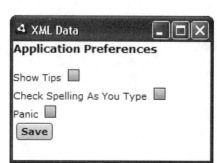

Figure 14.13 The choices the user makes for this application's (fake) preferences will be permanently stored in an XML file.

Script 14.6 The default XML preferences file that would ship with the application. It will be updated when the user changes their preferences (using Script 14.7).

```
1   <?xml version="1.0" encoding="UTF-8"?>
2   <preferences>
3       <showTips>false</showTips>
4       <checkSpelling>false</checkSpelling>
5       <panic>false</panic>
6   </preferences>
```

Then use the DOMParser object to turn the string into XML:

```
var xml = dp.parseFromString(data,
→ 'text/xml');
```

From there it's a matter of using rather verbose code to get the different element values. I'll explain more in the next sequence of steps.

To use XML data:

1. Create a new text document containing the following (**Script 14.6**):

    ```
    <?xml version="1.0" encoding="UTF-8"
    → ?>
    <preferences>
      <showTips>false</showTips>
      <checkSpelling>false</
      → checkSpelling>
      <panic>false</panic>
    </preferences>
    ```

    This is the initial XML preferences file. For this example, three preferences will be stored in it. Each preference will be a Boolean value, indicating that the user does (true) or does not (false) want to enable that setting. But in terms of the XML file, the preferences could just as easily store strings or numbers:

    ```
    <defaultLang>Eng</defaultLang>
    <historyCount>10</historyCount>
    ```

    Also note that XML files begin with the declaration: the opening and closing XML tags (<?xml and ?>) with attributes indicating the version (1.0 is fine) and the encoding.

2. Save the file as prefs.xml.

    Save the file in the project's directory and be sure to include that file when you build the actual AIR application.

continues on next page

HANDLING XML DATA

3. In your project's primary HTML file, create the necessary global variables (**Script 14.7**):

```
var file = air.File.
→ applicationStorageDirectory.
→ resolvePath('prefs.xml');

var stream = new air.FileStream();

var prefs = new Array('showTips',
→ 'checkSpelling', 'panic');
```

The application will use three global variables. The first two are for reading from and writing to the file (see Chapter 10, "Working with File Content," for details). The preferences file will be stored in the application's storage directory (which is the most logical place for it).

The third variable is an array of preference names. These names will be used in both the XML file and in the HTML. By storing them in an array, it makes it easier to quickly access them all.

continues on page 316

Script 14.7 This application reads in a user's preferences from an XML file. The user's current preferences are displayed in a window so they can be changed. When the user clicks the Save button, the updated preferences will be written to the XML file.

```
1   <html><!-- Script 14.7 -->
2      <head>
3         <title>XML Data</title>
4         <script type="text/javascript" src="AIRAliases.js"></script>
5         <script type="text/javascript">
6
7         // Create the objects:
8         var file = air.File.applicationStorageDirectory.resolvePath('prefs.xml');
9         var stream = new air.FileStream();
10
11        // List of preferences as an array:
12        var prefs = new Array('showTips', 'checkSpelling', 'panic');
13
14        // Function called when the application loads.
15        // This function retrieves the user's preferences.
16        window.onload = function() {
17
18           // Copy the preferences file to the storage
19           // directory if it's not already there.
20           if (!file.exists) {
21              var original = air.File.applicationDirectory.resolvePath('prefs.xml');
22              original.copyTo(file);
23           }
24
25           // Read the data from the file:
26           stream.open(file, air.FileMode.READ);
27           var data = stream.readUTFBytes(stream.bytesAvailable);
28           stream.close();
29
30           // Turn the file data into an XML object:
31           var dp = new DOMParser();
32           var xml = dp.parseFromString(data, 'text/xml');
33
```

(script continues on next page)

Script 14.7 *continued*

```
 34            // Set the preferences in the window:
 35            // Loop through each, adding its value to the data:
 36            for (var i = 0; i < prefs.length; i++) {
 37
 38                var item = xml.getElementsByTagName(prefs[i])[0].firstChild;
 39
 40                // If its value is 'true', check the box:
 41                if (item.nodeValue == 'true') document.getElementById(prefs[i]).checked = true;
 42
 43            } // End of for loop.
 44
 45        } // End of anonymous function.
 46
 47        // Function for writing the preferences to the file:
 48        function writePreferences() {
 49
 50            // Establish the OS-specific line ending:
 51            var CR = air.File.lineEnding;
 52
 53            // Start defining the data to be written:
 54            var data = '<?xml version="1.0" encoding="utf-8"?>' + CR;
 55            data += '<preferences>' + CR;
 56
 57            // Loop through each, adding its value to the data:
 58            for (var i = 0; i < prefs.length; i++) {
 59                data += '<' + prefs[i] + '>';
 60                data += (document.getElementById(prefs[i]).checked) ? 'true' : 'false';
 61                    data += '</' + prefs[i] + '>' + CR;
 62            }
 63
 64            // Close the root element:
 65            data += '</preferences>';
 66
 67            // Write the data to the file:
 68            stream.open(file, air.FileMode.WRITE);
 69            stream.writeUTFBytes(data);
 70            stream.close();
 71
 72            alert('Preferences saved!');
 73
 74        } // End of writePreferences() function.
 75
 76        </script>
 77    </head>
 78    <body>
 79    <h3>Application Preferences</h3>
 80    Show Tips <input type="checkbox" id="showTips"><br>
 81    Check Spelling As You Type <input type="checkbox" id="checkSpelling"><br>
 82    Panic <input type="checkbox" id="panic"><br>
 83    <button onclick="writePreferences();">Save</button>
 84    </body>
 85 </html>
```

HANDLING XML DATA

4. Begin defining an anonymous onload function:

```
window.onload = function() {
    if (!file.exists) {
        var original = air.File.
        → applicationDirectory.
        → resolvePath('prefs.xml');
        original.copyTo(file);
    }
```

The first thing this anonymous function, which is called after the window has loaded, does is check for the existence of the preferences file. If it doesn't exist, which will be the case the first time the application is run, the original (found in the application's directory) should be copied to the storage directory.

5. Read the data in from the file:

```
stream.open(file, air.FileMode.READ);
var data = stream.readUTFBytes
→ (stream.bytesAvailable);
stream.close();
```

At this point in the application, `data` contains a string of text. See Chapter 10 for more on reading from a file.

6. Create a `DOMParser` object and convert the data to XML:

```
var dp = new DOMParser();
var xml = dp.parseFromString(data,
→ 'text/xml');
```

Now the `xml` variable stores the data from the file as usable XML.

7. Access each preference in a loop:

```
for (var i = 0; i < prefs.length;
→ i++) {
    var item = xml.getElementsByTagName
    → (prefs[i])[0].firstChild;
```

This part involves a bit of code but is actually simple in theory. To start, the `for`

loop will loop through the preferences array, accessing each item with each iteration. Within the loop a reference is made to the corresponding element in the XML data. So the first time the loop is run, `prefs[i]` will have a value of *showTips*. The first line of code inside the loop is therefore equivalent to

```
var item = xml.getElementsByTagName
→ ('showTips')[0].firstChild;
```

The `getElementsByTagName()` method returns an array of elements with a given tag name (in the first iteration of the loop, that's *showTips*). This method always returns an array, even if there's only one element with that name, as in this case. So to refer to just that one element, `[0]` is added, indicating the first element in the array. The code up to that point would refer to the `<showTips>false</showTips>` part of the XML data.

Unfortunately, getting the value out of the element (i.e., *false*) takes a bit more effort. That value is actually a *text node* (i.e., a subelement or child) of the parent element `showTips`. Thus, the `firstChild` attribute will refer to this text node.

8. Check the corresponding check box, if appropriate.

```
    if (item.nodeValue == 'true')
    → document.getElementById
    → (prefs[i]).checked = true;
} // End of for loop.
```

The first line of the `for` loop, in step 7, retrieves a reference to the preference element's text node. To refer to that node's value, use `.nodeValue`. If this value equals *true* (the string, in quotes), the corresponding check box, which will have the same ID value as the preferences element, should be checked.

9. Complete the anonymous function:

```
} // End of anonymous function.
```

10. Begin defining the `writePreferences()` function.

```
function writePreferences() {
    var CR = air.File.lineEnding;
```

This function will write the user's preferences to the file. It will be called when the user clicks Save. It starts by associating the operating-specific line ending character with the variable CR (the `air.File.lineEnding` attribute is also introduced in Chapter 10).

11. Start defining the data to be written to the file:

```
var data = '<?xml version="1.0"
→ encoding="utf-8"?>' + CR;
data += '<preferences>' + CR;
```

Each time the user saves the preferences, the entire preferences file has to be rewritten from scratch. This may seem unnecessary, but it would take even more work to update just the parts of the file that have changed. So the point of this function is to re-create all the data in `prefs.xml` (see Script 14.6), starting with the XML declaration and root element.

12. Add each preference to the data:

```
for (var i = 0; i < prefs.length;
→ i++) {
    data += '<' + prefs[i] + '>';
    data += (document.getElementById
    → (prefs[i]).checked) ? 'true' :
    → 'false';
    data += '</' + prefs[i] + '>'
    → + CR;
}
```

A second `for` loop will be used to read in each preference from the HTML page. Within the loop, a line will be added to the `data` variable in the format

<name>value</name>

To determine the value, the ternary operator is used to see if the check box is clicked or not. The third line of code is, therefore, equivalent to

```
if (document.getElementById
→ (prefs[i]).checked) {
    data += 'true';
} else {
    data += 'false';
}
```

13. Write the data to the file:

```
data += '</preferences>';
stream.open(file, air.FileMode.
→ WRITE);
stream.writeUTFBytes(data);
stream.close();
```

To complete the string of data to be written to the file, the root element must be closed. Then the file is opened for writing, which will also erase any current contents. The data is written there and the file is closed.

continues on next page

HANDLING XML DATA

14. Complete the `writePreferences()` function:

```
    alert('Preferences saved!');

} // End of writePreferences()
→ function.
```

The alert just provides a visual cue to the user that the save process worked (**Figure 14.14**).

15. Within the body of the page, create the check boxes and a Save button:

```
Show Tips <input type="checkbox"
→ id="showTips"><br>

Check Spelling As You Type
→ <input type="checkbox"
→ id="checkSpelling"><br>

Panic <input type="checkbox"
→ id="panic"><br>

<button onclick="writePreferences();">
→ Save</button>
```

The `id` value of each element needs to exactly match that in the `prefs` array as well as the element names in the `prefs.xml` file. The Save button needs to invoke the `writePreferences()` function.

16. Save, test, debug, and run the completed application (**Figure 14.15**).

✔ Tips

■ As another example of an XML file (besides `prefs.xml`), check out the application descriptor file that is associated with every Adobe AIR application.

■ You can also read XML data (quite easily, in fact) by performing an `XMLHttpRequest` on the file. You can't write XML data this way, though (which is why this method isn't used in this example).

Figure 14.14 The result after the user clicks the Save button (assuming nothing went awry).

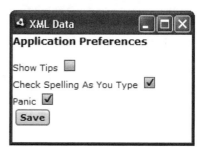

Figure 14.15 Restarting the application after changing and saving the preferences confirms that the entire process worked (compare with Figure 14.13).

SECURITY TECHNIQUES

The average Web developer does not have to delve too much into security issues. HTML has few, if any, security concerns because of the limitations it has within the Web browser. When you start working with JavaScript, let alone client-side technologies like PHP or ASP.NET, security becomes more of an issue because poor handling of malicious input can impact a site's visitors (and therefore your business). Because an AIR application runs on the user's computer with the same powers and privileges as any other program, it's important that Web developers making applications with the Adobe Integrated Runtime take extra time to consider several security-related problems and solutions.

This chapter looks at application security in two ways. The first two-thirds of the chapter explain and demonstrate the AIR security model. The model is simple in theory but complex in its details. To best convey this critical information, the first two examples are more demonstrative than practical, but the knowledge being taught leads up to instructions on creating a real-world, and secure, AIR application.

The remaining pages outline dozens of techniques, both general and specific, for tightening an application's security. Some of these pertain to JavaScript in particular and others are more applicable to AIR as a whole.

The AIR Security Model

The content—HTML, JavaScript, Shockwave, Flash, and so forth—that an application uses runs within one of two *sandboxes*: restricted areas in which the content "plays." All content will either be within the *application* or the *non-application* sandbox.

Only content in the application's installation directory—which should mean content bundled and installed with a program—can run within the application sandbox. Content in this sandbox can use the AIR APIs (Application Programming Interface), but cannot take advantage of some common but potentially dangerous HTML and JavaScript features (see the "Dynamic Code Execution"

sidebar). For example, such content can manipulate files and directories on the user's computer but is restricted in how it uses the JavaScript eval() function and cannot include a remote JavaScript file like so:

```
<script type="text/javascript"
→ src="http://www.example.com/
→ fileName.js"></script>
```

Simply put, application sandbox content is given more power but loses some freedoms that ordinary HTML pages have. Content in the non-application sandbox has just the opposite powers and privileges. For example, non-application sandbox content can include remote JavaScript files and use eval() to its full extent but can't manipulate files and

Dynamic Code Execution

One of the primary reasons AIR uses separate security sandboxes comes from the potential for executing *dynamically generated code*. In the applications you create, the JavaScript will be hard-coded (i.e., permanently defined in the content). As long as you aren't writing this application in order to do harm to people's computers, such JavaScript can be trusted (because, when it runs, it will do only what you programmed it to do). Conversely, dynamically generated code won't be known until the program runs. Therefore, there's no guarantee as to what said code will actually do.

Dynamically generated code can come from several situations. One would be inclusion of a remote script (like a JavaScript file stored online somewhere). If a hacker altered the contents of that file, your application will be at risk. Dynamically generated code can also arise from assigning data to an element's innerHTML or outerHTML values. If the data assigned is something like `<script type="text/javascript">Dangerous Code</script>`, that dangerous code will be executed. So if the data being assigned comes from a source that could be compromised, this is again an area for concern. Use of the JavaScript document.write() function has the same problem. The JavaScript eval() function also has a high risk factor, perhaps the highest. This function executes whatever code is passed to it, no matter what the ramifications are. If that code comes from outside of the content you created, your application is at risk for having malicious code executed.

In order to force a higher level of security on applications written using AIR, the methods that can be used to execute dynamically generated code are not usable within application sandbox content. And even though they are allowed within non-application sandbox content, you should still be very careful when using them. The last two sections of the chapter cover data validation and other security techniques to be applied in such cases.

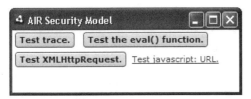

Figure 15.1 These four elements can be clicked to test the results of different actions within the application sandbox.

Script 15.1 This script will first be run within the application sandbox to see how air.trace(), eval(), XMLHttpRequests, and using *javascript:* for an href value will work.

```
1    <html><!-- Script 15.1 -->
2    <head>
3    <title>AIR Security Model</title>
4    <script type="text/javascript"
     src="AIRAliases.js"></script>
5    <script type="text/javascript">
6
7    // Function to test use of air.trace().
8    function testTrace() {
9        try {
10           air.trace('testing trace');
11       } catch (e) {
12           alert(e);
13       }
14   } // End of testTrace() function.
15
16   // Function to test use of the eval()
     function.
17   function testEval() {
18       try {
19           eval('alert("testing eval()")');
20       } catch (e) {
21           alert(e);
22       }
23   } // End of testEval() function.
24
25   // Function to test XMLHttpRequests.
26   function testXHR() {
27       var xhr = new XMLHttpRequest();
28       xhr.onreadystatechange = function() {
29           if (xhr.readyState == 4) {
30               alert( xhr.responseText );
31           }
32       }
33
```

(script continues on next page)

folders on the user's computer. Generally speaking, non-application sandbox content behaves more like a conventional Web page: techniques that could execute JavaScript code dynamically are allowed, because there's a limit to how much damage they can do on the user's computers. That limit is in part because non-application sandbox content can't use code that begins with air. or window.runtime.

With very few exceptions, most of the examples in this book run in the application sandbox. They are relatively simple scripts that don't attempt actions not allowed by the security model. As this next example will demonstrate, attempting tasks not allowed by the security model will result in error messages or no response at all. To get a sense of what content can do based on the sandbox it's in, let's make a dummy example that tests four different concepts (**Figure 15.1**).

To test the application sandbox:

1. In your project's primary HTML file, create three buttons and a link (**Script 15.1**):

   ```
   <button onclick="testTrace();">Test
   → trace.</button>
   <button onclick="testEval();">Test
   → the eval() function.</button>
   <button onclick="testXHR();">Test
   → XMLHttpRequest.</button>
   <a href="javascript:alert('testing
   → javascript: URL');">Test
   → javascript: URL.</a>
   ```

   This application will test four concepts that an AIR application can use. The first is a call to AIR's trace() function. The second is the use of the eval() function. The third will be a cross-domain XMLHttpRequest. The fourth will be the use of *javascript:* as the href value of a link (which has the end result of executing some JavaScript code when the link is clicked).

continues on next page

2. Within the JavaScript code block, define the testTrace() function:

```
function testTrace() {
    try {
        air.trace('testing trace');
    } catch (e) {
        alert(e);
    }
} // End of testTrace() function.
```

This function will simply call air. trace(), printing the text *testing trace* (**Figure 15.2**). To be notified of an error should one occur, the trace() function will be called within a try…catch block. If an error occurs, it'll be "caught" and assigned to the e variable (short for *error*), which is then printed in an alert. So, in short, this function will either successfully invoke trace() or will print (in an alert dialog) any error that is triggered.

Figure 15.2 Calls to the air.trace() function result in text being printed within the console.

THE AIR SECURITY MODEL

Script 15.1 *continued*

```
34      try {
35          xhr.open('GET', 'http://www.
            dmcinsights.com/air/ch13vars.txt');
36          xhr.send(null);
37      } catch (e) {
38          alert(e);
39      }
40  } // End of testXHR() function.
41
42  </script>
43  </head>
44  <body>
45
46  <button onclick="testTrace();">Test trace.</button>
47  <button onclick="testEval();">Test the eval() function.</button>
48  <button onclick="testXHR();">Test XMLHttpRequest.</button>
49  <a href="javascript:alert('testing javascript: URL');">Test javascript: URL.</a>
50
51  </body>
52  </html>
```

3. Define the testEval() function:

```
function testEval() {
    try {
        eval('alert("testing eval()")');
    } catch (e) {
        alert(e);
    }
} // End of testEval() function.
```

This function calls the JavaScript eval() function, passing it the code alert("testing eval()"). In other words, the eval() function is being told to execute code that would create an alert dialog.

If the eval() function can be called in the current sandbox, the text *testing eval()* will be printed in the alert dialog. If eval() cannot be called, an error will occur and it'll be printed in an alert (**Figure 15.3**).

4. Begin defining the testXHR() function:

```
function testXHR() {
    var xhr = new XMLHttpRequest();
    xhr.onreadystatechange =
    → function() {
        if (xhr.readyState == 4) {
            alert( xhr.responseText );
        }
    }
}
```

This function makes an XMLHttpRequest. The returned response will simply be printed in an alert (the importance of this example isn't in using the response but seeing what happens when an XMLHttpRequest is made within different sandboxes). See the example in Chapter 4, "Basic Concepts and Code," for explanations on what these particular lines mean (if you don't already know).

continues on next page

Figure 15.3 Content running within the application sandbox is restricted in its use of the eval() function. Attempts to use it could result in an error message like this one.

5. Complete the `testXHR()` function:

```
try {
    xhr.open('GET', 'http://www.
    ⇥ dmcinsights.com/air/
    ⇥ ch13vars.txt');
    xhr.send(null);
} catch (e) {
    alert(e);
}
} // End of testXHR() function.
```

If an error occurs in executing an `XMLHttpRequest`, it'll happen when its `open()` or `send()` methods are called. For this reason, this part of the request process is placed within a `try...catch` block. The URL being requested comes from Chapter 13, "Networking." The `ch13vars.txt` file just contains a small string of text (**Figure 15.4**).

6. Save, test, debug, and run the completed application.

You should see that this script, running in the application sandbox (which it will be when it's the program's primary HTML page), can use `trace()` (see Figure 15.2), cannot call `eval()` like it tries to (see the error in Figure 15.3), and can make a cross-domain `XMLHttpRequest` (see Figure 15.4). You'll also find that clicking on the link does nothing whatsoever.

✔ Tips

■ All the details as to what content can do in which sandbox are rather complicated. For example, application sandbox content can call `eval()` using any argument before the page has loaded but can only use certain kinds of arguments after that. See the online AIR documentation for all the gory details.

■ Content running in the application sandbox will have an `air.Security.sandboxType` value equal to the constant `air.Security.APPLICATION`. You can use a conditional to check for this value prior to attempting any action that you know to be restricted.

■ The non-application sandbox can be broken down into four subtypes: *remote*, *local-trusted*, *local-with-networking*, and *local-with-filesystem*. These four categories come from the Flash Player security model and are more pertinent to Flash and Shockwave content.

Figure 15.4 The result of the `XMLHttpRequest` shows the content returned by the requested page.

Using Non-Application Sandbox Content

The first example in this chapter demonstrates some of the tasks that can and cannot be done by content running in the application sandbox. To contrast this, let's create another example that runs in the non-application sandbox. One way that content runs in that sandbox is if it's loaded from outside the application installation directory. But there is another way to run content within the non-application sandbox—by associating it with another domain. To do that, include the content as an iframe with a different sandboxRoot domain:

```
<iframe src="example.html" sandboxRoot=
→ "http://www.example.com/air/"
→ documentRoot="app:/">
</iframe>
```

An iframe, like the older frame tag, creates a separate content area within a window. Its src attribute indicates the file to be used for the frame's content. The sandboxRoot attri-

bute is an addition to the iframe tag in Adobe AIR. It allows you to state that the frame's content is coming from a different domain. Its value must begin with *file*, *http*, or *https*, even if it's a made-up value. You can use *http://www.example.com* as the domain (as shown) or *http://localhost/*. For rather complicated reasons that I won't go into here, you should add a subdirectory to the sandboxRoot value, even if it doesn't exist (e.g., use *http://localhost/air/*, not just *http://localhost/*).

AIR also adds a documentRoot attribute to the iframe tag. It's used to find the content on the user's computer. Its value must begin with *file*, *app*, or *app-storage* and cannot be a made-up value (or else the content won't be found).

Looking back at this example code, even though the example.html file may be installed in the same place as the file that includes it (i.e., the file that has the iframe), the assignation of a different sandboxRoot value places example.html within the non-application sandbox. This is because content from different domains cannot be in the same security sandbox (and the parent HTML file is already in the application sandbox).

Now, you might think that you'd always want content to run within the application sandbox, but there are two common reasons you might want to have content run in the non-application sandbox:

- ◆ If the content uses features not allowed within the application sandbox. This may be the case when a third-party framework is being used.

- ◆ If the content doesn't need the full powers allowed in the application sandbox and you want to play it safe.

To compare and contrast the application and non-application sandboxes, this next script will run Script 15.1 within an iframe to test those same features in the non-application sandbox (**Figure 15.5**).

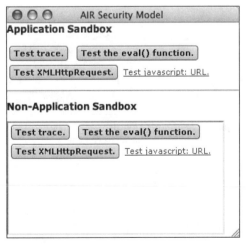

Figure 15.5 The top portion of the application is content running within the application sandbox. The bottom portion is the same content running within a non-application sandbox (because it's in an iframe with a different domain value).

To test the non-application sandbox:

1. Open Script 15.1 in your text editor or IDE, if it is not already.

2. In the body of the page, add an iframe (**Script 15.2**).

   ```
   <iframe src="script_15_01.html"
   → sandboxRoot="http://localhost/
   → air/" documentRoot="app:/">
   ```

   Change the src value here to whatever name you gave Script 15.1 (for the purposes of this book, I named that script, appropriately enough, *script_15_01.html*).

3. If you want, add some headers and a horizontal rule to clearly indicate the two sandboxes.

   Before the original set of buttons, add

   ```
   <h3>Application Sandbox</h3>
   ```

   Before the iframe, add

   ```
   <p><hr></p><h3>Non-Application
   → Sandbox</h3>
   ```

4. Save this file under a new name.

   You can use any name as long as it's different than the one you gave Script

15.1 (because that script will be used for the iframe source). Save the file in your project's directory.

5. Test, debug, and run the completed application (**Figures 15.6**, **15.7**, **15.8**, and **15.9**).

   The application sandbox content—the top section—still behaves the same; non-application sandbox content—the bottom section—will have different results as shown in the figures.

✔ Tips

■ As you can see in Figure 15.8, cross-domain XMLHttpRequests are not allowed within the non-application sandbox (this is also true for Web pages). In Adobe AIR, you can overrule this default setting by adding this code to your iframe tag:

   ```
   allowCrossDomainXHR="true"
   ```

■ If an application has two iframes, each of which loads content from a different domain—say, *www.example.com* and *localhost*, those two iframes run within separate non-application sandboxes.

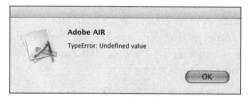

Figure 15.6 Because non-application sandbox content cannot use AIR APIs, a call to air.trace() results in this error.

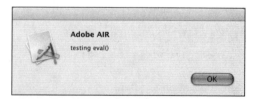

Figure 15.7 The eval() function can be fully used within non-application sandbox content.

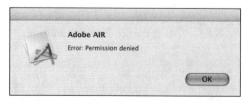

Figure 15.8 Unless special steps are taken (see the first tip), non-application sandbox content cannot perform cross-domain XMLHttpRequests.

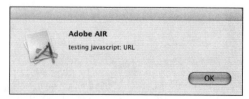

Figure 15.9 Non-application sandbox content also allows for uses of *javascript:* in an href value.

Script 15.2 This script is the same as Script 15.1, except that it also includes Script 15.1 as an iframe. That content will run in the non-application sandbox.

```
1    <html><!-- Script 15.2 -->
2    <head>
3    <title>AIR Security Model</title>
4    <script type="text/javascript" src="AIRAliases.js"></script>
5    <script type="text/javascript">
6
7    // Function to test use of the eval() function.
8    function testEval() {
9        try {
10           eval('alert("testing eval()")');
11       } catch (e) {
12           alert(e);
13       }
14   } // End of testEval() function.
15
16   // Function to test use of air.trace().
17   function testTrace() {
18       try {
19           air.trace('testing trace');
20       } catch (e) {
21           alert(e);
22       }
23   } // End of testTrace() function.
24
25   // Function to test XMLHttpRequests.
26   function testXHR() {
27       var xhr = new XMLHttpRequest();
28       xhr.onreadystatechange = function() {
29           if (xhr.readyState == 4) {
30               alert(xhr.responseText);
31           }
32       }
33
34       try {
35           xhr.open('GET', 'http://www.dmcinsights.com/air/ch13vars.txt');
36           xhr.send(null);
37       } catch (e) {
38           alert(e);
39       }
40   } // End of testXHR() function.
41
42   </script>
43   </head>
44   <body>
45
46   <h3>Application Sandbox</h3>
47
48   <button onclick="testTrace();">Test trace.</button>
49   <button onclick="testEval();">Test the eval() function.</button>
50   <button onclick="testXHR();">Test XMLHttpRequest.</button>
51   <a href="javascript:alert('testing javascript: URL');">Test javascript: URL.</a>
52
53   <p><hr></p><h3>Non-Application Sandbox</h3>
54
55   <iframe src="script_15_01.html" sandboxRoot="http://localhost/air/" documentRoot="app:/">
56   </iframe>
57
58   </body>
59   </html>
```

Using the Sandbox Bridge

In the AIR security model, applications are limited by a "same-origin" policy: Content is restricted from directly interacting with content from another source. With this previous example, this means that content in the application sandbox (Script 15.2) is limited in what it can do with content in the non-application sandbox (Script 15.1) and vice versa. To overcome this limitation, you can use the *sandbox bridge*.

Adobe AIR adds two properties to the `window` object: `childSandboxBridge` and `parent-SandboxBridge`. These properties can be used to make objects and functions in one script accessible to another. This concept can be hard to visualize, so I'll walk through some hypotheticals before implementing a real-world example.

Say you have a parent file, called `parent.html`, which includes the child file, `child.html`, in an iframe:

```
<iframe id="nas" src="child.html"
→ sandboxRoot="http://localhost/air/"
→ documentRoot="app:/"></iframe>
```

The iframe has an `id` value of *nas* (short for *non-application sandbox*).

The `parent.html` file has a function called *doThis*, which doesn't do anything:

```
function doThis() {}
```

The `child.html` file cannot call this function unless a bridge is made to it. To do that, `parent.html` needs this line:

```
document.getElementById('nas').
→ contentWindow.parentSandboxBridge =
→ doThis;
```

Now, for `child.html` to call this function, all it needs to do is refer to (**Figure 15.10**)

```
window.parentSandboxBridge.doThis().
```

As an example of making child content available in the parent, I'll walk through a different example. Say you want to make both a variable and a function available to the parent page. In the `child.html` page, start by defining an object containing a function and a variable:

```
var square = new Object();
square.side = 14;
square.getArea = function() {
    return this.side * this.side;
}
```

The first line creates a new variable of type generic `Object`. The second line creates an attribute in this object called *side* with a value of 14. The remaining code creates a method in the object called *getArea*. The method takes no arguments and returns the value of the `side` attribute times itself (`this` in OOP always refers to the current object, so `this.side` refers to this object's `side` attribute).

```
<!-- parent html -->
<script type="text/javascript">
function doThis() {}

document.getElementById
('nas').contentWindow.parentSandboxBridge = doThis;

</script>
</head>
<body>

<iframe id="nas" src="child.html" sandboxRoot="http://
localhost/air/" documentRoot="app:/">

    <!-- child.html -->
    <script type="text/javascript">

    window.parentSandboxBridge.doThis();

    </script>

</iframe>

</body>
</html>
```

Figure 15.10 The content in an iframe can call a function in the parent file, like `doThis()`, if the function is made available via the `parentSandboxBridge`.

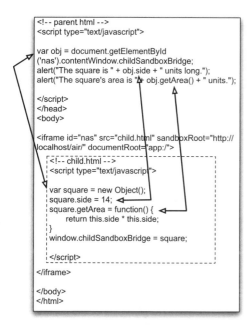

```
<!-- parent html -->
<script type="text/javascript">

var obj = document.getElementById
('nas').contentWindow.childSandboxBridge;
alert("The square is " + obj.side + " units long.");
alert("The square's area is " + obj.getArea() + " units.");

</script>
</head>
<body>

<iframe id="nas" src="child.html" sandboxRoot="http://
localhost/air/" documentRoot="app:/">

    <!-- child.html -->
    <script type="text/javascript">

    var square = new Object();
    square.side = 14;
    square.getArea = function() {
        return this.side * this.side;
    }
    window.childSandboxBridge = square;

    </script>

</iframe>

</body>
</html>
```

Figure 15.11 A parent file can use an object defined in the child file made available through the childSandboxBridge property.

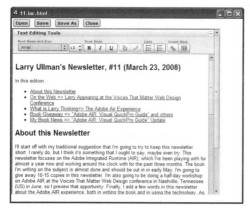

Figure 15.12 Thanks to the Yahoo! User Interface framework, a textarea is turned into an HTML editor.

Then, to make the object available in the parent, do this:

```
window.childSandboxBridge = square;
```

Now `parent.html` must get a reference to the object. To do that, it refers to the iframe element window's `childSandboxBridge` attribute:

```
var obj = document.getElementById('nas').
→ contentWindow.childSandboxBridge;
```

And finally, `parent.html` can refer to `obj.side` and `obj.getArea()` (**Figure 15.11**).

This next example should help you best understand how the AIR security model, the sandboxes, and the sandbox bridge would be used into a real-world application. This program (**Figure 15.12**) will be an expansion on the text editor created in Chapter 10, "Working with File Content." By incorporating the Yahoo! User Interface (YUI; http://developer.yahoo.com/yui/), the application will work as a WYSIWYG HTML editor. The application is complicated, from a security perspective, because it needs the ability to write to and read from files on the user's computer (i.e., AIR functionality), but it also needs to load remote JavaScript files and use the `innerHTML` property (both of which are restricted within application sandbox content). The solution will be to place all the AIR functionality in one file, load the YUI editor in an iframe (that runs within the non-application sandbox), and use a sandbox bridge to communicate between the two.

This example will require just two scripts. Most of the file-related logic comes from Script 10.2, with a couple of nice additions. The specifics for getting the YUI editor to work come from its own documentation, but I'll explain the relevant code in the following steps. Finally, with respect to the sandbox bridge, I'll make some of the child's (i.e., the frame's) functionality available in the parent but won't be making any parent functionality available in the child (the bridge only needs to go one way for this to work). Let's start by creating the frame's content, which is the HTML editor.

To use a sandbox bridge:

1. In an HTML file, include all the necessary YUI files (**Script 15.3**):

```
<link rel="stylesheet" type="text/
→ css" href="http://yui.yahooapis.
→ com/2.5.1/build/assets/skins/
→ sam/skin.css">

<script type="text/javascript"
→ src="http://yui.yahooapis.
→ com/2.5.1/build/yahoo-dom-event/
→ yahoo-dom-event.js"></script>

<script type="text/javascript"
→ src="http://yui.yahooapis.com/
→ 2.5.1/build/element/element-beta-
→ min.js"></script>

<script src="http://yui.yahooapis.
→ com/2.5.1/build/container/
→ container_core-min.js"></script>

<script src="http://yui.yahooapis.
→ com/2.5.1/build/editor/
→ simpleeditor-beta-min.js">
→ </script>
```

These lines come verbatim from the YUI library documentation. Including these scripts is necessary to create the "simple editor" (Yahoo!'s term). Note that these files are all being included from Yahoo!'s Web site; they are not packaged with the application and loaded from there. This is one reason that this content can't be placed within the application sandbox.

2. In the body of the script, create a textarea with an id value of *editArea*:

```
<textarea name="editArea"
→ id="editArea"></textarea>
```

This textarea will be where the user edits all text. The id value will be used by the code that generates the editor. This is all that the body of the page needs to contain.

3. In a JavaScript block, create a function to be called after the page has loaded:

```
window.onload = function() {

}
```

This anonymous function will do all the setup for the text editor and the child page as a whole.

4. Within the anonymous function, create the editor:

```
var yuiEditor = new YAHOO.widget.
→ SimpleEditor('editArea', {height:
→ '100%', width: '100%', collapse:
→ true});

yuiEditor.render();
```

Again, these two lines of code come from the YUI documentation. The first creates a SimpleEditor object associated with the *editArea* textarea. The second line creates the actual editor on the page by calling the render() method.

5. Create an object to be used by the sandbox bridge:

```
var forParent = new Object();
```

This object will be made available to the script running in the application sandbox (i.e., the parent to this file). It will enable the parent to access the text being edited so that the parent can write that text to a file (and, conversely, load the editor with text read in from a file).

6. Define a function that assigns the text to be edited:

```
forParent.setContents =
→ function(str) {
   yuiEditor.setEditorHTML(str);
}
```

continues on page 332

Script 15.3 A few lines of code and some files included remotely from Yahoo!'s Web site will create an HTML editor to be run in a non-application sandbox.

```
1    <html><!-- Script 15.3 -->
2    <head>
3    <title>Editor</title>
4    <script type="text/javascript" src="AIRAliases.js"></script>
5    <link rel="stylesheet" type="text/css" href="http://yui.yahooapis.com/2.5.1/build/assets/skins/
     sam/skin.css">
6    <script type="text/javascript" src="http://yui.yahooapis.com/2.5.1/build/yahoo-dom-event/
     yahoo-dom-event.js"></script>
7    <script type="text/javascript" src="http://yui.yahooapis.com/2.5.1/build/element/
     element-beta-min.js"></script>
8    <script src="http://yui.yahooapis.com/2.5.1/build/container/container_core-min.js"></script>
9    <script src="http://yui.yahooapis.com/2.5.1/build/editor/simpleeditor-beta-min.js"></script>
10   <script type="text/javascript">
11
12   // When the page loads, do the prep work:
13   window.onload = function() {
14
15       // Create the editor on the page:
16       var yuiEditor = new YAHOO.widget.SimpleEditor('editArea', {height: '100%', width: '100%',
         collapse: true});
17       yuiEditor.render();
18
19       // Create an object for parent file access:
20       var forParent = new Object();
21
22       // Function for setting the editor's contents:
23       forParent.setContents = function(str) {
24           yuiEditor.setEditorHTML(str);
25       }
26
27       // Function for returning the editor's contents:
28       forParent.getContents = function() {
29           yuiEditor.saveHTML();
30           return yuiEditor.get('element').value;
31       }
32
33       // Make the forParent object available
34       // via the sandbox bridge:
35       window.childSandboxBridge = forParent;
36
37   } // End of anonymous function.
38
39   </script>
40   </head>
41   <body class="yui-skin-sam">
42   <textarea name="editArea" id="editArea"></textarea>
43   </body>
44   </html>
```

USING THE SANDBOX BRIDGE

This code adds to the `forParent` object a method called *setContents*. This method will take a string as an argument (assigned to the variable `str`). The body of the method calls the `yuiEditor.setEditorHTML()` function. That function is used to assign to the textarea the actual text to be edited. In other words, the `forParent` object's `setContents()` method, which will eventually be callable by the parent script, acts as an alias to the `yuiEditor.setEditorHTML()` method.

7. Define a function that returns the text being edited:

```
forParent.getContents = function() {
    yuiEditor.saveHTML();
    return yuiEditor.get('element').
    → value;
}
```

These two lines also come from the YUI documentation. To get the edited text, call the `saveHTML()` method, and then return the `SimpleEditor` object's `get('element').value` attribute. This code is wrapped inside a function definition and is defined as the `getContents()` method of the `forParent` object.

8. Make the `forParent` object available to the parent script:

```
window.childSandboxBridge =
→ forParent;
```

Now the `forParent` object, and its `setContents()` and `getContents()` methods, can be used by the parent file (to be written next).

9. Save the file as `editor.html` in your project's directory.

10. In your project's primary HTML file, create four buttons in the body of the page (**Script 15.4**).

```
<button onclick="openFile();" id=
→ "btnOpen" disabled>Open</button>
<button onclick="writeData();" id=
→ "btnSave" disabled>Save</button>
<button onclick="saveFileAs();" id=
→ "btnSaveAs" disabled>Save As
→ </button>
<button onclick="closeFile();" id=
→ "btnClose" disabled>Close</button>
```

These four buttons will be used to provide basic functionality: opening a file for editing, saving a file, saving a file as a new file, and closing of a file. Each calls an associated JavaScript function. Each is also disabled to start. The Save and Close buttons are disabled because there's nothing to save or close until the user has opened a file. The Open and Save As files are disabled because the application needs to make some preparations first.

11. Add an iframe:

```
<iframe id="nas" src="editor.html"
→ sandboxRoot="http://localhost/
→ air/" documentRoot="app:/"
→ width="90%" height="90%">
→ </iframe>
```

The iframe has an id value of *nas* and its source is the `editor.html` file (Script 15.3). The domain for this content is *http://localhost/air/*: a made-up value that will place this content in a non-application sandbox. The documentRoot is `app:/`, meaning that the file will be found in the application's installation directory.

12. Within a JavaScript block, create three global variables and an anonymous function to be called once the page has loaded:

```
var mode, file, editor = null;
window.onload = function() {
}
```

continues on page 335

Script 15.4 This script will run in the application sandbox and include Script 15.3 in an iframe. This page manages all the AIR file-related functionality and uses a sandbox bridge to interact with the HTML editor.

```
1    <html><!-- Script 15.4 -->
2    <head>
3    <title>Text Editor</title>
4    <script type="text/javascript"
     src="AIRAliases.js"></script>
5    <script type="text/javascript">
6
7    // Global variables:
8    var mode, file, editor = null;
9
10   // When the page loads, do the prep work:
11   window.onload = function() {
12
13       // Get a reference to the child object
14       // made available through the sandbox
         bridge:
15       editor = document.getElementById('nas').
         contentWindow.childSandboxBridge;
16
17       // Create a new File object:
18       makeNewFileObject();
19
20       // Enable the Open and SaveAs buttons:
21       document.getElementById('btnOpen').
         disabled = false;
22       document.getElementById('btnSaveAs').
         disabled = false;
23
24   } // End of anonymous function.
25
26   // This function creates a new File object.
27   function makeNewFileObject() {
28
29       // Make the object:
30       file = air.File.documentsDirectory;
31
32       // Need an event listener for selecting
         the file:
33       file.addEventListener(air.Event.SELECT,
         fileWasSelected);
34
35   } // End of makeNewFileObject() function.
36
37   // Function called when the selection
     event occurs.
38   function fileWasSelected(e) {
39
```

Script 15.4 *continued*

```
40   // Call the right function depending
     upon the mode:
41   if (mode == 'open') {
42       readData();
43   } else if (mode == 'save') {
44       writeData();
45   }
46
47   // Set the title as the file's name:
48   document.title = file.name
49
50   // Enable the Save and Close buttons:
51   document.getElementById('btnSave').
     disabled = false;
52   document.getElementById('btnClose').
     disabled = false;
53
54   } // End of fileWasSelected() function.
55
56   // Function called when the user clicks
     Open.
57   function openFile() {
58
59       // If a file is already open, close it
         first:
60       if (!file.isDirectory) closeFile();
61
62       // Set the mode:
63       mode = 'open';
64
65       // Limit what kinds of files can be
         opened:
66       var filter = new air.FileFilter('Text',
         '*.txt;*.html;*.css;*.js');
67
68       // Create the dialog:
69       file.browseForOpen('Choose a text
         file:', [filter]);
70
71   } // End of openFile() function.
72
73   // Function called when the user clicks
     Save As.
74   function saveFileAs() {
75
76       // Set the mode:
77       mode = 'save';
78
```

(script continues on next page)

Script 15.4 *continued*

```
79      // Prompt to select the file's name
        and location:
80      file.browseForSave('Save As');
81
82   } // End of saveFileAs() function.
83
84   // Function called when the user clicks
     Close.
85   function closeFile() {
86
87      // Ask if the file should be saved:
88      if (confirm('Save before closing?')) {
89         if (!file.isDirectory) {
90            writeData();
91         } else {
92            saveFileAs();
93         }
94      }
95
96      // Reset the File object:
97      makeNewFileObject();
98
99      // Disable the Save and Close buttons:
100     document.getElementById('btnSave').
        disabled = true;
101     document.getElementById('btnClose').
        disabled = true;
102
103     // Reset the page title:
104     document.title = 'Text Editor';
105
106     // Clear the textarea:
107     editor.setContents('');
108
109  } // End of closeFile() function.
110
111  // Function that reads in the data.
112  function readData() {
113
114     // Open the file for reading:
115     var stream = new air.FileStream();
116     stream.open(file, air.FileMode.READ);
117
118     // Read the contents and send them to
        the editor:
119     editor.setContents(stream.
        readUTFBytes(stream.bytesAvailable));
```

Script 15.4 *continued*

```
120
121     stream.close();
122
123  } // End of readData() function.
124
125  // Function that writes the data to the
     file.
126  function writeData() {
127
128     // Get the text and convert line
        endings:
129     var data = editor.getContents();
130     data = data.replace(/\n/g, air.File.
        lineEnding);
131
132     // Open the file for writing:
133     var stream = new air.FileStream();
134     stream.open(file, air.FileMode.WRITE);
135
136     // Write the data:
137     stream.writeUTFBytes(data);
138
139     // Close the file:
140     stream.close();
141
142  } // End of writeData() function.
143
144  </script>
145  </head>
146  <body>
147
148  <button onclick="openFile();" id="btnOpen"
     disabled>Open</button>
149  <button onclick="writeData();" id="btnSave"
     disabled>Save</button>
150  <button onclick="saveFileAs();"
     id="btnSaveAs" disabled>Save As</button>
151  <button onclick="closeFile();"
     id="btnClose" disabled>Close</button>
152
153  <iframe id="nas" src="editor.html"
     sandboxRoot="http://localhost/air/"
     documentRoot="app:/" width="90%"
     height="90%"></iframe>
154
155  </body>
156  </html>
```

The three variables will be needed by multiple functions, so they must be global. The anonymous function will do the preparatory work for the application.

13. Within the anonymous function, get a reference to the forParent object found in editor.html (Script 15.3):

```
editor = document.getElementById
→ ('nas').contentWindow.
→ childSandboxBridge;
```

This line assigns to the editor variable the object made available by the child page. So now the parent file's editor variable is the same as the child file's forParent object.

14. Still within the anonymous function, call the makeNewFileObject() function and enable the Open and Save As buttons:

```
makeNewFileObject();

document.getElementById('btnOpen').
→ disabled = false;

document.getElementById
→ ('btnSaveAs').disabled = false;
```

This script uses a separate function for creating the necessary File object. The File object, of course, is used to refer to the file being edited. The makeNewFileObject() function will be called when the application is first started or after a file is closed. It's a good idea to make a new File object after closing an edited file to avoid bugs when the user goes to edit or create a new file. In other words, when the user is editing file A and then opens file B, all references to file A will first be wiped clean.

Once the File object has been created (by calling the function), it's safe to enable the Open and Save As buttons (**Figure 15.13**).

15. Define the makeNewFileObject() function:

```
function makeNewFileObject() {
    file = air.File.
    → documentsDirectory;
    file.addEventListener(air.Event.
    → SELECT, fileWasSelected);
}
```

First, file is assigned the value of a new File object, pointing to the user's documents directory. Then the event listener is added that states when a SELECT event occurs, the fileWasSelected() function should be called.

16. Begin defining the fileWasSelected() function:

```
function fileWasSelected(e) {
    if (mode == 'open') {
        readData();
    } else if (mode == 'save') {
        writeData();
    }
```

continues on next page

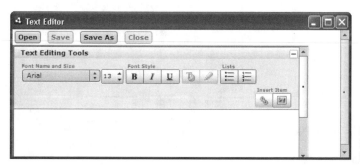

Figure 15.13 The application once it has fully loaded but before a file has been opened.

USING THE SANDBOX BRIDGE

This function will be called in two situations: when the user opens a file for editing and when the user chooses what to save a file as. If the file has been opened, the data should be read from it. If the file has been selected for saving, the data should be written to it. To know which is the case, despite the fact that the same event is triggered both times, the global mode variable is used in a conditional. This same logic is also used in Script 10.2 (see that example if this explanation isn't sufficient for you).

17. Complete the fileWasSelected() function:

```
document.title = file.name
document.getElementById
→ ('btnSave').disabled = false;
document.getElementById
→ ('btnClose').disabled = false;
} // End of fileWasSelected()
→ function.
```

After either reading in the data from the selected file or saving the data to it, these three lines are executed. The first changes the title of the application to the name of the file (compare Figures 15.12 and 15.13). This is just a nice little feature that's easy to implement.

Also, the Save and Close buttons are finally enabled because now that a file has been chosen (for reading from or writing to), the user should be able to perform either of those tasks.

18. Define the openFile() function:

```
function openFile() {
    if (!file.isDirectory)
    → closeFile();
    mode = 'open';
    var filter = new air.FileFilter
    → ('Text', '*.txt;*.html;*.css;
    → *.js');
```

```
file.browseForOpen('Choose a text
→ file:', [filter]);
}
```

This function needs to set the value of the mode variable (so that the conditional in the fileWasSelected() function, see step 16, will work), and then generate the browse for open prompt (**Figure 15.14**). The user is restricted to only opening files with certain extensions, thanks to the FileFilter object (again, see Chapter 10).

The first line of the function states that if the file object is not a directory, the closeFile() function should be called. I'll explain why...

When the File object is first created, it will refer to a directory (specifically, the user's documents directory). After the user uses the Open or Save As buttons, the file will no longer represent a directory, meaning that this conditional will be true. In either of those cases, this function is being called because the user has clicked Open again (to open a different file), even though a file is already open. Because this application can only edit one file at a time, the closeFile() function will be called, closing the current file before opening the new one.

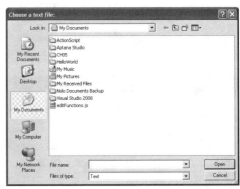

Figure 15.14 The browse for open prompt, which starts the user off in their documents directory.

USING THE SANDBOX BRIDGE

19. Define the `saveFileAs()` function:

```
function saveFileAs() {
    mode = 'save';
    file.browseForSave('Save As');
}
```

This function is called when the user clicks the Save As button. The user would do so under one of two circumstances: when the user wants to save the file being edited under a new name or when the user is creating a new file that needs a name in order to be saved. This function sets the mode, and then creates a browse for save prompt (**Figure 15.15**).

20. Begin defining the `closeFile()` function:

```
function closeFile() {
    if (confirm('Save before
    → closing?')) {
        if (!file.isDirectory) {
            writeData();
        } else {
            saveFileAs();
        }
    }
}
```

This function will be called when the user clicks Close or when the user clicks Open

while a file is already open (see step 18). It starts by asking the user whether to save the file before closing it (**Figure 15.16**). If the user clicks OK, the existing data needs to be written to a file.

If the user was editing a file that was opened or previously saved, the `file` object is not a directory, the second conditional is true, and the data just needs to be written to the file. If the user just started the application and began typing and now the user wants to save what was done prior to opening a new file, the `file` object is a directory and the user needs to be prompted as to what name the data should be saved as (see Figure 15.15).

21. Still in the `closeFile()` function, reset the application:

```
makeNewFileObject();
document.getElementById('btnSave').
→ disabled = true;
document.getElementById('btnClose').
→ disabled = true;
document.title = 'Text Editor';
```

This code takes some steps to return the application to its original state. The first

continues on next page

Figure 15.15 The Save As prompt, which also starts the user off in their documents directory.

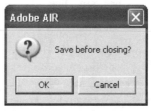

Figure 15.16 Before closing the current file, the user is asked whether to save the file first.

line regenerates the File object, so its current values are forgotten. The next two lines disable the Save and Close buttons, because there's nothing to be saved or closed (after closing the current file). Finally, the title of the page is reset to its default value.

22. Complete the closeFile() function:

```
    editor.setContents('');
} // End of closeFile() function.
```

The last thing this function should do is clear out the contents of the text editor. To do that, it needs to call the iframe's forParent.setContents() function, providing it with an empty string. Since the editor variable represents the functionality made visible to the parent by the child file, calling its setContents() method has the effect of calling editor. html's forParent.setContents() method.

23. Define the readData() function:

```
function readData() {
    var stream = new air.
FileStream();
    stream.open(file, air.FileMode.
    ↪ READ);
    editor.setContents(stream.
    ↪ readUTFBytes(stream.
    ↪ bytesAvailable));
    stream.close();
}
```

This function reads in the contents of the text file and assigns the contents to the textarea in the iframe. The code for reading in the contents comes from Chapter 10 (note that for simplicity sake synchronous reading and writing is performed). To place the file's contents in the textarea, the editor.setContents() method is called. For its argument, which is the text to be edited, the value returned by stream.readUTFBytes() is used.

24. Define the writeData() function:

```
function writeData() {
    var data = editor.getContents();
    data = data.replace(/\n/g,
    ↪ air.File.lineEnding);
    var stream = new air.FileStream();
    stream.open(file, air.FileMode.
    ↪ WRITE);
    stream.writeUTFBytes(data);
    stream.close();
}
```

This code is also explained in Chapter 10. To fetch the content from the textarea, the editor.getContents() method is called. Then the new lines in the content are replaced with the system-specific line ending characters. The file is opened for writing, the data is written there, and the file is closed.

25. Save, test, debug, and run the completed application.

You should see that this very practical, real-world application works rather well (and, thanks to AIR, it's cross-platform compatible!). To flesh this out, I would probably customize the toolbar (see the YUI documentation for details) and include the necessary YUI files in the application so it can be run when the user is offline.

✔ Tips

■ Remember that the AIR model purposefully separates potentially dangerous combinations. When using a sandbox bridge to create an application that functions within these confines, be careful that you don't undermine the AIR security model.

■ Some frameworks take into account the AIR security model. Check out a framework's Web site to see if it will work within the AIR application sandbox.

Storing Encrypted Data

Chapter 10 discusses all the information you need to create, write to, and read from files in an Adobe AIR application. The data written to files using those techniques have only limited security protections: They're just files on the computer and are accessible by any user or application. The same goes for the ideas covered in Chapters 11, "Working with Databases," and 12, "Database Techniques": Data stored in an SQLite database is accessible by any user or application.

A more secure method of storing data is to use AIR's `EncryptedLocalStore` class. This class gives an application the ability to permanently store and retrieve data in a way that's only usable by the application that created it. You can store up to 10 MB of data this way, which is plenty for any application. Because the data is still being stored in a file on the user's computer, it'll continue to be available the next time the user runs the program.

To start, you'll need to create a `ByteArray` object, because the data is stored in binary format. The `ByteArray` class is introduced in Chapter 10, but here's how you would create such an object:

```
var output = new air.ByteArray();
```

Figure 15.17 The application with a form for requesting the user's information and buttons to both retrieve and reset that information.

Reading from and writing to `ByteArrays` is accomplished using the same methods as reading from and writing to `FileStream` objects. To write plain text to a `ByteArray`, you would use:

```
output.writeUTFBytes('some text);
```

Once you've stored data in the `ByteArray`, call the `EncryptedLocalStore` class's `setItem()` method to store it in an encrypted format. Its first argument is a string name you give to the data, the second argument is the data itself:

```
air.EncryptedLocalStore.setItem('thing',
→ output);
```

Note that you don't create or use an object of type `EncryptedLocalStore`, you just call its methods directly.

To retrieve data stored this way, call the `getItem()` method, passing it the name of the stored item:

```
var input = air.EncryptedLocalStore.
→ getItem('thing');
```

Now the `input` variable is a `ByteArray` of the stored data. To find its string value, you would need to read that from the `ByteArray`:

```
var data = input.readUTFBytes(input.
→ length);
```

To delete an existing stored value, call `removeItem()`:

```
air.EncryptedLocalStore.
→ removeItem('name');
```

To remove every stored value, call `reset()`:

```
air.EncryptedLocalStore.reset();
```

A logical use of `EncryptedLocalStore` is to store a user's access credentials (like to an online resource). Toward that end, this next example will take some information from the user, store it in an encrypted format, and then retrieve it when a button is clicked (**Figure 15.17**).

To use an encrypted local store:

1. In your project's primary HTML file, create the form (**Script 15.5**):

   ```
   <p>Username: <input type="text"
   → id="name"></p>
   <p>Password: <input type="password"
   → id="password"></p>
   <p><button onclick=
   → "submitAccessInfo();">Submit
   → </button></p>
   ```

   The form contains one text input, one password input, and a button that submits the values to be stored.

2. After the form, create two more buttons:

   ```
   <p><button onclick="clearData();">
   → Reset Access Information</
   → button></p>
   <p><button onclick=
   → "getAccessInfo();">
   → Retrieve Access Information
   → </button></p>
   ```

   The first button, when clicked, will clear out the stored data. The second button, when clicked, will display the previously stored values in an alert (**Figure 15.18**).

3. In the JavaScript section, define the clearData() function:

   ```
   function clearData() {
      air.EncryptedLocalStore.reset();
   }
   ```

   To clear out the previously stored values, this function executes the reset() method of the EncryptedLocalStore class.

4. Begin defining the submitAccessInfo() function:

   ```
   function submitAccessInfo() {
      clearData();
      var name = document.
   → getElementById('name').value;
      var password = document.
   → getElementById('password').
   → value;
   ```

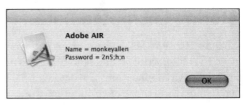

Figure 15.18 For demonstrative purposes, this application will display the stored values using an alert.

Script 15.5 This application securely stores user-submitted data in an encrypted format.

```
1    <html><!-- Script 15.5 -->
2    <head>
3    <title>Local Access Store</title>
4    <script type="text/javascript"
     src="AIRAliases.js"></script>
5    <script type="text/javascript">
6
7    // Function for clearing the stored data.
8    function clearData() {
9        air.EncryptedLocalStore.reset();
10   }
11
12   // Function that stores the form values.
13   function submitAccessInfo() {
14
15       // Clear the current values, just in
         case:
16       clearData();
17
18       // Get the form data:
19       var name = document.getElementById
         ('name').value;
20       var password = document.getElementById
         ('password').value;
21
22       // Create a ByteArray object:
23       var output = new air.ByteArray();
24
25       // Store the value:
26       output.writeUTFBytes(name);
27       air.EncryptedLocalStore.setItem('name',
         output);
28
29       // Repeat for the password:
30       output = new air.ByteArray();
31       output.writeUTFBytes(password);
32       air.EncryptedLocalStore.setItem
         ('password', output);
33
```

(script continues on next page)

Storing Encrypted Data

Script 15.5 *continued*

```
 34    // Reset the form:
 35    document.getElementById('name').value =
       null;
 36    document.getElementById('password').
       value = null;
 37
 38    // Notify the user:
 39    alert('The information has been stored
       securely!');
 40
 41  } // End of submitAccessInfo() function.
 42
 43  // Function that retrieves the form values.
 44  function getAccessInfo() {
 45
 46    // Get the stored ByteArray data:
 47    var name = air.EncryptedLocalStore.
       getItem('name');
 48    var password = air.EncryptedLocalStore.
       getItem('password');
 49
 50    // Place the values in a string:
 51    var msg = 'Name = ';
 52    msg += (name != null) ? name.
       readUTFBytes(name.length) : '<no value>';
 53    msg += '\nPassword = ';
 54    msg += (password != null) ? password.
       readUTFBytes(password.length) : '<no
       value>';
 55
 56    // Print the string:
 57    alert(msg);
 58
 59  } // End of getAccessInfo() function.
 60
 61  </script>
 62  </head>
 63  <body>
 64
 65  <h3>Enter your access information:</h3>
 66  <p>Username: <input type="text"
     id="name"></p>
 67  <p>Password: <input type="password"
     id="password"></p>
 68  <p><button onclick="submitAccessInfo();">
     Submit</button></p>
 69  <hr>
 70  <p><button onclick="clearData();">Reset
     Access Information</button></p>
 71  <p> <button onclick="getAccessInfo();">
     Retrieve Access Information</button></p>
 72
 73  </body>
 74  </html>
```

This function will be called when the user clicks the Submit button. It needs to store the form values in an encrypted format. It starts by calling the `clearData()` function. Doing so prevents bugs from occurring. Then the function retrieves the values from the form.

5. Store the data using the `EncryptedLocalStore`:

```
var output = new air.ByteArray();
output.writeUTFBytes(name);
air.EncryptedLocalStore.
→ setItem('name', output);
output = new air.ByteArray();
output.writeUTFBytes(password);
air.EncryptedLocalStore.
→ setItem('password', output);
```

A `ByteArray` object is created first. Then the `name` value is written to the `ByteArray`. Next the `setItem()` method is called, providing it with a label of *name* and the `ByteArray`, which represents the actual data. Then this process is repeated for the password.

6. Complete the `submitAccessInfo()` function:

```
document.getElementById('name').
→ value = null;
document.getElementById
→ ('password').value = null;
alert('The information has been
→ stored securely!');
} // End of submitAccessInfo()
→ function.
```

continues on next page

After clearing out the form values, the user is alerted that the data was stored (**Figure 15.19**).

7. Begin defining the `getAccessInfo()` function:

```
function getAccessInfo() {
   var name = air.EncryptedLocal
   → Store.getItem('name');

   var password = air.EncryptedLocal
   → Store.getItem('password');
```

This function will be called when the user clicks the Retrieve Access Information button. It starts by fetching the encrypted data from the local store, assigning it to the name and password variables. At this point, both are objects of type `ByteArray`, which is what the `getItem()` method returns.

8. Create the alert message:

```
var msg = 'Name = ';
msg += (name != null) ?
→ name.readUTFBytes(name.length) :
→ '<no value>';
msg += '\nPassword = ';
msg += (password != null) ?
→ password.readUTFBytes(password.
→ length) : '<no value>';
```

The alert message will be a string like

Name = somename

Password = somepass

You can see this in Figure 15.18. To generate that message is fairly simple: Just apply the `readUTFBytes()` function to each `ByteArray` to get the stored value. However, it is possible that this function will be called before any values are stored,

so to test for that, a condition confirms that each `ByteArray` doesn't have a `null` value. Using the ternary operator makes quick work of this conditional, but you could also write each out like this:

```
if (name != null) {
   msg += name.readUTFBytes(name.
   → length);
} else {
   msg += '<no value>';
}
```

Figure 15.20 shows the result if this function is called when no values have been stored.

9. Complete the `getAccessInfo()` function.

```
   alert(msg);
} // End of getAccessInfo() function.
```

10. Save, test, debug, and run the completed application.

✔ Tips

- The `EncryptedLocalStore` uses CBC 128-bit encryption, in case you were curious.

- Only content in the application security sandbox can access `EncryptedLocalStore` data.

- Uninstalling an application does not remove the stored data from the user's computer.

- The `setItem()` method takes an optional third argument that increases the security of stored data. If you set this value to `true`, the stored data is "strongly bound" to the application that stored it. This means that even an updated version of the same application can't access that data.

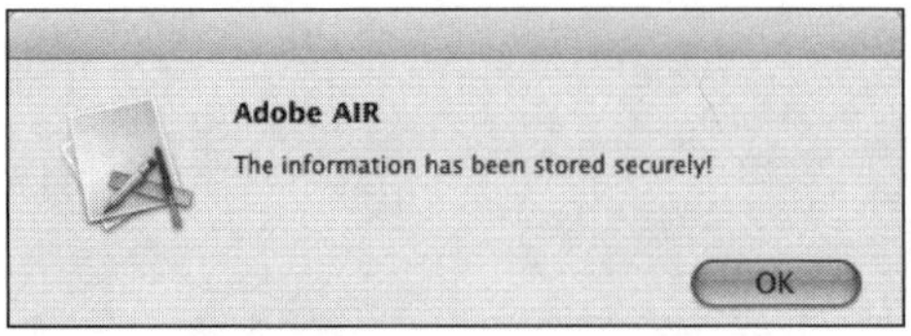

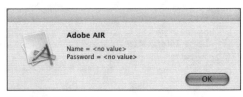

Figure 15.19 The result after the form data has been securely placed in an `EncryptedLocalStore`.

Figure 15.20 If no values are stored in the encrypted local store, the alert will look like this.

Validating Data

One of the most important security techniques that any application, written using any technology, should use is validation of external data. Use of external data with little or no validation is the primary way malicious users can manipulate an application or script to wreak all sorts of havoc on a computer. External data is anything that's not written into the application, including values such as those:

◆ Submitted by an application's user

◆ Retrieved from a database

◆ Found in an included file

◆ Read from an online resource

The fact is you cannot trust external data, even if it's coming from your own Web site or a database you created!

With an AIR application built using HTML, the validation would take place within the JavaScript code, so I outline some best JavaScript validation practices in this next series of bullet points. The one overriding rule is that how you go about validating any piece of data is based on the data's type, its expected or unexpected values, and how that data will be used. Not all techniques will be applicable in every situation, but you should use the most restrictive approach possible for all external data.

To validate data:

◆ For strings, at the very least, make sure they have a positive length to confirm that they aren't empty.

◆ For numbers, check that a value is in an appropriate range.

◆ Use type casting to force a value to be of a specific type.

This is a very useful validation technique, particularly for numeric values. The JavaScript `parseInt()` and `parseFloat()` functions will force a value into a numeric format, if they can. If a value cannot be parsed as an integer or a float, the result will be the special value *NaN*, short for not a number.

So to validate an age value, you might do this:

```
if ( (parseInt(age) != NaN) &&
→ (age > 0) && (age < 120) ) { // OK!
```

◆ Test values against explicit acceptable values.

This isn't always possible, but, for example, if an application uses a gender value, you know it can only be equal to *M* or *F* (or *Male* or *Female*).

◆ Apply regular expressions whenever possible.

Regular expressions are an advanced but very important topic when it comes to security, and they are supported in JavaScript. Note that regular expressions can only be used when a clearly identifiable pattern exists: For example, you can effectively validate an email address with them but not a mailing address.

◆ Watch for and strip tags from strings.

If you search online you'll find code for stripping HTML and JavaScript code from a string. If you apply the techniques you find, you'll go a long way toward improving the security of your JavaScript code. Even looking for the start of a tag can help:

```
if (strName.search(/</)) { //
→ Potential problem.
```

This assumes that there's no valid reason the less than symbol (which is the start of any tag) would be in the value.

Best Security Practices

I'll conclude this chapter with more recommendations as to how you can improve an application's security. Many of these techniques have been mentioned elsewhere in the book and some may be common sense, but it's often useful to have a quick reference for such things.

One last word on security, though: Many people, particularly those new to the topic, think of security as a binary state—that something is either *secure* or *insecure*. This is definitely not the case. The security of a script or application ranges from more secure to less secure. The goal of any developer, therefore, is to make an application as secure as possible.

To improve an application's security:

◆ Avoid using `eval()`, if at all possible.

◆ Avoid using *javascript:* in an `href` value.

◆ Watch uses of `innerHTML` and `outerHTML` properties.

These first three bullets also speak toward the kinds of actions that are not possible in the application sandbox, because of their potential harm.

◆ Besides validating data used in database queries, use prepared statements (see Chapter 12) for better database-related security.

◆ Never, ever have a program alter its application directory.

Because content in the application's installation directory can be run in the application sandbox (i.e., with the most power), an application should never manipulate the contents of this directory. If it does, and a malicious user gets the application to write something harmful there, the user's entire computer could be compromised.

◆ Use secure connections for sensitive network activity.

Although the examples in Chapter 13, "Networking," use HTTP connections, you can also use HTTPS connections as warranted.

◆ Be especially careful when using external data for a file or directory's name.

◆ Purchase and use a professional certificate for signing your applications from an accredited company like Thawte or VeriSign.

Most of the techniques in this chapter speak toward improving the security of an application from the developer's perspective. The security of an application from the perspective of the user installing it rests largely on the reassurances provided by the certificate of authenticity. If you're going to distribute applications you create, a self-signed certificate is totally unacceptable.

DEPLOYING APPLICATIONS

16

This final chapter in the book discusses the finishing touches that your complete Adobe AIR application might include. To start, the first two sections explain the optional application descriptor file elements. These can be used to provide more information to the end user, customize the application's installation, or have your application use its own icons.

The third topic in this chapter describes how to provide a *seamless installation* of your applications. This installation method—where the application will be installed after the user clicks a link on a Web page—can be simpler for the end user, more so than having the user formally download and run the `.air` file. After that discussion, the chapter provides an example that details three more general techniques that a running application might use. The chapter concludes with a longish but useful example to demonstrate how to make an application update itself.

More Application Descriptor File Options

Chapter 2, "Creating an Application," walks through the required application descriptor file elements, which are

◆ id

◆ filename

◆ version

◆ initialWindow

◆ content (within initialWindow)

But the application descriptor file contains many optional elements, all of which I'll introduce here. The sidebar "Associating File Types" goes into a bit more detail on the optional fileTypes element, and the next section of the chapter explains how to use the icon element. Of course, if you open the descriptor-template.xml file, which is found within the SDK's templates directory, you'll see all these elements, along with additional descriptions of them.

To use optional application settings:

◆ Use the name, description, and copyright elements to personalize your application.

Although it's optional, you should almost always provide a name value. It's displayed by the installer (**Figure 16.1**) and used to determine where the application should be installed (within the default installation folder). The description value also shows up during the installation process (see Figure 16.1). Including a copyright value, which will appear in an About dialog box on Mac OS X, is a legal protection for you, the developer.

◆ Customize the main application window using the initialWindow element.

The initialWindow element is required, as is its child element named content.

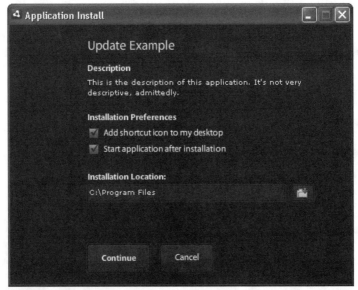

Figure 16.1 Some of the information in the application descriptor file, like name and description, appear during the application's installation.

But the `initialWindow` element can also have these subelements:

- ▲ `title`
- ▲ `systemChrome`
- ▲ `transparent`
- ▲ `visible`
- ▲ `minimizable`
- ▲ `maximizable`
- ▲ `resizable`
- ▲ `width`
- ▲ `height`
- ▲ `x`
- ▲ `y`
- ▲ `minSize`
- ▲ `maxSize`

Many of these settings play into the material covered in Chapter 6, "Making Windows," and they all apply to only the first application window (the primary content window). For example, if you'd like the window to have a set size and location, use the `width`, `height`, `x`, and `y` values.

I'll also add that although the `visible` element is optional, you'll want to use it if the user should be able to see your application, because this element's default value is *false*.

◆ Set an `installFolder` value to affect where the application will be installed.

This element allows you to specify a subdirectory within the default installation directory where the application should be installed (**Figure 16.2**). You might want to do this if the program is part of a suite, so that all the applications are grouped together.

Similarly, the `programMenuFolder` element dictates a subdirectory in which to place the Start/Programs menu shortcut on Windows.

continues on next page

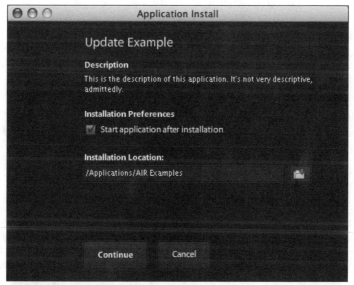

Figure 16.2 If the application descriptor file's `installFolder` element is used, the Installation Location value will be a subfolder with that name (here, *AIR Examples*) within the default AIR application folder (`/Applications` on Mac OS X as shown here).

MORE APPLICATION DESCRIPTOR FILE OPTIONS

- Use the `customUpdateUI` element to create your own update interface.

  If a user installs a newer version of the same application, by default, the AIR application installer will handle that update. If you'd rather have your program manage the update process, set this element's value to `true`. Later in this chapter you'll see an example of how to have an application update itself.

- Set `allowBrowserInvocation` if you want this program to be startable through a Web link.

  Using a Shockwave file, a link in a Web page can be used to start a desktop AIR application if this element's value is set to `true`.

✔ Tips

- Your application can access all the application descriptor file's settings by using this code:

  ```
  var data = air.NativeApplication.
  nativeApplication.
  applicationDescriptor;
  ```

  After that line, `data` is a string of text. You'll then need to turn it into XML using a `DOMParser` object (see Chapter 14, "Using Other Media") to access the element values. You can see an example of this in the "Updating an Application" section of this chapter.

- The publisher ID of the current program is available in `air.NativeApplication.nativeApplication.publisherID`. This value comes from the digital certificate used to sign the application.

- The application ID of the current program, which is defined within the application descriptor file, is available in `air.NativeApplication.nativeApplication.applicationID`.

Associating File Types

Your application descriptor file can also indicate what types of files should be associated with the application. If the named file type (or types) isn't already associated with another program on that computer, the AIR application will become the default program for files of that type.

To associate a file type with a program, add a `fileTypes` element with one `fileType` subelement for each associated file type. The `fileType` element has required `name` and `extension` subelements, along with optional `description` and `icon` subelements (the `descriptor-template.xml` file that comes with the AIR SDK has all this spelled out for you). There's also an optional `contentType` subelement, which refers to the file's MIME type. Although it's optional, it's generally best to use this element, too.

An AIR application can also invoke the `NativeApplication.setAsDefaultApplication()` method to instruct the operating system to make this program the default for the current file type. Your programs should never do this without the user's express permission.

Using Custom Icons

In the previous section of this chapter, several of the application descriptor file elements are highlighted. Here, I'll discuss one more element: icon. The icon element contains four subelements, each representing the name of the icon file in a particular size:

```
<icon>
    <image16x16>icon16.png</image16x16>
    <image32x32>icon32.png</image32x32>
    <image48x48>icon48.png</image48x48>
    <image128x128>icon128.png
    → </image128x128>
</icon>
```

You can use these elements to identify the icons used to represent your application. If you don't take this step, the application will use the default Adobe AIR icon (**Figure 16.3**).

The rules for creating your own application icons are as follows:

◆ The icons must be of PNG type.

◆ The icons must be included in the built application (i.e., added when you create the .air file).

◆ You must provide at least one icon using any of the listed sizes.

As for this last rule, ideally you would provide a version of the icon in each of the sizes. If you don't, the operating system will scale the closest available icon to the size it needs.

To specify an application's icon:

1. Create an icon for your application.

   Use any program (I'm pretty sure Adobe has one) to make the image that best represents your application or just looks cool—or, in my case, one that you put together in five minutes because you have limited artistic skills (**Figure 16.4**).

2. Save the icon in PNG format in four sizes: 128x128, 48,x48, 32x32, and 16x16.

   It's not required, but you should indicate the size in the filenames—*MyApp_ 16.png*, *MyApp_32.png*, *MyApp_48.png*, *MyApp_128.png*—so they'll be easy to reference in the application descriptor file.

3. Copy the icons to your project's directory.

   I recommend putting them within their own icons folder, so they're kept separate from the rest of the application content.

continues on next page

Figure 16.3 The generic icon used by default for Adobe AIR applications.

Figure 16.4 My sample application's visual representation (with acknowledgments to Piet Mondrian).

USING CUSTOM ICONS

4. Edit the project's application descriptor file so that it uses the icon element (**Script 16.1**).

If you placed the icons within an `icons` folder, the XML to add would be

```
<icon>
    <image16x16>icons/MyApp_16.png
    → </image16x16>
    <image32x32>icons/MyApp_32.png
    → </image32x32>
    <image48x48>icons/MyApp_48.png
    → </image48x48>
    <image128x128>icons/MyApp_128.png
    → </image128x128>
</icon>
```

This can go anywhere in the application descriptor file as long as it's a child of the root element (i.e., not placed within another element like `initialWindow`).

5. Be certain to include the icons when you go to build the application.

How you do this depends on how you build the application. See Chapter 4, "Basic Concepts and Code," for demonstrations using Aptana Studio, Adobe Dreamweaver, or the command-line `adt`.

6. After installing the application, confirm that it uses the custom icon (**Figure 16.5**).

✔ Tip

- As you'll see later in the chapter, an application's icon is also used in alert dialogs on Mac OS X.

Figure 16.5 The AIR application now uses its own custom icon instead of the default one (Figure 16.3).

Script 16.1 By using the `icon` element within the application descriptor file, an application can use custom icons.

```
1   <?xml version="1.0" encoding="utf-8" ?>
2   <application xmlns="http://ns.adobe.com/
    air/application/1.0">
3
4       <id>com.dmci.air.Ch16</id>
5       <filename>Update Example</filename>
6       <name>Update Example</name>
7       <version>2.1</version>
8       <description>This is the description
        of this application. It's not very
        descriptive, admittedly.</description>
9       <copyright>2008</copyright>
10
11      <initialWindow>
12          <content>script_16_02.html</content>
13          <visible>true</visible>
14      </initialWindow>
15
16      <installFolder>AIR Examples
        </installFolder>
17      <programMenuFolder>AIR Examples
        </programMenuFolder>
18
19      <icon>
20          <image16x16>icons/MyApp_16.png
            </image16x16>
21          <image32x32>icons/MyApp_32.png
            </image32x32>
22          <image48x48>icons/MyApp_48.png
            </image48x48>
23          <image128x128>icons/MyApp_128.png
            </image128x128>
24      </icon>
25
26  </application>
```

USING CUSTOM ICONS

Seamless Installations

Chapter 1, "Running AIR Applications," shows how a user can install an AIR application once the user has the .air file. Because installing an application using that file works easily, you can distribute your applications in the same way you might distribute any file, via:

◆ CD-ROM

◆ Email

◆ FTP server

◆ Flash drive

You can also make the file available for download from your Web site. However, if that's how you're distributing an AIR application, an alternative is to use the *seamless installation* feature. A seamless installation installs the application on the user's computer, including the AIR runtime, if necessary, without the user formally downloading and executing the file. In other words, it's a one-click-while-surfing installation.

Seamless installation uses the badge.swf file that comes with the AIR SDK (in the samples/badge folder). It works with browsers that have Flash Player version 9, update 3, or later installed.

To provide a seamless install:

1. Create, test, debug, and build your AIR application.

   For the sake of these steps, let's say you end up with a file called MyApp.air.

2. Create an image for the seamless installer.

   The seamless installer code will create a "badge" containing an image with some text underneath (**Figure 16.6**). The image should be approximately 215 pixels wide and 100 pixels tall.

3. Open a copy of default_badge.html in your text editor or IDE.

   This file, also found within the SDK's samples/badge folder, contains all the code necessary for placing the seamless install link on an HTML page. Although you'll eventually want to copy the proper code out of this page and place it within your own site's context, it's best to start with this sample file to make sure it all works properly.

continues on next page

Figure 16.6 The sample badge that comes with the AIR SDK.

4. Find the call to the AC_FL_RunContent() function:

```
AC_FL_RunContent(
'codebase','http://fpdownload.
→ macromedia.com/pub/shockwave/
→ cabs/flash/swflash.cab',
'width','217',
'height','180',
'id','badge',
'align','middle',
'src','badge',
'quality','high',
'bgcolor','#FFFFFF',
'name','badge',
'allowscriptaccess','all',
'pluginspage','http://www.
→ macromedia.com/go/getflashplayer',
'flashvars','appname=
→ My%20Application&appurl=
→ myapp.air&airversion=
→ 1.0&imageurl=test.jpg',
'movie','badge' );
```

This function, which is defined within the AC_RunActiveContent.js file that's included by this page, does all the work. The function call in the HTML page is several lines long, with lots of values being sent to the function.

5. Within the function call found in step 4, change the value that starts with *app-name=* and ends with *test.jpg* to match the values for your application.

This value, which comes after *flashvars*, is a string of *name=value* pairs that are used to customize the seamless installation link. To edit this, you'll want to leave the names, equal signs, and ampersands intact, changing the values that come after each equals sign.

The *appname* value should be the colloquial name of the application. Note that this needs to be encoded as it might be in a URL (for example, the name *My Application* becomes *My%20Application*). For the *appurl* value, use an absolute URL to the .air file on your Web site (e.g., *http://www.example.com/MyApp.air*). The *airversion* value reflects the minimum version of the Adobe AIR runtime required.

The *imageurl* value should be the URL (absolute or relative) for the image file created in step 2. It is optional. Two more optional *name=value* pairs you can add are *buttoncolor* and *messagecolor*. The former is the color of the download button and the latter is the color of the text message displayed if the AIR runtime is not installed. Both take hex values.

In the end, you might edit this string to read:

appname=My%20App&appurl=http://www.example.com/MyApp.air&airversion=1.0&imageurl=images/badge.png&buttoncolor=f7f26e&messagecolor=000000

6. Upload default_badge.html, badge.swf, AC_RunActiveContent.js, the image, and the .air file to your server.

7. Load the Web page in your browser (**Figure 16.7**).

Figure 16.7 The customized seamless installer badge created for my application.

8. Click the Install Now link to confirm that the seamless install will work.

If the badge is configured properly, the user (which is to say you, for now) should be prompted after clicking that link (**Figure 16.8**). Clicking the Open option in the prompt will begin the installation process.

9. If the seamless install works, take the necessary code out of `default_badge.html` and place it within your own Web page.

✔ Tips

- You can create your own Shockwave file, replacing `badge.swf`, to further customize the seamless installation process. This process is covered in the online documentation.

- To ensure that your server properly delivers manually downloaded AIR files to the end users, tell the Web serving application (Apache, IIS, etc.) to associate the `.air` extension with *application/ vnd.adobe.air-application-installer- package+zip*. Alternatively, you could zip the `.air` file so it's always just downloaded to the user's computer.

Figure 16.8 When the user clicks on the badge, the user will be given the choice of opening the file (i.e., installing it immediately), saving it, or canceling the operation.

More Application Ideas

In this next example, I'll discuss three more techniques that applications can incorporate. The first is detecting whether or not the application has been run before. This is useful to know so that the program can do whatever setup is required the first time the program runs. This may include getting information from the user, setting up a database, and so forth.

The second technique is having the program automatically start when the user logs in. To do that, set air.NativeApplication.native-Application.startAtLogin equal to true. Prior to taking this step, you should always first confirm that the user *wants* the application to launch when she or he logs in.

The third technique is detecting whether the user is actively using the computer (i.e., using the keyboard and mouse) or is idle. To do that, add event listeners to the NativeApplication object. You'll want to listen to USER_IDLE and USER_PRESENT events. A user is considered idle when the mouse or keyboard hasn't been used for longer than the air.NativeApplication.nativeAppli-cation.idleThreshold value (by default this is five minutes). So, by default, after five minutes of inactivity, a USER_IDLE event is triggered. Whenever the user does use the mouse or keyboard again, the USER_PRESENT event is triggered. You might use this information to tidy up an application's use of resources when the user goes idle (for example, disconnecting from a database or closing an open file).

To use these new techniques:

1. In your project's primary HTML file, create a File object (**Script 16.2**):

```
var file = air.File.
→ applicationStorageDirectory.
→ resolvePath('prefs.xml');
```

Most applications use a preferences file, which is what this object is a reference to. That file will contain XML data and be stored in the application's storage directory. Chapter 14 demonstrates this concept in a fully functional example. You'll also want to copy the prefs.xml file (Script 14.6) into this project's folder.

2. Begin an anonymous function to be called after the application has loaded:

```
window.onload = function() {
```

3. If the preferences file doesn't exist, copy one from the application directory:

```
if (!file.exists) {
    var original = air.File.
    → applicationDirectory.
    → resolvePath('prefs.xml');
    original.copyTo(file);
```

If there is no prefs.xml file in the application storage directory, the one that comes with the installed application needs to be copied there, which is what the second and third lines do.

Most important, for the sake of this example, the conditional is a good and simple test to see if the application is being run for the first time. Unless something went awry, the preferences file will not exist (in the storage directory) only the first time the user runs this program.

4. If the user wants this application to automatically launch, establish that:

```
if (confirm('Always start
→ application when you log in?')) {
    air.NativeApplication.
    → nativeApplication.startAtLogin =
    → true;
}
```

continues on page 356

MORE APPLICATION IDEAS

Script 16.2 Three new ideas are demonstrated by this program: checking if it has run before, setting it to automatically open when the user logs in, and watching for user activity and inactivity.

```
1    <html><!-- Script 16.2 -->
2        <head>
3            <title>Three New Ideas</title>
4            <script type="text/javascript" src="AIRAliases.js"></script>
5            <script type="text/javascript">
6
7            // Create the object associated with the preferences file:
8            var file = air.File.applicationStorageDirectory.resolvePath('prefs.xml');
9
10           // Function called when the application loads.
11           window.onload = function() {
12
13               // If the preferences file doesn't exist,
14               // the user hasn't run this program before.
15               if (!file.exists) {
16
17                   // Copy the preferences file to its final destination:
18                   var original = air.File.applicationDirectory.resolvePath('prefs.xml');
19                   original.copyTo(file);
20
21                   // See if the user wants the program to start automatically:
22                   if (confirm('Always start application when you log in?')) {
23                       air.NativeApplication.nativeApplication.startAtLogin = true;
24                   }
25
26               } // End of !file.exists IF.
27
28               // Check if this program is automatically launching:
29               if (air.NativeApplication.nativeApplication.startAtLogin) {
30                   document.getElementById('launch').checked = true;
31               }
32
33           } // End of anonymous function.
34
35           // Adjust idle time to 30 seconds:
36           air.NativeApplication.nativeApplication.idleThreshold = 30;
37
38           // Add event listeners:
39           air.NativeApplication.nativeApplication.addEventListener(air.Event.USER_IDLE, userIdle);
40           air.NativeApplication.nativeApplication.addEventListener(air.Event.USER_PRESENT, userActive);
41
42           // Function called when the user goes idle:
43           function userIdle(e) {
44               document.getElementById('idle').checked = true;
45           }
46
47           // Function called when the user returns:
48           function userActive(e) {
49               document.getElementById('idle').checked = false;
50           }
51
52           </script>
53       </head>
54       <body>
55       <h3>Some Application</h3>
56       Automatically Launch: <input type="checkbox" id="launch"><br>
57       Idle: <input type="checkbox" id="idle">
58       </body>
59    </html>
```

MORE APPLICATION IDEAS

For simplicity sake, a simple confirmation dialog (**Figure 16.9**) will ask the user if this program should automatically start when the user logs in. If the user clicks OK, the operating system is notified of this request by assigning the Boolean value true to `air.NativeApplication.nativeApplication.startAtLogin`.

5. Check if the program is set to automatically launch:

```
if (air.NativeApplication.
→ nativeApplication.startAtLogin) {
  document.getElementById('launch').
  → checked = true;
}
```

A check box in the application's window will reflect the user's decision (**Figure 16.10**). The first time the user runs this application, if the user clicked OK in the confirmation dialog, this conditional will naturally be true. It will also be true every subsequent time the application is loaded (again, assuming the user clicked OK).

6. Complete the anonymous function:

```
} // End of anonymous function.
```

7. Set the idle time to a small value:

```
air.NativeApplication.
→ nativeApplication.idleThreshold
→ = 30;
```

To demonstrate the concept of the user (i.e., you) being idle or active, this value will be set at 30 seconds, so you don't have to sit around for five minutes to see the results.

8. Add two event listeners to the native application object:

```
air.NativeApplication.
→ nativeApplication.addEventListener
→ (air.Event.USER_IDLE, userIdle);
air.NativeApplication.
→ nativeApplication.addEventListener
→ (air.Event.USER_PRESENT,
→ userActive);
```

The first line specifies that when the user is officially idle, which means that it's been more than 30 seconds since the user used the mouse or keyboard, the `userIdle()` function should be called. The second line specifies that when the user is idle and then does something again (uses the mouse or keyboard), the `userActive()` function should be called.

9. Define the `userIdle()` function:

```
function userIdle(e) {
  document.getElementById('idle').
  → checked = true;
}
```

Figure 16.9 This prompt will appear the first time the user runs the application.

Figure 16.10 The simple application with the first check box reflecting the user's choice in the confirmation dialog (Figure 16.9).

This function checks a box in the application window when the user goes idle (**Figure 16.11**).

10. Define the `userActive()` function:

```
function userActive(e) {
    document.getElementById('idle').
    → checked = false;
}
```

This function unchecks the box that indicates the user is idle.

11. Within the body of the page, create the two requisite check boxes:

```
Automatically Launch: <input
→ type="checkbox" id="launch"><br>
Idle: <input type="checkbox"
→ id="idle">
```

In a more complete application, when the user unchecked the Automatically Launch check box, a function would be called that assigned a value of `false` to `air.NativeApplication.nativeApplication.startAtLogin`.

12. Save, test, debug, and run the completed application.

To fully test this, you should build and actually install the program; don't just use the Adobe Debug Launcher (`adl`). Make sure that you also include a `prefs.xml` file in the packaged application.

Figure 16.11 After 30 seconds of inactivity, the second check box will automatically be checked by the application.

The first time you run this program, the preferences file will be moved to the application's storage directory and you'll see the confirmation dialog. Click OK, and then log out and log back in. The application should automatically launch, and the check box should reflect your choice.

To test the idle/active check box, don't do anything for 30 seconds. It doesn't matter if this application is currently active or not, it will still watch for the idle and present events.

✔ Tips

■ To stop this application from automatically opening every time you log into your computer, you'll need to have it set `air.NativeApplication.nativeApplication.startAtLogin` to `false`, and then rerun the application. Alternatively, you can search online for operating system–specific instructions for removing a program from the automatically start list.

■ You can see how long it has been since the last time the user did something by referring to `air.NativeApplication.nativeApplication.timeSinceLastUserInput`.

■ To react to the user making the application active (i.e., turning back to it after using other applications), watch for an ACTIVATE event:

```
air.NativeApplication.
→ nativeApplication.addEventListener
→ ( air.Event.ACTIVATE, nowActive);
```

Updating an Application

One way to update an application is to have the user download and install the latest version of it. When a user installs the new version with the same application ID but a later version number (both from the application descriptor file) of an AIR application they have already installed, the user will be prompted to update it (**Figure 16.12**).

Another option is to have an application check for and handle updates itself. To do so, the application needs to check for the existence of a more current version. This means that the application first needs to know its own version number, which is defined in the application descriptor file. You can get that data by referring to `air.NativeApplication.nativeApplication.applicationDescriptor`. The returned string then needs to be turned into XML and parsed to get the version information (this next script will demonstrate all that).

The next step is for the application to communicate with your server to see if a newer version is available. The easiest way to accomplish that is to create a plain text page on your server that stores the current application version. Then the application could perform an `XMLHttpRequest` to that page to retrieve the value. Or the application could use a `URLLoader` object to read in the information (see Chapter 13, "Networking").

If a new version is available, the application should download it. That will require creating a `URLRequest` object referring to the new version on the server and loading the new version into a `URLStream`. Then that data will be written to a new file on the user's computer.

After all that has been accomplished, the updating process starts with an `Updater` object:

```
var updater = new air.Updater();
```

You'll also need a reference to the downloaded file (the latest version of the application):

```
var file = air.File.desktopDirectory.
↪ resolvePath('MyApp.air');
```

Finally, call the `update()` method of the `Updater()` object. It takes the file object as the first argument and the new version number as the second:

```
updater.update(file, version);
```

Figure 16.12 The AIR installer will ask the user whether to replace the current version of an application with a newer version.

As soon as the update() method is called, the current invocation of the application will terminate, the new version will be installed, and then the new version will be opened. It's all very professional, and this next script will demonstrate all the necessary code. As you can already tell, there are many steps to this process and the application I've created uses seven user-defined functions. But it's still all accomplished within a little more than 50 lines of code (not including comments and blank lines).

To use the Updater class:

1. In your project's primary HTML file, declare the necessary global variables (**Script 16.3**):

```
var thisVersion, currentVersion,
→ xhr, newAppFile, data,
→ urlStream = null;
```

continues on page 361

Script 16.3 This script has all the code required for an application to update itself.

```
                                    Script
1    <html><!-- Script 16.3 -->
2       <head>
3          <title>Update Example</title>
4          <script type="text/javascript" src="AIRAliases.js"></script>
5          <script type="text/javascript">
6
7          // Declare the global variables:
8          var thisVersion, currentVersion, xhr, newAppFile, data, urlStream = null;
9
10         // Function called when the application loads.
11         // This function begin the updating process.
12         // It gets the two application versions.
13         window.onload = function() {
14
15             // Get the version of the running application:
16             getThisVersion();
17
18             // Get the most current version:
19             getCurrentVersion();
20
21         } // End of anonymous function.
22
23         // Function gets the version of the running
24         // application from the application descriptor file.
25         function getThisVersion() {
26
27             // Get the data:
28             var appData = air.NativeApplication.nativeApplication.applicationDescriptor;
29
30             // Turn the file data into an XML object:
31             var dp = new DOMParser();
32             var xml = dp.parseFromString(appData, 'text/xml');
33
34             // Parse out and return the version value:
35             var version = xml.getElementsByTagName('version')[0].firstChild;
36             thisVersion = version.nodeValue;
37
38         } // End of getThisVersion() function.
39
```

(script continues on next page)

UPDATING AN APPLICATION

Script 16.3 *continued*

```
40      // This function performs an XMLHttpRequest to get the
41      // version number of the most recent release.
42      function getCurrentVersion() {
43
44          // Perform the request:
45          xhr = new XMLHttpRequest();
46          xhr.open('get', 'http://www.example.com/air/version.txt');
47          xhr.onreadystatechange = askAboutUpdate;
48          xhr.send(null);
49
50      } // End of getCurrentVersion() function.
51
52      // This function asks the user if they want to update
53      // the application, if appropriate.
54      function askAboutUpdate() {
55
56          // Check the readyState value:
57          if (xhr.readyState == 4) {
58
59              // Get the current version:
60              currentVersion = xhr.responseText;
61
62              // If the current version is greater, ask the user:
63              if (currentVersion > thisVersion) {
64                  if (confirm('Update to the newest version?')) {
65                      downloadNewVersion();
66                  }
67              } else {
68                  alert('The current version is up to date.');
69              }
70
71          } // End of readyState IF.
72
73      } // End of askAboutUpdate() function.
74
75      // This function downloads the latest version.
76      function downloadNewVersion() {
77
78          // Create the variables:
79          var addr = 'http://www.example.com/air/MyApp.air';
80          var url = new air.URLRequest(addr);
81          urlStream = new air.URLStream();
82          data = new air.ByteArray();
83
84          // Add an event listener:
85          urlStream.addEventListener(air.Event.COMPLETE, saveNewVersion);
86
87          // Get the data:
88          urlStream.load(url);
89
90      } // End of downloadNewVersion() function.
91
92      // Function that writes the downloaded data to a file:
93      function saveNewVersion(e) {
94
```

(script continues on next page)

UPDATING AN APPLICATION

Because this script uses so many functions, a number of global variables are required (because each of these will be referred to in more than one function). They are each initially given a null value.

2. In an anonymous onload function, get the ball rolling:

```
window.onload = function() {
  getThisVersion();
  getCurrentVersion();
}
```

As I said, there are seven functions involved (a figure later in the chapter will show the logic), beginning with this one. The premise is that after the application has loaded, a check would be made to see if a newer version of the application is available. To do that,

calls to the getThisVersion() and getCurrentVersion() functions are made.

3. Begin the getThisVersion() function:

```
function getThisVersion() {
  var appData= air.
NativeApplication.nativeApplication.
→ applicationDescriptor;
  var dp = new DOMParser();
  var xml = dp.parseFromString
  → (appData, 'text/xml');
```

Very similar to code found in Chapter 14, this function starts by reading the contents of the application descriptor file into the appData variable. You can do this by simply referring to air. NativeApplication.nativeApplication. applicationDescriptor.

continues on next page

Script 16.3 *continued*

```
95          // Read the downloaded data into the 'data' variable:
96          urlStream.readBytes(data, 0, urlStream.bytesAvailable);
97
98          // Write the data to a file:
99          newAppFile = air.File.desktopDirectory.resolvePath('MyApp.air');
100         var fileStream = new air.FileStream();
101         fileStream.open(newAppFile, air.FileMode.WRITE);
102         fileStream.writeBytes(data, 0, data.length);
103         fileStream.close();
104
105         // Call the function that performs the update:
106         updateApplication();
107
108      } // End of saveNewVersion() function.
109
110      // This function performs the actual update.
111      function updateApplication() {
112
113          var updater = new air.Updater();
114          updater.update(newAppFile, currentVersion);
115
116      } // End of updateApplication() function.
117
118      </script>
119   </head>
120   <body>
121      <h3>Update Example</h3>
122   </body>
123 </html>
```

Then a new object of type `DOMParser` is created, and the `appData` string is turned into an XML object.

4. Complete the `getThisVersion()` function:

```
var version = xml.getElementsByTag
→ Name('version')[0].firstChild;
thisVersion = version.nodeValue;
} // End of getThisVersion() function.
```

This cumbersome code is best explained in Chapter 14. In short, the first line returns the first item from the XML data whose element name is *version*. There will only be one such element, but `getElementsByTagName()` always returns an array. The `firstChild` attribute of that element is the value of the element, which will be a text node. Finally, the value of that text node, which is the value of the element—e.g., 1.2 or 3.59—will be assigned to the global `thisVersion` variable.

5. Define the `getCurrentVersion()` function:

```
function getCurrentVersion() {
    xhr = new XMLHttpRequest();
    xhr.open('get', 'http://www.
    → example.com/air/version.txt');
    xhr.onreadystatechange =
    → askAboutUpdate;
    xhr.send(null);
} // End of getCurrentVersion()
→ function.
```

This function finds out what the most recent version of the application is. That value will be stored in a text file on a server (presumably the same Web site where the user downloaded the program in the first place). This code performs a basic `XMLHttpRequest` for that document. The `askAboutUpdate()` function will be called when the request's `readyState` value changes.

6. Begin defining the `askAboutUpdate()` function:

```
function askAboutUpdate() {
    if (xhr.readyState == 4) {
        currentVersion = xhr.
        → responseText;
```

This function is called as the `XMLHttpRequest` object's `readyState` value changes. Once that value equals 4, the request is complete and the response (which is the entire contents of the `version.txt` file) will be assigned to the global `currentVersion` variable. This code as written will only work if the text file contains just a number and absolutely nothing else.

7. If there's a newer version of the application available, ask the user whether to install it:

```
if (currentVersion > thisVersion) {
    if (confirm('Update to the newest
    → version?')) {
        downloadNewVersion();
    }
} else {
    alert('The current version is up
    → to date.');
}
```

At this point in the script, the two numbers are stored in variables. One reflects the most recent version of the application available (fetched from the Web), and the other reflects the version of the currently running application. If the former is greater than the latter, a new version is available and the user can be asked whether to update the application (**Figure 16.13**).

Otherwise, the user is notified that the version running is the most current one available (**Figure 16.14**). You may not want to do this in a real application, but here it confirms that the process works.

8. Complete the askAboutUpdate() function:

```
    } // End of readyState IF.
} // End of askAboutUpdate()
→ function.
```

9. Begin defining the downloadNewVersion() function:

```
function downloadNewVersion() {
    var addr = 'http://www.example.
    → com/air/MyApp.air';
    var url = new air.URLRequest(addr);
    urlStream = new air.URLStream();
    data = new air.ByteArray();
```

If the user clicks OK in the confirmation dialog (Figure 16.13), this function will be called. It downloads the newest version of the application from the server. To do that, it first identifies the full URL of the file to be downloaded. Then it creates three new objects: one URLRequest, one URLStream, and one ByteArray. The first two are discussed in Chapter 13 and the third is introduced in Chapter 10, "Working with File Content."

10. Complete the downloadNewVersion() function:

```
    urlStream.addEventListener(air.
    → Event.COMPLETE, saveNewVersion);
    urlStream.load(url);
} // End of downloadNewVersion()
→ function.
```

To perform the download, there are two final steps. First, an event listener is added to the URLStream object, stating that the saveNewVersion() function should be called when the entire file has been downloaded. Second, the file is loaded into the stream.

11. Begin defining the saveNewVersion() function:

```
function saveNewVersion(e) {
    urlStream.readBytes(data, 0,
    → urlStream.bytesAvailable);
```

This function will take the data read from the server and store it as a file on the computer (so that it can be used for the update). To start, it takes the data loaded into the URLStream and writes it into the data global variable.

12. Write the data to a file:

```
newAppFile = air.File.
→ desktopDirectory.resolvePath
→ ('MyApp.air');
var fileStream = new air.
→ FileStream();
fileStream.open(newAppFile,
→ air.FileMode.WRITE);
fileStream.writeBytes(data, 0,
→ data.length);
fileStream.close();
```

continues on next page

Figure 16.13 If a new version of the application is available, the user is asked whether to perform an update.

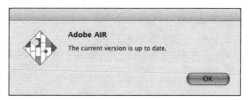

Figure 16.14 If no new version of the application is available, a simple statement says as much.

UPDATING AN APPLICATION

The global `newAppFile` variable will be a `File` object that points to the new version of the application. By default, this will be on the user's desktop and be given a name of *MyApp.air*. A `FileStream` object is created, the file is opened for writing, all the data is written to the file, and the file stream is closed.

13. Complete the `saveNewVersion()` function:

    ```
        updateApplication();

    } // End of saveNewVersion()
    → function.
    ```

    Now that the newest version of the application is on the user's computer, the last step is to actually perform the update. That will take place in the `updateApplication()` function, called here after the file has been saved. **Figure 16.15** shows the complete logic flow of this application.

14. Define the `updateApplication()` function:

    ```
    function updateApplication() {
        var updater = new air.Updater();
        updater.update(newAppFile,
        → currentVersion);
    }
    ```

    Ironically, the function that does the most important part is the easiest to write. An object of type `Updater` is created, and then its `update()` method is called. Its first argument is the file that represents the new version of the application. Its second argument is the version number.

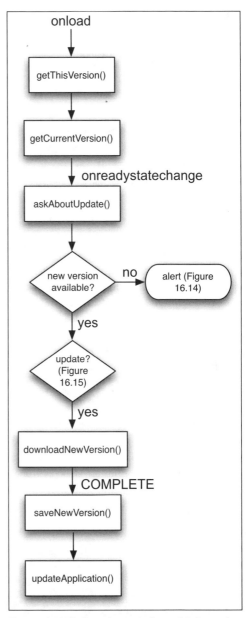

Figure 16.15 The long, but actually straightforward, logic of this application.

15. Create a file called `version.txt` that stores just a version number and place it on your server.

The version number needs to be a simple integer or real number: *1* or *2.3* or *6.34*. It cannot be *v1* or *2.3.45*. The number cannot be followed by any spaces, newlines, or carriage returns.

16. Go back to the code explained in step 5 and change the URL to match your server, if they don't match already.

This whole application will not work unless the two URLs used by it are accurate.

17. Make sure the version of this application, as defined in the application descriptor file, matches the version number you put in `version.txt`.

The `update()` method takes two arguments: the file to be used for the update and the version number. If the file (i.e., the new version of the application) does not use the same version number as that in the text file (and therefore, as that used in the `update()` method), the update won't proceed.

18. Save and build the completed application.

This first build will represent the "newer" version of the application.

19. Place the finished `.air` file on your server.

Make sure that it has a name and location that matches the URL used in step 9.

20. Change the version of the application, as defined in the application descriptor file, to be lower than that used in the already built version.

This next build will represent the "older" version of the application. So if you built the previous version of this application as version 2.3, this version needs to be 1.0 or 1.8, or 2.23—anything less than 2.3.

21. Save, build, install, and run the completed application.

It's very important that you actually install and run the application. You cannot test all of this using the command-line `adl`.

When you run the program, you should see a prompt like that in Figure 16.13. Click OK: The file will be downloaded, the application will close, be updated, and restart, generating the alert in Figure 16.14. Depending on the speed of your Internet connection and your computer, all of this should happen rather quickly (because the application file is really small).

✔ Tips

- As an alternative, the `version.txt` file on the server could be called `version.xml`, storing more information:

```
<?xml version="1.0" encoding=
→ "UTF-8"?>
<update>
    <majorVersion>2</majorVersion>
    <minorVersion>3</minorVersion>
    <minFreeUpgradeVersion>2.0
    → </minFreeUpgradeVersion>
</update>
```

Then the `XMLHttpRequest` would refer to the `responseXML` instead of `responseText`.

- Keep in mind that every AIR application is associated with a certificate, and self-signed certificates are only valid for five years. This means you can only provide updates for a self-signed application for five years. After that you'll need to create a new application (with a new application ID) associated with a new certificate. This is another reason why professional applications require legitimate signing certificates.

INDEX

INDEX